Part of the **award-winning** MyLanguageLabs suite of online learning and assessment systems for basic language courses, MyLatinLab brings together—in one convenient, easily navigable site—a wide array of language-learning tools and resources, including an interactive version of the *DISCE!* student text, an online Student Activities Manual, and all materials from the audio program. Chapter tests, tutorials, and English grammar readiness checks personalize instruction to meet the unique needs of individual students. Instructors can use the system to make assignments, set grading parameters, listen to student-created audio recordings, and provide feedback on student work. MyLatinLab can be packaged with the text at a substantial savings. For more information, visit us online at http://mylanguagelabs.com/books.html

A GUIDE TO *DISCE!* ICON

Text Audio Program — This icon indicates that recorded material to accompany *DISCE!* is available in MyLatinLab, on audio CD, or the Companion Website.

VOLUME 1

Disce!

An Introductory Latin Course

Kenneth F. Kitchell, Jr.
University of Massachusetts Amherst

Thomas J. Sienkewicz
Monmouth College

Historical Consultant: Gregory Daugherty
Randolph Macon College

Prentice Hall
Boston   Columbus   Indianapolis
New York   San Francisco   Upper Saddle River
Amsterdam   Cape Town   Dubai   London
Madrid   Milan   Munich   Paris   Montréal   Toronto
Delhi   Mexico City   São Paulo   Sydney
Hong Kong   Seoul   Singapore   Taipei   Tokyo

Library of Congress Cataloging-in-Publication Data

Kitchell, Kenneth.
  Disce! / Kenneth Kitchell, Thomas Sienkewicz.—1st ed.
    p. cm.
  ISBN 0-13-158531-2
  1. Latin language—Study and teaching. 2. Latin language—Textbooks for foreign speakers.
3. Latin language—Grammar—Problems, exercises, etc. I. Sienkewicz, Thomas J. II. Title.
  PA2087.5.K54 2010
  478.2'421–dc22

2010022509

Executive Acquisitions Editor: Rachel McCoy
Executive Editor, MyLanguageLabs: Bob Hemmer
Editorial Assistant: Noha Amer Mahmoud
Executive Marketing Manager: Kris Ellis-Levy
Marketing Coordinator: William J. Bliss
Senior Managing Editor for Product Development: Mary Rottino
Associate Managing Editor: Janice Stangel
Production Project Manager: Manuel Echevarria
Project Manager: Assunta Petrone, Preparé, Italy
Audio-Visual Project Manager: Gail Cocker
Development Editor for Assessment: Melissa Marolla Brown
Media Editor: Meriel Martínez
Senior Media Editor: Samantha Alducin
Senior Art Director: Pat Smythe
Interior/cover Designer: Wanda España
Cartographer: Peter Bull Art Studio
Line Art Studio: Peter Bull Art Studio
Senior Manufacturing and Operations Manager, Arts and Sciences: Nick Sklitsis
Operations Specialist: Cathleen Petersen
Publisher: Phil Miller

Cover image: ML Sinibaldi/CORBIS

This book was set in 12/14 Times New Roman.

10 9 8 7 6 5 4 3 2 1

Prentice Hall
is an imprint of

www.pearsonhighered.com

	ISBN 10:	ISBN 13:
Disce! An Introductory Latin Course, Volume 1	0-13-158531-2	978-0-13-158531-7
Disce! An Introductory Latin Course, Volume 2	0-205-83571-6	978-0-205-83571-3

Brief Contents

Table of Contents

CHAPTER 5   In Forō **52**

ORBIS TERRĀRUM RŌMĀNUS

ANGULUS GRAMMATICUS

LECTIŌNĒS
LECTIŌ PRĪMA

LECTIŌ SECUNDA

APPENDIX

IPSISSIMA VERBA

For a brief description
of this anthology of authentic
Latin readings, see MyLatinLab under
Online Resources in the Preface

Preface

DISCE! is a fully integrated Latin program designed expressly for classrooms and students of the 21st century. It consciously seeks to combine the best of pedagogical theory and classroom practice to produce a single textbook that serves students with varying abilities and learning styles as well as instructors who teach in a wide range of institutions and curricula. The unwavering goal of the book is to bring students to the point where they can read Latin fluently and readily and to guide them in a gradual and controlled manner toward reading original Roman authors and their texts.

Philosophy

DISCE! is based on the belief that both the "reading first" and the "grammar first" approaches have pedagogical value and thus combines the best features of both.

- The guiding principle at any moment is what is best for the student and for the particular items being studied. Some grammar is readily learned by induction whereas other concepts are best learned through prior explication of the grammar.

- *DISCE!* makes use of many of the pedagogical techniques found in modern foreign language books, especially combining language and culture, integrating the student's own experiences into the learning process, and providing a wide variety of practice exercises (grammatical, cultural, conversational, written, etc.).

- From the reading method approach *DISCE!* uses a unified story line with controlled introduction of vocabulary and grammar in context. *DISCE!* is committed to the belief that students are better able to follow, and will profit more from, stories with rich and fully developed characters than they will from a series of unconnected practice sentences or readings.

- *DISCE!* is committed to exposing students to authorial Latin as soon as possible.

- From the grammar first approach *DISCE!* maintains a belief that many students profit from a structured explication of the grammar and periodic review. Thus, grammatical charts are given in the body of the text as an aid for such students, but never as a primary goal in and of themselves.

As a hybrid text, *DISCE!* presents the material in a carefully structured way. In each chapter, students are first exposed to the basics of a grammatical concept—just enough grammar is explained to enable students to read the *lectiō* that immediately follows the explanation. In this *lectiō* each instance of the target grammar is indicated by a special typeface. Following this exposure through reading, the grammar is explained in more depth. The story line, as well as the cultural materials in each chapter, are designed to serve the single purpose of engaging and readying students to read advanced Latin.

The Standards for Classical Language Learning[1]

DISCE! has been carefully created according to the *Standards for Classical Languages* established by the American Classical League and the American Philological Association. A

---

[1]Richard Gasoyne et al. *Standards for Classical Language Learning. A Collaborative Project of The American Classical League and The American Philological Association and Regional Classical Associations.* (Miami, OH: American Classical League, 1997).

thoughtful Latin teacher at any level should have these "5Cs" in mind over the course of his or her classes: Communication, Culture, Connections, Comparisons, and Communities. As the original document states, "Each goal is one strand in a fabric that must be woven into curriculum development."

COMMUNICATION. From the earliest chapters students are communicating directly with the ancient Romans and with each other. *DISCE!* strives to ensure that this communication involves four skills: reading, listening, writing, and speaking.

CULTURE. The culture of the Romans is not relegated to specific little niches, but is woven directly into the narratives the students read and is reinforced by written discussions and extensive visual aids (photographs of ancient sites, artifacts, maps, etc.).

CONNECTIONS AND COMPARISONS. From the *Quid Putās?* and *Latīna Hodierna* sections through the constant stress on the role of Classical culture in the world today, links are made between Latin and modern languages and between Roman practices and modern culture. *DISCE!* encourages students at all times to learn and learn from other languages and to see the ways in which Classical culture has evolved into significant portions of today's multicultural world.

COMMUNITIES. *DISCE!* makes frequent reference to the cultures of ancient Rome and the diverse people in its empire. It also makes cultural comparisons between Roman and modern life and regularly draws attention to modern foreign languages derived from Latin. Such exposure encourages students to think about and to explore the communities of the world, both ancient and modern.

The Story Line

The story is set in Rome c. 9 B.C. and follows the lives of two families, one well-to-do, and one working class. The patrician family is that of Marcus Servilius Severus, who lives on the Viminal Hill and hopes for social and political advancement within the Augustan bureaucracy. He has two children by a previous marriage that ended in divorce (Marcus, age 21 and Servilia, age 16), and one son with his current wife Caecilia (Lucius, age 10). This family's plot line takes us through elections, a literary banquet designed to curry favor with Augustus, the young Marcus' trip to Greece to study rhetoric, Lucius' adventures as a young child in school, and Servilia's attempts to marry the young man of her dreams (Cordus) rather than her father's chosen mate (Iullus Antonius). Also in the house is the titular *pater familiās* (the *avus* or grandfather), and a full panoply of slaves, upon whom the story often focuses to give a more rounded picture of urban life in Rome.

The plebeian family is headed by a matriarch named Valeria. She was living in Verona on a farm and her son Licinius was serving in the army in Germany under Tiberius when her husband died, leaving her unable to run the farm on her own. Now in Rome, she runs a snack shop near the Forum, aided by her very pregnant daughter named Licinia who is married to Aelius, a blacksmith, and by a German slave girl named Flavia. Having put all her money into the store, Valeria and her family (which also includes Plotia, Valeria's mother, and Socrates, a pet monkey) are strapped for cash and live in the Subura, providing a glimpse into a frequently overlooked area of Roman life. Their story line includes childbirth, the terrors of urban fire, worries about money and lodging, street life, fortune tellers, and ultimately, a patron-client relationship with the Servilius family.

Grammar

From the grammar first method the authors provide orderly and clear grammar explanations that are presented in every chapter. It is a fact based upon of experience that not all grammar is best (or most quickly) learned by induction. Charts and short clear grammar explanations are helpful to many learners and learning styles, and are used accordingly.

DISCE! is unique in offering, in each chapter, both "core" grammar/morphology and a "More on the Language" section entitled *Angulus Grammaticus*. The core grammar, presented in the body of each chapter, offers students just enough explanation to enable them to read and comprehend the language as quickly as possible. But for those teachers and students who desire more, each chapter also has an *Angulus Grammaticus* where more traditional and in-depth explanations and terminology are presented.

The order of the grammar presented in the book is in accordance with the frequency with which given forms or usages appear in the Latin authors.[2]

Vocabulary

Vocabulary is also presented in order of occurrence in the major authors, following a list created by the authors based on previous studies.[3] This vocabulary is divided into *Verba Ūtenda*, which are to be used while reading, but not committed to memory, and *Verba Discenda*, which are for memorization. Where appropriate, *Verba Discenda* are accompanied by English derivatives. *Verba Ūtenda* are always given the first time they appear but gradually disappear if used frequently enough. The *Verba Discenda* are introduced according to the frequency rules discussed in the previous section and, whenever feasible, a word is used as a *Verba Ūtendum* prior to its becoming a *Verbum Discendum*. The *Verba Omnia*, a comprehensive list of all the Latin words used in *DISCE!*, is also provided in the appendix.

Macrons are used throughout on the principle that students learn vocabulary faster and more accurately when they say and hear the words pronounced properly. Choices had to be made constantly between different theories of where to indicate long vowels (especially over internal vowels long by nature, e.g., *rōstrum* vs. *rostrum*) and the authors chose to follow the *Oxford Latin Dictionary* in such cases.

Chapter Structure

DISCE! consists of two volumes with 20 chapters in each volume. In these chapters all the grammar and syntax needed for a student to begin to read authentic Latin is introduced. Each chapter is divided into two sections, each centered on a reading of approximately 250 Latin words in a connected narrative about one of our two families. Each chapter contains the following sections:

Antequam Legis (Before You Read)

This section provides students with the information needed to read the following *lectiō*. This can include cultural material, a short explanation of the new grammar being presented, pre-reading questions, and an exercise designed to reinforce the new grammatical material. The focus is on getting the student directly into the chapter with the minimum preparation possible and thus the exercise is commonly done just prior to or in conjunction with the reading.

---

[2]Paul Distler. *Teach the Latin, I Pray You*. (Chicago: Loyola University Press, 1962, reprinted 2000, Wimbledon Publishing Co.) Offers a convenient survey of this information.

[3]The vocabulary frequency lists used in *DISCE!* are based on: (1) "300 Most Frequent Latin Words" from Paul Diederich's "The frequency of Latin words and their endings" (1938 University of Chicago dissertation; http://www.users.drew.edu/jmuccigr/latin/diederich/); (2) "Tolle, lege! The Fourteen Hundred" by Vojin Nedeljkovic (http://dekart.f.bg.ac.yu/~vnedeljk/TL/apropos/wordlist.html), a list of 1400 most common Latin words based on *Grund- und Aufbauwortschatz Latein* by E. Habenstein, E. Hermes and H. Zimmermann (Stuttgart: Ernst Klett Schulbuchverlag 1990); (3) The entire mastery list for elementary Latin contained in the New York State Syllabus in Latin for 1956, available in the Latin-English Vocabulary of *Our Latin Heritage II* by Lillian M. Hines, Edward J., and Joseph W. Hopkinson (New York: Harcourt, Brace and World, Inc., 1966); and (4) Frequency of use in *Fabulae Faciles* by Francis Ritchie (Chicago: Longman, Green and Co., 1914).

Lectiō Prīma (First Reading) and Lectiō Secunda (Second Reading)

In each *lectiō* the target grammar and/or usage is used in context. Moreover, the target grammar for each reading is set typographically to enable students to see it in action and in context as they read. In many cases, adapted passages from authentic Latin authors have been worked into the narratives. For example, audience members at a production of Plautus' *Amphitruō* hear a modified version of its prologue. In another, a lovesick girl consoles herself with words from a Catullus poem, and later, the menu at a banquet is taken directly from Petronius.

Postquam Lēgistī (After You Have Read)

This section, immediately following the *lēctiō*, consists of a series of comprehension questions about the reading. Some of these are to be answered in English, others in Latin.

Grammatica (Grammar)

This grammar section follows each *lēctiō* and provides a more detailed presentation of the target grammar introduced in *Antequam Legis*. Each *Grammatica* includes exercises on the material introduced. Exercises in the textbook are designed for classroom use whereas those in the Student Activities Manual are designed for work outside of class.

Mōrēs Rōmānī (Roman Customs)

This section presents cultural material appropriate to the chapter *lectiōnēs*. An attempt has been made to address all levels of Roman life: the privileged and the disenfranchised; male and female; urban and rural; free and enslaved. The goal is to encourage students to see the broad span of Roman culture. Usually in this section (but sometimes in one of the next two sections), passages from ancient Roman authors are introduced in abbreviated or simplified form. These readings are always connected to the cultural material presented in the chapter.

Latīna Hodierna (Latin Today)

Here the influence of Latin in today's world is demonstrated by discussing etymologies, Latin borrowings, and the connection between Latin and living Romance languages.

Orbis Terrārum Rōmānus (The Roman World)

Addressing the fact that the narrative of the readings is largely confined to the Rome of 9 B.C., this section offers students a broad geographic introduction to Rome, Italy, and the Roman Empire. Each topic is somehow linked to the chapter readings.

Quid Putās? (What Do You Think?)

Following the *Orbis Terrārum Rōmānus* cultural sections, this section encourages students to put Roman civilization in meaningful contexts.

Exerceāmus! (Let's Practice!)

Every chapter contains a number of exercises offering pre-readings, comprehension, grammar and vocabulary review, composition, and oral drills intended for in-class work. These exercises always include some practice with the *Verba Discenda*. In addition, *Scrībāmus* exercises facilitate composition and *Colloquāmur* exercises encourage basic oral work in Latin. The goal here and in the Student Activity Manual is to present a wide variety of types of exercises to alleviate boredom and predictability while appealing to various learning styles.

Angulus Grammaticus (The Grammar Corner)

This section offers an in-depth explanation of a point of grammar of interest to many students and instructors. The information contained in this section is confined to explanations that are not necessary to enable the student to read Latin.

Program Components

Innovative supplements provide ample opportunities for practicing lexical and grammatical features while extending the breadth and depth of the cultural presentation and the introduction to the Roman world. New and sophisticated electronic components build on *DISCE!'s* pedagogical and cultural presentations in interesting, creative ways.

Student Resources

AUDIO CDs. Each chapter's two *lectiōnēs*, are on the Audio CDs and can also be found in the MyLatinLab and Companion Website. Additional recorded materials include: the Verba Utenda and Verba Discenda from all the chapters, plus the vowel and diphthong charts, the stress chart, and the first four exercises from Chapter One. This additional audio can be found exclusively in the *MyLatinLab*. Recorded material is indicated by an icon in the textbook, making it easy to find selections and incorporate them into class activities or assign as homework.

STUDENT ACTIVITIES MANUAL (SAM). The Student Activities Manual consists of written exercises providing meaningful and communicative practice, incorporating the vocabulary and structures introduced in each chapter, a review of previous material, and additional process-oriented activities. Each chapter of the SAM concludes with a **How Closely Did You Read?** section offering a review of major themes, terms, and concepts covered in the chapter.

ANSWER KEY TO ACCOMPANY THE SAM. A separately bound **Answer Key** is available for optional inclusion in course packages. It includes answers for all discrete and short-answer exercises in the SAM.

Instructor Resources

INSTRUCTOR'S RESOURCE CENTER (IRC). The IRC provides password protected instructor access to the Instructor's Resource Manual and Testing Program, in downloadable format. The IRC is located at *www.pearsonhighered.com*

INSTRUCTOR'S RESOURCE MANUAL (IRM). An extensive introduction to the components of the *DISCE!* program is included in the Instructor's Resource Manual (IRM). The IRM is available in downloadable format via the Instructor's Resource Center and MyLatinLab. Sample syllabi for two- and three-term course sequences are outlined, along with numerous sample lesson plans. The extensive cultural annotations are a unique feature of this IRM, providing further information about topics introduced in the textbook. Information-gap activities, ready for classroom use, are also provided for each chapter.

TESTING PROGRAM. A highly flexible testing program allows instructors to customize tests by selecting the modules they wish to use or by changing individual items. This complete testing program, available in downloadable format via the Instructor's Resource Center and MyLatinLab, includes quizzes, chapter tests, and comprehensive examinations that test reading and writing skills as well as cultural knowledge. For all elements in the testing program, detailed grading guidelines are provided.

Online Resources

MYLATINLAB™. This new, nationally hosted online learning system was created specifically for students in college-level language courses. It brings together—in one convenient, easily navigable site—a wide array of language-learning tools and resources, including an interactive version of the SAM and all materials from the audio programs. Readiness checks and grammar tutorials presented in English individualize instruction to meet the needs of each student. Instructors can use the system to make assignments, set grading parameters, listen to student-created audio recordings, and provide feedback on student work as well as to access the IRM, the Testing Program, and all the line-art images featured in the textbook. Instructor access is provided at no charge to adopting institutions. Students can purchase access codes online or at their local bookstore.

IPSISSIMA VERBA (THE VERY WORDS). This section of *DISCE!* presents an anthology of authentic Latin readings that can serve as the beginning of the students' reading of unadapted Latin, or it can be used as a class progresses through the book. *DISCE!* is unique in that much of this material has already been seen by the student. Most chapters contain bits of original Latin adapted for the current reading level of students. Some are in the *lectiōnēs,* others appear in the *Mōrēs Rōmānī* section. Selections of such readings are provided online in the section entitled *Ipsissima Verba* which contains the unchanged, original text accompanied by full lexical assistance and notes. The *Ipsissima Verba* can be found in MyLatinLab.

COMPANION WEBSITE. The Companion Website (CW) is organized by chapter and offers open access to the *lectiōnēs* audio recordings.

To the Student

Why did you choose to study Latin? Many students of Latin do so to improve their English vocabulary, to improve their knowledge of grammar, and to read ancient Roman authors in their own words. *DISCE!* is designed to help you meet these goals. Using this program will enable you to:

- Understand the Latin language well enough to read major Latin authors with the help of a dictionary.

- Gain an understanding of the structure of the Latin language: its pronunciation, grammar, and vocabulary. In the process you many even learn to understand your native language better!

- Become familiar with many features of everyday life and culture in ancient Rome. You will have the opportunity to reflect on how your life in North America and your values compare with those of ancient Romans.

- Understand the Latin basis of English vocabulary.

- Recognize the ties between Latin and Romance languages like Spanish, Italian, and French.

- Write simple sentences in Latin.

- Understand basic phrases spoken in Latin.

- Hold simple conversations in Latin.

Assuring Your Success

Use What you Already Know

Whether or not you have already studied Latin, you already have a head start on learning it. Many words of Latin origin are used in English. For example of the 52 words in the Preamble to the Constitution of the United States, 27 (marked in bold below) are directly derived from Latin:

> We the **People** of the **United States, in Order** to **form** a more **perfect Union, establish Justice, insure domestic Tranquility, provide** for the **common defense, promote** the **general** Welfare, and **secure** the Blessings of **Liberty** to ourselves and our **Posterity,** do **ordain** and **establish** This **Constitution** for the **United States** of **America.**

Such a high percentage of English words derived from Latin is not unusual.

Some people say that Latin is a dead language. Although it is true that no one today is a native speaker of the language of ancient Rome, anyone who speaks or understands one of the Romance languages such as French, Spanish, Italian, Portuguese, and Romanian is speaking a language based on Latin. So if you know any of these languages, you will find many similarities with Latin.

You also bring to the study of Latin your knowledge of general human activities, the world in general, and of specific events, which you can use to anticipate what you read in Latin. You can use your knowledge of a particular topic, as well as accompanying photos, drawings, or titles, to anticipate what will come next. Finally, the reading and listening skills you have learned for your native language will also prove useful as you study Latin.

Take the Long View

The study of any language, including Latin, is like building a house. If you start with a solid foundation, the rest of the structure will be stronger and more solid. So, if you learn carefully as you go along, you will build an ever stronger foundation for learning later materials.

Think like an athlete in training. Before going to class prepare each lesson carefully as directed by your instructor. Be sure to complete assignments required by your instructor and review regularly, not just for an exam. It is the daily practice in the language that ensures success.

Acknowledgments

We owe great debts of thanks to many people for their gracious help in creating *DISCE!* First is Rachel McCoy, our Executive Acquisitions Editor who first saw the need for such a book and was its most constant advocate. Likewise, a virtual army of editors and support team at Pearson did help guide us through the maze of publishing such a complicated project. Our thanks to all of them including Phil Miller, Publisher; Noha Amer Mahmoud, Editorial Assistant; Mary Rottino, Senior Managing Editor; Janice Stangel, Associate Managing Editor; Manuel Echevarria, Project Manager; Gail Cocker, Line Art Manager; Melissa Marolla Brown, Development Editor for Assessment; Meriel Martínez, Media Editor; Samantha Alducin, Senior Media Editor and Bob Hemmer, Executive Editor for MyLanguageLab, for their assistance in creating the state-of-the-art MyLatinLab; Kris Ellis-Levy, Executive Marketing Manager and Bill Bliss, Marketing Coordinator. The copyeditor, Patricia Ménard, did a tremendous job in assuring accuracy of the copy and the keen eyes of Keith Woodell (PhD student at the University of New Mexico) and Amy Chamberlain proved to be an invaluable resource to ensure that nothing slipped through the cracks. Any remaining errors, however, are our own.

The generosity of our colleagues all across the world was fathomless. First, thanks to Greg Daugherty, our historical consultant. His advice helped formulate the story line and his constant passion for accuracy shows on every page. Likewise, the eventual format of *DISCE!* was shaped in great part by the thoughts of those who attended sessions at professional meetings (CAAS, 2005; CANE, 2007; CAMWS 2006, 2008) and shared their advice and encouragement. Special thanks to the members of the 2008 CAMWS panel Barbara Hill, Wilfred Major, Cynthia White.

During the writing of the actual text, countless people offered their expertise on a wide variety of areas. Surely we will omit some names in the following list and we begin with our apologies to any generous person we may inadvertently omit: Marie Bolchazy, Brian Breed, Stephen Brunet, Lawrence Crowson, Eric DeSena, Nick Dobson, Hans Gluecklich, Nicholas Gresens, John Gruber-Miller, Virginia Hellenga, Melissa Henneberry, Liane Houghtalin, Elizabeth Keitel, Donald Kyle, Anne Mahoney, Thomas Mann, Eric Poehler, Teresa Ramsby, Anna Dybis Reiff, Dawn McRoberts Strauss, John Traupman, Stephen L. Tuck, Tony Tuck, Rex Wallace, and Vicki Wine.

Special thanks to our family, colleagues, and students who gave us permission to use their photographs in this book and who sometimes even took a photo specifically for *DISCE!*: Susan Bonvallet, Marilyn Brusherd, Nelson Eby, Robert Hellenga, Leigh Anne Lane, Victor M. Martinez, Daniel McCaffrey, Hunter Nielson, Julia A. Sienkewicz, William L. Urban, and Thomas Watkins.

It is only fitting that thanks should go to the many students who helped form *DISCE!* in many ways. First, thanks to students in our own introductory Latin classes who helped us improve this book in many ways. Thanks also to the many students who participated in the field testing of *DISCE!* across the country. Special thanks to University of Massachusetts MAT students Ryan Williamson, Wade Carruth, Simon Desantis, and to all the other MAT students who taught from the book and contributed to its improvement in many ways. Dennis Mui did crucial work as a fact checker for vocabulary.

The following teachers arranged field testing at their schools, endured the imperfections of a preliminary edition, and provided valuable feedback: Monica Cyrino and Keith Woodell of the University of New Mexico; Eddie Lowry of Ripon College; Stephen Brunet, Anna Newman, and Richard Clairmont of the University of New Hampshire; Jeremy Miranda and Cynthia White of the University of Arizona; Ronnie Ancona, Tamara Green, Yvonne Bernardo, and William Mayer of Hunter College; Benjamin Haller of Virginia Wesleyan University; John Gruber-Miller and Eric Ross at Cornell College; and our colleagues at Monmouth College and the University of Massachusetts Amherst.

Countless thanks to Andrea Crum at Monmouth College and Lisa Marie Smith at the University of Massachusetts for their cheerful support with scanning, faxing, copying, and mailing manuscripts.

Finally, and most importantly, to Theresa Kitchell and Anne Sienkewicz for their patient acceptance of *DISCE!*—a demanding stepchild in their lives who consumed the time they so richly deserved.

Reviewers

Joseph McAlhany, *Carthage College*
Andrew S. Becker, *Virginia Tech*
James Brehany, *St. Bernard's Central Catholic High School, MA*
Steven M. Cerutti, *East Carolina University, NC*
Catherine Connors, *University of Washington Seattle*
Gregory N. Daugherty, *Randolph-Macon College, VA*
Sally Davis, *VA*
Ed DeHoratius, *Wayland High School, MA*
Thomas Dinsmore, *University of Cincinnati - Clermont College, OH*
Mary C. English, *Montclair State University, NJ*
George Edward Gaffney, *Montgomery Bell Academy, TN*
Maria Giacchino, *Cambridge Rindge & Latin School, MA*
Judith P. Hallett, *University of Maryland, College Park*
Brian McCarthy, *Newington High School, CT*
T. Davina McClain, *Scholars' College at Northwestern State University*
Pauline Nugent, *Missouri State University*
Claude Pavur, *Saint Louis University*
Emma Scioli, *University of Kansas*
Janice Siegel, *Hampden-Sydney College, VA*
Linda Mitchell Thompson, *University of Maryland*
Maureen Toner, *Boston College High School*
Elizabeth Tylawsky, *Norwich Free Academy, CT*
Rose Williams
Eliot Wirshbo, *University of California, San Diego*

1

Intrōductiō

Augustus

Some Advice from a Roman Emperor

As you begin your study of Latin, consider this proverb, which was a favorite of the emperor Augustus:

FESTĪNĀ LENTĒ Make haste slowly!

This seeming contradiction (we call this an oxymoron) offers some good advice. You certainly want to move ahead quickly in your study of Latin, but not so fast that you do not learn well as you go along.

Notice how the proverb is written all in capital letters with long marks (macrons) over some vowels. We will explain later in this chapter why this was done.

Antequam Legis

Drāmatis Persōnae

As you learn Latin in this book, you will read a story in Latin about two fictional families who live in Rome in the year 9 B.C. One of these families is upper class. The other is lower class. In this *drāmatis persōnae* (characters in the drama) are some brief introductions of the most important characters you will encounter. Others will be introduced as they appear.

GRAMMATICA
Writing Latin
The Latin Alphabet
Pronouncing Latin
Parts of Speech

ORBIS TERRĀRUM RŌMĀNUS
Iūdaea et Arcus Titī

MŌRĒS RŌMĀNĪ
Inscriptiōnēs Rōmānae

LATĪNA HODIERNA
English Loan Words

ANGULUS GRAMMATICUS
The Birth of "W" and "J"

Meet the members of the Familia Valeriae and the Familia Servilii.

Familia Valeria (the lower-class family)

Plōtia (*aet.* 59) = **Valerius** (†)

C. Licinius († 14 B.C.) = **Valeria** (*aet.* 40)

M. Aelius (*aet.* 25) = **Licinia** (*aet.* 18)   **C. Licinius C.f.** (*aet.* 20) [*Leg. XVIII trans Rhēnum*]

M. Aelius M.f. (*infans*) ("Maximus")

Key:	†	=	deceased
	aet.	=	*aetātis* (age)
	C.	=	Gaius
	M.	=	Marcus
	C.f.	=	*Gaiī fīlius* (son of Gaius)
	M.f.	=	*Marcī fīlius* (son of Marcus)

Valeria, a 40-year-old widow of the farmer Licinius from Verona. Unable to run the farm alone and with her son in the army, she moved to Rome from Verona after the death of Licinius a few years ago. In Rome she now runs a snack shop stand near the Forum. Valeria put all the money she had into the shop, and as a result, she and her family live in a less respectable part of town called the Subura.

C. Licinius C.f., the son of Valeria and her late husband. While technically the legal head of the family, Licinius is in the army on the German border and has left his mother in charge of the family.

Licinia, Valeria's 18-year-old, married daughter, who works with Valeria at the snack shop stand. Licinia is pregnant.

Aelius, Licinia's husband. He works as a blacksmith in his own small shop near their apartment in the Subura.

Flāvia, a German slave girl who works in the shop and helps around the house.

Sōcratēs, Licinius' pet monkey. Licinius left the monkey with his mother when he enlisted. Socrates now "works" in Valeria's shop as entertainment for her customers.

Familia Servīliī (the upper-class family)

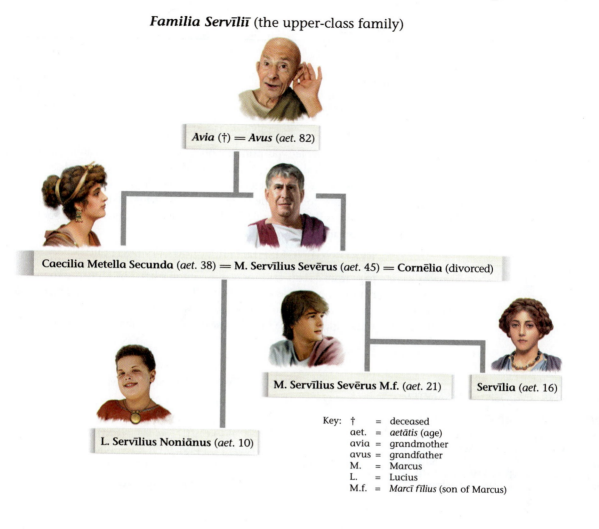

Key:	†	=	deceased
	aet.	=	*aetātis* (age)
	avia	=	grandmother
	avus	=	grandfather
	M.	=	Marcus
	L.	=	Lucius
	M.f.	=	*Marcī fīlius* (son of Marcus)

M. Servilius Severus, actually existed. He was consul in 3 A.D. At the time of this story he is 45 years old and is running for the office of praetor. Servilius had two children by his first wife, Cornelia, from whom he is now divorced: a 21-year-old son also named M. Servilius Severus and a 16-year-old daughter named Servilia.

M. Servilius Severus M.f., the 21-year-old son of Servilius. Marcus is preparing to study rhetoric in Greece before beginning his political career.

Servilia, Marcus' 16-year-old sister. She is anticipating marriage in the near future.

Caecilia Metella Secunda, present wife of Servilius.

L. Servilius Nonianus, the 10-year-old son of Servilius and Caecilia Metella. Known better as Lucius, he attends a school run by the grammarian Chiron and has a *paedagogus* (slave assigned to his education) named Hermes.

POSTQUAM LĒGISTĪ

1. How does the composition of the Licinia and Servilia families compare to that of modern American families and especially to your own family?
2. What kinds of lives do the characters in their twenties lead? How does this compare to the lives of you and your friends from high school?

Grammatica A

Writing Latin

A Roman living in the year 9 B.C. would have written the emperor Augustus' favorite proverb, *Festīnā lentē,* all in capital letters with little or no space between the words. It would have looked something like this:

FESTINALENTE

By the time that the moveable-type printing press was invented by Johannes Gutenberg (c.1450), small letters and real spacing between words had been introduced. So the earliest books printed in Latin used a font much like the one used in this book. This means that the capital letters we use in this book are the same ones the Romans used, but the small letters are different. Reading Latin as it is written in this book is easy for us, but it would not have been easy for an ancient Roman, any more than

READINGENGLISHINTHISFORMATISEASYFORUS.

Below at left is a page from a sixth-century manuscript of a letter by Pliny the Younger now in the Pierpont Morgan Library in New York. Notice how all the letters are capitalized and run together with no punctuation or spaces between the words.

At right is a transcription of the first lines at the top of the manuscript page (Book 3, iii):

EPISTVLARVM

·C·PLINIVS · CALVISIO SVO SALVTEM

Nescioanvllvmivcvndivstempvs
exegerimqvamqvonvperapvdspv
rinnamfviadeoqvidemvtneminem
magisinsenectvtesimodosenesce
redatvmestaemvlarivelimnihil
estenimillovitaegeneredistin
ctivs

Cōdex Latīnus

EPISTVLARVM

·C·PLINIVS · CALVISIO SVO SALVTEM

NESCIO AN VLLVM IVCVNDIVS TEMPVS
EXEGERIM QVAM QVO NVPER APVD SPV
RINNAM FVI ADEO QVIDEM VT NEMINEM
MAGIS IN SENECTVTE SI MODO SENESCE
RE DATVM EST AEMVLARI VELIM NIHIL
EST ENIM ILLO VITAE GENERE DISTIN
CTIVS

and here is how these lines would be written today:

Epistulārum
C. Plinius Calvisiō suō salūtem.
Nesciō, an ullum iucundius tempus exēgerim, quam quō nuper apud Spurinnam fuī, adeō quidem, ut nēminem magis in senectūte, si modo senēnescere datum est, aemulārī velim; nihil est enim illō vītae genere distinctius.

Which version is easier for you to read? Which one would be easier for an ancient Roman?

The Latin Alphabet

English has 24 letters that are ultimately derived from the Latin alphabet.

A B C D E F G H I K L M N O P Q R S T U V X Y Z

a b c d e f g h i k l m n o p q r s t u v x y z

The letter V was also used for U. The small letters came later.

Pronouncing Latin

It is important to remember that we have no recordings of ancient Romans speaking Latin, so our modern pronunciations of Latin words are approximations. We know that there were many variations of pronunciation across the Roman Empire. The same is true for English of course. Just ask people from London, Boston, and Brooklyn to say "horse" or "murder."

Moreover, Latin was a living language spoken across the Mediterranean and Europe for millennia. Different pronunciations arose in various geographical areas and historical periods.

There are two major pronunciation systems in use today. The "classical" Latin pronunciation represents our best reconstruction of what the Latin of authors like Cicero and Caesar sounded like. The system called "ecclesiastical," "church," or "medieval" was more influenced by the sound of Italian. We use classical pronunciation in this book, but you will often hear church Latin sung in concert halls.

Remember always that you only get better by trying and that your ear needs to hear the language to help your brain understand it. So the only rule is to keep trying and model yourself on the pronunciation of your teacher and the online drills.

General Rules for Pronouncing Latin

There are two important keys to pronouncing Latin:

- There are no silent letters. Even final e's are pronounced. Latin is essentially WYSIWYG (What you see is what you get!).
- Unlike English, Latin is quite consistent in the sound a letter represents. This is especially true of vowels. Once you get used to a few rules and patterns, you can easily predict the pronunciation of a Latin word.

Consonants

Though the majority of Latin consonants are pronounced much as they are in English, the sounds of the letters are not always identical in the two languages. Note the following differences:

C   C is always hard, sounding like a K. *Cicerŏ* is pronounced "Kickero."

G   G is always hard, as in "great." It is never soft, as in "gem."

J/I   There is no J in classical Latin. The letter I took its place. The consonant "I" is pronounced like the Y in "yes."

R   The R was slightly rolled in Latin as it is in many modern languages.

S   Almost always a pure S sound, as in "guess." Try not to make it a Z as in "rays."

V   V is pronounced like the English letter W. Thus, the Latin *vector* is pronounced "wector" and *vortex* is pronounced "wortex."

W   There is no W in Latin.

X   Between vowels, X is pronounced as it is in English. Sometimes it begins a word (usually a Greek loan word). In this case, pronounce it like "KS."

Notā Bene: Pronounce every consonant. You pronounce *committō* (I commit) as *com-mit-tō*, with the first two syllables beginning **and** ending with a consonant.

Consonant Blends

GN This is **not** pronounced as if in two words (e.g. "big nosed"). It is a nasal blend. Try to make it sound a bit like the "gn" in the Italian "lasagna."

QU As in English, rather like the "kw" sound in "quiet."

CH Latin CH is pronounced like the "ch" in "choir" or "chiropractor," **not** like the CH in the English word "church." Most Latin words with "ch" come from Greek letter "chi."

PH Although many Latin students and teachers pronounce this like an "f," technically this combination of letters is pronounced like "p" followed by a breath. Most Latin words with PH come from the Greek letter "phi."

TH Although many Latin students and teachers pronounce this like the "th" in "the," technically this combination of letters is pronounced like "t" followed by a breath. Most Latin words with TH come from the Greek letter "theta."

EXERCEĀMUS!

1-1 Pronouncing the Latin G

Many Latin words come into English largely unchanged in spelling. These are called Latin loan words. We need to pay attention, however, to the Latin pronunciation of these words. For example, we use the Latin hard "g" in the word "gladiator." Sometimes, however, we change the Latin hard "g" to a soft one. Try pronouncing the g in each of the following words like the g in "girl." That is how the Romans pronounced it!

genius (spirit)   *agenda* (the things that must be done)

rigidus (stiff)   *magicus* (magical)

1-2 Pronouncing the Latin C

The same applies to the letter C which, like the Romans, we pronounce hard in words like "campus" and "clamor." Frequently, however, we make the "c" soft in words we borrowed from the Romans. So try pronouncing a hard "c" in each of the following Latin words.

circus (racecourse)   *Cerēs* (goddess of grain)

censor (judge)   *biceps* (two-headed)

facile (easy)   *speciēs* (type)

Vowels

The same five vowels exist in Latin and English:

a   e   i   o   u

In Latin, vowels have two pronunciations depending upon whether they are long or short. In *DISCE!* a long mark (macron) is placed over long vowels to help you recognize them: ā, ē, ī, ō, ū. Romans did not use or need these macrons, but you should pay attention to these marks—they can be as important to meaning as the difference in English between the sounds of "meet" and "met" or "read" and "read" (past tense).

Here is a chart showing how vowels are pronounced in Latin:

SHORT VOWELS		LONG VOWELS	
Vowel	**English Example**	**Vowel**	**English Example**
a	ahead	ā	father
e	bet	ē	may
i	bin	ī	see
o	off	ō	role
u	put	ū	mood

Y   Extremely rare in Latin, this letter was introduced to spell words borrowed from Greek, like *peristȳlium* (a court surrounded by columns). The sound of "y" was equivalent to that of Greek upsilon, a sharp "u" sound made by combining the sounds "ee" and "u" together. Unlike English, it is always a vowel in Latin.

EXERCEĀMUS!

1-3 **Pronouncing Latin Vowels**

Now apply the guidelines for the pronunciation of Latin vowels to these words from Exercises 1-1 and 1-2.

HINT: Don't forget to pronounce the g and c the classical Latin way!

genius	*agenda*
rigidus	*magicus*
facile	*circus*
Cerēs	*censor*
biceps	*speciēs*

Diphthongs

In addition to these simple or single vowels, Latin also combines two vowels to create a single sound. These double vowels are called diphthongs. Diphthongs are always long.

Here is a chart of Latin diphthongs:

DIPHTHONG	EXAMPLE
ae	**ai**sle
au	**ou**t
ei	**ei**ght
eu	**ey-oo**
oe	t**oi**l
ui	Ph**ooey**!

EXERCEĀMUS!

1-4 **Pronunciation: Vowels and Diphthongs**

Use the key to pronounce the Latin words written in bold.

HINT: Always stress the first syllable in a two-syllable word.

Vowel	English Example	Latin Word	English Meaning
a	ahead	*at*	but
		capax	spacious
e	bet	*et*	and
		ede	eat
i	bin	*in*	in
		is	he
o	off	*odor*	scent
		dolor	sorrow
u	put	*ut*	in order to, that
		ulcus	ulcer
ā	father	*āla*	wing
		amās	you love
ē	may	*Lēthē*	river of forgetfulness
		nē	indeed
ī	see	*quī*	who
		sīc	thus
ō	rotate	*dōs*	talent
		ōrō	I pray
ū	mood	*ūsūs*	use
		frūx	crops
ae	**ai**sle	*aes*	bronze
		faex	sediment
au	**ou**t	*aut*	or
		pauper	poor
ei	n**eigh**	*ei*	alas!
		eia	wow!
eu	**ey-oo**	*seu*	or if
		neuter	neither
oe	t**oi**l	*Oedipūs*	Oedipus
ui	ph**ooey**!	*cui*	to whom

Syllables

Now that you know how to pronounce Latin consonants, vowels, and diphthongs, let's talk a little more about pronouncing whole words. Here are a few simple rules to remember:

1. There is a syllable for every vowel or diphthong

   rabiēs (ra·bi·es)   3 syllables

   vacuum (va·cu·um)   3 syllables

2. A consonant between two vowels is pronounced with the second vowel.

   rabiēs (ra·bi·es not rab·i·es)

3. When two or more consonants are between two vowels, only the last consonant is pronounced with the second vowel.

spectātor (spec·ta·tor)   *consortium* (con·sor·ti·um)

Stress

Word stress is important in English. Consider these sentences:

> I **refuse** to pick up the **refuse**.
> He cannot **conduct** the orchestra because of his previous **conduct**.
> Why do you **project** such negative vibes about my **project**?

In Latin stress is regular and predictable. The stress lands only on one of three syllables. Grammarians give them formal names. The technical terms are Latin-based. Let's look at *Rōmānī*, the Latin word for Romans.

	RŌ	**MĀ**	**NĪ**
Formal name	antepenult	penult	ultima
Latin meaning	before the next to last	next to last	last
Disce! nickname	S3 (syllable 3)	S2 (syllable 2)	S1 (syllable 1)

Rules for Stress

The following rules for syllable stress in Latin are simplified and omit the obvious (e.g., a one-syllable word takes the stress on the first syllable!), but they will get you started. Exceptions will be introduced when they are important.

1. The stressed syllable can never go further back than **S3**.
   Thus: Ō·ce·a·nī is impossible. The stress is Ō·**CE**·a·nī
2. Always stress the first syllable of a two-syllable word.
3. For words of three or more syllables,
   - if **S2** is short, the stress tends to fall back to **S3**,
   - if **S2** is long, it attracts the stress.

A syllable can be long two ways. It is long if:
1. it contains a long vowel, as in *fē·mi·NĀ·rum*
2. it comes before a double consonant like the *e* followed by *nd* in *a·GEN·da*

(There are exceptions to this, but you needn't worry about them right now.)

Latin Stress—Examples

	S3/ANTEPENULT	S2/PENULT	S1/ULTIMA
one-syllable word			*AT* *IN*
two-syllable word		*ACtor* *CAMpus* *FIat*	
three syllables or more, S2/penult long		*aGENda* *reGĀLia* *imiTĀtor*	
three syllables or more, S2/penult short	*FAcile* *HAbitat* *IAnitor*		

Grammatica B

Parts of Speech

Latin has the eight parts of speech similar to ours:

Verb (*verbum*, word): expresses an action or state of being. Here are some Latin verbs and their English equivalents. The English words in parentheses are derived from the Latin words and are called **derivatives**.

dūcit	leads (induce)	*dīcit*	says (dictate)
ambulat	walks (perambulate)	*respondet*	replies (respond)

Noun (*nōmen*, name): the name of a person, place, or thing.

fēmina	woman (femininity)	*taberna*	shop (tavern)
vir	man (virility)	*Forum*	forum

All of the nouns listed can serve as the subject of the Latin verbs we listed above, like this:

Fēmina ambulat.   The woman walks./A woman walks.

Adjective (*adiectum*, added to): describes a person, place, or thing.

bona fēmina	a good woman	*taberna parāta*	a prepared shop
magnus vir	a large man	*Forum meum*	my Forum

Notice that the endings on the adjectives change.

Pronoun (*prōnōmen*, instead of a noun): takes the place of a noun.

ego	I	*tū*	you
mē	me	*nōs*	we

Adverb (*adverbum*, to the verb): modifies a verb, an adjective, or another adverb.

valdē	very	*nōn*	not
nunc	now	*mox*	soon

Preposition (*praepositum*, placed before): expresses direction or relation.

in	in, on	*ē, ex*	out of
ad	to, toward	*sub*	under

Conjunction (*coniunctum*, joined together): connects two words, phrases, or sentences together.

et	and	*sed*	but

Interjection (*interiectum*, thrown between): an expression of surprise or emphasis.

Ō!	Oh! Hey!	*Heu!*	Alas!

Notā Bene: Unlike English, Latin has no words for "the" or "a," so you can translate any Latin noun the ways we translate *fēmina* here:
fēmina woman, the woman, a woman

Arcus Titī

Orbis Terrārum Rōmānus

Iūdaea et Arcus Titī

Although most of the action in the narrative of *Disce!* takes place in the city of Rome, the city was the capital of a wide empire spanning east to west from Syria to Spain and north to south from the Danube to the Sahara. In order to illustrate this connection between Rome and her empire, we offer the Arch of Titus in the Roman Forum and its ties with Rome's Jewish Wars in the first century A.D.

Judaea became a Roman province in 6 A.D., but the territory had been under Roman control for decades before that date. The Jews revolted against Roman rule from 66 to 72 A.D. Jerusalem fell in 70 A.D. and the Jewish temple was destroyed. The Jews were defeated at Masada in 72 A.D. by the general Titus, son of the emperor Vespasian. Titus erected a triumphal arch in the Roman Forum to commemorate his victory in 80 A.D. Decoration on the arch includes the Roman army carrying plunder from Jerusalem.

Triumphus Titī

A series of coins were issued to celebrate the suppression of the revolt in Judaea in 70–71 A.D. In the coin at right a female figure representing captured Judaea sits under a palm tree while a Roman stands victorious at left with the inscription *Iūdaea Capta* ("Judaea Captured"). The abbreviation S.C. stands for "by the Decree of the Senate.

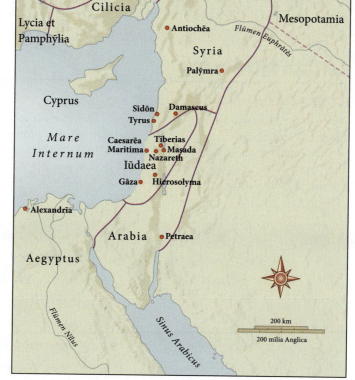

Iūdaea capta

Iūdaea

Mōrēs Rōmānī

Inscriptiōnēs Rōmānae

Romans often carved writing onto buildings and other stone objects. Such writing is called an **inscription**. You can see such an inscription on the façade of the Arch of Titus. Notice how the inscription is written all in capital letters with no division between the words and no macrons. Here is a transcription of the inscription.

SENATVS
POPVLVSQVEROMANVS
DIVOTITODIVIVESPASIANIF
VESPASIANOAVGVSTO

Inscriptiō Arcūs Titī

Now here is the inscription written with word divisions and with the one abbreviation in the inscription expanded and underlined:

SENATVS
POPVLVSQVE · ROMANVS
DIVO · TITO · DIVI · VESPASIANI · <u>FILIO</u>
VESPASIANO · AVGVSTO

And here is how this inscription reads in English:

The Senate
And the Roman People
To the Divine Titus Vespasian Augustus
Son of the Divine Vespasian

Arcus Americānus in Eborāco Novō

The emperor Vespasian reigned 69–79 A.D. His son Titus reigned 79–81 A.D. The Romans often called their emperors divine after they died. Abbreviations are very common in Latin inscriptions, but the only abbreviation in this one is F[ILIO] "to the son"). Also notice the V's in *POPVLUS, ROMANVS,* and *AVGVSTVS,* which are usually transcribed as U's.

Latīna Hodierna

English Loan Words

Many of the Latin words in the exercises should look familiar to you because they are actually English words borrowed from Latin. Remember that the pronunciation and stress of these words is not necessarily the same in Latin and English. This is also true for the meanings of these words. Here are a few examples of English loan words that have meanings different from the parent Latin word.

LATIN WORD	LATIN MEANING	ENGLISH MEANING
arēna	sand	enclosed area for competition
habitat	he lives	place where an animal or plant lives
minister	servant	a member of the clergy; a government official
rabiēs	madness	a disease of the nervous system
serum	whey, watery part of milk	clear part of blood used for medicinal purposes
trivia	places where three roads meet	commonplace or unimportant facts

QUID PUTĀS?

1. Compare the English proverb "Haste makes waste" to the Latin *Festīnā lentē*. Which proverb do you prefer and why?
2. Why do you think the English word "arena" comes from the Latin word for sand?
3. Why and where might you find Latin inscriptions on modern American buildings? Look for inscriptions on some of your campus buildings. Are any of them in Latin? If so, find out what they mean.

Use this *Verba Ūtenda* for the exercises that follow.

Gemma

Verba Ūtenda and *Verba Discenda:* Words marked in **bold** in the *Verba Ūtenda* (words to be used) become *Verba Discenda* (words to be learned) in that chapter. So

   ***nōmen, nōminis* n. name**

is becoming a *Verbum Discendum* in this chapter. Right now the form *nōmen* makes sense to you but *nōminis* does not, but we always list *Verba Discenda* the way they are found in a Latin dictionary. We will explain the second form soon. The n. stands for neuter gender, which will also be explained later.

VERBA ŪTENDA

ambulat walks	*fēmina* woman	*respondet* responds
clāmat shouts	*fīlia* daughter	*stat* stands
currit runs	*fīlius* son	***tibi* your, to you**
dat gives	***mihi* my, to me**	*vendit* sells
dīcit speaks	***nōmen, -inis* n. name**	*vir* man
dūcit leads	***quid* what?**	
***est* is**	*quis* who?	

EXERCEĀMUS!

1-5 Colloquāmur

Practice the following dialogue with other people in your class.

Dialogue: *Quid est nōmen tibi?*   What is your name?

      Mihi nōmen est _____.   My name is _____ .

1-6 Colloquāmur

(To be done after Exercise 1-5.)
Point at student A and ask student B, *Quis est?* (Who is this?). Student B responds *John est.* Then student B points to student C and asks, *Quis est?* etc.

1-7 Scrībāmus

Make ten simple Latin sentences by taking a noun from column A and linking it with a verb in column B. Be sure to make at least one sentence with each verb. In order to do this, you will have to use the nouns in column A more than once. Follow the model below.

A	**B**
fēmina (woman)	*currit* (runs)
vir (man)	*ambulat* (walks)
fīlia (daughter)	*dīcit* (speaks)
fīlius (son)	*respondet* (responds)
	est (is)
	dat (gives)
	clāmat (shouts)
	stat (stands)
	vendit (sells)
	dūcit (leads)

→ *Fēmina currit.*

1-8 Translation

Now translate each of the Latin sentences you made in Exercise 1-7 into English. Follow the model.

→ *Fēmina currit.* "The woman runs."

1-9 Verba Discenda

Use your knowledge of English to determine the part of speech of each of the *Verba Discenda*. Follow the model.

 VERBA DISCENDA

est is	**nōmen, nōminis** n. name	**tibi** to you, your
mihi to me, my	[nomenclature, nominate]	
	quid what? [quid pro quo]	

Verbum	Part of Speech
mihi	→ to me (pronoun)
nōmen	
est	
quid	
tibi	

Angulus Grammaticus

The Birth of "W" and "J"

The letter V originally stood for both for the consonant W and for the vowel U. It is now common practice to write Latin with the consonant V and the vowel U, but the Latin word *vacuus* (empty) was originally written as *VACVVS* or *vacvvs.* Only after the fall of the Roman Empire was the letter U used to distinguish the vowel from the consonant. Occasionally the Latin letter V became a W in English. Here are some examples:

Latin Word	Latin Meaning	English Word
vallum	rampart, palisade	wall
vastus	waste, deserted	waste
vīnum	wine	wine

Similarly, the letter I originally stood for both the consonant J and the vowel I. Occasionally in Latin texts, J is used as a consonant along with I as a vowel. Look at how this affects the change from Latin words to English words.

Latin	English
iniūria	injury
iānitor	janitor
iūnior	junior

2

In Tabernā

Lectiō Prīma

Antequam Legis

The Family of Valeria

The three women in this *lectiō* form the core of one of the families who appear in the narrative of *Disce!* Valeria, the mother, runs the shop. Her daughter, Licinia, helps her in the shop. Licinius, husband of Valeria and father of Licinia, died a few years before in Verona. Valeria could not run their farm alone and therefore sold it and moved to Rome to make her way as best she could, running a snack shop near the Forum. You will learn more about shops like these in the *Mōrēs Rōmānī* section in Chapter 3. The third woman is Flavia, a German slave girl who helps run the shop. Notice that her dress is different from that of free women. You will learn more about the family and its other members as the story progresses.

As you read *Lectiō Prīma,* pay attention to the verbs. There are three of them: *est* (is), *sunt* (are), and *vendit* (sells).

EXERCEĀMUS!

2-1 Subjects and Verbs

As you read, notice that verbs are marked in **bold** and their subjects are marked in ***bold italics***. List all the subjects line by line in the subject column and all the verbs in the verb column. Then translate the subjects and verbs together. Follow the model.

Line	Subject	Verb	Translation
→ 1	fēminae	sunt	the women are

Now use the subjects to determine why some verbs end in *-t* and others end in *-nt*.

In tabernā

GRAMMATICA
The Present Tense (3rd Person)
Principal Parts
Latin Derivatives in English
The Concept of "Person" and Personal Endings
Simple Greetings and Imperatives

MŌRĒS RŌMĀNĪ
Nōmina Rōmāna

LATĪNA HODIERNA
Salutatorians and Valedictorians

ORBIS TERRĀRUM RŌMĀNUS
The *Argīlētum*

ANGULUS GRAMMATICUS
Tense and Aspect

LECTIŌNĒS:
TRĒS FĒMINAE
and
MERĪDIĒS

We meet Valeria and her daughter Licinia who run a snack shop near the Roman Forum.

🔊 TRĒS FĒMINAE

In pictūrā trēs *fēminae* **sunt**. *Fēmina* ad sinistram Valeria **est**. *Valeria* Ītala **est**. *Fēmina* prope Valeriam Licinia **est**. *Valeria* **est** māter. *Licinia* fīlia **est**. Tertia *fēmina* in pictūrā Flāvia **est**. *Flāvia* Germānica **est**. *Flāvia* ancilla **est** et *Valeria* domina
5 **est**. In tabernā *Valeria* pōtum et cibum **vendit**.

In pictūrā trēs fēminae sunt.

🔊 VERBA ŪTENDA

ad sinistram to the left	*fēmina, -ae* **f. woman**	*māter* mother	*taberna, -ae* **f. snack shop**
ancilla maid servant	*fīlia* daughter	*pictūrā* picture	*tertia* third
cibum food	*Germānica* German	*pōtum* (n.) drink	*trēs* three
domina mistress	*in* **in, on, into**	*prope* near	*vendit* (she) sells
et **and**	*Ītala* Italian	*sunt* **(they) are**	

POSTQUAM LĒGISTĪ

1. What is the relationship between Valeria and Licinia?
2. What is the relationship between Valeria and Flavia?
3. What is the nationality of Valeria? What is Flavia's nationality?
4. What does Valeria sell in her shop?

Grammatica A

The Present Tense (3ʳᵈ Person)

What did you learn from *Exercise 2-1*? In the following sentences, observe the change in verb endings.

Vir **est**.	He **is** a man.	singular verb
Virī **sunt**.	They **are** men.	plural verb
Fēmina **vendit**.	The woman **is selling**.	singular verb
Fēminae **vendunt**.	The women **are selling**.	plural verb

The endings of these verbs indicate that the subject is singular or plural.

- *-nt* indicates a plural subject, "they"
- *-t* indicates a singular subject, "he," "she," or "it"
- This concept is called the **number** of a verb.

Latin Verb Ending	Number	English Translation
-t	singular	he/she/it
-nt	plural	they

Principal Parts

Every Latin verb form consists of endings added to a **stem**. These stems are made from one of the four **principal parts** of every Latin verb.

English has principal parts as well. You have certainly spent a lot of time memorizing things like "sing, sang, sung" or "go, went, gone." English also uses them to form our tenses (e.g., I am going, I have gone). You can read more about English and Latin principal parts in the *Angulus Grammaticus* in Chapter 5.

Most Latin verbs have four principal parts. All four principal parts are given for *Verba Discenda*, but for now, we will focus only on the first two principal parts. Here are the first two principal parts of three verbs from this chapter.

- The 1st principal part is the 1st person singular of the present tense (i.e., I run, I see).
- The 2nd principal part is the infinitive (i.e., to run, to see).

1ST PRINCIPAL PART	TRANSLATION	2ND PRINCIPAL PART	TRANSLATION
ambulō	I walk	*ambulāre*	to walk
videō	I see	*vidēre*	to see
vendō	I sell	*vendere*	to sell

Here is how the 3rd person singular and plural are formed for these verbs:

SINGULAR		PLURAL	
ambulat	he/she/it walks	*ambulant*	they walk
videt	he/she/it sees	*vident*	they see
vendit	he/she/it sells	*vendunt*	they sell

Notā Bene:

- The Latin verb *vendit* can be translated three different ways: he/she/it sells, he/she/it is selling, he/she/it does sell.
- Latin verbs have a variety of vowels before the endings (*ambulat, videt, vendit, vendunt*). For now, simply use the *-t* or *-nt* ending to decide how to translate a given form, using "he, she, it" or "they."

EXERCEĀMUS!

2-2   Principal Parts

Here are the first two principal parts of the *Verba Discenda* for this chapter.

ambulō, ambulāre **walk**
bibō, bibere **drink**
dō, dare **give**
veniō, venīre **come**

Use this information to complete the following chart.

1ST PRINCIPAL PART	TRANSLATION	2ND PRINCIPAL PART	TRANSLATION
ambulō	I walk		
		bibere	
	I give		
			to come

Lectiō Secunda

Antequam Legis

Latin Derivatives in English

How many English words did you recognize in *Lectiō Prīma*? Here are some you might have found: feminine from *fēmina*; tavern from *taberna*; and maternal from *māter*. Finding English derivatives of Latin words is a good practice as you learn to read Latin. But you need to be cautious. Just looking like one particular Latin word does not necessarily mean that an English word is derived from it. You need to compare the meanings of the Latin and English words to make sure. When necessary, you should consult a dictionary. Look for more derivatives as you read *Lectiō Secunda,* in which you meet some of Valeria's customers.

Continue to pay attention to verb endings and watch for the plural *-nt* (they) versus the singular *-t* (he/she/it).

Also observe the way characters greet each other in this reading with the words *salvē*, and *valē*, and you will learn how to say "hello" and "goodbye" in Latin.

EXERCEĀMUS!

2-3 Recognizing Derivatives

Before you read *Lectiō Secunda*, use an English dictionary to determine whether either or both of the two English words are derivatives of the Latin word. All of these Latin words are marked in the reading.

Line	Latin Word	Meaning	Possible English Derivatives	
1	*merīdiēs*	noon	**mer**ry	**meri**dian
1	*sōl*	sun	**sol**arium	**sol**itary
1	*altus*	high	**alt**er	**alt**itude
1	*caelō*	sky	**cel**ebrant	**cel**estial
1	*urbe*	city	**urb**an	t**urb**an
2	*multī*	many	**multi**plex	**multi**lateral
2	*viīs*	roads	**vi**aduct	**vi**tal
3	*populī*	people	**popul**ace	**popul**ar
3	*ambulant*	walk	**ambu**scade	**ambu**latory
4	*ūnus*	one	**un**favorable	**un**ique
4	*vir*	man	**vir**gin	**vir**ile
4	*venit*	comes	con**ven**tion	**ven**ial
5	*placet*	pleases	com**plac**ent	**plac**ard
6	*aquam*	water	**aqu**atic	**aqui**line

MERĪDIĒS

Merīdiēs est et **sōl altus** in **caelō** est. In **urbe** Rōmā **multī** Rōmānī in **viīs** sunt. Diēs aestuōsus est et multī **populī**, dum **ambulant**, bibunt.

Ūnus **vir** ad tabernam **venit** et "Salvē, Valeria," in-
5 quit. "Dā mihi calidum, sī **placet**."

Alius venit et **aquam** poscit.

Tertius venit. Valdē iēiūnus est et "Salvē," inquit, "dā mihi pānem et fīcōs, sī tibi placet." Valeria cibum dat. "Gratiās, domina," vir inquit, "Valē!"
10 "Valēte," Valeria respondet.

In urbe Rōmā multī Rōmānī in viīs sunt.

VERBA ŪTENDA

ad to, toward
aestuōsus hot
alius another
altus, -a, -um high
ambulō, ambulāre, ambulāvī, ambulātum walk
aqua, -ae f. water
bibō, bibere, bibī drink
caelō sky
calidum a hot drink

cibus, -ī m. food
dā mihi give (to) me
diēs day
dō, dare, dedī, datum give
domina ma'am
dum while
fīcōs figs
gratiās! Thanks!
iēiūnus hungry
inquit he says
merīdiēs midday, noon

multus, -a, um much, many
pānem bread
populī people
poscō, poscere to ask for
respondeō, respondēre reply
Rōmānī Romans
salvē hi, hello
sī (tibi) placet please ("if it pleases you")

sōl sun
sunt (they) are
tertius third
ūnus one
urbe city
valdē very
valē, valēte goodbye
veniō, venīre, vēnī, ventum come
viīs roads
vir, virī m. man

POSTQUAM LĒGISTĪ

1. What time of day is it?
2. What is the weather like?
3. What are some of the things Valeria's customers order from her?
4. How many customers does Valeria serve?

Grammatica B

The Concept of "Person" and Personal Endings

English verbs change to conform to their subject. Consider these examples:

- **Tom has** five dollars, but **I have** ten. Between us, **we have** fifteen.
- **Sally sees** the glass as half full, but **I see** it as half empty.

The English verb changes

by **number** (i.e., singular or plural) ⟶   he has, they have
by **person** (i.e., by the subject) ⟶   I have, you have

Gemma

inquit: This word is used to indicate that someone is speaking. Notice how it always comes after or even in between what the person says. You will only see this verb in the 3rd person singular (*inquit* he/she/it says) or the 3rd person plural (*inquiunt* they say).

Gemma

altus, -a, -um; *multus, -a, -um:* Both of these *Verba Discenda* are adjectives. The *-us, -a, -um* endings indicate different gender forms of these adjectives (masculine, feminine, neuter).

What is "person"?

		Singular	Plural
1st person	= the one(s) speaking	I	we
2nd person	= the one(s) spoken to	you	you (all)
3rd person	= the one(s) spoken about	he/she/it	they

In Latin, the endings on the verb's stem indicate person and number. These endings are called **personal endings** because they show the "person" of the subject:

English Pronoun	Person	Number	Latin Personal Ending
he, she, it	3rd	singular	*-t*
they	3rd	plural	*-nt*

EXERCEĀMUS!

2-4 **Verb Analysis**

Fill in the grid following the pattern of the first examples. Don't worry about what these verbs mean. Just focus on the personal endings.

	NUMBER (SINGULAR, PLURAL)	ENGLISH PRONOUN (HE/SHE/IT, THEY)
videt	singular	he/she/it
vident	plural	they
significant		
est		
sunt		
adveniunt		
advenit		
dant		

Simple Greetings and Imperatives

Notice how Valeria greets her customer with the word *Salvē*. As a customer leaves, he says *Valē*. Valeria says goodbye to her customers with the word *Valēte*. In Latin, the greetings "Hello" and "Goodbye" are actually commands meaning "Be well." Latin distinguishes between a command to one person (singular) and to more than one person (plural).

	Singular	Plural
Hello	*Salvē*	*Salvēte*
Goodbye	*Valē*	*Valēte*

Notā Bene: *-ē* is used to address one person and *-ēte* is used to address more than one person. This form of the verb is called an imperative.

MŌRĒS RŌMĀNĪ

Nōmina Rōmāna

You have already seen how Romans used abbreviations (*contractiōnēs*) in the inscription on the Arch of Titus. Abbreviating is also common in Roman names. Do you remember from

Chapter 1 how *fīlius*, the Latin word for "son" is abbreviated "F" on the Arch of Titus and in the family charts of the characters in our narrative? Well, the Romans used abbreviations in a wide variety of written contexts.

There is only a small set of possible male first names (*praenōmina*), for example, and these were almost always abbreviated when written. Here are some of the more common ones:

Praenōmina
Twelve Common Men's First Names

A.	*Aulus*	*P.*	*Pūblius*
App.	*Appius*	*Q.*	*Quintus*
C.	*Gāius*	*S.*	*Sextus*
Cn.	*Gnaeus*	*Ser.*	*Servius*
L.	*Lūcius*	*T.*	*Titus*
M.	*Marcus*	*Ti(b).*	*Tiberius*

In addition to one of these *praenōmina*, or first names, a Roman male also could have

- a *nōmen*, i.e., a *gēns* (tribe or clan) name
- a *cognōmen*, a third name that could
  mark a family branch of a *gēns*
  indicate that a son was born after the death of his father (*Postumus*)
  show that the man had been adopted (via a name ending in *-iānus*)

Very illustrious Romans could have more than one *cognōmen* but less illustrious men often had fewer. Here are some examples:

Praenōmen	Nōmen	Cognōmen	Cognōmen	Cognōmen
M.	Tullius	Cicerō		
C.	Iulius	Caesar		
C.	Iulius	Caesar	Octaviānus	Augustus
M.	Servīlius	Sevērus		
M.	Aelius			

Servilius' son, also known as M. Servilius Severus, could add M.f. (*Marcī fīlius*) to distinguish himself from his father. Note how a lower-class Roman like Aelius often had no *cognōmen*, whereas emperors like Augustus could accumulate multiple *cognōmina*.

- Augustus was born C. Octavius.
- After his adoption by Julius Caesar he became C. Iulius Caesar Octaviānus.
- After he became emperor he took the *cognōmen* Augustus ("revered") and was often called by that name.

Roman women had far fewer options. All the daughters in a family simply bore the name of their father's *gens* or clan. So Servilius' daughter is Servilia, and Licinia bears the name of her father, Licinius. If there were more than one daughter in the family, they were often distinguished by formal nicknames like *Māior* (the Elder) and *Minor* (the Younger). If there were more daughters, they might be known as *Tertia* (the Third), *Quarta* (the Fourth), etc. These names were not abbreviated. For example, if Julius Caesar had had two daughters, the first would have been known as *Julia Māior* and her younger sister would have been *Julia Minor*. A Roman woman kept this birth name even after she was married.

When Romans sent letters, they also used abbreviations. Very often a Roman began a letter with the abbreviation S.D., which stands for the expression *salūtem dīcit/dīcunt* (he/she/it sends greetings or they send greetings). Notice how letter writers refer to themselves in the third person.

Gemma

The Latin abbreviation S.D. is sometimes used today in college diplomas in a formulaic way: "The college sends greetings to…"

Here is how the statesman Cicero addressed letters to his friend Atticus:

> CICERO ATTICO SAL.
> CICERO ATTICO S.D.
> CICERO SAL. DIC. ATTICO

All of these expressions stand for:

> CICERO ATTICO SALVTEM DICIT   Cicero sends greetings to Atticus.

Here is how Julius Caesar addressed a letter to Cicero and how Cicero replied. The abbreviation *imp.* stands for *imperātor* or "general."

> CAESAR IMP. S.D. CICERONI IMP.
> CICERO IMP. S.D. CAESARI IMP.

Another important abbreviation in letter writing is S.V.V., which stands for *Si valeās, valeō.* (If you are well, I am well.)

Latīna Hodierna

Salutatorians and Valedictorians

Did your high school graduation have a salutatorian and a valedictorian? The salutatorian is the one who says *Salvē* or "Hello" at the beginning of the ceremony and the valedictorian is the one who says *Valē* or "Goodbye." Here are some related English words. Remember that the essential idea is "Be well!" If you don't know the meaning of one of these English words, look it up!

Salvē!	*Valē!*
salutatorian	valedictorian
salutatory	valedictory
salutation	valediction
salutary	valetudinarian
salute	valetudinary

Orbis Terrārum Rōmānus

The *Argīlētum*

Valeria's *taberna* is imagined to be in an excellent location on a street called the Argiletum just off the Roman Forum, the chief political and commercial center of the city and the empire. The Argiletum is marked in red on the map on the next page. As you can see in the photographs at the left, the Argiletum leading out of the Forum essentially disappeared in the Imperial period and is not visible today.

Argīlētum ē Forō hodiē

Argīlētum ad Forum hodiē

Argīlētum ē Forō ad Subūram

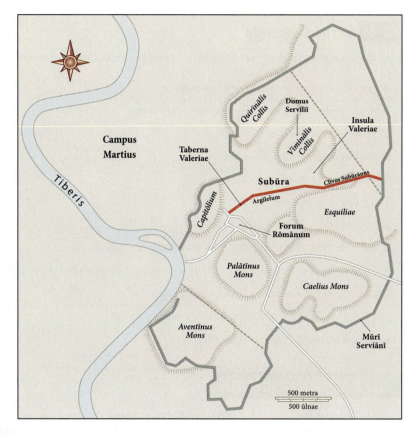

QUID PUTĀS?

1. How does the Roman use of abbreviations in letter writing compare to modern practice, especially in text messaging?
2. What does their elaborate system of naming males tell you about Romans and their society?
3. Use the Roman system of naming women to rename a visible today.woman in your family. For example, your mother would be known by her father's family name.
4. What observations about the role of women in Roman society can you make based on the way Roman women were named?

EXERCEĀMUS!

2-5 **Colloquāmur**

Use the following Latin phrases to say hello and goodbye to people in your class:

Salvē, magister.	Valē, magister.	(if your teacher is male)
Salvē, magistra.	Valē, magistra.	(if your teacher is female)
Salvē, discipule.	Valē, discipule.	(a male student)
Salvē, discipula.	Valē, discipula.	(a female student)
Salvēte, discipulī.	Valēte, discipulī.	(more than one student)

🔊 VERBA ŪTENDA

discipula student (female)   *discipulus* student (male)   *magistra* teacher (female)   *magister* teacher (male)

2-6 **Verba Discenda**

Find the Latin word in the *Verba Discenda* that best fits each of the statements. Follow the model.

→ one of your female classmates: *discipula*

1. word used to indicate when a person is speaking:

2. a place where you can buy a snack:

3. used to describe Mt. Vesuvius:

4. connects two words together:

5. the opposite of a *vir*:

6. used to address your teacher:

7. the verb used to get from Valeria's shop to the Forum on foot:

8. the verb used to describe what Valeria's customers come to her shop to do:

9. a word used to describe a lot of something:

10. a word used to describe what Valeria's customers eat:

11. a drink served at Valeria's shop:

🔊 **VERBA DISCENDA**

ad **to, toward, for**
altus, -a, -um **high**
   [altitude]
ambulō, ambulāre,
   ambulāvī, ambulātum
   walk [ambulatory,
   perambulation]
aqua, -ae **f. water**
   [aqueous, aquatic]
bibō, bibere, bibī **drink**
   [imbibe]
cibus, -ī **m. food**
discipula, -ae **f. student**
   (female) [disciple]

discipulus, -ī **m. student**
   (male)
dō, dare, dedī, datum **give**
   [data]
et **and**
fēmina, -ae **f. woman**
   [feminine]
in **in, on, into**
inquit, inquiunt **say(s)**
magister, -trī **m. teacher**
   (male)
magistra, -ae **f. teacher**
   (female) [magisterial,
   magistrate]

multus, -a, -um **much,**
   many [multitude]
sum, esse, fuī **be (see** *est*
   and *sunt*) [essence]
sunt **(they) are**
taberna, -ae **f. snack shop**
veniō, venīre, vēnī,
   ventum **come** [advent,
   prevention]
vir, virī **m. man** [virile,
   virility]

Angulus Grammaticus

Tense and Aspect

In English, **tense** primarily refers to the time of the action: past, present, or future. So far we have only talked about the present tense in Latin. You will, of course, be introduced to other tenses as we move along. But you should think about more than time when you talk about tense in Latin. You should also think about what is called **aspect**, i.e., the kind of action of the verb. In English we indicate aspect by adding helping verbs. Here are some examples:

he sells	simple action
he is selling	continuous action
he does sell	emphatic action

One way to distinguish a simple action from a continuous action is to think in terms of a photograph and a video of the same event. "He sells" is the photographic shot of an action, whereas "he is selling" is a video.

All three types of aspect are indicated by the Latin present tense, so the Latin word *vendit* can be translated in three different aspects:

he sells
he is selling
he does sell

Now try translating *vendunt* into English in three different aspects.

Although Latin is very subtle in many ways, English is more nuanced in its use of aspect. There can be a big difference in aspect in English present tense. Consider this little dialogue about Bill, the automobile salesman.

- **He sells** cars, doesn't he?
- Yes, **he does sell** cars.
- In fact, **he is selling** them right now.

In Latin, all three words in bold would be the same—*vendit*. Context will help you decide which aspect to use when you translate into English from Latin.

3

Negōtium Bonum

Taberna in Herculaneō

GRAMMATICA

The Concept of Case

The Nominative Case

The Accusative Case

Nominative and Accusative Endings

The 1st and 2nd Declensions

The Predicate Nominative

Word Order in Latin

MŌRĒS RŌMĀNĪ

The *Taberna* or *Thermopōlium*

LATĪNA HODIERNA

Taberna and Tavern

ORBIS TERRĀRUM RŌMĀNUS

Forum Rōmānum

ANGULUS GRAMMATICUS

Inflection vs. Word Order

LECTIŌNĒS:
MULTA PECŪNIA
and
MĒ ADIUVĀTE!

Valeria and her daughter Licinia tend to
the business of the snack shop.

Lectiō Prīma

Antequam Legis

Subjects and Objects

In this *lectiō*, Valeria continues to serve her customers. You should be able to read this narrative fairly easily even though it uses some noun endings you have not yet studied. These endings indicate the **subject** and the **object** of a sentence.

The **subject** of a verb is the one who performs the action (or simply "is," if there is no action):

> **John** hit the wall.

> **John** is in a world of pain.

The **direct object** receives the action of a verb:

> John hit **the wall**.

EXERCEĀMUS!

3-1 **Subjects and Objects**

Before you read *Lectiō Prīma*, make a line-by-line list of the subjects (marked in **bold**) and the objects (marked in ***bold italics***). Find the verb that goes with each subject. Then try to put the three words together into an English sentence. Follow the models.

Line	Subject	Object	Verb	Translation
→ 1	Valeria	cibum	dat	Valeria gives food.
→ 1	Valeria	pōtum	dat	Valeria gives drink.

🔊 MULTA PECŪNIA

Valeria *cibum* et *pōtum* dat et ūnus vir "Grātiās," inquit "domina." **Aliī** *nihil* dīcunt sed sōlum edunt et bibunt. **Virī** *pecūniam*
dant et "Valē," inquiunt "Valeria." "Valēte!" Valeria respondet.
Tunc virī ad Forum ambulant.

5   Subitō, **multī virī** simul ad tabernam adveniunt et
fēminās vident. Et *cibum* et *pōtum* simul poscunt. **Valeria**
virōs videt et "Salvēte!" inquit. Valeria et Licinia et ancilla
Flāvia strēnuē labōrant sed domina laeta est, quod **multī virī**
multam pecūniam significant. Hodiē negōtium bonum est.

Valeria cibum et pōtum dat.

🔊 VERBA ŪTENDA

adveniunt come to
aliī others
cibum food
dīcō, dīcere say
domina mistress, ma'am
edō, edere eat
et... et... both... and...
Forum, -ī n. Forum, the city
   center
grātiās thanks

hodiē today
labōrō, labōrāre work
laeta happy
negōtium business
nihil nothing
nōn not
pecūnia, -ae f. money
poscō, poscere ask for
pōtum (a) drink
quod because

respondeō, respondēre,
   respondī, responsum
   reply, answer
Salvē!/Salvēte! Hello! Hi!
sed but
significō, significāre mean,
   signify
simul all at once, together
sōlum only
strēnuē hard

subitō suddenly
tū you (sing.)
tunc then
ūnus one
valeō, valēre, valuī, valitum
   be well *Valē!/Valēte!*
   Farewell! Goodbye!
videō, vidēre, vīdī, vīsum
   see, perceive
vīnum, -ī n. wine

POSTQUAM LĒGISTĪ

Answer the questions in both Latin and English.
   1. What does Valeria give the men?
   2. What do the men give Valeria?
   3. Where are the men going?
   4. Why is Valeria happy?

Gemma

Et cibum et pōtum simul
poscunt: When there are two
et's joining words in a
sentence, the first *et* means
both and the second **and**.

Grammatica A

The Concept of Case

With the vocabulary you know, you probably have no problem translating sentences like
these:

*Ūnus **vir** ad tabernam advenit.*	One man comes to the shop.
*Multī **virī** ad tabernam adveniunt.*	Many men come to the shop.
*Subitō, Valeria ūnum **virum** videt.*	Suddenly, Valeria sees one man.
*Subitō, Valeria multōs **virōs** videt.*	Suddenly, Valeria sees many men.

These differing forms of the word *vir* demonstrate a crucial part of Latin grammar—the concept of **case**.

- The **case** of a word (nouns, adjectives, pronouns) indicates the **function** that word plays in the sentence (subject, direct object, showing possession, etc.). Words have a **case ending** that indicates this function.
- The **case endings** also vary by number (singular and plural).
- There are five major cases in Latin and we will learn them one at a time. In this chapter, you will learn the **nominative** and the **accusative** cases.

The Nominative Case

The **nominative case** is used for the **subject** of the sentence—that is, the person, place, or thing that is **being** or is **doing** an action.

The **woman** is working hard.	*Fēmina strēnuē labōrat.*
The **man** comes up to the shop.	*Vir ad tabernam advenit.*
The **man** is **happy**.	*Vir laetus est.*

In the last example, notice that the adjective *laetus* is nominative because it refers to the man, who is the subject of the sentence. This is an important concept to which we will return shortly.

The Accusative Case

The **accusative case** is used for the **direct object** of the verb. A **direct object** is a noun or pronoun that receives the direct action of a transitive verb.

The man sees the **woman**.	*Vir fēminam videt.*
The woman sees the **man**.	*Fēmina virum videt.*

A **transitive verb** is one that takes a direct object. The quick rule of thumb is that if you can do it to something else, then it is **transitive**. If the verb does not do something directly to something else, then it is **intransitive** (e.g., to exist or to seem).

Nominative and Accusative Endings

The following chart shows the nominative and accusative endings of some nouns you have learned so far. Note how the endings (in **bold**) change to indicate their case.

CASE	SINGULAR	PLURAL
Nominative	fēmin**a**	fēmin**ae**
Accusative	fēmin**am**	fēmin**ās**
Nominative	tabern**a**	tabern**ae**
Accusative	tabern**am**	tabern**ās**
Nominative	vir	vir**ī**
Accusative	vir**um**	vir**ōs**
Nominative	discipul**us**	discipul**ī**
Accusative	discipul**um**	discipul**ōs**

The 1ˢᵗ and 2ⁿᵈ Declensions

You probably noticed patterns in the endings you just learned. For example, all the accusative singulars end in *-m* and the accusative plurals in *-s*. But note *-ās* vs. *-ōs*. So the patterns are not exact matches. Still, they do tend to come in groups. We call these groups **declensions**, that is, groups of nouns that use the same endings.

English nouns also occur in certain groups that act alike with some degree of regularity. Most nouns make their plural by adding a simple **-s**, sometimes with vowel changes before the **-s**.

SINGULAR	PLURAL
house	houses
bed	beds
dog	dogs
party	parties

Others do not form the plural this way, and there are several groups of nouns that more or less act the same way.

SINGULAR	PLURAL
mouse	mice
louse	lice
goose	geese
tooth	teeth
man	men
woman	women
child	children

As you know from speaking English, the number of ways to make plurals seems infinite. It is a great problem for non-native speakers. Latin is, in fact, much tidier than English in this regard.

Most inflected languages are like this and sort their nouns into groups that tend to follow the same patterns. In Latin, there are five declensions and the majority of nouns occur in the first three. In this chapter, we have used mostly 1ˢᵗ and 2ⁿᵈ declension nouns:

	1ˢᵗ DECLENSION		2ⁿᵈ DECLENSION		
	Singular				
Nominative	fēmina	**-a**	discipulus	vir	**-us**
Accusative	fēminam	**-am**	discipulum	virum	**-um**
	Plural				
Nominative	fēminae	**-ae**	discipulī	virī	**-ī**
Accusative	fēminās	**-ās**	discipulōs	virōs	**-ōs**

Gemma

If it helps, you can think of the accusative singular ending as the same in English and Latin: *fēminam* and *virum* vs. "whom" and "him."

Notā Bene:
- The accusative singular ending for many Latin nouns, regardless of declension, is -**m** (*fēmina**m***, viru**m**).
- There are six major cases in Latin, singular and plural.
- Latin nouns, adjectives, and pronouns have case.
- There are five declensions of Latin nouns.
- Three of these declensions are used for Latin adjectives.
- There is some flexibility in the nominative singular as shown by *vir* and *discipulus*.

EXERCEĀMUS!

3-2 Nominative and Accusative

Use the chart of case endings to help you determine the case and number of the words marked in bold in each of the following sentences. Follow the model.

	CASE	NUMBER
→ **Fēmina** labōrat.	*nominative*	*singular*
1. **Fēminae** pōtum dant.		
2. **Virī** veniunt.		
3. **Vir** respondet.		
4. Fēmina **virum** videt.		
5. Vir **fēminās** videt.		
6. Virī **discipulum** vident.		
7. **Magistrī** respondent.		
8. Discipulae **pecūniam** vident.		
9. Fēmina multōs **virōs** videt.		
10. **Discipulī** respondent.		
11. Magistra **fēminam** videt.		

Lectiō Secunda

Antequam Legis

Things get quite busy in Valeria's shop as more and more customers appear. *Lectiō Secunda* also gives you practice with **word order**, **direct objects**, and **predicates**. A predicate nominative is a noun or an adjective linked to the subject by an intransitive verb. Remember: transitive verbs take direct objects, intransitive verbs do not.

*Vir **fēminam** videt.*
The man sees the woman.

Videt is a transitive verb and takes a **direct object**, *fēminam*.

*Vir **laetus** est sed fēmina nōn **laeta** est.*
The man is happy, but the woman is not happy.

Est is an intransitive verb and does not take a direct object. Both *laetus* and *laeta* are **predicate nominatives**.

*Valeria **fēmina** est.*
Valeria is a woman.

A noun can also be a predicate nominative.

In *Lectiō Secunda* the transitive verbs that have objects are in **bold** and the intransitive verbs are in ***bold italics***.

Word Order

In English, word order is everything. John Bogart, a former editor of the *New York Sun* reportedly said that if the headline reads "Dog bites man," it isn't news, but if the headline reads "Man bites dog," then you have yourself a news story. This is the power of word order in English—it controls meaning. But in Latin the endings rule.

In English our word order is fixed. We usually place the subject first, then the verb, and then the direct object.

Subject	**Verb**	**Object**
The man	sees	the woman.

In Latin the preferred word order is:

Subject	**Object**	**Verb**
Vir	*fēminam*	*videt.*

BUT: This sentence is also possible, is good Latin, and means the same thing:

Object	**Subject**	**Verb**
Fēminam	*vir*	*videt.*

Moreover, you have the endings to help you figure out which is which. As you read *Lectiō Secunda* pay attention to the word order of the Latin sentence.

EXERCEĀMUS!

3-3   Skimming the Lectiō

Find the answers to these questions before you read *Lectiō Secunda*. Give the answer in both Latin and English. Follow the model.

→ Whom does Valeria see in line 1? *multōs virōs* (many men)

1. What does Valeria ask Licinia to put in the cup in line 1?

2. What falls on the floor in line 3?

3. What do the men give Valeria in line 4?

4. What is Valeria's mood in line 5?

5. As you translate *Lectiō Secunda*, sort the Latin verbs below into "Transitive" and "Intransitive" groups. For each transitive verb, list the direct object. For each intransitive verb list the two words being linked. Follow the model.

Transitive		**Intransitive**	
→ videt	*virōs*	→ est	*Valeria* and *laeta*

adiuvāte
implē
dā
capit
sunt
habent
dant
est

🔊 MĒ ADIUVĀTE!

Valeria multōs virōs **videt** et clāmat: "Mē **adiuvāte!** Licinia, **implē** pōculum vīnō et **dā** mihi pānem. Ubi *est* Flāvia? Flāvia! **Dā** mihi ficōs!" Flāvia ficōs **capit,** sed quīnque ficī ad terram cadunt. Valeria nōn laeta *est,* sed nihil **dīcit.** Nunc virī laetī **sunt** quod cibum et pōtum **habent.** Pecūniam **dant** et ad Forum ambulant.
5 "Valēte!" Valeria clāmat. "Et tū, valē!" virī respondent. Valeria valdē laeta *est* quod multam pecūniam **habet.** Ubi negōtium bonum *est,* Valeria semper laeta est!

Dā mihi fīcōs!

🔊 VERBA ŪTENDA

adiuvāte! help!
bonus, -a, -um
  good
cadunt fall
capiō, capere, cēpī,
  captum **take**
clāmat shouts
ficī / ficōs figs

Forum, -ī n. Forum, the city
  center
habet has
implē fill!
laetus, -a, -um **happy**
mē **me**
negōtium business
nihil **nothing**

nunc **now**
pecūnia, -ae **f. money**
pānem bread
pōculum cup
quīnque five
quod **because**
sed **but**
semper **always**

terra the ground
tū **you (sing.)**
ubi when
valdē very
videō, vidēre, vīdī, vīsum
  see, perceive
vīnō with wine

POSTQUAM LĒGISTĪ

Find the Latin words that answer each of the following questions. Then answer the question in English.
  1. Why does Valeria call to Licinia and Flavia?
  2. What accident occurs in this reading?
  3. How does Valeria react to the accident?
  4. Why are Valeria's customers happy?
  5. Why is Valeria happy?
  6. Where do the customers go after they leave the shop? How do they get there?

Grammatica B

The Predicate Nominative

Compare these two Latin sentences:

> *Flāvia ficōs capit.*
> *Valeria nōn laeta est.*

In the first sentence *capit* is a transitive verb that takes a **direct object** in the accusative case (*ficōs*). But not all verbs take direct objects. Some verbs, like "is" and "are" link things together. Since they are saying that A = B, this means that, in Latin, the nouns joined by words like *est* and *sunt* are in the nominative case. For example,

> *Valeria fēmina est.*   Valeria is a woman.

In this sentence, both *Valeria* and *fēmina* are nominative case. That is because in this sentence the subject *Valeria* is linked with the word *fēmina* by the verb "is" and thus lies in the part of the sentence called the **predicate**. That is why this construction is called the **predicate nominative**.

The *est* acts like an equals sign. Therefore, the predicate nominative is also in the same number as the subject.

> *Valeria fēmina est.*
> *Valeria et Flavia fēminae sunt.*

So **transitive** verbs take **direct objects** in the accusative case, whereas some **intransitive** verbs (like "is") take **predicate nominatives**.

Word Order in Latin

Now let's look more closely at the word order of some of the sentences you read in *Lectiō Secunda* and make some more observations about Latin word order. Remember that these are just tendencies and that Latin word order is more flexible than English word order.

Personal verbs, i.e., verbs with personal endings, tend to be placed at the end of a sense unit or sentence in Latin:

> *Flāvia ficōs **capit**, sed quīnque ficī ad terram **cadunt**.*

The **subject**, if expressed, usually comes first.

> ***Flāvia*** *ficōs capit.*
> ***Valeria*** *nōn laeta est.*

The **direct object** most often comes between the subject and the verb.

> *Flāvia **ficōs** capit.*
> *Nunc virī **cibum** et **pōtum** habent.*

The **predicate nominative** comes between the subject and the verb.

> *Valeria valdē **laeta** est.*
> *Valeria semper **laeta** est!*

Orders or **imperatives**, however, come at the beginning or early in the sentence:

> ***Implē*** *pōculum vīnō et **dā** mihi pānem.*

EXERCEĀMUS!

3-4 **Translation**

Practice your grasp of endings (and Latin word order) by translating the following sentences. Let the endings be your guide, not your sense of English word order.

1. Vir fēminam videt.
2. Vir laetus est.
3. Laetī sunt virī.
4. Fēmina virum videt.
5. Fēminam virī vident.
6. Virī fēminās vident.
7. Vir fēminās videt.
8. Virum fēminae vident.
9. Fēminae virōs vident.
10. Fēmina laeta est.
11. Fēminae laetae sunt.

Mōrēs Rōmānī

The *Taberna* or *Thermopōlium*

Snack shops like Valeria's were a common feature of any Roman city or town. The Latin word for this type of eatery was *taberna*, but a form of the Greek word *thermopōlium* ("hot shop") is also found. Many examples of these shops can be seen today at the archaeological excavations at Pompeii, Herculaneum, and Ostia. These shops were often open to the street and had stone counters into which earthenware jars were set. The jars would keep food and

drink warm. Customers could walk up to the counter from the street to place an order. Sometimes, however, customers would have to step inside to find the food counter. Especially popular at a *taberna* was *calidum*, a hot spiced wine. Foods were mostly snack foods that could be eaten in the customers' hands, such as eggs, fruit, cheese, or meat.

Ancient Romans liked to conduct business in the street so much that the emperor Domitian (A.D. 81–96) passed an edict forbidding the use of the public thoroughfare for business purposes. This led the 1st-century A.D. poet Martial to comment in one of his poems:

> *Nunc Rōma est, magna taberna fuit.*
>
> Martial VII. 61.10

Taberna antīqua Pompēiīs

🔊 VERBA ŪTENDA

fuit was

magna big

Latīna Hodierna

Taberna and Tavern

The Romans borrowed the word *thermopōlium* (hot shop) from Greek, but the Latin word *taberna* (shop) has lived on in modern languages. Look what happens to *taberna* in these languages:

Latin	**taberna**
Italian	taverna
Spanish	taverna
French	taverne
English	tavern

Orbis Terrārum Rōmānus

Forum Rōmānum

Cūria Iūlia

Valeria's shop is very close to the *Forum Rōmānum*. Located in a valley between the Capitoline and Palatine hills, the Forum was the heart of the ancient city and consisted of an unplanned mix of buildings and monuments built over a long period of time on land that was once a swamp. Originally the central market of the city, the Forum became the religious, political, and legal center of Rome. During the reign of Augustus, Rome's first emperor, there was a great deal of construction in the Forum. Many of the buildings visible in the Forum today date from this period.

Three important Forum landmarks are very near the Via Argiletum and Valeria's shop:

- The *Cūria Iūlia* or the **Roman Senate House**, the traditional meeting place of the Roman Senate. The construction of this building, which still stands today, was begun by Julius Caesar to replace one that had burned down. The building was finished by Augustus and dedicated in 27 B.C.

- The *Rostra*, was a platform just to the right and in front of the Curia, where speakers addressed the people. The platform is called *Rostra*, which means "beaks" in Latin, because of the bronze ship prows that were placed there after a Roman naval victory in 260 B.C. The *Rostra* was rebuilt according to the plans of Julius Caesar and finished by Octavian, the future emperor Augustus in 42 B.C. Mark Antony gave his funeral speech about Caesar from the unfinished *Rostra*.

- The *Basilica Paullī* was originally built in 179 B.C. by M. Aemilius Lepidus and M. Fulvius Nobilior. This large law court was reconstructed in the late 1st century B.C. when some shops were built into the front façade. The basilica burned in a fire in 14 B.C., shortly before the time in which our story is set, and was rebuilt by Augustus. It is commonly known by a later name, Basilica Aemilia.

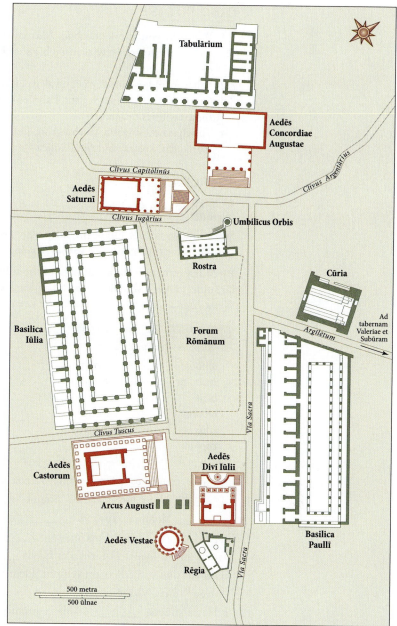

Forum Rōmānum

Rostra hodiē

Rostra Rōmāna

Basilica Paullī hodiē

QUID PUTĀS?

1. What do you think the poet Martial was suggesting about Rome's past when he described the former city as just a big shop? What does he mean when he says that now the city is "Rome"?
2. What would the modern equivalent of Valeria's snack shop be?
3. Compare the meaning of the Latin *taberna* with its English derivative "tavern." How are these facilities different?
4. To what buildings in Washington, D.C., or in your state capital could you compare the Curia, the Rostra, and the Basilica Paulli?

EXERCEĀMUS!

3-5 Scrībāmus

What follows is a version of the story with some blanks in it. Fill in the blanks with one of the Latin words provided in the *Verba Ūtenda*.

HINT: Pay attention to the number of the subject of the sentence, and remember that a singular subject takes a singular verb and a plural subject takes a plural verb. Not every word in the *Verba Ūtenda* is used but some can be used more than once.

🔊 VERBA ŪTENDA

ambulant	clāmant	habent	poscunt
ambulat	clāmat	habet	respondent
bibit	dant	inquit	respondet
bibunt	dat	inquiunt	vident
capit	edit	labōrant	videt
capiunt	edunt	labōrat	

Fēminae cibum et pōtum dant. Valeria cibum _____ et Licinia et Flāvia pōtum _____. Ūnus vir "Gratiās," inquit "domina." Tunc edit et bibit. Aliī virī "Grātiās," _____, "domina." Tunc virī _____ et _____. Ūnus vir pecūniam _____ et "Valē," inquit "Valeria." Aliī virī pecūniam _____ et "Valē," _____ "Valeria," "Valēte!" Valeria respondet. "Valēte!" Licinia et Flāvia _____. Tunc ad Forum virī _____. Subitō, multī virī simul ad tabernam veniunt. Licinia et Flāvia virōs vident. Valeria virōs _____ et "Salvēte!" dīcit. Virī fēminās _____ et cibum et pōtum simul _____. Licinia et ancilla Flāvia strēnuē _____. Valeria strēnuē _____. Nunc virī laetī sunt quod cibum et pōtum _____. Virī pecūniam _____ et ad Forum _____. "Valēte!" Valeria clāmat. "Et tū, valē!" virī _____. Valeria valdē laeta est quod multam pecūniam _____.

3-6 Colloquāmur

Use the narrative you created in Exercise 3-5 to tell the story to a classmate.

3-7 Verba Discenda

List the verbs from the *Verba Discenda* in one column, the nouns and pronouns in a second, and the adjectives in a third. Follow the model.

Verbs	Nouns, Pronouns	Adjectives
→ capiō	pecūnia	bonus, -a, -um

🔊 VERBA DISCENDA

bonus, -a, -um good [bona fide]

capiō, capere, cēpī, captum take [capture, captive]

laetus, -a, -um happy

mē me

nihil nothing [nihilism]

nōn not

nunc now

pecūnia, -ae f. money [impecunious, pecuniary]

quod because

respondeō, respondēre, respondī, responsum reply, answer [respondent, responsive]

Salvē!, Salvēte! Hello, Hi, Be well!

sed but

sōlum only [solitary]

semper always

tū you (sing.)

tunc then

valeō, valēre, valuī, valītum be strong, be well; Valē!, Valēte! Farewell, Goodbye, Be well! [valedictorian]

videō, vidēre, vīdī, vīsum see, perceive [invisible, video game]

vīnum, -ī n. wine

Angulus Grammaticus

Inflection vs. Word Order

Latin is an inflected language. **Inflection** is the modification of a word to indicate grammatical information, such as gender, tense, number, or person. As you have seen, the endings on a Latin verb change to indicate 3rd person singular (*videt*) and 3rd person plural (*vident*), and the endings of a Latin noun change to distinguish subject (*fēmina*) from object (*fēminam*). Although Modern English does not inflect as much as Latin does, here are some important examples: "I see" vs. "he see**s**," "ask" and "ask**ed**," and "horse" vs. "horse**s**." Instead of inflection, English uses word order to indicate subject and object. This was not always the case. Old English was also inflected.

Compare the Modern English and Old English sentences

The **father** loved his son.	*Sé **fæder** lufode þone sunu.*
	*þone sunu lufode sé **fæder**.*
	*Lufode sé **fæder** þone sunu.*
The son loved his **father**.	*Sé sunu lufode þone **fæder**.*
	*þone **fæder** lufode sé sunu.*
	*Lufode þone **fæder** sé sunu.*

Notice how changing the order of "father" and "son" completely changes the meaning of the Modern English sentence, whereas in Old English, subject and object are not distinguished by word order but by inflection. Thus *sé fæder* (father) or *sé sunu* (son) are subjects and *þone fæder* (father) and *þone sunu* (son) are objects, no matter where they appear in the sentence.

Latin is more like Old English than Modern English. The same sentences can be written in Latin like this:

The **father** loved his son.	***Pater** filium amāvit.*
	*Fīlium **pater** amāvit.*
The son loved his **father**.	*Fīlius **patrem** amāvit.*
	***Patrem** filius amāvit.*

So remember, in Latin the **endings** make the **meanings**.

Paedagōgus

Intrat Hermēs

Lectiō Prīma

Antequam Legis

Meet Hermes, the *Paedagōgus* of Lucius Servilius

In this chapter we meet **Hermes**, a slave of M. Servilius Severus, the ambitious head of a fairly well-to-do family living on the Viminal Hill. Servilius' younger son, Lucius, age ten, attends school in a shop (a common practice) near Valeria's snack shop. He is brought to and from school every day by Hermes, his *paedagōgus*. The Latin word *paedagōgus* is borrowed directly from Greek and means "one who leads a child." A *paedagōgus* was a slave, often a Greek, who predictably formed a bond with the young boy and took a major role in his education.

The Genitive Case

We introduce a new case called the **genitive case** in this chapter. Here are some Latin nouns in the genitive case with their English equivalents.

fēminae	of the woman, the woman's
fēminārum	of the women, the women's
virī	of the man, the man's
virōrum	of the men, the men's

Each **genitive** in the story is marked in **bold**. For now, when you see a genitive, simply translate it with "of" or use the apostrophe form.

LECTIŌNĒS:
HERMĒS PAEDAGŌGUS
and
HERMĒS IN TABERNĀ

Hermes, the *paedagōgus* for the Servilius family, comes to pick up his young charge. He stops at the shop of Valeria for a drink while he waits.

EXERCEĀMUS!

4-1 **Finding Genitives**

Make a line-by-line list of all the genitive words (marked in **bold**) in *Lectiō Prīma*. Then translate each word both with "of" and with an apostrophe to show possession. Follow the model.

Line	Genitive	"Of" Translation	Apostrophe Translation
→ 1	Valeriae	of Valeria	Valeria's

HERMĒS PAEDAGŌGUS

Postrīdiē Valeria, Licinia, et Flāvia iterum in **Valeriae** tabernā sunt. Hodiē, sīcut herī, aestuōsus est. Multī populī in Forō ambulant et ad tabernās veniunt. Nunc Hermēs quoque ad **Valeriae** tabernam venit.

Hermēs paedagōgus **Lūciī** est. Lūcius fīlius **Servīliī** est. Cotīdiē māne
5 Lūcius ad lūdum **magistrī** venit. Chīrōn magister **lūdī** est. Cotīdiē māne Hermēs Lūcium ad scholam **magistrī** dūcit et tunc, merīdiē, Lūcium domum ad prandium dūcit. Tunc ad lūdum reveniunt. Sērius Hermēs Lūcium domum rursus dūcit.

Nunc Hermēs dūcere Lūcium domum parātus est. Venit ad **Valeriae**
10 tabernam et eam salūtat.

Hermēs paedagōgus

VERBA ŪTENDA

aestuōsus hot
Chīrōn Chiron, Lucius' teacher. The centaur Chiron was the tutor of both Achilles and Hercules.
cotīdiē daily, every day
domus, -ī f. home, house domum home, to a house

dūcō, dūcere, dūxī, ductum lead
eam her
fīlius, -ī m. son
herī yesterday
Hermēs m. Hermes, Lucius' *paedagōgus* or tutor. He shares his name with the Greek messenger god.
hodiē today

in Forō in the Forum
***iterum* again, for a second time**
lūdus, -ī m. school, game
***māne* early in the morning**
merīdiē at noon
paedagōgus a slave assigned to a young boy, a tutor
parātus prepared
populī people

postrīdiē the next day
prandium lunch
quoque also
rursus again
salūtō, salūtāre, salūtāvī, salūtātum greet
scholam school
sērius later
sīcut just as, like
venit, veniunt come(s)

POSTQUAM LĒGISTĪ

1. How does the weather in this story compare to the weather in the previous story?
2. How many times a day does Hermes take Lucius to school? At what times?
3. Why is Chiron a good name for a teacher?
4. Why is Hermes a good name for a *paedagōgus*?

Grammatica A

The Genitive Case

Use the following chart to see the genitive endings, singular and plural. Compare the endings of the genitive with those of the nominative and accusative.

	1ST DECLENSION		2ND DECLENSION		
Singular					
Nominative	-a	fēmina	-us, -er, -ir	discipulus	magister	vir
Genitive	**-ae**	**fēminae**	**-ī**	**discipulī**	**magistrī**	**virī**
Accusative	-am	fēminam	-um	discipulum	magistrum	virum
Plural					
Nominative	-ae	fēminae	-ī	discipulī	magistrī	virī
Genitive	**-ārum**	**fēminārum**	**-ōrum**	**discipulōrum**	**magistrōrum**	**virōrum**
Accusative	-ās	fēminās	-ōs	discipulōs	magistrōs	virōs

Notā Bene:

- Whenever we show you a new case or ending, we will include the ones you already know to provide context.
- To identify the stem of a noun, drop the -ī on the genitive singular. This is especially important for words like *magister, magistrī*, in which the e in the nominative singular drops out in all the other case forms. More on this later.
- *Fēminae* and *virī* can, by form, be either nominative plural or genitive singular. A nominative plural is followed by a plural verb, but a genitive is linked to a nearby noun. What is the case of the word in bold in each of the following sentences?

  Fēminae *ad Forum ambulant.*
  Fēminae *taberna cibum et pōtum habet.*
  Paedagōgī *in Forō sunt.*
  Paedagōgī *pōtum vīnum est.*

- Translate the genitive as "of" or use an appropriate form of the apostrophe. Be careful to follow proper English usage:

  Valeriae of Valeria, Valeria's　　　*Servīliī* of Servilius, Servilius'
  fēminae of the woman, the woman's　　*virī* of the man, the man's
  fēminārum of the women, the women's　*virōrum* of the men, the men's

Notice how the genitive case indicates **possession**. Other uses of the genitive case will be introduced later.

EXERCEĀMUS!

 **4-2** **Translation**

Find the Latin phrase that best translates each English phrase.

1. Valeria's snack shop:
   a. *Valeriae taberna*
   b. *Valeriam taberna*
   c. *Valeriam tabernae*

2. the money of the man:
   a. *vir pecūnia*
   b. *virī pecūnia*
   c. *virōrum pecūnia*

3. the name of the mistress:
   a. *domina nōmen*
   b. *dominam nōmen*
   c. *dominae nōmen*

4. the men's daughters:
   a. *vir fīliae*
   b. *virōrum fīliae*
   c. *virī fīliae*

5. the daughters' maid servants:
   a. *fīliārum ancillae*
   b. *fīliae ancillae*
   c. *fīliās ancillae*

Dictionary Entry for Nouns

Now that you know about the genitive case, you can understand the dictionary entry for nouns.

- The nominative form is the main entry in your dictionary.
- The second form is genitive, usually abbreviated. The genitive tells you what declension a noun belongs to, so *-ae* means 1ˢᵗ declension and *-ī* means 2ⁿᵈ.
- The third item is gender: m. = masculine; f. = feminine, and n. = neuter.
- The last item is the meaning of the word.
- Drop the genitive ending to get the stem of a noun. So the stem of the 1ˢᵗ declension noun is *discipulae* is *discipul-* and the stem of the 2nd declension noun *discipul-* is also *discipul-*.

Thus, when you see the entry for *discipulus* in your dictionary, here is how to interpret it:

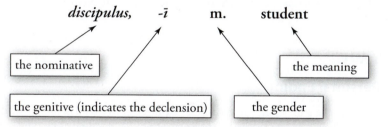

From now on, we will always give you the full dictionary entry for 1ˢᵗ and 2ⁿᵈ declension nouns in the *Verba Ūtenda*.

EXERCEĀMUS!

4-3 **Dictionary Entries**

Your turn. Take this dictionary form and identify its parts.

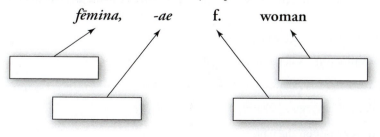

Lectiō Secunda

Antequam Legis

-ne and *-que*

Words with *-ne* attached at the end indicate that a question is being asked.

- *cupis* you want
- *cupisne* do you want?

Attaching *-que* at the end of a word is another way to say **and** in Latin.

- *vīnum aqua**que*** = *vīnum **et** aqua*

Personal Endings

You already know the verb endings *-t* (he, she, it) and *-nt* (they). In this reading you will see the Latin verb endings used for the English subjects I, we, and you. Here is how it works:

SINGULAR		PLURAL	
-ō	I	-mus	we
-s	you	-tis	you (all)
-t	he/she/it	-nt	they

Thus: *ambulās* you walk *ambulāmus* we walk

As you read *Lectiō Secunda* use this chart and the context to help determine how these endings work.

EXERCEĀMUS!

4-4 Personal Endings

Before you read, make a list of all the verbs marked in **bold** in *Lectiō Secunda*. Underline the personal ending. Then translate the verb into English. Follow the model. Use the chart of personal endings to help you.

Line	Verb	Translation
1	ambula<u>t</u>	he, she, it walks

4-5 Skimming the *Lectiō*

Skim *Lectiō Secunda* to find the answers to these questions. Give the answers in both Latin and English.

1. Whom does Hermes see when he enters the snack shop?

2. How is business for Valeria today?

3. What does Hermes order?

4. What does Hermes give Valeria?

5. What does he put on the table?

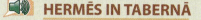

HERMĒS IN TABERNĀ

Ad Valeriae tabernam Hermēs **ambulat**. Paedagōgus Valeriam **videt salūtat**que. "Salvē, Valeria!"

"Et tū, salvē," Valeria **inquit**. "Quid **agis** hodiē?"

"**Valeō**. Et tū? Quid tū et Licinia **agitis**? Et quid **agit** familia tua?"

"Bene! Omnēs **valēmus**. Et negōtium bonum est hodiē. Multī populī cibum pōtumque **cupiunt**. Iēiūnusne **es**?

5 Sitiensne **es**? **Cupis**ne aut cibum aut pōtum?"

Hermēs sitiens est et pōtum **poscit**. "Bibere **cupiō**," **inquit**, "dā mihi vīnum aquamque, sī **placet**."

Valeria vīnum aquamque in pōculō **pōnit**. Hermēs vīnumque aquamque **bibit** et laetus **est**. Rōmānī frequenter et vīnum et aquam in pōculō singulō **bibunt**, et in tabernā vīnum semper calidum **est**. Hermēs pecūniam **dat** et saccum in mensā **pōnit**.

VERBA ŪTENDA

agō, agere, ēgī, actum lead, drive

aut or; **aut... aut** either... or

bene well

calidum hot

cibum food

cupiō, cupere, cupīvī / cupiī, cupitum wish, want to

et and, also, even; **et... et** both... and

familia, -ae f. family

frequenter frequently

iēiūnus hungry

in tabernā in the tavern

mensā table

multī many

-ne asks a yes/no question

negōtium business

omnēs everyone

paedagōgus a slave assigned to a young boy, a tutor

pōculō cup

pōnō, pōnere, posuī, positum put

populī people

poscit asks for, orders

pōtum a drink

-que and; **-que... -que** both... and

Quid agis? How are you?; Quid agit familia tua? How is your family doing?

quoque also

saccus money sack

salūtō, salūtāre, salūtāvī, salūtātum greet, say Salvē

sī if

sī placet "if it pleases," "please"

singulō one, a single

sitiens thirsty

tua your

POSTQUAM LĒGISTĪ

1. What do Hermes and Valeria talk about right after they greet each other?
2. Why does Valeria say business is good?
3. In what way is the Roman custom of wine drinking different from typical practice today?
4. In what way is Hermes careless in this *lectiō*?

> **Gemma**
>
> Compare *et... et* and *que... que*. They both mean *both... and* but their position is different:
>
> *vīnum**que** aquam**que** et vīnum et aquam*

Grammatica B

The Present Stem

The Latin verbs *ambulat* and *respondet* consist of a **present stem** plus a personal ending.

VERB	PRESENT STEM	PERSONAL ENDING
ambulat	ambulā-	-t
respondet	respondē-	-t

> **Gemma**
>
> *Quid agis?* Sometimes expressions cannot be translated literally from one language to another. This is a good example. Literally it means "What are you doing?" but it is equivalent of "How are you doing?" in English. Such expressions are called **idioms**.

You can usually determine the stem of a verb, at least for now, by dropping the personal ending from the end of the verb. Note that the stem of verbs like *ambulō* ends in *ā* and the stem of verbs like *respondeō* ends in *ē,* but these vowels can be long or short in the full form of the verb (*ambulās* vs. *ambulat*).

The 1st and 2nd Persons

In the previous chapter, you saw verbs in the present tense ending in *-t* (he, she, it) and *-nt* (they). You learned that these are the **3rd person** endings for the verb in Latin, but there are two more persons. Here is a summary of how person works in English:

		Singular Pronoun	Plural Pronoun
the speaker	1st person	I	we
the one spoken to	2nd person	you	you
the one spoken about	3rd person	he, she, it	they

In English we make minimal change to the actual verb and use personal pronouns to indicate the subject of the verb.

	Singular	Plural
1st person	I walk	we walk
2nd person	you walk	you walk
3rd person	he, she, it walks	they walk

The English verb form only changes in the third person singular ("walks" instead of "walk"). Latin, being inflected, has a whole set of **personal endings**, and they are attached to the stem of the verb to indicate the person of the subject.

Here is a summary of how "person" works in Latin:

		Singular	Plural
the speaker	1st person	*-ō* (or *-m*)	*-mus*
the one spoken to	2nd person	*-s*	*-tis*
the one spoken about	3rd person	*-t*	*-nt*

Thus:

Person	Singular		Plural	
1st	ambul**ō**	I walk	ambulā**mus**	we walk
2nd	ambulā**s**	you walk	ambulā**tis**	you walk
3rd	ambula**t**	he, she, it walks	ambula**nt**	they walk
1st	responde**ō**	I respond	respondē**mus**	we respond
2nd	respondē**s**	you respond	respondē**tis**	you respond
3rd	responde**t**	he, she, it responds	responde**nt**	they respond

Notā Bene:
- Latin verbs consist of a stem plus a personal ending.
- The vowel between the stem and the personal ending changes according to the verb's conjugation or grouping.
- Latin always distinguishes between "you" singular and "you" plural, whereas English generally uses "you" to refer to either one or more than one person. But compare our American dialectical plurals: "y'all" (southern), "youse" (northern), and "yinz" (southern Pennsylvanian and Appalachian).
- English shows gender in the third person singular (he, she, it) but Latin does not.
- The first person singular of a verb like *ambulō* is the only one of these forms for which you cannot obtain the present stem by dropping the personal ending. This is because *ambulā* + *-ō* → *ambulō*. (If you want, you can remember it this way: "O's eat A's!")
- Although you will not encounter 1st person singular verbs ending in *-m* until later, here is a memnonic you can use to remember the personal endings:

    MOST (*-m -o, -s, -t*)   MUST (*-mus*)   ISN'T (*-tis, -nt*)

EXERCEĀMUS!

4-6 **Conjugation**

Use the foms for *ambulō* and *respondeō* as models to fill in the charts for *salūtō* and *valeō*.

PERSON	SINGULAR		PLURAL	
1st	*salūtō*	I greet		
2nd				
3rd			*salūtant*	they greet
1st	*valeō*	I am well		
2nd				
3rd			*valent*	they are well

Asking Yes/No Questions

To ask a yes/no question in English we usually put the verb first and the subject second and add a question mark. Sometimes we add "do/does."

He is prepared to run.	Is he prepared to run?
You are hungry.	Are you hungry?
He wants wine.	Does he want wine?

To ask a yes/no question in Latin, add *-ne* to the first word in the sentence.

Currere parātus est.   *Est**ne** parātus currere?*
He is prepared to run.   Is he prepared to run?

Iēiūnus es.   *Es**ne** iēiūnus?*
You are hungry.   Are you hungry?

Vīnum cupit.   *Vīnum**ne** cupit?*
He wants wine.   Does he want wine?

Sitiens es.	*Sitiens**ne** es?*
You are thirsty.	Are you thirsty?
Cupis aliquid bibere aut edere.	*Cupis**ne** aliquid bibere aut edere?*
You want something to eat or drink.	Do you want something to eat or drink?

Notā Bene: *-ne* is not used when another interrogative word appears in the sentence.

Quid tibi nōmen est?	What is your name?
Ubi es?	Where are you?

Mōrēs Rōmānī

Wine in Ancient Rome

Prēlum antīquum Pompeiīs

Although grapes for wine had been grown north of Rome in Etruria and in Greek southern Italy for centuries, the cultivation of wine grapes and the consumption of wine did not become popular in Rome until the second century B.C. The earliest written work on wine in Rome was translated from Punic shortly after the end of the Third Punic War in 146 B.C. The first Roman to write about the topic was Cato the Elder in a work called *Dē Agrī Cultūrā* (*On Agriculture*). One of the most important documents on Roman wine production and use appears in Book XIV of *Historia Nātūrālis* (*Natural History*) by Pliny the Elder (23–79 A.D).

Vine cultivation in Rome spread quickly, and by the middle of the second century B.C., Rome was a major producer of wine grapes. In fact, in 154 B.C. the Roman Senate prohibited the cultivation of vines north of the Alps to preserve the market for Roman producers. Wine was cultivated on large estates worked by slaves. By the first century A.D., wine consumption in Rome was so high that wines were imported from provinces in Spain and France.

Romans especially liked sweet wines produced from very ripe grapes. *Mulsum,* a wine drink heavily flavored with honey, was especially popular among the lower classes. *Lōra,* a drink made from grape skins soaked in water and fermented, was often served to slaves.

Many Roman authors discuss multiple types of wine but especially praised a wine called Falernian, produced from grapes grown on Mount Falernus south of Rome.

Some of the finest Italian wines were produced in antiquity on the slopes of Mt. Vesuvius. The picture at left shows Bacchus, the god of wine, dressed in grapes and standing on the slope of the mountain, which is covered by grape vines. Evidence for wine production in this area includes the wine press (*prēlum, -ī* n.) depicted in the picture.

Vesuvius et Bacchus

Latin continues to have a presence in modern wine-making: *Est! Est!! Est!!!* is a white wine produced in Montefiascone, north of Rome near Lake Bolsena. The name of the wine is attributed to a German bishop named Johann Fugger, who was going to Rome for the coronation of Henry V in the year 1125. Fugger sent a servant ahead of him to mark the inns with the best wine with *Est* (for *Vīnum bonum est*). At one inn in Montefiascone the servant apparently liked the wine so much that he wrote *Est! Est!! Est!!!*

The Romans had a lot to say about drinking wine. With the help of the *Verba Ūtenda,* you can understand what they said.

One of the earliest Roman writers to refer to wine is the 2nd-century B.C. playwright Plautus, who said:

> *Magnum hoc vitium in vīnō est. Vīnum pedēs captat prīmum;*
> *Vīnum luctātor dolōsus est.*
>
> Pseudolus (act V, 1, 5)

A Roman proverb quoted by Pliny the Elder, reads:

> *In vīnō vēritās (est).*

Doc Holliday also quoted this proverb in Latin in the 1993 film *Tombstone*.

In poem I.7 of his *Carmina* (*Odes*), the poet Horace (65–27 B.C.) said:

> *Nunc vīnō pellite cūrās.*

In Petronius' *Satyricon 34* (1st century A.D.), a character named Trimalchio said:

> *Vīta vīnum est.*

Finally, in his discourse *Dē Īrā* (*On Anger*, 2.19) the philosopher Seneca the Younger (c. 4 B.C.–65 A.D.) said:

> *Vīnum incendit īram.*

 VERBA ŪTENDA

captat (he, she, it) seizes	*luctātor* wrestler	*vīta* life
cūra, -ae f. care, concern	*pedēs* feet	*vīnō* with wine
dolōsus clever, crafty	*Pellite!* Banish!	*vīnum* despite the *-um*
hoc this	Drive away!	ending, this word is
incendit sets fire to, burns	*prīmum* first	nominative
īra, -ae f. anger	*vēritās* truth	*vitium* vice

Gemma

Cavē! (Beware!) The stem of *vīta* (life) is *vīt-* and the stem of *vitium* (vice) is *viti-*. That final *-i* can make all the difference in Latin between "life" and "vice." The macron in *vīta* certainly helps, but how can the declension endings also be useful here?

Orbis Terrārum Rōmānus

Urbs Rōma

The major geographical landmarks of the city of Rome are the Tiber River (*Tiberis, -is* m.), which runs through the city, the *Campus Martius* (Field of Mars), and the following seven hills:

Capitoline (*Capitōlīnus Collis, Capitōlīnī Collis* m.; also *Capitōlium, -iī* n.)

Palatine (*Palātīnus Mons, Palātīnī Montis* m.; *Palātium, -iī* n.)

Esquiline (*Esquiliae, -ārum* f. pl.)

Caelian (*Caelius Mons, Caeliī Montis* m.)

Viminal (*Vīminālis Collis, Vīminālis Collis* m.)

Quirinal (*Quirīnālis Collis, Quirīnālis Collis* m.)

Aventine (*Aventīnus Mons, Aventīnī Montis* m.; *Aventīnum, -ī* n.)

Septem collēs Rōmae

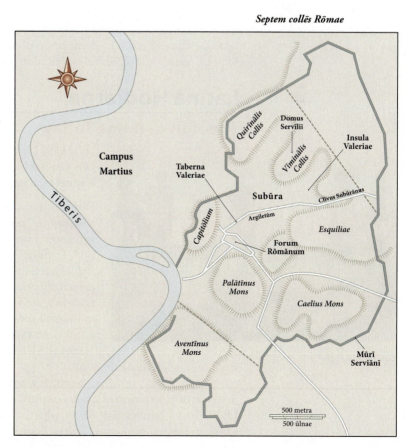

Dē Forō Rōmānō ad Capitōlium hodiē

Forum Rōmānum et Palātium hodiē

The Roman Forum is located in the valley between the Palatine and the Capitoline. It was on the Palatine Hill that the founders of Rome, Romulus and Remus, were said to have been nursed as infants by a she-wolf. On the Capitoline Hill were located the chief temples of the city, especially the Temple of Jupiter Capitolinus (*Capitōlium, -iī* n.), the most important temple in the city. Victorious generals led their triumphal processions along the Via Sacra through the Forum up to the *Capitōlium*. The route of the Via Sacra runs between two more hills, the Esquiline and the Caelian. The Viminal and the Quirinal Hills lie to the north of the Esquiline. The Velia is the projection of the Esquiline toward the Palatine. The seventh hill, the Aventine, lies to the south of the Palatine. In the valley between the Palatine and the Aventine was the Forum Boarium, an important market area, and the open space that eventually became the Circus Maximus. In the Imperial period, all seven of these hills, but not the Campus Martius, were enclosed within fortification walls.

Latīna Hodierna

The Hills of Rome Today

Capitōlium hodiē

"Hey kids, I have a **capitol** idea! Let's go to the nation's **capitol**, and visit **Capital** Hill where we can see all the Greek **capitols** on the **Capital** building!"

Did you spot the spelling errors in that sentence? Both "capital" and "capitol" come from Latin. Once you know their origins, you will never misspell them again.

"Capitol," in English, refers to the building in Washington, D.C., that houses the Congress. It stands on Capitol Hill and it is named after the *Capitōlium* in Rome, implying a clever identification with the Temple of Capitoline Jupiter on the Capitoline Hill in Rome. Likewise, the building in which a state legislature meets is called the capitol (lower case). These uses, and the Capitol Reef National Museum in Utah, are the only common forms of the words in English that end in -ol.

"Capital" with an -al can be either a noun or an adjective. As a noun it can mean: the official seat of government of a state, country, or the like; wealth, as in "capital funds"; CAPITAL LETTER; or column top. As an adjective "capital" means "chief" or "excellent." Both -al words are derived from *caput, -itis* n. head, main part.

So now you know that the paragraph at the beginning of this section *should* have read: "Hey kids, I have a **capital** idea! Let's go to the nation's **capital**, and visit **Capitol** Hill where we can see all the Greek **capitals** on the **Capitol** building!"

The city of Richmond, Virginia, is built on seven hills. The state capitol is located (naturally) on Capitol Hill.

Several of Rome's hills have taken on special meaning in some modern languages. For example, because Augustus and later emperors built elaborate homes on the Palatine hill, *Palātium* is the source of the word for "palace."

The president of modern Italy lives in a palace on the Quirinal Hill, so "Quirinale" in Italian means "the presidential palace." In English and French, "Quirinal" can also refer to the palace of the Italian president.

Now look at some other derivations:

Capitōlium Americānum

LATIN	ENGLISH	FRENCH	ITALIAN	SPANISH
Capitōlīnus	Capitoline	Capitole	Campidoglio Monte Capitolio	Capitolio
Capitōlium	Capitol	Capitole	Campidoglio	Capitolio
caput, capitis	capital	capitale	capitale	capital
Palātium	palace	palace	palazzo	palacio

QUID PUTĀS?

1. Why do you think *schola* and *lūdus*, two Latin words for "school," both originally referred to leisure and games?
2. Compare the Roman statements about wine to modern attitudes toward wine. Which of the Roman statements best express your own attitude toward wine. Why?
3. How have modern wine drinking tastes changed from Roman times?
4. Why do you think that the U.S. Capitol building has such close linguistic ties with the Capitoline Hill in Rome?

EXERCEĀMUS!

4-7 Scrībāmus

Answer each of these questions in Latin. Use complete sentences. You may use *ita* or *sīc* (yes) and *nōn* (no/not) in your answers as well. Follow the model.

HINT: All of these sentences are based on the quotations about wine in the *Mōrēs Rōmānī* section.

→ Estne vēritās in vīnō? *Ita, vēritās in vīnō est!*

1. Estne magnum vitium in vīnō?

2. Captatne vīnum prīmum pedēs?

3. Estne vīnum luctātor?

4. Pellitne vīnum cūrās?

5. Vītane vīnum est?

6. Incenditne vīnum īram?

4-8 Colloquāmur

As you ask a classmate the following questions, use one of the words suggested in parentheses. Then have your classmate respond as she or he thinks fit. Follow the pattern in the model and experiment with word order.

 Estne vēritās (in aquā, in cibō, in pōculō)?

Student #1   *Estne vēritās in aquā?*

Student #2   *Nōn, vēritās in aquā nōn est.*   or

Nōn, vēritās nōn in aquā est.   or

Ita, vēritās in aquā est.   or

Sīc, in aquā vēritās est.

1. Valeriāne (cibum, pecūniam, pōtum) in pōculō pōnit?

2. Vītāne (vīnum, aqua, saccus, negōtium) est?

3. Hermēsne (aquam, Valeriam, pōculum) in mensā pōnit?

4. Cupiuntne omnēs (pecūniam, negōtium bonum, vīnum calidum)?

4-9 Verba Discenda

For each of the following English words, list the *Verbum Discendum* that is its source. Be sure to include the meaning of the Latin word. Then use the meaning of the Latin word to define the English word. Follow the model.

HINT: If you need help, use an English dictionary.

→ reactivate: *agō, agere, ēgī, actum* do, drive; to make to do again

1. depopulate
2. beneficiary
3. introduction
4. deposition
5. ludicrous

6. salutation
7. affiliation
8. iteration
9. domicile
10. cupidinous

🔊 VERBA DISCENDA

agō, agere, ēgī, actum act, do, lead, drive [agile, active]

aut or; *aut... aut* either... or

bene well [benefactor]

cupiō, cupere, cupīvī / cupiī, cupītum wish, want to [Cupid, cupidity]

domus, -ī f. home, house *domum* home, to a house [domicile]

dūcō, dūcere, dūxī, ductum lead [duct, induct]

et and, also, even; *et... et* both... and

familia, -ae f. family [familiarity]

fīlius, -ī m. son [filial]

hodiē today

iterum again [reiterate]

lūdus, –ī m. school, game [ludicrous]

māne early in the morning

-ne asks a yes/no question

pōnō, pōnere, posuī, positum put, place [position]

populus, -ī m. people [popularity]

-que and; *-que... -que* both... and

Quid agis? Quid agitis? How are you?

salūtō, salūtāre, salūtāvī, salūtātum greet [salutation, salutatorian]

Angulus Grammaticus

Enclitics and Word Stress

Did you notice anything unusual about *-ne* and *-que*, two words introduced in this chapter? They are not really independent words. Rather the hyphen tells you that they are always attached to another word. This type of linguistic element is called an **enclitic**. Technically, an enclitic is an element that has no stress or accent of its own and is tightly bound to the word that precedes it.

One question that arises with enclitics in Latin is the issue of pronunciation and stress. Though everyone agrees that enclitics like *-ne* and *-que* are never stressed themselves, there is debate as to how they affect the accent of the words to which they are attached.

Early Roman grammarians claimed that the enclitic was a sort of "accent magnet" and always attracted the accent to the syllable before the enclitic, whether that syllable was long or short. This would yield forms like:

*ac**TOR**que*

*imitā**TOR**que*

This approach is the one most commonly used in classrooms today. But some later grammarians tend to believe that in the time of Augustus, the enclitic affected stress little or not at all and that the word was subject to the normal rules of stress. This would yield forms such as:

***AC**torque*

*imi**TA**torque*

Final certainty is not possible. As in English, there were probably variants even in antiquity. In various parts of America you might hear either version of this sentence:

"Don't forget your umbr**EL**la because if you catch
cold and die, we have no ins**UR**ance."

or

"Don't forget your **UM**brella because if you catch
cold and die, we have no **IN**surance."

How do you pronounce this sentence?

Forum Rōmānum

GRAMMATICA

Asking Questions: *Num* and *Nōnne*

Prepositions

The Concept of Conjugation

More Principal Parts

MŌRĒS RŌMĀNĪ

Marmor et Templa Rōmāna

ORBIS TERRĀRUM RŌMĀNUS

Mausōlēum Augustī

LATĪNA HODIERNA

Animālia Rōmāna

ANGULUS GRAMMATICUS

Principal Parts in English and Latin

LECTIŌNĒS:
SĪMIA SŌCRATĒS
and
SĪMIA SAGAX

While at Valeria's snack shop, Hermes teases Socrates, the shop's pet monkey. Socrates snatches Hermes' money bag, and the angry *paedagōgus* chases the monkey through the Roman Forum.

In Forō

Lectiō Prīma

Antequam Legis

Socrates the Monkey

While Hermes is at Valeria's *taberna*, he makes the mistake of teasing Socrates, the pet monkey in Valeria's shop. As you can see in the relief from Ostia in the *lectiō*, monkeys were often found in such shops. In this scene, two untied monkeys sit on the counter of a food store. (The rabbits are undoubtedly not pets, but are rather for sale.) Keeping pets in stores to attract customers is a phenomenon common to this day.

As you read about Hermes and the monkey, look out for more ways to ask questions in Latin.

Asking Questions with *Num* and *Nōnne*

Read this sentence aloud: "He wants to eat chicken."

Now read this sentence aloud: "He wants to eat chicken?"

Notice that we can tell that a spoken sentence is a question from the tone of voice, but a written question requires a punctuation mark. Spanish wisely puts an inverted question mark at the beginning of a question.

¿Dónde está el pollo?

Like Spanish, Latin puts its question indicators at the beginning of the sentence. There are three such Latin words, and each expects a different kind of answer:

*Habēs**ne*** sīmiam?	a yes/no question	Do you have a monkey?
Nōnne sīmiam habēs?	expects a "yes" answer	You do have a monkey, don't you?
Num sīmiam habēs?	expects a "no" answer	You don't have a monkey, do you?

EXERCEĀMUS!

5-1 Asking Questions

Translate the following questions, using the chart as a guide.

1. Valeriane tabernam habet?
   Num Valeria tabernam habet?
   Nōnne Valeria tabernam habet?

2. Sīmiaene nōmen Sōcratēs?
   Nōnne sīmiae nōmen Sōcratēs?
   Num sīmiae nōmen Sōcratēs?

3. Nōnne Rōmānī vīnum bibunt?
   Rōmānīne vīnum bibunt?
   Num Rōmānī vīnum bibunt?

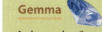

Gemma

Is the monkey Socrates male or female? *Sīmia, -ae* is 1st declension where most words are feminine. But some words are "common" gender, i.e., masculine or feminine.

Now watch for *-ne*, *nōnne*, and *num*, marked in **bold**, in *Lectiō Prīma*.

Sīmiae in tabernā Rōmānā

🔊 SĪMIA SŌCRATĒS

Subitō Hermēs sīmiam in tabernā videt. Nōmen sīmiae Sōcratēs est et in Valeriae tabernā cōtīdiē sedet et lūdit.

Hermēs rīdet. "Salvē, sīmia!" paedagōgus
5 inquit. "Quid agis? Habēs**ne** nōmen?"

Sīmia nihil respondet sed "Nōmen sīmiae," inquit Valeria, "Sōcratēs est." Sīcut Sōcratēs philosophus, sīmia habet nāsum plānum, ergō nōmen Sōcratēs est.

"Hermēs "Cupis**ne**," inquit vīnum, Sōcratēs?" et pōculum ostendit.
10 "**Num** vīnum," Licinia, Valeriae fīlia, clāmat, "eī das?!"

Error est. Sīmiae nōn vīnum amant, sed semper iocōs amant et Sōcratēs subitō saccum paedagōgī rapit.

"Ecce!" Hermēs clāmat. "Sīmia saccum meum habet. **Num**, sīmia, pecūniam meam cupis? **Nōnne** vīnum cupis? Dabis**ne** mihi saccum?"

Subitō Hermēs ad sīmiam salit, sed eum nōn capit. Sīmiae valdē celerēs sunt. Sōcratēs ē tabernā currit.

🔊 VERBA ŪTENDA

ad (+ acc.) **to, toward**
amō, amāre, amāvī, amātum love
clāmō (1) **shout**
celerēs fast, swift
cōtīdiē daily
currō, currere, cucurrī, cursum **run**
dabisne? will you give?
ē / ex (+ abl.) **out of, from**
Ecce! Look!
eī to him

ergō therefore
error mistake, error
eum him
fīlia, -ae f. daughter
habeō, habēre, habuī, habitum **have, hold**
in (+ abl.) **in, on, at;** (+ acc.) **into, against**
iocus, -ī m. joke
lūdō, lūdere play
meus, -a, -um **my**
nāsus, -ī m. nose

nōnne asks a question **expecting a yes answer**
num asks a question **expecting a no answer**
ostendō, ostendere show
philosophus, -ī m. philosopher
plānum flat
pōculum, -ī n. cup
poscō, poscere, poposcī **ask for, demand, request**
Quid agis? How are you doing?

rapiō, rapere seize
rīdeō, rīdēre laugh
saccus, -ī m. money sack
saliō, salīre leap
sedeō, sedēre sit
sīcut just like
sīmia, -ae f. **monkey**
Sōcratēs, -is m. Socrates, a Greek philosopher
subitō suddenly
valdē very

Sōcratēs philosophus nāsum plānum habet.

Answer the first four questions in both Latin and English. Answer question 5 in English.

1. Why is the monkey called Socrates?
2. What mistake does Hermes make?
3. What does the monkey take from Hermes?
4. How does Hermes react?
5. What do you think is going to happen next?

Grammatica A

Asking Questions: *Num* and *Nōnne*

You have learned that to ask a yes/no question in Latin, you add the enclitic *-ne* to the first word in the sentence. Here are a few examples:

Currere parātus est.	*Est**ne** currere parātus?*
He is prepared to run.	Is he prepared to run?
Iēiūnus es.	*Es**ne** iēiūnus?* or *Iēiūnus**ne** es?*
You are hungry.	Are you hungry?

The person asking these questions is looking for simple yes/no information and is not anticipating a particular response.

It is possible, however, to ask the same questions in expectation of a particular answer. For example:

You are hungry, aren't you?	(expects the answer "yes" or "certainly")
You aren't hungry, are you?	(expects the answer "no" or "not at all")

Here is how Latin asks the same questions:

Nōnne iēiūnus es?	(expects the answer *ita* or *ita vērō*)
Num iēiūnus es?	(expects the answer *nōn* or *nōn vērō*)

EXERCEĀMUS!

5-2 **Answering Questions**

Use *Lectiō Prīma* to answer the following questions by saying either *ita/(sīc)* (yes) or *nōn* (no) and repeating the verb. Follow the models.

→ Q: Vide**ne** Hermēs sīmiam in tabernā?
  A: Ita, videt.

→ Q: **Num** sedet Sōcratēs in tabernā Valeriae cotīdiē?
  A: Nōn sedet.

1. **Num** sīmiae vīnum amant?
2. **Nōnne** rapit Sōcratēs saccum paedagōgī?
3. **Nōnne** amant sīmiae iōcōs semper?
4. Currit**ne** Sōcratēs ē tabernā?
5. **Num** sīmiae nōmen Hermēs est?
6. Capit**ne** Hermēs sīmiam?

Lectiō Secunda

Antequam Legis

Prepositions

In this *lectiō* Hermes chases Socrates through the Forum. The map will help you trace their route. **Prepositions** are parts of speech used with nouns or pronouns to express direction (in, on, around, through, under), the source of an action (by, on account of, etc.), or relationship (about, concerning, etc.). In English, the preposition does not affect the appearance of the noun or pronoun but in Latin it does. Note the following examples:

into the shop	*in tabernam*
in the shop	*in tabernā*
out of the shop	*ē tabernā*
through the shop	*per tabernam*

As these examples show, prepositions in Latin are used with either the **accusative case** or the **ablative case**. You are already familiar with the accusative. You will meet the ablative in the next chapter.

EXERCEĀMUS!

5-3 **Prepositional Phrases**

Before you read *Lectiō Secunda*, make a line-by-line list of 10 of the prepositions marked in **bold**. Then find the object of each preposition and decide whether the object is in the accusative or ablative case. Then translate the prepositional phrase. Follow the model.

HINT: You can recognize prepositions in the vocabulary because they are followed by **+ abl.** or **+ acc.** in the *Verba Ūtenda* to tell you which case they take.

REMEMBER: If it's not accusative, it's ablative!

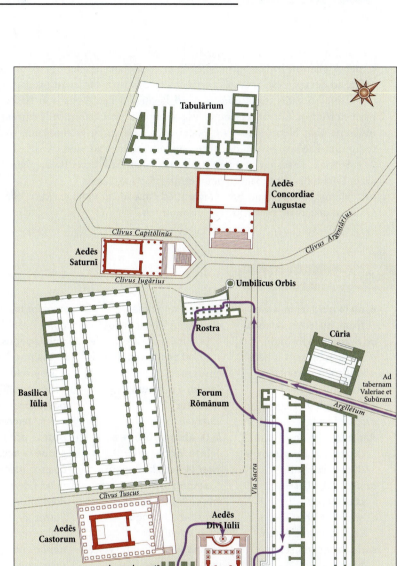

Iter Sīmiae Pedagōgīque in Forō

Line	Preposition	Object	Case	Translation
→ 1	ad	Forum	acc.	to the Forum

SĪMIA SAGAX

Sīmiā Sōcratēs

Sōcratēs **ā** tabernā **ad** Forum currit. Taberna Valeriae **prope** Argīlētum est et **per** Argīlētum **in** Forum nunc currunt et Sōcratēs et Hermēs. Mox, **in** Forō sunt. Cūria, ubi Senātus Rōmānus sedet, **ad** dextram est. Sōcratēs currit et **super** Rostrīs stat et **ad** paedagōgum clāmat.

Tunc Sōcratēs **trans** Forum et **ad** Basilicam Paullī currit et basilicam intrat. **Per** basilicam currit et tunc **ē** basilicā rumpit. Sōcratēs nunc **in** Viā Sacrā est. Sīmia latēre vult et **post** Dīvī Iūliī templum quiescit. Sed nōn diū quiescit, nam Hermēs advenit. Sōcratēs iterum currit et nunc stat medius **inter** Vestae templum et Castorum templum. Paedagōgus, valdē īrātus, sīmiam videt et **ad** eum currit.

Sōcratēs fessus est, sed adhūc saccum tenet. Sed, ecce! Paedagōgus valdē īrātus iam adest! Sōcratēs territus **ad** āram Dīvī Iūliī currit. Salit in āram et magnā vōce clāmat.

Hermēs **prope** āram stat. Sīmiam territum **in** āra videt et rīdet. "Sīmia sagax es, Sōcratēs. **In** āra sacrā salvus es! Dā mihi pecūniam meam et omne bonum est."

VERBA ŪTENDA

ā, ab (+ abl.) from, away from; by (with persons)
ad dextram to the right
adest he is present, is here
adhūc to this point, still, yet
adveniō, advenīre come
āra, -ae f. altar
Argīlētum the Argiletum, (a street leading into the Roman Forum)
basilica, -ae f. basilica, courthouse
Castorum of the Castors, i.e., Castor and Pollux
cūria, -ae f. curia, senate house
dā! give! (command)

diū for a long time
dīvus Iūlius "divine Julius" (Julius Caesar was made a god posthumously)
fessus tired
forum, -ī n. forum, city center
iam now
in (+ abl.) in, on; (+ acc.) into, onto
inter (+ acc.) between, among
intrō, intrāre enter
īrātus, -a, -um angry
lateō, latēre hide
magnā vōce in a loud voice
medius midway
mox soon

nam for, because
omne everything
paedagōgus, -ī m. a slave assigned to a young boy, a tutor
per (+ acc.) through
poscō, poscere, poposcī ask for, demand, request
post (+ acc.) behind, after
prope (+ acc.) near
quiescō, quiescere rest
rīdeō, rīdēre laugh
Rōmānus, -a, -um Roman
Rostra, -ōrum n. pl. speaker's platform
rumpō, rumpere burst
sacra sacred, holy
sagax wise

saliō, salīre leap
sedeō, sedēre, sēdī, sessum sit
senātus senate
sīmia, -ae f. monkey
stō, stāre, stetī, stātum stand
super (+ acc. or abl.) over, on top of
templum temple
territus afraid, scared
trans (+ acc.) across
tunc then
ubi where, when
via, -ae f. road, way
valdē very
Vesta, -ae f. Vesta, goddess of the hearth
vult he wishes, wants

POSTQUAM LĒGISTĪ

Answer the following questions in English.

1. Where does Socrates run when he leaves Valeria's snack shop?
2. What is the Curia used for?
3. Which building does Socrates enter?
4. What does Socrates want to do once he gets to the Via Sacra?
5. Between which two temples does Socrates stand?
6. Where does the chase end?
7. Why does Hermes tell Socrates he is a wise monkey?

Grammatica B

Prepositions

Here are several prepositional phrases you saw in the reading:

per Argīlētum	through the Argiletum
ad āram Dīvī Iūliī	to the altar of Divine Julius
trans Forum	across the Forum
ad Forum	to the Forum
post Dīvī Iūliī templum	behind the temple of Divine Julius
ad Basilicam Paullī	to the Basilica Paulli

Notice how all of these prepositions are followed by nouns in the accusative case. These words are called the **objects of the prepositions**. The preposition plus its object is called a **prepositional phrase**.

Not all objects of prepositions are accusative. Some are ablative, a case you will learn in the next chapter. Here are some ablative objects of prepositions you have already seen.

ā tabernā	away from the snack shop
ē tabernā	out of the snack shop
in tabernā	in the snack shop
in ārā	on the altar
super Rostrīs	on top of the Rostra

Notā Bene: *ā* and *ē* tend to be used before consonants, *ab* and *ex* before vowels.

The Concept of Conjugation

You have noticed that verbs have a variety of vowels before their personal endings. Which vowel to use with which verb depends on that verb's **conjugation**. Latin verbs are grouped into four categories or **conjugations** depending upon which vowel appears before the *-re* of the infinitive.

CONJUGATION	INFINITIVE	STEM	VOWEL SIGN
1st	*ambulāre*	*ambulā-*	stem ends in *-ā*
2nd	*respondēre*	*respondē-*	stem ends in *-ē*
3rd	*vendere*	*vende-*	stem ends in *-e*
4th	*venīre*	*venī-*	stem ends in *-ī*

In your dictionary, each verb is listed with its four **principal parts**, and these, too, help you create various tenses and forms of the verb. For now we are focusing on 1st and 2nd conjugation verbs.

More Principal Parts

You will find a Latin verb listed in the dictionary under its 1st person singular form, generally followed by three other forms. These four forms are called principal parts (PP). Here is what you will find for the verb *salūtō*:

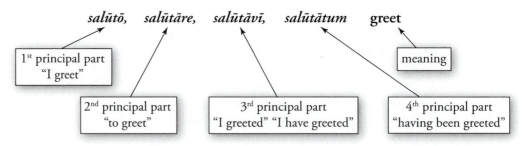

salūtō,   salūtāre,   salūtāvī,   salūtātum   greet

| 1st principal part "I greet" | 2nd principal part "to greet" | 3rd principal part "I greeted" "I have greeted" | 4th principal part "having been greeted" | meaning |

Notā Bene: The pattern of principal parts for 1st conjugation verbs like *salūtō* is so predictable that, from now on, we will only list them in *Verba Discenda* like this: *salūtō* (1).

EXERCEĀMUS!

5-4 **Dictionary Entries**

Your turn. Take this dictionary form and identify its parts.

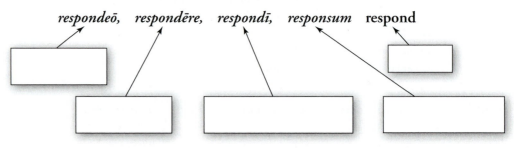

respondeō,   respondēre,   respondī,   responsum   respond

Mōrēs Rōmānī

Caesar Augustus Dīvus Iūlius

Marmor et Templa Rōmāna

The Romans themselves justly boasted of their impressive forum and its history. They often noted with pride that the area filled with majestic buildings in the time of Augustus was once only swampland. Here the poet Ovid (43 B.C.–17 A.D.) describes the site:

hōc ubi nunc fora sunt, palūdēs ūdae tenuēre

Fasti vi.401

The Emperor Augustus himself boasted about his own building projects. He said:

(Urbem) marmoream relinquō, quam latericiam accēpī

Suetonius *Dīv Aug* 28

🔊 VERBA ŪTENDA

accēpī I accepted, received
hōc here
latericiam made of brick
marmoream made of marble

palūdēs swamps
quam which
relinquō, relinquere leave

tenuēre (they) held
ūdus, -a, -um wet
urbem city

Ironically, the marble veneer has generally been removed from the surviving monuments of the Augustan Age, and only their brick infrastructure remains, as you can see on the tomb of Augustus in Rome today. We often have to use our imagination to appreciate how the monuments originally appeared.

Aedēs Vestae et Aedēs Castorum hodiē

Many of these Augustan monuments are temples. The Romans considered these buildings to be homes for the cult statues of the gods, not buildings in which large congregations could worship. The typical Roman temple (*templum, -ī* n.; also *aedēs, aedis* f.) was rectangular. It was fronted by a tall staircase leading to a collonaded portico. Though the columns of a Greek temple commonly ran around all four sides of the building, the columns on a Roman temple were usually only in front. Inside were the cult statue of the deity and other sacred objects.

Aedēs Castorum, the Temple of Castor and Pollux, follows this design. Originally built after the Battle of Lake Regillus in 496 B.C., a Roman victory where the twin gods (also known as *Geminī*) were thought to play a major role in Roman victory, the temple burned down in 14 B.C. Its reconstruction was not finished until 6 A.D. when it was rededicated by the Emperor Tiberius. So when Hermes chases Socrates through the Forum, the new temple is still under construction (as is the Basilica Paulli).

Aedēs Vestae, the Temple of Vesta (Roman goddess of the hearth), is unusual in that its design is circular instead of rectangular. Here the Vestal Virgins, the priestesses of Vesta, always kept a fire burning on the public hearth of the city. The temple was built in the 3rd century B.C. and was rebuilt after the famous fire of 64 A.D. during the reign of Nero. This is one of the few buildings in the Forum that Augustus did not construct or rebuild.

Aedēs Dīvī Iūliī hodiē

Aedēs Dīvī Iūliī was built on the site where Julius Caesar's body was cremated after his assassination on the Ides of March in 44 B.C. The temple was dedicated to the deified Caesar by Augustus on August 18, 29 B.C. On one side of the Roman coin depicted at left, Julius Caesar is celebrated as divine. Note the comet with eight rays, one with a tail, which is said to have been seen in 44 B.C. after his death. The other side of the coin shows the image of Augustus. As long as Socrates sat on the altar in front of this temple, he was protected by the ancient law of suppliants, which said that anyone being chased could seek sanctuary or protection from pursuers by taking refuge at such a religious spot.

Āra Dīvī Iūliī hodiē

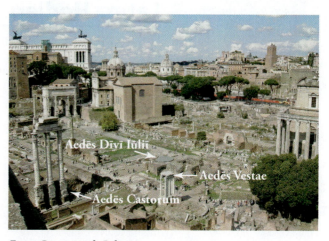

Forum Rōmānum dē Palātīnō

Orbis Terrārum Rōmānus

Mausōlēum Augustī

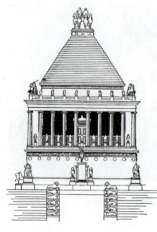

Exemplar Mausōlēī Halicarnassī

Augustus started building his own mausoleum in Rome in 28 B.C., three years after he defeated Mark Antony and Cleopatra at the Battle of Actium. In planning this tomb, Augustus certainly had in mind monuments like the Mausoleum of Halicarnassus, built in 353 B.C. and one of the Seven Wonders of the Ancient World. Only the foundations of Mausolus' tomb remain today, but ancient descriptions provide some idea of its appearance. Mausolus' tomb was so famous that "mausoleum" became the name for any tomb. Compare its design with the Masonic House of the Temple of Scottish Rite in Washington, D.C.

Inside Augustus' mausoleum were the cinerary urns of the emperor and his family. This fragmentary inscription from the Mausoleum commemorates Augustus' sister Octavia:

OCTAVIA . C . F | SOROR | AVGV

And here is a fuller version of the text with the abbreviations explained in brackets and the possible missing text supplied in parentheses.

OCTAVIA . C[AII]. F[ILIA] | SOROR | AVGV(STI . CAESARIS)

Can you translate this on your own?

Mausōlēum Augustī hodiē

Imitātiō Mausōlēī Halicarnassī

Latīna Hodierna

Animālia Rōmāna

English has borrowed many Latin words for animals. Here are just a few examples:

Latin	Animal	English
sīmia, sīmiae	monkey	**simi**an
canis, canis	dog	**can**ine
fēlēs, fēlis	cat	**fel**ine
bōs, bovis	bull, cow	**bov**ine
piscis, piscis	fish	**pisc**ine
serpens, serpentis	snake, serpent	**serpent**ine

Notice how the English word is often derived from the genitive (rather than nominative) form of the Latin word. The general rule is that the stem of a Latin word is determined by dropping the ending on the genitive singular form of the Latin word. So the stem of *sīmia* is *sīmi-* from *sīmiae* and the stem of *serpens* is *serpent-* from *serpentis*.

QUID PUTĀS?

1. Compare the design of Roman temples described in *Mōrēs Rōmānī* with a place of worship with which you are familiar.
2. Are there any modern parallels to the right of sanctuary that prevents Hermes from seizing Socrates on the Altar of Divine Julius?
3. Using the *Latīna Hodierna* as a guide, can you find any more English words based on the Latin word for an animal followed by the suffix **-ine**?

EXERCEĀMUS!

5-5   Scrībāmus

Answer the following questions with complete Latin sentences based on the *Lectiōnēs* in this chapter. The result will be a paragraph about *Lectiō Prīma*. We have started the narrative for you.

→ Does Socrates sit in Valeria's snack shop every day?
   Sōcratēs in tabernā Valeriae cotīdiē sedet.

1. Does the monkey love wine?

2. Does Socrates snatch the *paedagōgus's* wallet?

3. Do monkeys always love jokes?

4. Does Socrates run from the snack shop?

5. Where does Socrates run?

6. Does Hermes catch the monkey?

5-6   Colloquāmur

Practice asking and answering the questions in Exercise 5-5 with other members of your class, but change each sentence a bit before you ask it. For example:

→ Q: Does the monkey like money?
   A: Ita, sīmia pecūniam amat.

5-7   Verba Discenda

Draw a simple house (*casa, -ae* f). Then, pick out all the prepositions from the *Verba Discenda* and illustrate each one with the house you have drawn. Thus, *in casam* would have an arrow going into the house.

🔊 **VERBA DISCENDA**

ā, ab (+ abl.) away from
ad (+ acc.) to, toward
clāmō (1) shout
currō, currere, cucurrī,
    cursum run [curriculum,
    cursor]
ē / ex (+ abl.) out of, from
forum, -ī n. forum, city center
habeō, habēre, habuī,
    habitum have, hold
    [habit]

in (+ abl.) in, on, at; (+ acc.)
    into, onto
inter (+ acc.) between,
    among [intermediary]
meus, -a, -um my
nōnne asks a question
    expecting a yes
    answer
num asks a question
    expecting a no
    answer

paedagōgus, -ī m. a slave
    assigned to a young
    boy, a tutor [pedagogy]
per (+ acc.) through
poscō, poscere, poposcī ask
    for, demand, request
post (+ acc.) after, behind
prope (+ acc.) near
    [propinquity]
sedeō, sedēre, sēdī, sessum
    sit [sedentary]

sīmia, -ae m. monkey [simian]
stō, stāre, stetī, stātum
    stand [stationary,
    station]
trans (+ acc.) across
    [transfer]
ubi where, when [ubiqui-
    tous, ubiquity]
via, -ae f. road, way
    [viaduct]
vult (s)he wishes, wants

Angulus Grammaticus

Principal Parts in English and Latin

Though most Latin verbs have four principal parts, English verbs typically have only three.

Base	**Past**	**Past Participle**
walk	walked	walked

What are these principal parts? These are the words you need to use the verb in all its forms. Here are examples of forms you can make from each principal part:

Base	**Past**	**Past Participle**
I walk	I (have) walked	(having) walked
walking		

Many English verbs are fairly regular and form their principal parts, on the **-ed** model.

dance	danced	danced
work	worked	worked
tie	tied	tied
try	tried	tried

But we are all aware of the number of irregular verbs English has.

go	went	gone
bring	brought	brought
lie	lay	lain
lay	laid	laid

What others can you think of?

So how does a person learning English learn such forms? By trial and error and by memorization. We have all heard a child say, "Yesterday we goed to the zoo." You will have to do the same as you learn Latin. There are some general patterns that can help.

1ˢᵗ conjugation verbs are generally so regular that we can write their principal parts in shorthand in your vocabulary lists.

Thus, *ambulō* (1) stands for

    ambulō   *ambulāre*   *ambulāvī*   *ambulātum*

Notā Bene: This is how we list 1st conjugation verbs in *Disce!* So *temptō* (1) means "this is a regular 1st conjugation verb."

2nd conjugation verbs have a few more patterns to their principal parts:

videō	*vidēre*	*vīdī*	*vīsum*
teneō	*tenēre*	*tenuī*	*tentum*

3rd conjugation verbs have the most variation of all, but a few patterns can help you with the 3rd PP. Notice verbs like:

dūcō	*dūcere*	*duxī*	*ductum*
regō	*regere*	*rexī*	*rectum*
mittō	*mittere*	*mīsī*	*missum*

Such verbs form the perfect stem (here, the 3rd PP) by adding an *-s* to the stem.

$$\text{dūc} + \text{s} \longrightarrow \text{dux-}$$
$$\text{rēg} + \text{s} \longrightarrow \text{rex-}$$
$$\text{mitt} + \text{s} \longrightarrow \text{mīs-}$$

Some verbs reduplicate (repeat) the first consonant of their stem.

currō	*currere*	*cucurrī*	*cursum*
cadō	*cadere*	*cecidī*	*casum*

But in many instances, you simply have to memorize the stem. It is important! It is often the only thing that differentiates a form:

dūcit	she leads	*dūxit*	she led
fugit	he flees	*fūgit*	he fled

4th conjugation verbs have a large group that parallels the 1st conjugation format.

dormiō	*dormīre*	*dormīvi*	*dormītum*

Others act rather like third conjugation verbs.

veniō	*venīre*	*vēnī*	*ventum*

Again, pay attention!

equus venit	the horse is coming
equus vēnit	the horse has come

Ludī magister cum discipulīs

GRAMMATICA
The Ablative Case
Translating the Ablative
Prepositions and Case
The Verb *Sum*
The Infinitive
The Imperative
Mood

MŌRĒS RŌMĀNĪ
Magistrī Rōmānī

LATĪNA HODIERNA
Latin Words in American Education

ORBIS TERRĀRUM RŌMĀNUS
Hispānia

ANGULUS GRAMMATICUS
Ablatives with and without Prepositions

LECTIŌNĒS:
MAGISTER CHĪRŌN
and
CHĪRŌN ĪRĀTUS
Hermes returns from the Forum to the school (*lūdus*) run by the freedman Chiron. He watches events at the school for a while and then begins the journey home with Lucius.

In Lūdō Chīrōnis

Lectiō Prīma

Antequam Legis

In this chapter we meet Chiron, Lucius' *magister* (teacher). He is a *lībertīnus* (freedman), a slave who has been freed. Some freedmen became very wealthy and influential in Rome, but a teacher was seen as a lower-class worker. Like Hermes, Chiron bears a name his master thought was funny. Chiron was the centaur who tutored the heroes Achilles and Hercules.

The Verb *Sum*

The verb **to be** is irregular both in English and in Latin. These forms are in *italics* in *Lectiō Prīma*.

sum	I am	*sumus*	we are
es	you are	*estis*	you are
est	he, she, it is	*sunt*	they are
	esse	to be	

The Ablative Case

You have seen the ablative case already in previous readings, but now we introduce it formally. Here are a few facts:

- If the ablative is used with a preposition, simply translate the word according to the meaning of the preposition: e.g., *ē lūdō* **out of** the school, *sub tabulā* **under** the table.
- If the ablative is alone, remember the acronym **BWIOF**. This stands for:

By With In On From

When you see an ablative alone, substitute whichever of the BWIOF prepositions sounds the best. It is that simple.

EXERCEĀMUS!

6-1 Ablative Case

The ablatives in *Lectiō Prīma* are marked in **bold**. List their line number, indicate if they are used with a preposition and translate the ablative with the preposition or with BWIOF. Follow the models.

Line	Ablative	Preposition?	Translation
→ 1	tabernā	*in*	at the snack shop
→ 2	vīnō	no	with wine

MAGISTER CHĪRŌN

In **tabernā** Valeria Liciniaque īrātae *sunt* sed Hermēs nōn īrātus *est*. Sīmia territus sub **mensā** sē abdit. Licinia pōculum **vīnō** implet et aquam addit. Pōculum in **mensā** ponit et Hermēs vīnum cum **aquā** bibit. (Sīmia sub **mensā** semper est.)

"Domina," inquit Hermēs, "Nōn īrātus *sum*. Habeō saccum meum et omnem
5 pecūniam meam. Sine **culpā** *es* et sīmiae *sunt* sīmiae."

Respondet Valeria: "Benignus *es*, amīce. Hodie vīnum tuum sine **pretiō** *est*. Accipe pecūniam tuam!"

Paedagōgus cum **fēminīs** breviter confert et tunc ad lūdum magistrī Chīrōnis ambulat. Chīrōn lībertīnus et Hispānus *est*. Prō **lūdō** magistrī, decem puerī et duae
10 puellae in **terrā** sedent. Magister Chīrōn prō **discipulīs** stat, sed nōn docet. Omnēs puerī et puellae tabulās et stilōs habent, sed nōn scrībunt **stilīs** in **tabulīs**. Spectant Lūcium et magistrum. Sōlus Lūcius tabulam et stilum nōn habet. Chīrōn tabulam et stilum Lūciī tenet et tabulam inspectat. In **tabulā** pictūram videt et pictūra pulchra nōn *est*. Pictūra *est* figūra virī. In **pictūrā** vir nāsum longum et sōlum trēs capillōs longōs habet.

15 Chīrōn prō **puerō** stat. Valdē īrātus *est*. "Puer," inquit, "quis *est* in **pictūrā**? Num in **pictūrā tuā** *sum*?"

"Nōn in **pictūrā** *es*, magister. **Nūllō modō** caput tuum *est*! Tū omnīnō calvus *es* et ille vir trēs capillōs habet!"

In pictūrā vir nāsum longum et sōlum trēs capillōs longōs habet.

VERBA ŪTENDA

abdō, abdere hide
accipiō, accipere take
addō, addere add
amīcus, -ī m. friend
benignus, -a, -um kind
calvus, -a, -um bald
capillus, -ī m. hair
caput head
cogitō (1) think
conferō, conferre talk together
culpa, -ae f. blame, fault
cum (+ abl.) with
decem ten
doceō, docēre teach

domina ma'am
duae two
figūra, -ae f. shape
Hispānus, -a, -um Spanish
iam now, already
ille that
impleō, implēre fill
inspectō (1) look at
īrātus, -a, -um angry
libertīnus, -ī m. freedman
longus, -a, -um long
mensa, -ae f. table
nāsum, -ī n. nose
nūllō modō in no way
omnem all

omnīnō completely
pictūra, -ae f. picture
pretium, -iī price, cost
prō (+ abl.) in front of, before
pulchra pretty
puella, -ae f. girl
puer, -ī m. boy
quis? who?
saccus, -ī m. money bag
scrībō, scrībere, scrīpsī, scrīptum write
sē himself
sedeō, sedēre sit
sine (+ abl.) without

stilus, -ī m. stilus, pen
sōlum only
spectō (1) look at
sub (+ abl.) under, from under; (+ acc.) under
tabula, -ae f. slate, tablet
teneō, tenēre, tenuī, tentum hold
terra, -ae f. land, ground
territus afraid
trēs, tria three
tuus, -a, -um your (sing.)
valdē very

1. How does Hermes explain and justify Socrates' behavior? Do you agree with him?
2. How do the women try to make amends to Hermes for what Socrates did?
3. How does Chiron's classroom compare to modern schoolrooms?
4. Do you think the reply Lucius gives to Chiron's questions at the end of the reading will make the schoolmaster angry or happy? Why?
5. What does Lucius' reply to Chiron tell you about Lucius' personality?

Grammatica A

The Ablative Case

Here are the endings of the **ablative case** for the first two declensions.

	1ST DECLENSION		2ND DECLENSION		
Singular					
Nominative	-a	fēmina	-us, -er, -ir	discipulus	magister	vir
Genitive	-ae	fēminae	-ī	discipulī	magistrī	virī
Accusative	-am	fēminam	-um	discipulum	magistrum	virum
Ablative	**-ā**	**fēminā**	**-ō**	**discipulō**	**magistrō**	**virō**
Plural					
Nominative	-ae	fēminae	-ī	discipulī	magistrī	virī
Genitive	-ārum	fēminārum	-ōrum	discipulōrum	magistrōrum	virōrum
Accusative	-ās	fēminās	-ōs	discipulōs	magistrōs	virōs
Ablative	**-īs**	**fēminīs**	**-īs**	**discipulīs**	**magistrīs**	**virīs**

Notā Bene:
- The ablative singular form in both declensions has a long vowel (*-ā* or *-ō*).
- The ablative plural form is the same in both declensions (*-īs*).
- Add the ablative ending to the stem of the noun. The stem is the genitive singular minus the ending, so *magistrō*.

Translating the Ablative

You probably have no trouble translating the following phrases because of the prepositions that precede them. All the words in ***bold italics*** are in the **ablative case**.

*in **tabernā***	*in **terrā***	*in **pictūrā***	*prō **puerīs***
in the shop	on the ground	in the picture	before the boys

Did you also notice these ablative phrases, which have no preposition in Latin?

*Licinia pōculum **vīnō** implet.*	Licinia fills the cup **with wine**.
*Discipulī nōn scrībunt **stilīs** in tabulīs.*	The students are not writing **with stiluses** on their tablets.

In both of these sentences, the English preposition is understood with the Latin ablative.

Notā Bene:
- Translate the preposition if there is one. If not, supply one using BWIOF.
- Most uses of the ablative have grammatical names:
  If Valeria fills the cup with wine (*vīnō*) or the boys write with styluses (*stilīs*), this is called an **ablative of means**.
  If Valeria is shouting with Joy or Chiron is acting with anger, this is an **ablative of manner**.

More information on these constructions can be found in the *Angulus Grammaticus*.

Prepositions and Case

In Chapter 5, we introduced prepositions that took the accusative case. Now look at some prepositional phrases that take the ablative case:

***cum** fēminīs*	with the women	***in** tabernā*	in the snack shop
***dē** amīcīs*	concerning friends	***in** tabulā*	on the tablet
***ē** lūdō*	out of the school	***sub** mensā*	under the table

Now study these accusative prepositional phrases:

per Argīlētum	through the Argiletum
ad āram Dīvī Iūliī	to the altar of Divine Julius
trans Forum	across the Forum

Do you see any patterns here?

Hints:
- If the prepositional phrase expresses "motion toward," the object is generally accusative.
- If the prepositional phrase expresses location (e.g., in, on), the object is generally ablative.
- If the phrase expresses motion away from (e.g., out of, away from, down from), the object is generally ablative.
- When you learn a Latin preposition, it is important to learn in what case its object is placed.

Here is a list of prepositions by case:

Ablative **Location / Motion Away From**	Accusative **Motion Toward / Position in a Series**
ā, ab from, away	*ad* to, toward
cum with	*inter* between
dē from, down from	*per* through, across
ē, ex out of, from	*in* into
in in, on	*post* after, behind
prō in front of	*sub* under
sine without	*super* over
sub under	*trans* through, across
super over	

Notā Bene:

- Some prepositions can take either the accusative or the ablative, depending on whether they are showing location or movement toward:

Super Rostrīs stat.	He stands on top of the Rostra.
Super Rostra currit.	He runs over the top of the Rostra.

- The preposition *in* can be translated three different ways in English, depending on context:

  in + accusative = into:
  > **In** *basilicam currit.* He runs **into** the basilica.

  in + ablative = in, on
  > **In** *basilicā est.* He is **in** the basilica.
  > *Saccum* **in** *mensā pōnit.* He puts his money bag **on** the table.

  Consider the *taberna* in the following sentences:

Sīmia in tabernam currit.	The monkey runs **into** the snack shop.
Sīmia in tabernā sedet.	The monkey is sitting **in** the snack shop. The monkey is sitting **on** the snack shop.

The Verb *Sum*

Notice that although the verb *sum* is irregular, it actually uses the personal endings you already know, except in the 1st person singular:

Gemma

The *-m* in *sum* is an alternative 1st person singular ending you will see on many Latin verbs later on.

	SINGULAR	PLURAL
1st person	su**m**	su**mus**
2nd person	e**s**	es**tis**
3rd person	es**t**	su**nt**
Infinitive	esse	

Now you can understand why that mnemonic for personal endings begins with *m-*:

MOST MUST ISN'T

Notā Bene:

- The stem of this verb is irregular. Sometimes it appears as *su-* (*sum, sumus, sunt*) and sometimes as *es-* (*es, est, estis*).
- The personal endings are the same as those used for other verbs like *ambulō* except in the 1st person singular, where *-m* is used instead of *-ō*.
- The infinitive *esse* does not end in *-re* (as in *ambulāre*).

EXERCEĀMUS!

6-2 **Agreement**

Use the English prompts provided in parentheses to write the correct Latin form of *sum* needed to complete each sentence. Follow the model.

→ In lūdō laeta (you sing.) _____: *es.* You are happy in school.

1. In lūdō laetus (I)

2. In lūdō laetī (we)

3. In lūdō laetī (they)

4. In lūdō laetus (he)

5. In lūdō laetae (you pl.)

Lectiō Secunda

Antequam Legis

The Infinitive

In English infinitives are made by adding "to" in front of a verb: to give, to speak, etc. All the infinitives marked in ***bold italics*** in the *lectiō* end in *-re*.

The Imperative

Imperatives are used to give commands or orders. You have seen them already in forms like *Salvē!* or *Valēte!* Here are a few others:

Tabulae stilusque

Singular	Plural	Translation
Spectā!	*Spectāte!*	Look!
Sedē!	*Sedēte!*	Sit down!

In Latin most negative imperatives consist of two words: *Nōlī* or *Nōlīte* (Don't!) plus an infinitive.

Singular	Plural	Translation
Nōlī dare!	*Nōlīte dare!*	Don't give!
Nōlī adiuvāre!	*Nōlīte adiuvāre!*	Don't help!

In the *lectiō*, we have marked all the imperatives in **bold**.

EXERCEĀMUS!

6-3 **Imperatives**

As you read, make line-by-line lists of infinitives and imperatives and translate each into English. Remember that infinitives are marked in ***bold italics*** and imperatives in **bold**. Follow the models.

	Infinitives	Imperatives
→ Line 3		Observā!
→ Lines 4–5	verberāre	Nōlī verberāre

🔊 CHĪRŌN ĪRĀTUS

Omnēs puerī et puellae rīdent et, in viā, Hermēs quoque rīdet. Sōlus Chīrōn nōn rīdet, sed virgam capit et ad Lūcium ruit. "Puer male! Numquam *discere* vīs! **Observā!**" Lūcius valdē timet. Sedet sub virgā magistrī et tremit. Chīrōn virgam altē tollit sed tunc Hermēs magnā vōce clāmat: "**Nōlī**, magister,
5 puerum *verberāre*! Bonus puer, sed animōsus, est."

Chīrōn paulīsper cōgitat et virgam dēpōnit. Magistrī saepe discipulōs virgā pulsant, et Chīrōn Lūcium *verberāre* vult, sed Chīrōn Servīlium, patrem Lūciī, *irrītāre* nōn vult. Servīlius vir potens Rōmae est.

Chīrōn in sellā sedet et "Discipulī," inquit "**Sedēte** et **scrībite** in tabulīs
10 vestrīs. **Este** quiētī et **nōlīte** sonum *facere*!"

Puerī puellaeque clāmant, "Nōnne sumus bonī discipulī, magister?" et stilīs in tabulīs *scrībere* incipiunt. Sōlus sonus in lūdō est sonus stilōrum. Chīrōn surgit et circum discipulōs *ambulāre* incipit. Pauca post mōmenta nōn iam īrātus est. Prō puerīs et puellīs magister stat et "Discipulī," inquit.
15 "Domum **īte**! Fīnis studiōrum est. **Discite** trēs sententiās Publiliī Syrī et **revenīte** crās!"

Hermēs ad Lūcium ambulat. "Puer," inquit, "ambulā mēcum! Iēiūnusne es? Aliquid *edere* cupis?"

Puer "Rēctē dīcis," inquit, "iēiūnus sum. **Dūc** mē ad cibum!" Puer
20 paedagōgusque ad Valeriae tabernam eunt priusquam domum eunt.

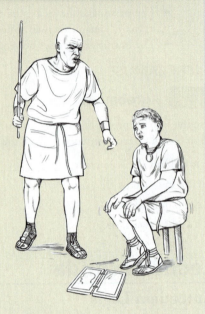

Magister īrātus virgam altē tollit. Lūcius valdē timet.

🔊 VERBA ŪTENDA

aliquid something
altē high
animōsus, -a, -um spirited
circum (+ acc.) around
crās tomorrow
cupiō, cupere want
dēpōnō, dēpōnere lay down
discō, discere, didicī learn
dīcō, dīcere speak
Dūc! Lead!
edō, edere eat
Este! Be!
eunt they go
**faciō, facere, fēcī, factum
   make, do**
fīnis end
iēiūnus, -a, -um hungry
incipiō, incipere begin
inquam, inquit say
īrātus, -a, -um angry

īte! go!
irrītō (1) upset
malus, -a, -um bad
mēcum = cum mē, with me
mōmentum, -ī n. moment
nōn iam not any longer
numquam never
observō (1) pay attention (to)
omnēs all
paulisper for a little while
patrem father
pauca a few
potens powerful
priusquam before
**prō (+ abl.) in front of,
   before**
Publilius Syrus Publilius the
   Syrian, author of a book
   of proverbs.
puella, -ae f. girl

puer, -ī m. boy
pulsō (1) beat
quiētus -a, -um quiet
quoque also
rēctē rightly, correctly
reveniō, revenīre come
   back
rīdeō, rīdēre laugh
Rōmae at Rome
ruō, ruere rush
**scrībō, scrībere, scripsī,
   scriptum write**
saepe often
sella, -ae f. chair
sententia, -ae f. proverb,
   saying
**sōlus, -a, -um only,
   alone**
sonum, -ī n. sound
stilus, -ī m. pen

**studium, -iī n. study,
   eagerness**
**sub (+ abl.) under,
   from under; (+ acc.)
   under**
surgō, surgere get up
tabula, -ae f. slate,
   tablet
timeō, timēre fear
tollō, tollere raise
tremō, tremere
   tremble
trēs, tria three
valdē very, a lot
verberō (1) beat
**vester, vestra, vestrum
   your (pl.)**
virga, -ae f. rod
vīs you want
vōce voice

POSTQUAM LĒGISTĪ

1. Who is laughing and who is not at the beginning of this *lectiō*? What is the reason for this laughter? (HINT: Think back to *Lectiō Prīma*.)
2. What does Hermes not want Chiron to do to Lucius? Why?
3. How is Chiron's behavior different from the way a teacher would respond in a modern classroom?
4. Why does Chiron follow Hermes' advice?
5. Describe the atmosphere in the classroom after this incident.
6. What homework does Chiron assign?
7. Where do Hermes and Lucius go after school? Where do they stop on the way? Why?

Grammatica B

The Infinitive

The infinitive is generally described as a "verbal noun." That means it does certain things that both a verb and a noun do.

I love **to play ball.**	*Pilā lūdere* amō.
I want **to play ball.**	*Pilā lūdere* volō.
To play ball is good.	*Pilā lūdere* bonum est.

These infinitives are surely verbs, but they also function as nouns. In the first sentence, for example, the infinitive is a direct object, no different in function than the direct object in the sentence "I love cookies." In the last example, the infinitive is the subject of the sentence.

The Imperative

The Romans had an impressive number of ways to give commands, as befits a martial people. The **imperative mood** is the simplest way to do this. Here are the simple formulae for making imperatives in Latin:

The **singular imperative** = the present stem (2nd principal part *-re*):

1st conjugation	*Vocā!* Call!
2nd conjugation	*Implē!* Fill!
3rd conjugation	*Scrībe!* Write!
4th conjugation	*Venī!* Come!

The **plural imperative** = present stem + **-te**:

1st conjugation	*Vocāte!* Call!
2nd conjugation	*Implēte!* Fill!
3rd conjugation	*Scrībite!* Write! (note: *-ete* → *-ite*)
4th conjugation	*Venīte!* Come!

A **negative imperative** = nōlī (sing.) or nōlīte (pl.) + infinitive:

Singular:	*nōlī* + infinitive	*Nōlī vocāre!*	Don't call!
Plural:	*nōlīte* + infinitive	*Nōlīte vocāre!*	Don't call!

Gemma

studium, -iī n. study, eagerness, zeal: Note the -iī ending in the genitive. This tells you that the stem of *studium* is *studi-* and that genitive singular is *studiī*.

Gemma

pauca post mōmenta Notice this word order in line 14. Latin sometimes likes to put the preposition between its object and an adjective describing that object. English would never do this. So translate "few after moments" as "after a few moments."

REGULAR IMPERATIVE					
		1ST	**2ND**	**3RD**	**4TH**
Singular	Present Stem	*Vocā!*	*Implē!*	*Scrībe!*	*Venī!*
Plural	Present Stem + -te	*Vocāte!*	*Implēte!*	*Scrībite*	*Venīte*
NEGATIVE IMPERATIVE					
Singular	*nōlī* + infinitive	*Nōlī vocāre!*	*Nōlī implēre!*	*Nōlī scrībere!*	*Nōlī venīre!*
Plural	*nōlīte* + infinitive	*Nōlīte vocāre!*	*Nōlīte implēre!*	*Nōlīte scrībere!*	*Nōlīte venīre!*

Notā Bene:

- Latin imperatives always distinguish between singular and plural, while English does not. Is the phrase "Call the cops!" directed at one or many bystanders? In Latin *Vocā!* is used for one person and *Vocāte!* is for more than one.
- The imperative forms of *sum* are irregular:

Es! (singular)	Be!	*Este!* (plural)
Es sine culpā!	Be without worry!	*Este sine cūrā!*

- Other irregular imperatives include:

Dīc!	Speak!
Dūc!	Lead!
Fac!	Do it!
Fer!	Carry!

These verbs lack a vowel at the end. Remember: "*Dīc, dūc, fac,* and *fer,* lack the e that ought to be there."

Which of these irregular imperatives did you see in *Lectiō Secunda*?

Mood

When we think of "mood" in English, we are talking about states of mind. When we think of "mood" in Latin, it is a grammatical term, more akin to "mode" or "manner" than to "mood."

The verbs you have met in the earlier chapters are in the **indicative mood**. That is, they "indicate" a fact. *Ambulat* denotes a fact: he/she/it is walking. This mode is easy to understand and, for day-to-day purposes, can be said to be the mood that indicates a fact, while the **imperative mood** indicates a command or order.

EXERCEĀMUS!

6-4 Imperatives

Match each of the following Latin imperative phrases with the appropriate English command. Indicate whether the command is addressed to one person (singular) or more than one (plural). Follow the model.

Revenīte crās!	Venī hūc!	Observā!
Sedēte!	Dūc mē ad cibum!	Nōlīte sonum facere!

ENGLISH COMMAND	LATIN COMMAND	NUMBER
→ Pay attention!	Observā!	Singular
1. Come here!		
2. Return tomorrow!		
3. Sit!		
4. Lead me to the food!		
5. Don't make a sound!		

Mōrēs Rōmānī

Magistrī Rōmānī

Here is a description of a schoolteacher in an epigram written by the poet Martial. We have modified the epigram slightly to make it easier to read. This schoolteacher keeps the poet Martial and his neighbors awake with his pedagogical techniques. Keep in mind that Roman classrooms, like Chiron's, were usually out in the open.

> Ō scelerāte magister lūdī, caput tuum invīsum ā puerīs et puellīs est!
> Mane iam murmure saevō verberibusque tonās. Mītior clāmor in
> magnō amphitheātrō est, ubi turba victōrem applaudat. Tuī vīcīnī
> somnum—nōn tōtā nocte—rogāmus: nam vigilāre leve est, pervigilāre
> grave est. Discipulōs tuōs dīmitte. Quantum pecūniae, ō garrule, vīs
> accipere ut clāmēs, ut taceās?

> *Epigrams.* IX.68

Gemma

There are two ways to refer to the dates surrounding the life of poet like Martial.
40–c.102–103 A.D.: *c.* stands for Latin *circa* (about) and means that we do not know the exact date of his death.
Fl. 86–103 A.D.: *fl.* Stands for *floruit* and indicates that "he flourished," or was writing his poetry, around those dates.

🔊 VERBA ŪTENDA

ā puerīs et puellīs by boys and girls
accipiō, accipere accept, receive
applaudō (1) applaud
caput head (Martial means not only his head but his whole body)
clāmor cry, uproar
dīmittō, dīmittere send away
garrule chatterer, chatterbox
grave a serious thing, a big deal
iam already
invīsus, -a, -um hated
leve easy, no big deal (refers to *vigilāre*)
magnus, -a, -um great

mane in the morning
mītior softer
murmure with a murmur, growling (ablative)
nōndum not yet
pervigilō (1) be awake all night, be up all night
quantum pecūniae… A tricky phrase. "Are you willing to take as much money to do X as to do Y?" Martial is offering to buy off the noisy teacher.
rogō (1) ask for
scelerāte wicked (vocative masc. sing.) "O wicked person!"

saevō furious (describes *murmure*)
somnum, -ī n. sleep
taceās you be quiet
tam so
tonō (1) thunder
tōtā nocte the whole night through
turba, -ae f. crowd
tuus, -a, -um your (sing.)
ut clāmēs to shout
ut taceās to be quiet
verberibus with blows (ablative)
victōrem a victorious fighter
vīcīnus, -ī m. neighbor
vigilō (1) wake up, be awake
vīs are you willing

Magister Chīron et Achilles discipulus

Education in ancient Rome was private rather than public. Children only went to school if their families could afford to pay tuition to a teacher like Chiron. Some education certainly took place in the home, where children could begin their studies with their parents or family slaves. A *lūdus* like Chiron's offered the earliest formal schooling beginning around the age of seven. Here, pupils (mostly boys and occasionally upper-class girls) learned to read, write, and count from a teacher called the *lūdī magister* or *litterātor*. Sometimes Greek was also taught in the *lūdus*. Much of the learning was by rote, and the instruction was often reinforced by physical punishment like the rod with which Chiron threatens Lucius in the story.

Once students had mastered the basics, some, at about the age of eleven, would move on to a *grammaticus*, who would instruct them in the literature of Rome and Greece. Many Romans, especially the upper-class ones, were bilingual and knew both Latin and Greek. About the age of sixteen, a select few might then move to a *rhētor* or rhetorician who would introduce them to the art of public speaking.

Latīna Hodierna

Latin Words in American Education

Many of the words we use in our schools and colleges come from Latin. Here are just a few. Notice how the meaning of the English word or phrase is often slightly different from the Latin word or phrase.

ENGLISH TERM	LATIN WORD OR PHRASE AND MEANING
college	*collēgium, -ī* n. corporation, brotherhood
campus	*campus, -ī* m. field
university	*ūniversitās, -tātis* f. community
dormitory	*dormītōrium, -ī* n. a place for sleeping
alma mater	*alma māter* foster mother
alumna; alumnus	*alumna, -ae* f. foster daughter; *alumnus, -ī* m. foster son
cum laude	*cum laude* with praise

Orbis Terrārum Rōmānus

Hispānia

The Romans spent more than two centuries trying to conquer Spain. This task was not completed until 19 B.C., under the reign of Augustus. After this the peninsula was divided into three provinces: *Hispānia Tarrconensis, Hispānia Baetica*, and *Lusitania*.

During the imperial period, the region was a major source of metals, grains and wine, and its inhabitants became increasingly Romanized. Latin became so well established as the

Macaca sylvanus

language of the inhabitants that Latin survived the fall of the Roman Empire and evolved on the Iberian peninsula into the Romance languages Spanish and Portuguese.

Some famous Romans from the Iberian peninsula include: **Quintilian**, a famous rhetorician (c. 35–c. 100 A.D.); **Seneca the Elder**, rhetorician and scientist (c. 54 B.C.–c. 39 A.D.), author of model debate texts called *Suasōriae* and *Contrōversiae*; **Seneca the Younger**, nephew of the Elder Seneca, Stoic philosopher, tragedian and tutor of the emperor Nero (c. 4 B.C.–65 A.D.), born in Corduba; **Martial**, the poet (40–c.102–103 A.D.), born in Bilbilis; and the emperor **Trajan** (53–117 A.D.).

Several modern Spanish cities have Roman roots, including Mérida (Emerita Augusta); Córdoba (Corduba); Tarraco (Tarragona); and Barcelona (Barcino).

Hispānia Rōmāna

QUID PUTĀS?

1. Read through Martial's poem to determine what hours the school must have kept.
2. Compare the American educational system to Roman practice.
3. Do you think Chiron the schoolmaster is well named after the centaur Chiron? Why or why not?
4. Why was the schoolmaster in Martial's poem so disturbing to his neighbors? What solution does Martial propose to the problem? Can you think of a comparable situation today?
5. Explain how the *campus*, the Latin word for "field" acquires its modern English meaning. Can you apply the word "field" to any part of a college campus?
6. Compare the meaning of the Latin word *ūniversitās* to the meaning of its English derivative "university".
7. What evidence of the Roman occupation of the Iberian peninsula survives today?

EXERCEĀMUS!

6-5　Scrībāmus

Theātrum Rōmānum in Emeritā Augustā hodiē

Make each of the following singular imperatives negative. Then make the singular imperatives plural. Follow the model.

Singular	Negative	Plural	Negative
→ Ambulā!	Nōlī ambulāre!	Ambulāte!	Nōlīte ambulāre!
1. Venī!			
2. Stā!			
3. Sedē!			
4. Clāmā!			

6-6 **Colloquāmur**

Take turns addressing the command in Exercise 6-5 to one or more people in your class. If you wish, you can make this into a "Simon dīcit" type game.

6-7 **Verba Discenda**

Substitute the word in **bold** in each sentence with one derived from a *Verbum Discendum*. Follow the model.

→ Magellan **sailed around** the world. *circumnavigated*

1. When it comes to term papers, I tend to **put things off to tomorrow**.

2. Gandhi had many **student followers**.

3. Don't make him so **angry**!

4. The police will catch the **evil doer**.

5. The gila monster's bite is very **stubborn**.

6. I just ordered an **annual contract** to receive *Newsweek*.

7. Superman lives in the Fortress of **Aloneness**.

8. The professor kept his books in his **room for learning things**.

Gemma

tuus and *vester*: Just as Latin distinguishes between "you" singular and "you" plural in verbs (*scrībis* vs. *scrībitis*), it does also with "your":

Scrībe in tabulā tuā!
Write on your tablet!

Scrībite in tabulīs vestrīs!
Write on your tablets!

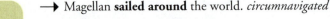

🔊 VERBA DISCENDA

circum (+ acc.) around [circumference]

crās tomorrow [procrastinate]

cum (+ abl.) with

discō, discere, didicī learn [discipline, discourse]

faciō, facere, fēcī, factum make, do [facile, factory, manufacture]

īrātus, -a, -um angry [irate]

malus, -a, -um bad [malodorous, malevolent]

prō (+ abl.) in front of, before, for [project]

puella, -ae f. girl

puer, -ī m. boy [puerile]

quis? who?

saepe often

scrībō, scrībere, scripsī, scriptum write [scribe, script]

sine (+ abl.) without [sincere]

sōlus, -a, -um only, alone [solitary, solitude]

studium, -iī n. study, eagerness, zeal [studious]

sub (+ abl.) under, from under; (+ acc.) under [subsurface]

teneō, tenēre, tenuī, tentum hold [tenacious]

trēs, tria three [trifold, trifecta]

tuus, -a, -um your (sing.)

vester, vestra, vestrum your (pl.)

Angulus Grammaticus

Ablatives with and without Prepositions

Earlier you saw ablative phrases in which the ablative case is used without a preposition and the English preposition **with** is understood.

*Licinia ūnum pōculum **vīnō** implet.*	Licinia fills one cup **with wine**.
*Licinia alium pōculum **aquā** implet.*	Licinia fills another cup **with water**.
*Magistrī saepe discipulōs **virgā** pulsant.*	Teachers often strike students **with a rod**.

These are examples of an ablative called **ablative of means**. The rule about the ablative of means is that the ablative case is used alone, without a preposition, to indicate the instrument or tool used to perform an action. One way to recognize an ablative of means is by asking whether it makes sense to translate the ablative with the phrase "by means of."

Licinia fills the cup by means of wine (*vīnō*) and by means of water (*aquā*).

In Latin these tools must be physical objects. If Lucius cries out "with joy," for example, Latin would use the prepositional phrase *cum gaudiō*. This is called an **ablative of manner**.

But note the following. If Lucius cries out "with great joy," then the preposition is optional in Latin and, if the preposition **is** used, it is placed between the adjective and the noun. So,

Lūcius **cum gaudiō** *clāmat.*	ablative of manner with preposition
Lūcius **magnō gaudiō** *clāmat.*	ablative of manner with adjective and without preposition
Lūcius **magnō cum gaudiō** *clāmat.*	ablative of manner with adjective and with preposition in special position

Now, when you graduate *summa cum laude*, you will know why the words are in that order!

Actions performed with or by people **always** use a preposition in Latin. One example is the **ablative of accompaniment**. For example, if Lucius cries out "with the boys," Latin would use the prepositional phrase *cum puerīs*. The ablative of accompaniment indicates a person who performs an action "along with" or "together with" the subject of the verb. So here Lucius cries out along with the boys.

Lūcius clāmat **cum puerīs.**	ablative of accompaniment

Can you figure out which ablatives are means, which are manner, and which are accompaniment in the following sentences?

Magistrī saepe discipulōs **virgā** *pulsant.*

Magistrī saepe discipulōs **cum īrā** *pulsant.*

Magistrī saepe discipulōs **magnā īrā** *pulsant.*

Magistrī saepe discipulōs **magnā cum īrā** *pulsant.*

Magistrī saepe discipulōs **cum virīs** *pulsant.*

Notā Bene:

- It is usually not important for translation purposes to distinguish means from manner or accompaniment, and you can easily translate the ablatives without prepositions if you remember **BWIOF**. But the categories have a long history in the study of Latin.

Gemma

When the preposition *cum* is used with 1st person personal pronouns like *mē* or *tē*, the pronoun always comes first and the prepositional phrase is written as one word:

mēcum   with me

tēcum   with you

Note: In English a "vade mecum" (*Vāde mēcum!* "Go with me!") is an edition of a book small enough to be put in your pocket to take along on a trip.

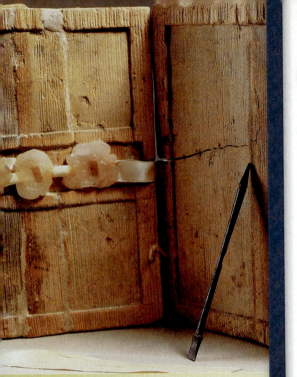

Post Lūdum

Lectiō Prīma

Antequam Legis

School is over. Hermes gives Lucius some mild advice about his behavior, while Chiron wonders whether he should even be a teacher. You will see many variations on wishing in this *lectiō*, because the Latin word for "wish" is an irregular verb.

Some Irregular Verbs

In this chapter we introduce you to four irregular but very common, verbs. Here are their principal parts and English meanings:

> *possum, posse, potuī* be able to, can
> *volō, velle, voluī* want to, wish to
> *nōlō, nōlle, nōluī* not want to, not wish to, be unwilling to
> *mālō, mālle, māluī* prefer to

You will recognize most of their endings—it is mostly their stems that are irregular.

EXERCEĀMUS!

7-1 Irregular Verb Forms

Before you read *Lectiō Prīma*, look for all of the irregular verb forms marked in **bold**. Make a list of them line by line. Then use the principal parts listed above and the personal endings you already know to determine a possible translation of each word. Follow the model.

Line	Irregular Verb	Personal Ending	Meaning
→4	*volunt*	-nt	they wish

🔊 DE LŪDŌ CHĪRŌNIS

Hermēs Lūcium ā lūdō ad tabernam dūcit. Dum ambulant, dē lūdī magistrō dīcunt.

Hermēs "Lūcī," rogat, "dīc mihi aliquid! Cūr puerī magistrum irrītāre **volunt**? Estne magister tam malus?"

5 Respondet puer: "Chīron nōn malus est, sed nōs dēlectāre nōn **potest**. Nōs puerī in lūdō male facere **nōlumus** sed aliquandō nōn aliter facere **possumus**!"

"Fortasse," inquit paedagōgus, "**nōn vultis**, sed nihilōminus male facitis. **Nōlī** male facere, puer. Tū et amīcī bonī esse **potestis**. Tū bonus
10 esse **potes**! **Nōlō** magistrum maestum vidēre. Chīron ōlim servus erat sīcut nunc ego servus sum. Esse benignior **potes**!"

Nunc puer paedagōgusque ad Valeriae tabernam adveniunt.

Valeria "Salvēte," clāmat.

Valeria "Puer," inquit, "aliquid bibere aut ēsse **vīs**? Puerī semper aliq-
15 uid ēsse **possunt**! Sed sīcut dīcit Publilius Syrus, 'is quī habet quod **vult**, est vir quī **velle** quod satis est **potest**.'"

Lūcius rīdet et fīcōs duās pānemque poscit.

"Et tū, Hermēs. Quid tū et puer bibere **vultis**?"

"**Mālō** vīnum bibere, sī placet, sed puer aquam bibere debet."
20 "Licinia!" clāmat Valeria, "Fer pōculum vīnī et alium pōculum aquae!"

Licinia ūnum pōculum vīnō et alium pōculum aquā implet.

Licinia ūnum pōculum vīnō et alium pōculum aquā implet. Puerī apud familiam vīnum bibere **possunt**, sed nōn in viā vīnum bibere debent!

Hermēs et Lūcius bibunt. Puer sīmiam videt et paedagōgus fābulam dē saccō narrat. Lūcius rīdet et "Iam,"
25 inquit, "Hermēs, dūc mē domum! Fessus sum!"

🔊 VERBA ŪTENDA

adveniō, advenīre come to
aliquandō sometimes
aliquid something
aliter otherwise
alium another
amīcus friend
apud familiam at home
benignior kinder
cūr why
dē (+ abl.) concerning, about, down from
dēbeō, dēbēre, dēbuī, dēbitum owe, ought
dīcō, dīcere, dīxī, dictum say, tell

dēlectō (1) amuse
dum while
duo, duae, duo two
edō, ēsse / edere , ēdī, ēsum eat
ego I
eō, īre, īvī / iī, itum go
erat was
fessus tired
fīcōs duās two figs
    [*Fīcōs* is feminine.]
fortasse perhaps
iam now
impleō, implēre fill
irrītō (1) annoy, bother

is quī habet…quod satis est potest "A person who has what he wants, is one who is able to want (only) what is enough."
maestus sad, gloomy
male facere to misbehave
mālō, mālle, māluī prefer
malus bad
nihilōminus nevertheless
narrō (1) to tell about
nōlō, nōlle, nōluī not want to, be unwilling

nōs we, us
ōlim once
pānem bread
possum, posse, potuī be able to, can
rīdeō, rīdēre, rīsī, rīsum laugh
rogō (1) ask
servus, -ī m. slave
sī if
sī placet! Please!
sīcut just as
tam so
volō, velle, voluī want to, be willing to

Pānem poscit

Try to answer these questions in Latin. The sentences can be short and you will find patterns for the answers in the *lectiō*. Follow the model.

→ What do Lucius and Hermes talk about as they walk from school?
Dē lūdō magistrī Chīrōnis dīcunt.

1. Why do the students act up in class?
2. What do Lucius and Hermes each drink at the snack shop?
3. Why don't they order the same thing?
4. What story does Hermes tell Lucius while they are in the snack shop?

Grammatica A

The Irregular Verbs *Volō*, *Nōlō*, and *Mālō*

	volō, velle, voluī		*nōlō, nōlle, nōluī*		*mālōm, mālle, māluī*	
Singular						
1st Person	*volō*	I want	*nōlō*	I do not want	*mālō*	I prefer
2nd Person	*vīs*	you want	*nōn vīs*	you do not want	*māvīs*	you prefer
3rd Person	*vult*	he/she/it wants	*nōn vult*	he/she/it does not want	*māvult*	he/she/it prefers
Plural						
1st Person	*volumus*	we want	*nōlumus*	we do not want	*mālumus*	we prefer
2nd Person	*vultis*	you want	*nōn vultis*	you do not want	*māvultis*	you prefer
3rd Person	*volunt*	they want	*nōlunt*	they do not want	*mālunt*	they prefer
Infinitive	*volle*	to want	*nōlle*	not to want	*mālle*	to prefer

Notā Bene:
- The personal endings are regular. It is the stem of the verb that changes.
- If you know *volō*, you can do *nōlō* and *mālō*.
- The forms of *nōlō* are basically *nōn* + *volō*, i.e., "I do not want." Sometimes they are contracted (as in *nōlumus*) and at other times not (*nōn vult*).
- You have already seen the imperative forms of *nōlō*: *nōlī* and *nōlīte*! (Do not wish to . . . ! Don't . . . !)
- The *ma-* of *mālō* is from the Latin *magis* meaning "more." Thus, the forms of *mālō* basically mean "to want more," that is, "to prefer." They are all contracted; e.g., **ma**(*gis*) + (*vo*)**lō** → *mālō*.

The Irregular Verb *Possum*

In many languages some very common verbs are irregular. This is especially true of the verb **to be** in both English and Latin.

Remember the conjugation of *sum*:

sum	I am	*sumus*	we are
es	you are	*estis*	you are
est	he/she/it is	*sunt*	they are
	esse	to be	

Now consider *possum* (I am able to, I can):

*pos**sum***	I can, I am able to	*pos**sumus***	we can, we are able to
potes	you can, you are able to	*potestis*	you can, you are able to
potest	he can, he is able to	*pos**sunt***	they can, they are able to

posse   to be able to

Notā Bene:
- The actual stem of *possum* is *pot-*. You can see this in words like *potēns* (powerful) or *potentia* (power) and in the English "potentate" or "potency."
- Put this stem in front of the normal form of *sum* to say "I am able." Notice what happens:

t + *s* ⟶ *ss*

potsum ⟶ *possum*

potsumus ⟶ *possumus*

potsunt ⟶ *possunt*

t + a vowel remains unchanged

potes, potest, potestis

Complementary Infinitives

Volō, nōlō, mālō, and *possum* are all usually followed by an infinitive, which completes the meaning of the verb. This infinitive is called a **complementary infinitive**.

*Cūr puerī magistrum **irrītāre volunt**?*
Why do the boys **want to annoy** the teacher?

*Puerī apud familiam vīnum **bibere possunt**.*
Boys **are able to drink** wine at home.
Boys **can drink** wine at home.

*Nōlō magistrum maestum **vidēre**.*
I **do not want to see** the teacher sad.

*Mālō vīnum **bibere**.*
I **prefer to drink** wine.

It will help you remember to look for these complementary infinitives if you get in the habit of translating these verbs like this:

volō	want **to**, wish **to**	*mālō*	prefer **to**
nōlō	not want **to**, not wish **to**	*possum*	be able **to**

Notā Bene:
- *Volō, nōlō,* and *mālō* can also be used with a direct object rather than an infinitive:

Vīnum volō. Aquam nōlō. Vīnum mālō.

I want wine. I don't want water. I prefer wine.

- *Possum* almost always needs an infinitive to complete its meaning.

Vīnum bibere possum.

I am able to drink wine.

I can drink wine.

EXERCEĀMUS!

7-2   *Volō, nōlō, mālō,* and *possum*

Translate each of the following forms of *volō, nōlō, mālō,* and *possum*. Then change the form from singular to plural. Finally, translate the word you made. Follow the model. Check the verb chart in *Grammatica A* if you do not remember how to conjugate these irregular verbs.

Singular	**Plural**
⟶ *possum* I can, I am able	*possumus* we can, we are able

1. vīs
2. nōlō

3. māvis
4. potest

5. vult
6. nōn vult

Lectiō Secunda

Antequam Legis

While Lucius is on his way home, his discouraged teacher Chiron lingers at the school and tries unsuccessfully to get some work done. Eventually he goes to Valeria's snack shop and finds comfort in wine and amusement in Socrates. As you read this *lectiō*, look more closely at verbs of the 3rd and 4th conjugations and the irregular verb *eō*.

The Irregular Verb *Eō*

This too is an irregular verb. The principal parts are: *eō, īre, īvī/iī, itum*.

SINGULAR		PLURAL	
eō	I go	*īmus*	we go
īs	you go	*ītis*	you go
it	he/she/it goes	*eunt*	they go
Ī!	Go!	*Īte!*	Go!
īre		to go	

The verb *eō* is extremely common and is found in many compounds that are easy to figure out by just combining "go" with the meaning of the preposition used as a prefix: *transeō* (go across), *adeō* (go toward), *abeō, ineō,* etc. Watch for these as you read. Forms of this verb are in **bold italics** in the *lectiō* that follows.

The 3rd and 4th Conjugations

In this reading you will be introduced formally to 3rd and 4th conjugation verbs. They should be no problem. In *Lectiō Prīma*, for example, you have already seen such 3rd and 4th conjugation verbs as:

dūcit	he leads
poscit	he asks for
*adveni**unt***	they arrive

Since the personal endings are the same for all four conjugations, just use what you know already and you should have little trouble understanding the 3rd and 4th conjugation verbs which are marked in **bold** in *Lectiō Secunda*.

EXERCEĀMUS!

7-3 **3rd and 4th Conjugation Verbs**

As you read, group the verbs in bold according to the vowels that link the stem to the personal endings. Thus, in line 1 *tollit* would go in the "i-group" and *legere* would go in the "e-group." Be sure to have a group for long "ī" as well as short "i."

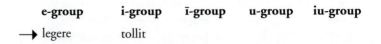

e-group	i-group	ī-group	u-group	iu-group
→ legere	tollit			

🔊 CHĪRŌN IN LŪDŌ

Chīrōn sōlus in lūdō sedet. Propter discipulōs malōs nōn laetus est. Librum **tollit** et **legere** temptat, sed nōn potest. Librum in mēnsam rursus **ponit**. Sōlum dē discipulīs malīs putat. **Scrībere** nōn potest. Pecūniam numerāre temptat, sed nōn **succēdit**.

5　　Chīrōn vītam suam dēplōrat et "Ēheu," inquit, "lībertīnus sum et nunc dominī servus nōn sum. Sed lūdī et discipulōrum malōrum servus sum. Cupiō docēre sed discipulī nōn **audiunt**, nōn **discunt** et nōn **discere cupiunt!**" Tunc Chīrōn ā lūdō *abit* et ad Valeriae tabernam *adit*. "Satis!" inquit, "'Nunc est bibendum!'" et rīdet.

10　　Ubi Sōcratēs magistrum in tabernā videt, sīmia dē mēnsā **currit** et in bracchia Chīrōnis **salit**. Sōcratēs Chīrōnis bonus amīcus est.

　　Chīrōn "Ō sīmia," inquit, "**Curris**ne ad mē? Tū saltem mē vidēre vīs. Discipulī mē aut vidēre aut **audīre** nōlunt et tē vidēre magis quam meōs discipulōs mālō!"

　　Sīmia dē magistrō **salit** et ad mensam **currit**. In mensā quattuor ficī sunt et Sōcratēs ūnam ē ficīs **capit** et ad

15　magistrum portat. Chīrōn ficum **capit** et clāmat: "Amīce, **venī**. Da mihi reliquās ficōs. *Ī*, sī tibi placet." Sīmia iterum ad mensam *adit* et aliās portat. "Bene, sīmia, **discis!**" Chīrōn rīdet et "Ecce, amīcī," inquit "sīmia bonus discipulus est. Poscō, et sīmia *it* et **facit!**" Omnēs prope tabernā **plaudunt** quod sīmia sagāx est. "Sīmia," Chīrōn inquit, "mē amat magis quam puerī. Fortasse nōn puerōrum, sed sīmiārum, magister esse dēbeō. Sed satis est! Nunc bibō!" Tunc Chīrōn tacitus vīnum **bibit** et ficōs **edit** dum omnēs **bibunt** et rīdent.

Sīmia ūnam ē fīcīs ad magistrum portat.

🔊 VERBA ŪTENDA

abeō, abīre, abīvī / abiī, abitum go away
adeō, adīre, adīvī / adiī, aditum go to
aliās "the other (figs)"
aliōrum other
amīcus, -ī m. friend
amō (1) love
audiō, audīre, audīvī / audiī, audītum hear, listen to
bibendum est "it's time to drink"
bracchia arms
dē (+ abl.) **down from, concerning**
dēbeō, dēbēre, dēbuī, dēbitum owe, ought
dīco, dīcere, dīxī, dictum say, tell

doceō, docēre teach
dēplōrō (1) lament
dum while
duo, duae, duo two
Ecce! Behold! Look!
edō, ēsse / edere, ēdī, ēsum eat
ēheu alas
eō, īre, iī / īvī, itum go
ficus, -ī f. fig
fortasse perhaps
in (+ acc.) translate here as "onto"
imperō (1) command
legō, legere read
liber, librī m. book
lībertīnus, -ī m. freedman
magis more
mālō, mālle, māluī prefer
mēnsa, -ae f. counter, table

nōlō, nōlle, nōluī not want to, be unwilling
numerō (1) count
omnēs everyone
plaudō, plaudere clap
portō (1) carry
possum, posse, potuī be able to, can
propter (+ acc.) on account of
putō (1) think
quam than
quattuor four
reliquās the remaining
rīdeō, rīdēre, rīsī, rīsum laugh
rursus again
sagāx wise
saltem at least
saliō, salīre leap, jump

satis enough
servus, -ī m. slave, servant
sī if
sī tibi placet please
sīcut just as
succēdō, succēdere succeed
suam "his"
tacitus silently
tē you (direct object)
temptō (1) try
tollō, tollere lift, raise
ūnam ē ficīs "one of the figs"
ūnus, -a, -um one
vīta, -ae f. life
volō, velle, voluī want to, be willing to

POSTQUAM LEGISTĪ

1. Why is Chiron unhappy? What does he do to try to distract himself without success?
2. So what does he do instead?
3. What finally cheers him up?
4. What advice would you give Chiron about his teaching techniques?

Grammatica B

The Irregular Verb *Eō*

Did you look for forms of the irregular verb *eō* in *Lectiō Secunda*? How many did you find? Besides *it* (he goes) and *Ī!* (Go!), did you notice words like *abit* (he goes away) and *adit* (he goes to), which contain forms of *eō*? These compound forms of *eō* are formed by adding directional prefixes like *ab-* and *ad-* to the verb. These two compounds become *Verba Discenda* in this chapter:

abeō, abīre, abīvī / abiī go away

adeō, adīre, adīvī / adiī go to

Compounding is easy:

SINGULAR		PLURAL	
abeō	I go away	*abīmus*	we go away
abīs	you go away	*abītis*	you go away
abit	he/she/it goes away	*abeunt*	they go away
abī!	Go away!	*abīte!*	Go away!
abīre		to go away	

What do you think these *eō* compounds mean?

exeō   subeō   intereō   transeō

Notā Bene:

- The stem of *eō* is usually *i-*, as in *īs, it,* and *īmus.*
- But the irregular forms use *e-*, as in *eō* and *eunt.*
- Look for more on compounding in the *Angulus Grammaticus* in *Chapter 10.*

Forming the Present Tense: All Four Conjugations

If you made the list requested in the *Antequam Legis*, it should look something like this:

E: legere, discere

I: tollit, discis, venit

Ī: audīre, venī

U: bibunt

IU: audiunt

You have discovered all the vowels that are used in 3rd and 4th conjugation verbs to link the stems to personal endings!

When you are reading Latin, the change in linking vowels causes little or no problem. But if you try to speak or write Latin (as you are sometimes asked to do), you need to know how to find the stem and what vowel is used to link it to its personal ending. There are many "formulas" you can learn for making the present tense, but the one presented here allows for the fact that 1st and 2nd conjugations form their present tenses one way whereas 3rd and 4th conjugation verbs use a different formula. It also helps you form the next two tenses you will learn.

Using the Present Stem for the 1st and 2nd Conjugations

You already know the general rule for forming present tense of verbs in the 1st and 2nd conjugations:

Present Stem (2nd principal part − -re) +   ō   mus

s   tis

t   nt

1st Conjugation

vocō, vocāre ⟶ Present Stem: *vocā*

vocā + ō ⟶ *vocō*   *vocā + mus* ⟶ *vocāmus*

vocā + s ⟶ *vocās*   *vocā + tis* ⟶ *vocātis*

vocā + t ⟶ *vocat*   *vocā + nt* ⟶ *vocant*

2nd Conjugation

moneō, monēre ⟶ Present Stem: *monē*

monē + ō ⟶ *moneō*   *monē + mus* ⟶ *monēmus*

monē + s ⟶ *monēs*   *monē + tis* ⟶ *monētis*

monē + t ⟶ *monet*   *monē + nt* ⟶ *monent*

Using the Short Present Stem for the 3rd and 4th Conjugations

For 3rd and 4th conjugation verbs we use a different stem, called the Short Present Stem (SPS), which is found by removing the -ō from the 1st principal part:

dūcō, dūcere ⟶ SPS *duc-*

audiō, audīre ⟶ SPS *audi-*

To this SPS add the following pattern of vowels and personal endings to form the present tense of 3rd and 4th conjugation verbs:

SPS +   ō   imus

is   itis

it   unt

Thus

3rd Conjugation

$$d\bar{u}c\bar{o} \longrightarrow \text{SPS } d\bar{u}c\text{-}$$

dūc + ō ⟶ *dūcō*	*dūc + imus* ⟶ *dūcimus*
dūc + is ⟶ *dūcis*	*dūc + itis* ⟶ *dūcitis*
dūcō + it ⟶ *dūcit*	*dūc + unt* ⟶ *dūcunt*

3rd Conjugation *-iō* Verbs

There is a special group of 3rd conjugation verbs called *-iō* verbs because their first principal part ends in *-iō* (*capiō, capere*) instead of *-ō* (*dūcō, dūcere*). You already know some of these verbs as *Verba Discenda*:

> *capiō, cap**ere**, cēpī, captum* take
> *cupiō, cup**ere**, cupīvī / cupiī, cupitum* wish, want to
> *faciō, fac**ere**, fēcī, factum* make, do

These 3rd conjugation *-iō* verbs work the same way as other 3rd conjugation verbs, but with one special rule: i + i ⟶ i. Thus, the correct 3rd person singular form of *capiō* is *capit*, not "capiit."

$$capi\bar{o} \longrightarrow \text{SPS } capi\text{-}$$

capi + ō ⟶ *capiō*	*capi + imus* ⟶ *capimus*
capiō + is ⟶ *capis*	*capi + itis* ⟶ *capitis*
capi + it ⟶ *capit*	*capi + unt* ⟶ *capiunt*

4th Conjugation

4th conjugation verbs also follow the rule of i + i ⟶ i:

$$audi\bar{o} \longrightarrow \text{SPS } aud\bar{i}\text{-}$$

audi + ō ⟶ *audiō*	*audi + imus* ⟶ *audīmus*
audīō + is ⟶ *audīs*	*audī + itis* ⟶ *audītis*
audī + it ⟶ *audit*	*audi + unt* ⟶ *audiunt*

And here is a summary of how 3rd, 3rd *-io*, and 4th conjugation verbs work. Notice how 3rd conjugation *-iō* verbs are sometimes like the regular 3rd conjugation verbs and sometimes like the 4th, but that the long marks of the 4th conjugation forms can be very helpful.

PERSON	3RD REGULAR		3RD -IŌ		4TH	
	Singular	**Plural**	**Singular**	**Plural**	**Singular**	**Plural**
1st	*dūcō*	*dūcimus*	*capiō*	*capimus*	*audiō*	*audīmus*
2nd	*dūcis*	*dūcitis*	*capis*	*capitis*	*audīs*	*audītis*
3rd	*dūcit*	*dūcunt*	*capit*	*capiunt*	*audit*	*audiunt*

Summary of Imperatives

And here is a summary of **imperatives**.

1st, 2nd, 4th conjugation	Singular imperative = Present Stem (2nd principal part – -re) Plural imperative = Present Stem + te		
	Vocā!	*Monē!*	*Audī!*
	Vocāte!	*Monēte*	*Audīte!*

3rd conjugation	Singular imperative = Present Stem (2nd principal part – -re) Plural imperative = Short Present Stem (1st principal part – -ō) + -ite	
	Mitte!	*Mittite!*
	Pone!	*Ponite!*

And remember: "*Dīc, dūc, fac,* and *fer* lack the *-e* that 'ought to' be there."

EXERCEĀMUS!

7-4   **3rd and 4th Conjugation Verbs**

Use the charts in *Grammatica B* to complete the following charts for *dīco, dīcere, dīxī, dictum* and *faciō, facere, fēcī, factum.* Be sure to watch out for irregular imperative forms! We have done some for you.

Person	3RD CONJUGATION		3RD CONJUGATION -IŌ	
	Singular			
1st	*dīcō*		*faciō*	
2nd				you do, you make
3rd			*facit*	
	Plural			
1st				
2nd				
3rd		they say		
Infinitive	*dīcere*			
Imperatives	*Dīc!*		*Fac!*	

Mōrēs Rōmānī

Slavery and the Manumission of Slaves

The relationships between the slave Flavia and her mistress Valeria and between the *paedagōgus* and Lucius illustrate the central role slavery played in ancient society and economy. Even a poor family like Valeria's would often own one or two slaves. These slaves would live in close quarters with their masters and, in fact, legally belonged to the *familia* of the master. In Latin the word *familia* includes not only parents, children, and other relatives, but also any slaves belonging to the *paterfamiliās*, or head of the family.

Pilleus lībertātis

A German woman like Flavia could have been born into slavery, or she could have been sold into slavery as a result of war. Unlike slavery in the American experience, Roman slavery was not racially based. Anyone could become a slave if they were in the wrong place at the wrong time.

Chiron is a *lībertīnus* or freedman. This means that he is a former slave who has managed to purchase his own freedom or who was freed by his master through the process of manumission, a formal legal process. The master and slave went before a judge to whom the master said *hunc hominem līberum volō* (I want this person to be free), while holding the slave with his hand. The master then let go (*ēmīsit ē manū*) of the slave who was then free. Note that the English word **manumission** describes the actual process of a Roman master releasing his slave. The newly freed slave then put on a special hat or cap of liberty (*pilleus, -eī* m.), seen at left on a coin issued by Brutus after the assassination of Julius Caesar in 44 B.C.

The two daggers represent the assassination of Julius Caesar. In the center of the coin is a *pilleus*, a cap of liberty, suggesting that Brutus brought liberty to Rome by assassinating Caesar. The letters below, EID • MAR are an abbreviation for ĪDIBUS MARTIĪS "on the Ides of March" (March 15th) referring to the date of the assassination.

The freed slave, now known as a *lībertīnus* or *lībertīna*, often took the *praenōmen* and *nōmen*, the names, of his or her former master. The master (*dominus*) became patron (*patrōnus, -ī* m.). Thus, when Cicero freed his secretary Tiro, he gave him the name Marcus Tullius Tīrō, who would legally append L. (for *lībertus*) after this name.

Lībertīnī could become wealthy and powerful members of Roman society. In fact, some of Rome's most important authors, including the playwrights Plautus and Terence, were once slaves.

Do you remember the homework assignment Chiron gave his pupils at the end of the last chapter? He told them to learn three *sententiae* of Publilius Syrus. *Sententiae* (The Sentences or Proverbs), a collection of Latin maxims, survives under the name of Publilius Syrus, who lived in the first century B.C. Syrus was born in Syria (hence *Syrus* "the Syrian") and came to Italy as a slave. Like Chiron, he was eventually freed and became a *lībertīnus*. He wrote mimes (*mīmus, -ī* m.), a popular, if somewhat lower class, farcical stage performance, which even Julius Caesar enjoyed. The mimes are lost, but a collection of his most famous sayings has survived, rather like the proverbs and maxims collected from the pen of "Poor Richard," Benjamin Franklin.

Here are some of his *Sententiae* featuring forms of the verb *volō*. You should be able to understand these with the help of the *Verba Ūtenda* provided.

> *Quod vult habet, quī velle quod satis est potest.*

(Valeria quotes a slightly simpler version of this *sententia* in *Lectiō Secunda*.)

> *Quod esse tacitum vīs, id nūllī dīxeris.*
> *Sī vīs beatus esse, cōgitā cogitā hoc prīmum: contemne contemnī.*
> *Imperium habēre vīs magnum? Imperā tibi!*

And here is one more famous maxim using a form of *volō*. This one is not by Publilius Syrus but by Publius Flavius Vegetius Renatus, whose work on military affairs, *Epitoma reī mīlitāris* (c. 400 A.D.), has been read by military tacticians into modern times.

> *Sī vīs pācem, parā bellum.*

Gemma

Parā Bellum: This short phrase by Vegetius has had significant impact in the modern world and illustrates the continuing use of Latin in our society. The famous German pistol that we know as the Luger was originally called the "Luger Parabellum" and derives its name from the second half of Vegetius' phrase.
The heavy metal group Metallica also uses the phrase (in English) in the lyrics of "Don't Tread on Me."

🔊 VERBA ŪTENDA

beātus happy	*contemnō, contemnere* scorn	*imperō* (1) rule, command	*quī* he who
bellum, -ī n. war		*nūllī* "to no one, to nobody"	*quod* that which
cōgitō (1) think about	*dīxeris* "you will have said"		*satis* enough
	id it	*pācem* peace	*tacitus, -a, -um* silent, secret
contemnī "to be scorned"	*imperium, -iī* n. supreme command	*parō* (1) prepare	
		prīmum first	*tibi* "yourself"

Latīna Hodierna

Volō in English

Latin is very helpful in building our English vocabulary, but you must be sure of the Latin word that lies at the root. Consider *volō, velle, voluī* "to wish" and *volō, -āre* "to fly." In English, their stems look alike, but which Latin verb provides the root of the following English words?

volatile   volition   volley

voluntary   volunteer

Notice how similarity in spelling is not a sure indicator that a specific English word is derived from a Latin word. You have to pay attention to meaning as well as spelling.

Nōlō appears in a variety of contexts in the modern world. Here is an example from art:

- **Noli me tangere.** "Don't touch me!" This refers to a type of painting based on the words of Jesus to Mary Magdalene after his resurrection (John 20:17). The 1511–1512 painting by the Italian artist Titian (Tiziano Vecellio), now in the National Gallery, London, is a good example.

We also find *nōlō* in the law.

- **Nolle prosequi.** "To be unwilling to continue." Used in law to refer to a plaintiff or prosecutor's decision not to pursue a case.
- **Nolo contendere.** "I do not wish to contest the charge." In criminal law, the accused has the option of making this plea instead of a declaration of guilt or innocence.

Nōlī mē tangere

Orbis Terrārum Rōmānus

Syria

Syria, the homeland of Publilius Syrus, was conquered by Pompey the Great in 64 B.C. and became a Roman province. With its strategic location on the border of the Parthian Empire, Syria was important militarily, and the governor of the province had several legions at his command in the first century A.D.

Major trade routes to Arabia and to the east, especially the Silk Road to China, passed through the province, and in the early empire, made its capital, Antioch (*Antiochēa ad Orontem*, Antioch on the Orontes), the largest city in the East, except for Alexandria. Besides Antioch, important cities of Roman Syria included Damascus and Palmyra (in modern Syria), and Tyre and Sidon (in modern Lebanon).

Syria was also an important producer of wine and vegetables (especially onions), and manufacturer of linens and wools for clothing.

Julia Domna (died 217 A.D.), the wife of the emperor Septimius Severus and the mother of his successor Caracalla, was born in Syria.

Porta quadrāta Palmyrae Rōmānae hodiē

Tyrus antīqua et hodierna

Ā Syria ad Sīnās

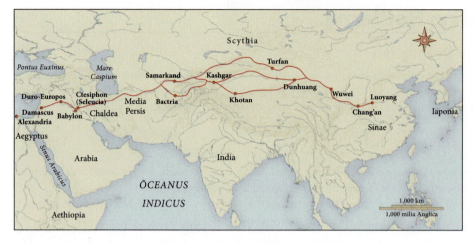

QUID PUTĀS?

1. Which of Publilius Syrus' *Sententiae* is most appealing to you? Why?
2. How would you describe the treatment of Flavia and Hermes as slaves?
3. How is the Roman practice of slavery similar to and different from slavery in the American experience?
4. How does the Roman practice of slavery affect your view of ancient Roman society?
5. Use the Roman practice of manumission of slaves to show how different the Roman institution of slavery was from the American experience.
6. Why would lawyers continue to use Latin expressions like *nolo contendere* in the modern world?

7. What cities could be compared to Antioch and Damascus as major trade crossroads in the modern world?

EXERCEĀMUS!

7-5   Scrībāmus

Refer to *Lectiō Prīma* to answer each of the following questions in Latin. Use either *ita / sic* or *nōn* and then give a complete-sentence answer. Follow the model.

→ Dūcitne Lūcius paedagōgum ad tabernam?

Nōn, paedagōgus Lūcium ad tabernam dūcit!

1. Estne Chīron Lūciī magister?
2. Vultne Hermēs magistrum maestum vidēre?
3. Eratne Chīron ōlim servus?
4. Estne Hermēs nunc lībertīnus?
5. Vultne Lūcius aliquid bibere?

7-6   Colloquāmur

Now practice asking and answering the questions in Exercise 7-5 with a classmate.

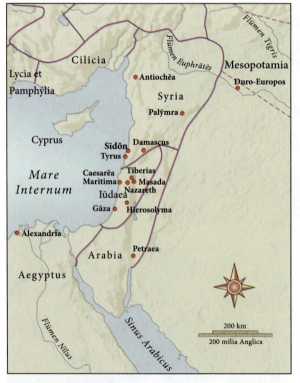

Rōmānī in Oriente

7-7   **Verba Discenda**

Refer to the *Verba Discenda* to answer the following questions.

1. What conjugation is *audiō* in?
2. What word means the opposite of *abeō*?
3. What numbers appear in this list?
4. Find a noun in this list. What does it mean?
5. What word means the opposite of *volō*?
6. Find a verb in the 2nd conjugation. How do you know?
7. What is the first principal part of *iī*?
8. The English word **adit** means a mine entrance. What verb is it from?
9. Find a verb in the 3rd conjugation.
10. Find a verb in the 4th conjugation.
11. What is the alternate form of *audīvī*?

🔊 VERBA DISCENDA

abeō, abīre, abīvī / abiī, *abitum* go away
adeō, adīre, adīvī / adiī, *aditum* go to
amīcus, -ī m. friend [amicable]
audiō, audīre, audīvī / *audiī, audītum* hear, listen to [audible, auditory]
dē (+ abl.) down from, concerning

dēbeō, dēbēre, dēbuī, *dēbitum* owe, ought, have to [debt, debit]
dīcō, dīcere, dīxī, dīctum say, tell [dictator, dictation]
duo, duae, duo two [dual]
edō, ēsse / edere, ēdī, *ēsum* eat
ego I [egotism, egotistical]

eō, īre, īvī / iī, itum go
mālō, mālle, māluī prefer
nōlō, nōlle, nōluī not want to, be unwilling
possum, posse, potuī be able, can [potential]
rīdeō, rīdēre, rīsī, *rīsum* laugh [risible, ridiculous]

servus, -ī m. slave, servant [servitude]
sī if
sī tibi placet! please!
sīcut just as
ūnus, -a, -um one [unicycle]
volō, velle, voluī want to, be willing to [volition]

Angulus Grammaticus

More Irregular Verbs in Latin and Modern Languages

The Latin verb *edō, ēsse / edere, ēdī, ēsum* (to eat) is irregular in the present tense. Here is its conjugation, compared to the verb *sum, esse, fuī* (to be).

EDŌ TO EAT		*SUM* TO BE	
edō	I eat	*sum*	I am
ēs	you eat	*es*	you are
ēst	he/she/it eats	*est*	he/she/it is
edimus	we eat	*sumus*	we are
ēstis	you eat	*estis*	you are
edunt	they eat	*sunt*	they are
ēsse *edere*	to eat	*esse*	to be

Note that the infinitives *ēsse* "to eat" and *esse* "to be" as well as some other forms (marked in bold) have the same spelling but are pronounced differently. Later in its history, Latin developed a regular infinitive *edere* to replace *ēsse*. But the long marks can make a difference. Consider this old Latin schoolboy's joke:

Mea mater mala sus est.

Without long marks or punctuation, it can mean either "My mother is a bad pig" or "My mother, the pig is eating apples!" See if you can put in the required punctuation and long marks for each meaning.

Knowing how irregular verbs like *sum, esse* work in Latin can help you understand some modern languages better. Here are some examples:

LATIN	ENGLISH	FRENCH	ITALIAN	SPANISH
sum	I am	*je suis*	*sono*	*soy*
es	you are	*tu es*	*sei*	*eres*
est	he/she/it is	*il/elle est*	*é*	*es*
sumus	we are	*nous sommes*	*siamo*	*somos*
estis	you are	*vous êtes*	*siete*	*sois*
sunt	they are	*ils/elles sont*	*sono*	*son*
esse	to be	*être*	*essere*	*ser*

Notā Bene:
- Notice how the three Romance languages, French, Italian, and Spanish transform the Latin personal endings.
- Like Latin, Spanish and Italian do not need personal pronouns with the verb. French, like English, does.
- The French and Italian forms of the verb "to be" are descended directly from Latin *sum, esse.*

One of the challenges for English speakers in learning Spanish is that Spanish has two forms of the verb "to be": *ser*, which is used to indicate identity and quality, and *estar*, which is used to indicate health, location, and state. *Estar* is derived from the Latin verb *stō, stāre* (to stand).

LATIN	SPANISH
stō	*estoy*
stās	*estás*
stat	*está*
stāmus	*estamos*
stātis	*estáis*
stant	*están*
stāre	*estar*

8

Eāmus Domum!

Lectīca ornāta

Lectiō Prīma

Antequam Legis

The Vocative Case

In Chapter 7 you learned about the imperative mood. Very often imperatives are accompanied by nouns indicating the person(s) or thing(s) being addressed. In English we often mark these nouns with interjections like "Hey, John" or "Oh, Melissa." Latin sometimes uses a similar interjection *Ō,* but always puts the one addressed into a case called the **vocative** (from *vocāre,* to call).

As you read this next episode, in which Lucius meets his older sister Servilia on his way home from school, look for the vocatives (marked in **bold**). Most vocative forms are the same as the nominative, but some have different endings.

EXERCEĀMUS!

8-1 **Vocatives**

As you read, put the vocatives (marked in **bold**) into two lists. The first list is for vocatives that look like a nominative form. The second list is for vocatives that do not look like a nominative.

LECTIŌNĒS:
IN LECTĪCĀ ORNĀTĀ
and
Ē TABERNĀ

While Lucius gets a ride home with his sister Servilia, Valeria and her daughter close up their shop for the day.

🔊 IN LECTĪCĀ ORNĀTĀ

Dum paedagōgus cum puerō ambulat, lectīcam ornātam in viā vident.
Lectīca familiae Servīliī est. Quattuor servī lectīcam portant et in lectīcā
sedet Servīlia, soror Lūciī et fīlia Servīliī. Prō lectīcā servus magnus ambulat
et hominēs ā viā āmovet. Post lectīcam ancilla Servīliae quoque ambulat.

5   Lūcius magnā vōce vocat: "**Servī**, sistite!" Servī lectīcam in terrā
pōnunt et sub arbore stant. Puer "Salvē," inquit, "**soror**! Quid agis?"

Servīlia Lūcium videt et perlaeta est. "**Lūcī**," inquit Servīlia, "Venī
hūc, et audī aliquid dē amīcō novō meō!" Servīlia sēdecim annōs nāta est
et marītum nōndum habet sed mox nūbere oportet. Lūcius decem annōs
10 nātus est.

"Intrā in lectīcam meam, ō **mī frāter**, et dum domum īmus, dē
novō amīcō meō audī!"

Lūcius nihil dē amīcīs puellārum cūrat, sed melius est in lectīcā
sedēre quam in viā ambulāre.

15 Ergō frāter respondet, "Bene, **Servīlia**, intrō" et in lectīcam intrat.

Nunc "**Mī paedagōge**," Lūcius inquit, "post lectīcam ambulā!" Subitō Servīlia clāmat; "Ō **servī**! Num fessī
estis? Nōlīte illīc stāre! Nōs portāte domum!"

Servī nōn laetī sunt quod nunc duōs et nōn ūnam portant, sed nihil dīcunt. Servī sagācēs semper nihil dīcunt.

Lectīcam ornātam in viā vident.

🔊 VERBA ŪTENDA

aliquid something	***fīlia, -ae* f. daughter**	*mox* soon	*puella, -ae* f. girl
āmoveō, āmovēre move away	*frāter* brother	*nātus, -a, -um* See *annōs nātus, -a est*	*quam* than
***ancilla, -ae* f. female servant**	*hominēs* people	*nōndum* not yet	*quattuor* four
	hūc here, to this place	***novus, -a, -um* new**	***quoque* also**
annōs nātus, -a est he/she is …years old	***iam* now, already**	*nūbō, nūbere* marry	*sagācēs* wise
	illīc there, over there	*oportet* (+ inf.) it is fitting that	***sēdecim* sixteen**
arbore tree	***intrō* (1) enter**		***sistō, sistere, stetī / stitī, statum* stop, stand still**
audiō, audīre hear	***inquam, inquit* say**	*ornātus, -a, -um* decorated	
cūrō (1) care	*lectīca, -ae* f. litter, sedan chair	*perlaetus, -a, -um* very happy	*soror* sister
decem ten			*subitō* suddenly
dum while	***magnus, -a, -um* large, great, loud**	*prō* (+ abl.) in front of	***terra, -ae* f. land**
***ergō* therefore**	*melius* better	***portō* (1) carry**	***vocō* (1) call**
***familia, -ae* f. family**	*mī* my (vocative)		*vōce* voice

POSTQUAM LĒGISTĪ

1. Describe how Lucius' sister Servilia travels through Rome. How would his sister travel today?
2. How old is Servilia? What are her plans and expectations for the immediate future?
3. What news does Servilia want to share with Lucius?
4. What does Lucius want to do?
5. In line 18 you read that the slaves carry *duōs et nōn ūnam*. To whom does *ūnam* refer? To whom does *duōs* refer? Note how Latin uses masculine gender to refer to male and female together.
6. Why are Servilia's slaves unhappy at the end of this story? What do they do about this? Why?

Grammatica A

The Vocative Case

Scan the list you made of vocative forms as you read *Lectiō Prīma*. Here are the rules for forming the vocative:

- Most vocative singulars and all vocative plurals are the same as their nominatives.
- The only exceptions are in the singular vocative of 2nd declension nouns ending in *-us* (re-read that—every word is important). And in such a case:

   The ending *-us* ⟶ *-e*

   Thus *amīcus* ⟶ *amīce!* or *paedagōgus* ⟶ *paedagōge!*

   The ending *-ius* ⟶ *-ī*

   Thus *fīlius* ⟶ *fīlī!* or *Lūcius* ⟶ *Lūcī!*

	1ST DECLENSION		2ND DECLENSION		
Singular					
Nominative	-a	fēmina	-us, er, ir	vir	discipulus	fīlius
Genitive	-ae	fēminae	-ī	virī	discipulī	fīliī
Accusative	-am	fēminam	-um	virum	discipulum	fīlium
Ablative	-ā	fēminā	-ō	virō	discipulō	fīliō
Vocative	**-a**	**fēmina**	**-e**	**vir**	**discipule**	**fīlī**
Plural					
Nominative	-ae	fēminae	-ī	virī	discipulī	fīliī
Genitive	-ārum	fēminārum	-ōrum	virōrum	discipulōrum	fīliōrum
Accusative	-ās	fēminās	-ōs	virōs	discipulōs	fīliōs
Ablative	-īs	fēminīs	-īs	virīs	discipulīs	fīliīs
Vocative	**-ae**	**fēminae**	**-ī**	**virī**	**discipulī**	**fīliī**

Notā Bene:

- 2nd declension words that do not end in *-us* have a vocative that *is* identical with the nominative. *Ō vir! Ō magister!*
- Be careful of confusing forms. *Ō amīcī* can fool the casual reader. It is plural. And compare *Ō fīlī* (sing.) with *Ō fīliī* (pl.). Forms like these cause fewer problems if you get into the habit of reading aloud. The ear is less easily fooled than the eye.

EXERCEĀMUS!

8-2 Vocative Fill-Ins

Choose the correct vocative form to complete the sentence. Pay attention to singulars and plurals! Follow the model.

⟶ (Lūcius / Lūcī), intrā in lectīcam meam. *Lūcī*

1. Venī, ō (Licinia / Liciniae).
2. (Serve / Servī), nōlīte illīc stāre!
3. Ō (fēminae / fēmina), venīte.
4. (Servīlia / Servīliae), portā Sōcratem!
5. Ō (paedagōgum / paedagōge), intrā in lectīcam meam.

Lectiō Secunda

Antequam Legis

Latin Expressions of Time

The next reading presents expressions of time, several using the word *hōra, -ae* (f. hour). They are marked in ***bold italics***.

- When the phrase is accusative, the English word "for" generally is the best translation.
- When it is ablative, try "at" or, if appropriate, "during."

The Perfect Tense

In the next reading, as Valeria closes up shop for the day, we introduce you to the **perfect tense**. To help you spot the new tense, we have put all perfects in *Lēctiō Secunda* in **bold**. For now, simply translate them in one of two ways:

as a **simple past tense**:   *salūtāvit* he/she/it **greeted**
                                     salūtāvērunt they **greeted**

as a **compound past tense**:   *salūtāvit* he/she/it **has greeted**
                                     salūtāvērunt they **have greeted**

You will see only 3rd person forms right now. The personal endings of these forms will be familiar because the singular ends in *-t* and the plural ends in *-nt*, just as in the present tense!

EXERCEĀMUS!

8-3   **Scanning the Text**

Before you read, scan the *lectiō* to find the answers to the following questions.

1. What time does business in the Forum begin to slow down?
2. Why is Valeria tired?
3. Why is she happy?
4. What are Valeria, Licinia, and Flavia no longer able to do today?
5. Now that the time for work is over, what is it time for?

🔊 Ē TABERNĀ

Octāva hōra est. Paucī hominēs aut in Forō aut in viīs nunc adsunt. Senātōrēs et mercātōrēs negōtium reī pūblicae **ēgērunt** et omne negōtium ad fīnem **prōcessit**. Nōn iam tempus negōtiī est, sed tempus ōtiī. Multī hominēs ā Forō ad familiās suās nunc prōcēdere incipiunt.

5   In tabernā, Valeria quoque parum negōtiī agit quod hominēs absunt. Fessa est, quia māne **surrexit** et ad tabernam **vēnit**. *Multās horās* **labōrāvit**. Licinia et Flāvia quoque *multās horās* **labōrāvērunt**. Valeria multōs virōs in tabernā **salūtāvit**. Multī virī in tabernā **ēdērunt** et **bibērunt**. Valeria laeta est quod multī virī multam pecūniam **dedērunt**.

10   Sed nunc *octāvā horā*, sine populō in viā, Valeria nūllum negōtium in tabernā agere **potuit**. Tempus negōtiī **fīnīvit**.

Valeria filiam ancillamque magnā voce **vocāvit** et eīs **dīxit**. "Ō Licinia! Flāvia!" **clāmāvit**, "Hūc venīte! Plūs negōtiī hodiē agere nōn possumus. Lābor iam **fīnīvit**. Tempus ōtiī est. Ergō, nōlīte illīc stāre! Eāmus domum!

Tempus negōtiī fīnīvit.

🔊 VERBA ŪTENDA

absum, abesse, āfuī be away, be absent
adsum, adesse, adfuī be present
ancilla, -ae f. female servant
aut…aut either …or
Eāmus! Let's go! (from *eō*)
ēgērunt "they did" (from *agō*)
eīs to them (i.e., Licinia and Flavia)
ergō therefore
fessus, -a, -um tired

fīlia, -ae f. daughter
fīnem end
fīniō, fīnīre, fīnīvī / fīniī, fīnītum finish
hūc here, to this place
hominēs people
hōra, -ae f. hour, time
iam now, already
illīc there
incipiō, incipere, incēpī begin
intrō (1) enter
lābor work

labōrō (1) work
magnus, -a, -um large, great, loud
mercātor merchant
negōtium, -iī n. business, task
nōn iam no longer
octāva hōra = eighth hour, about 2 P.M.
ōtium, ōtiī n. leisure, rest
parum (+ gen.) little
paucī few
plūs more

prōcēdō, prōcēdere, prōcessī proceed, advance
quia because
quoque also
reī pūblicae of the republic
senātōrēs senators
sine (+ abl.) without
suās their
surgō, surgere, surrexī to get up
tempus time
vōce voice
vocō (1) call

POSTQUAM LĒGISTĪ

1. Compare the time expressions *multās horās* in line 6 and *octāvā horā* in line 10. Note that one is in the accusative and one is in the ablative. How does Latin use case to indicate different kinds of time?
2. Does the timing of a Roman business day resemble any modern countries' commercial patterns?
3. What effect might the Italian climate have had on the Roman business day?
4. *Ōtium* means "leisure" and *negotium* is a compound (*nec* + *ōtium*) meaning "not leisure." What does this seem to say about Roman priorities?

Grammatica B

The Perfect Tense: 3ʳᵈ Person Singular and Plural

Did you find *salūtāvit, surrexit, vēnit* and *fīnīvit* in this scene? Compare these perfect forms with the present.

Present	*salūtat*	she greets
Perfect	*salūtāvit*	she greeted
Present	*surgit*	she gets up
Perfect	*surrexit*	she got up
Present	*venit*	she comes
Perfect	*vēnit*	she came
Present	*Labor fīnit.*	Work ends.
Perfect	*Labor fīnīvit.*	Work has ended.

- For now, you will see only the 3ʳᵈ person, singular and plural.
- The endings are: 3ʳᵈ singular *-it* and 3ʳᵈ plural *-ērunt*.
- Translate the perfect as a simple past or use the helping verb "has/have."

salūtāvit	she greeted	*salūtāvērunt*	they greeted
surrēxit	she has arisen	*surrēxērunt*	they have arisen
vēnit	she went	*vēnērunt*	they went
fīnīvit	it has ended	*fīnīvērunt*	they have ended

The Perfect Stem

The perfect stem (used to form three tenses) is found by dropping the *-ī* from the 3rd principal part.

1st PP	2nd PP	3rd PP	Perfect Stem
habitō	*habitāre*	*habitāvī*	*habitāv-*
videō	*vidēre*	*vīdī*	*vīd-*
dūcō	*dūcere*	*dūxī*	*dūx-*
veniō	*venīre*	*vēnī*	*vēn-*
sum	*esse*	*fuī*	*fu-*

Some stems are very close to each other and may seem hard for the eye to catch, such as *venit* (present, "he comes") vs. *vēnit* (perfect, "he came"). But for the Romans it was a matter of hearing the difference—*weh-nit* vs. *wey-nit*. It gave them no greater pause than this sentence gives you: "I love to **read**, so yesterday I **read** three books." Again, try reading aloud whenever you can.

Tense

A verb has tense as well as mood. The tense of a verb indicates the time of an action and the kind of action (simple or continuous). So far you have seen two tenses, **present** and **perfect**. For now, distinguish these two tenses in terms of time. The present tense indicates actions happening "now," whereas the perfect tense indicates actions that have happened in the past.

ambulat	he walks	now
ambulāvit	he walked	in the past

Later we will deal with other aspects of tense.

The 3rd Principal Part

The third form of a Latin verb listed in the dictionary is its 1st person singular perfect active form. This is called the third principal part. Here are examples for some verbs you have already learned.

1st Conjugation	*ambulō*	*ambulāre*	*ambulāvī*
	I walk	to walk	I walked
2nd Conjugation	*respondeō*	*respondēre*	*respondī*
	I reply	to reply	I replied
3rd Conjugation	*agō*	*agere*	*ēgī*
	I do	to do	I did
3rd Conjugation *-iō*	*capiō*	*capere*	*cēpī*
	I seize	to seize	I seized
4th Conjugation	*veniō*	*venīre*	*vēnī*
	I come	to come	I came
Irregular	*sum*	*esse*	*fuī*
	I am	to be	I was

Perfect stems vary widely, but there are some patterns:

PATTERN	PRESENT STEM	PERFECT STEM
add -v-	clāmā-	clāmāv-
add -u-	habē-	habu-
add -s-	dūc- scrīb-	dūx- scrips-
lengthen vowel	ven-	vēn-
reduplicate (double) initial sound	curr-	cucurr-
complete stem change	fer- ag-	tul- ēg-

EXERCEĀMUS!

8-4 3rd Principal Parts

Use the patterns described in the chart to identify the 1st principal part of each of the following *Verba Discenda*. Then describe the type of pattern change. Follow the model.

	1st PP	**Pattern**
→ vocāvī	*vocō*	add -v-
1. portāvī		
2. debuī		
3. dīxī		
4. ēdī		
5. didicī		
6. fuī		

Latin Time Expressions

Latin uses the accusative and the ablative cases to express time.

The **accusative case** is used to show how long an action lasted. This is called the **accusative of duration of time** or **accusative of extent of time** or, if you will, "the accusative of time how long." For example:

> *Multās hōrās labōrāvit.*   She worked **(for) many hours**.

The **ablative case** is used to show when an action took place or the time during which the action took place. These are usually called the **ablative of time when** and the **ablative of time within which**.

> *Octāvā hōrā dormīvit.*   **At the eighth hour** she was sleeping.
>
> *Nocte labōrāvit.*   She worked **at night**.

The biggest challenge posed by these expressions for English speakers is supplying the right English preposition, since Latin uses none. As a rule, you know it is **accusative of time** if you can use either **for** or no preposition in your translation, as in:

> "She worked **for many hours** on the homework assignment."
> "She worked **many hours** on the assignment."

In either case the English words become *multās hōrās* in Latin.

It is an **ablative of time** expression if you use the prepositions **at**, **during**, or **in,** as in

"She finished the assignment **at noon**."	⟶	*merīdiē*
"She finished the assignment **during the night**."	⟶	*nocte*
"She went home **at the eighth hour**."	⟶	*octāvā hōrā*

These three time expressions in **bold** become ablative in Latin: it is the reader's job to choose the English preposition that works the best.

Mōrēs Rōmānī

Tempus Fugit

Several Roman expressions about time have passed the test of time and have become proverbial expressions today. Perhaps the most famous of these is *Tempus fugit*, which we know in English as "Time flies." This expression can be traced back to a line in Vergil's *Georgics* (III.284), written in the late first century B.C. Use the *Verba Ūtenda* to help you translate.

> *Sed fugit intereā **fugit** irreparābile **tempus**.*

In one of his *Odes*, Vergil's friend Horace uses *aetās* instead of *tempus* as he offers a comment on time that you will recognize:

> *Dum loquimur, fūgerit invida*
> *Aetās: **carpe diem**.*
> > *Carmina* I.11.7–8

A generation later, the poet Ovid wrote the following in *Metamorphoses* XV.233:

> *Tempus edax rērum*

Notice how Ovid uses *edax* (devouring) from *edō, ēsse* to describe time here as the "devourer of things."

Finally, in his first speech against Catiline in 65 B.C., the famous orator Cicero (106–43 B.C.) also used an expression about time that is often quoted today:

> *Ō tempora, ō mōrēs!*

Cicero here is lamenting the bad state of affairs in Rome, that a man like Catiline, who was plotting to overthrow the Roman government, would dare to show his face in the Roman Senate. This speech became so famous that any Roman at the end of the 1st century B.C. would know many phrases from it by heart. This particular phrase is also quoted today when people want to complain about the present and to compare it unfavorably with the "good old days."

Sōlārium Rōmānum Pompēiīs

🔊 VERBA ŪTENDA

aetās age, period of time	*edax* devouring (from *edō*);	*intereā* meanwhile	*loquimur* we speak
carpō, carpere seize, pluck,	refers to *tempus*	*invida* envious (refers to	*mōrēs* customs, habits
enjoy	*fūgerit* "will have fled"	*aetās*)	*rērum* "of things"
diem day	*fugiō, fugere, fūgī* flee, run	*irreparābile* unrecoverable,	*tempora* times
dum while	away	irreparable	*tempus* time

The Romans had no mechanical clocks, so telling time during the day was not an exact science. They did, however, have the sundial (*sōlārium, -iī* n.) and the water clock (*hōrologium, -iī* n.). The *hōrologium* was especially useful for telling time during the dark hours. It worked by calibrating the level of water flowing from one vessel into another.

The Romans divided daylight time into twelve equal *hōrae* or hours, rather than assigning a fixed amount of time for each hour. Nighttime was divided into four equal *vigiliae* or watches. Since there is more daylight in summer than in winter, a Roman *hōra* ended up being much longer in summer than it was in winter. Thus, if sunrise were at 6 A.M., then *prīmā hōrā,* "at the first hour," would be 6–7 A.M. *Secundā hōrā,* "at the second hour," was thus 7–8 A.M.

Latīna Hodierna

Telling Time by the Romans

Though our ability to tell time today is much more exact than the Roman method, Latin words are still used in the modern vocabulary for telling time.

Latin	English	French	Italian	Spanish
hōra	hour	heure	ora	hora
hour, season, time				
hōrologia water clock		l'horloge	l'orologio	
minutia	minute	minute	minuto	minuto
from a stem meaning "tiny"				
secunda	second	seconde	secondo	segundo
that following first				
diēs	day			día
day, daylight				
diurnus, -a, -um,		jour	giornata	
daily				

Business travelers often receive a *per diem* allowance. This is a set amount for daily expenses. The phrase literally means "through the day, daily."

Orbis Terrārum Rōmānus

Campus Martius

The Campus Martius (Field of Mars) was an open, flat area north and west of the Capitoline Hill. An early temple of Mars gave the area its name. Since it was located outside the *pomerium* (the official, religious boundary) of the city of Rome, the Campus Martius was used frequently for military gatherings and exercises. It was also the place where citizens gathered to vote in the *comitia centuriata* (a political assembly). In the Republican period, several important structures were erected there including the Circus Flaminius (221 B.C.) and the Theater of Pompey (52 B.C.), where Julius Caesar was assassinated.

In the Augustan period, the Campus Martius saw several major building projects, including the Mausoleum of Augustus, the Ara Pacis, the original Pantheon (built by Agrippa) and the *Sōlārium Augustī,* a huge horological park near his Mausoleum. Augustus dedicated this monument in 10 B.C. to celebrate the restoration of Egypt to Roman power (after the battle of Actium in 31 B.C). He used an Egyptian obelisk as the arm of the sundial to mark not only the hours of the day but also the seasons of the year. This obelisk, now in the Piazza Montecitorio in Rome, appears in a photograph on page 102.

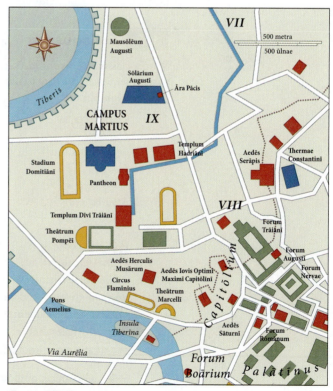

Campus Mārtius

Sōlārium (Hōrologium) Augustī in Campō Martiō

QUID PUTĀS?

1. "Time flies" is not an accurate translation of Vergil's *tempus fugit*. Can you give a better one based on what the verb *fugiō* really means? Which version do you like better and why?
2. Why does Vergil describe time as *irreparābile*? How is the literal meaning of the Latin word different from the English derivative "irreparable"?
3. Explain how each of the different possible meanings of the verb *carpō* adds new meaning to the phrase *Carpe diem.*
4. Where have you seen the phrase *Carpe diem* used today? Do you agree with this statement? Why or why not?
5. Compare the *sōlārium Augustī* illustrated in *Mōrēs Rōmānī* with the meaning of the English word "solarium." What do they have in common?
6. Compare the Campus Martius to a park or other open space in your home town. How are these spaces similar? How are they different?

EXERCEĀMUS!

8-5 Scrībāmus

Retell in the past tense the meeting between Socrates and Chiron that you read in the last chapter. In order to do this replace all the present tense verb forms (marked in bold in parentheses) with perfect ones. Follow the model.

Chīrōn ā lūdō ___*abīvit*___ (**abit**) et ad tabernam Valeriae _____ (**adit**). Ubi Sōcratēs magistrum in tabernā _____ (**videt**), sīmia dē mensā et in bracchia Chīrōnis _____ (**currit**). In mensā quattuor fīcī _____ (**sunt**) et Sōcratēs ūnum dē fīcīs _____ (**capit**) et ad magistrum _____ (**portat**). Sīmia fīcum _____ (**dat**) et magister _____ (**rīdet**). Chīrōn tacitus vīnum _____ (**bibit**) dum omnēs in tabernā _____ (**rīdent**).

8-6 Colloquāmur

With a classmate or your instructor, practice asking and answering the questions based on the pattern sentences. Be sure to use the vocative with your question and answer. Here is some vocabulary you can use:

Questions

Quid hoc est?
  (What is this?)
Ubi est . . . ?
  (Where is . . .)
Monstrā mihi . . .
  (Show me . . .)

Addressee

amīca (female friend)
amīce (male friend)
discipula (female student)
discipule (male student)
magister (male teacher)
magistra (female teacher)

Classroom Objects

charta (paper)
fenestra (window)
hōrologium (clock)
liber (book)
mensa (table, desk)
porta (door)
sella (chair)
stilus (pen or pencil)
tabula (notebook)

Words in Answers

hīc (here)
illīc (there)

 Q: Amīce, quid hoc est?   **A:** Hoc est sella!

 Q: Magistra, ubi est liber?   **A:** Liber hīc est.

8-7 **Verba Discenda**

Find the Latin word in the *Verba Discenda* that best answers each of the following questions.

→ Valeria would address Licinia with this word: *fīlia*

1. This noun can refer to the girl who accompanies Servilia:

2. This noun refers to Valeria, Licinia, and her husband as a group:

3. Servilia's age:

4. What is conducted in the Roman Forum:

5. There are twelve of these in a Roman day:

6. How Valeria and Licinia feel at the end of a hard day's work:

7. Use this verb to refer to an object that is no longer moving:

8. This noun is walked on:

🔊 VERBA DISCENDA

ancilla, -ae **f. female servant** [ancillary]
ergō **therefore**
familia, -ae **f. family** [familiar]
fessus, -a, -um **tired**
fīlia, -ae **f. daughter** [filial]
fīniō, fīnīre, fīnīvī / fīniī, fīnītum **finish** [infinity]

hōra, -ae **f. hour, time** [hour]
iam **now, already**
illīc **there**
intrō **(1) enter** [introduce]
magnus, -a, -um **large, great, loud** [magnitude]

negōtium, -iī **n. business, task** [negotiate]
novus, -a, -um **new** [novelty]
portō **(1) carry** [porter, portable]
praeter **(+ acc.) along, beyond; except**
quoque **also**

sēdecim **sixteen**
sistō, sistere, stetī / stitī, statum **stand still** [desist]
terra, -ae **f. land** [terrestrial]
vocō **(1) call** [vocative, vocation]

Angulus Grammaticus

More on 2nd Declension Vocatives

You know that the vocative case usually has the same endings as the nominative case and that ALL vocative plurals are identical to the nominative plural forms. The only significant exceptions occur in the 2nd declension singular. Here are the rules:

- If the nominative singular ends in *-r*, the vocative is the same as the nominative.

   puer   *Ō puer*

- If the nominative singular ends in *-us*, the vocative is *-e*.

   amīcus   *Ō amīce*

- If a nominative singular noun ends in *-ius*, the vocative is *-ī*.

   filius   *Ō filī*

- Rarely, if a nominative singular adjective ends in *-ius*, the vocative is *-ie*. There are not many of these.

    filius tertius   *Ō filī tertie*

- The vocative singular of *meus* is *mī*.

    meus amīcus   *Ō mī amīce*

Here is a chart summarizing how this works:

SINGULAR					
Nominative	vir	discipulus	filius	tertius	meus
Vocative	**vir**	**discipule**	**filī**	**tertie**	**mī**
PLURAL					
Nominative	virī	discipulī	filiī	tertiī	
Vocative	**virī**	**discipulī**	**filiī**	tertiī	

The interjection *Ō* is an easy way to recognize a vocative in a phrase, but it is not required. Just as, in English, we can say, "Hey, John, where are you?" or simply "John, where are you?" Latin says, *Ō Marce, ubi es?* or *Marce, ubi es?*

9

Per Viās Rōmānās

Lectiō Prīma

Antequam Legis

Subūra

In this chapter, Valeria, Licinia, and Aurelia walk home through a lively Roman neighborhood called the Subura, which was located in the valley between the Viminal and Esquiline hills. The Subura was a lower-class area with lots of activity, both legal and illegal, taking place in the street. All sorts of businesses set up shop in the street, including barbers, as you will see, and there were all sorts of street vendors and performers, as in many modern American cities.

One of the topics of conversation on the street is an upcoming performance of a play called *Amphitryō* by Plautus, a 2nd-century B.C. author of comedies. Later in this book, you will "attend" this performance.

As you read about life in the Subura, watch for more verbs in the perfect tense. **Note:** The following story intentionally mixes the present and perfect tenses. Be sure of the tense before you translate.

Uses of the Genitive Case

This reading introduces you to two new uses for the genitive, the **genitive of description** and the **genitive of the whole**. We use a **genitive of description** in English in phrases like "a man of great wisdom." Latin can say the same thing: *vir magnae sapientiae.*

Latin uses a **genitive of the whole** in expressions indicating the part of a whole, as in the phrase *plūs negōtiī* "more of business" = "more business."

Per viam Pompēiānam

GRAMMATICA
The Genitive of Description
and Genitive of the Whole
Possessive and Reflexive Adjectives

MŌRĒS RŌMĀNĪ
Fullōnica Rōmāna

LATĪNA HODIERNA
Latin in Modern Commerce

ORBIS TERRĀRUM RŌMĀNUS
Subūra

ANGULUS GRAMMATICUS
What Kind of Genitive Is That? Genitives
with Nouns and Adjectives

LECTIŌNĒS:
AD SUBŪRAM
and
VIA OCCUPĀTA

Valeria and her daughter walk home to the Subura. Along the way they experience Roman street life.

Gemma

Another idiom: *Quid novī?* Literally, "What of new?" We would say "What's new?"

EXERCEĀMUS!

9-1 Translating Genitives

As you read *Lectiō Prīma*, make a list of the genitives marked in **bold** along with the word that is linked to this genitive. Then identify each of them as either a **genitive of possession**, a **genitive of description** or a **genitive of the whole**. Follow the models.

Line	Genitive	Type
→ 1	plūs negōtiī	of the whole
→ 1	tabernā Valeriae	possession

🔊 AD SUBŪRAM

Plūs **negōtiī** nōn in Forō est. Multī hominēs ā Forō et ā tabernā **Valeriae** abīvērunt et ad familiās suās adīvērunt. Nunc, ergō, parum **negōtiī** in tabernā est. Labor **fēminārum fessārum** in tabernā finīvit.

Valeria Liciniaque tabernam clausērunt et per Argīlētum fēminae ambulāvērunt ad
5 Subūram, ubi **Valeriae** familia habitat. Dum ambulant, fēminae multa varia vīdērunt.

Dum Valeria et Licinia per viās eunt, hominēs multōs et variōs vīdērunt. Prīmum, **tonsōris** tabernam vīdērunt. Tonsor, vir **magnae statūrae**, prō tabernā suā stetit et virum **parvae statūrae** rāsit dum aliī virī circumstant et multa dē multīs dīcunt. In antīquitāte, sīcut hodiē, virī in tabernīs **tonsōrum** multa dīcunt!

10 "Quid **novī**, amīce?" ūnus **ē virīs** rogāvit.

Amīcus respondit: "Multī dē theātrō dīcunt." Alius addidit: "Mox in theātrō **Marcellī** *Amphitryō*, fābula **Plautī** erit."

Et tertius: "Quid dē rēbus **Augustī**?"

"St! Tacē, stulte!" monuit ūnus **ē virīs**. "Nōlī audēre talia verba dīcere! Fortasse aliquis **malī animī** nostra verba
15 audīre potest!" Nēmō **virōrum** magnā vōce dīcere voluit.

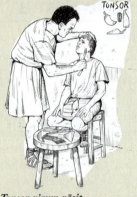

Tonsor virum rāsit

🔊 VERBA ŪTENDA

addō, addere, addidī add
aliquis someone
alius, -a, -um other, another
animus, -ī m. mind, spirit
antīquitāte antiquity
audeō, audēre, ausus sum dare
audiō, audīre, audīvī, audītum hear
circumstō, circumstāre, circumstetī stand around
claudō, claudere, clausī close, shut up
dum while
ē virīs of the men

ergō therefore
erit there will be
fābula, -ae f. play, story
fortasse perhaps
hominēs people
labor work
moneō, monēre, monuī warn
mox soon
multa dē multīs much about many things
multa varia many different things
nēmō no one, nobody
noster, nostra, nostrum our
nunc now

parum little
parvae small
plūs more
prīmum first, at first
prōnuntiō (1) pronounce, say
prō (+ abl.) before, in front of
rādō, rādere, rāsī shave
rēbus "the affairs"
rogō (1) ask
sīcut just as
st! shh! shush!
statūra, -ae f. stature
stulte! stupid!

suus, -a, -um his/her/its/their own
suā his (refers to the barber)
Subūra, -ae f. Subura, a neighborhood in Rome
taceō, tacēre, tacuī be silent
talia such
tertius a third (person)
theātrum, -ī n. theater; the Theater of Marcellus was new at the time
tonsōris "of a barber"
tonsōrum "of barbers"
varia various things
verba words

POSTQUAM LĒGISTĪ

Answer the following questions in Latin. You can easily find the material for your answer in the *lectiō*, but be sure your answers are in complete sentences. Follow the model.

→ Quid in viīs fēminae vīdērunt?
  Hominēs multōs et variōs vīdērunt.

1. Quid Valeria Liciniaque agunt?
2. Ubī Valeriae familia habitat?
3. Ubi virī multa dē multīs dīcunt?
4. Quid mox in theātrō erit?

Gemma

Compare the verbs *audēre* and *audīre*. If you remember that their stems are *audē-* (dare) and *audi-* (hear), you will be able to tell them apart.

Grammatica A

Genitive of Description and Genitive of the Whole

You have already seen the genitive used in phrases like *Servīlī fīlius* (Servilius' son), *Liciniae vir* (Licinia's husband), and *Valeriae taberna* (Valeria's shop) in which the genitive case was used to show **possession**. You see two other uses of the genitive in *Lectiō Prīma*: the **genitive of description** and the **genitive of the whole**, also known as the **partitive genitive**.

The **genitive of description** is used to describe the general characteristics of a person or a thing.

  vir magnae statūrae   a man of great stature

The **genitive of the whole** is used to indicate a part or portion of a larger whole.

  quid novī   "what of new" or "what's new"
  plūs negōtiī   "more of business" or "more business"

Now look over the list you created while you were reading the *lectiō*. Is there anything from Exercise 9-1 you need to put in a different category?

Notā Bene:
- Notice how the genitive of the whole can be translated into English without "of," as in "more business" instead of "more of business." In fact, English prefers it that way!
- In English we might say "many of the men" but Latin would rather say *multī virī* (many men).
- With numbers Latin prefers to use *ex* + the ablative instead of the genitive of the whole: *ūnus ē virīs* (one of the men)

EXERCEĀMUS!

9-2 **Translating Genitive Phrases**

Match the genitive phrase in column A with its English translation in column B.

	A		B
____	1. domus magnī spatiī	A.	a house of great space
____	2. fēminae magnae sapientiae	B.	a man of evil mind
____	3. fēminae taberna	C.	a tutor of few words
____	4. paedagōgus paucōrum verbōrum	D.	boys of little ambition
____	5. plūs spatiī	E.	more space
____	6. puerōs paucae industriae	F.	none of the men
____	7. nēmō virōrum	G.	the man's daughter
____	8. vīnum parvī pretiī	H.	the woman's snack shop
____	9. vir malī animī	I.	wine of small price (cheap wine)
____	10. virī fīlia	J.	women of great wisdom

Hint: Use the vocabulary you know to identify the words you don't know.

Lectiō Secunda

Antequam Legis

Reflexive Adjectives

As you read *Lectiō Prīma*, did you notice how the barber stood *prō tabernā suā* (in front of his shop)? *Suā* is a form of the adjective *suus, -a, -um*, a word that has no fixed translation, but rather means "the subject's own". This word is used to show possession by the subject. You can translate it as "his (own)," "her (own)," "its (own)," or "their (own)," depending on the subject of the sentence. Nothing like it exists in English. Note the following phrases and their translations.

*Valeria fīliam **suam** amat.*	Valeria loves **her** (own) daughter.
*Aelius uxōrem **suam** amat.*	Aelius loves **his** (own) wife.
*Licinia virum **suum** amat.*	Licinia loves **her** (own) husband.
*Sīmia familiam **suam** amat.*	The monkey loves **its** (own) family.
*Aelius et Licinia familiam **suum** amant.*	Aelius and Licinia love **their** (own) family.

Watch for more forms of this adjective marked in **bold** as you read about all the people in the streets of the Subura.

EXERCEĀMUS!

9-3 **Translating Reflexive Adjectives**

As you read *Lectiō Secunda*, make a line-by-line list of all the forms of *suus, -a, -um*. Then identify the subject of the sentence in which the word is found. This subject will tell you whether to translate the word as **his**, **her**, **its**, or **their**.

Line	Form of *suus, -a, -um*	Subject	Translation
→ 3	suam	actōrēs	their

VIA OCCUPĀTA

Porrō fēminae ambulāvērunt et multōs aliōs hominēs vīdērunt.

Hīc in viā sunt musicī et saltātōrēs. Actōrēs magnī ingeniī quoque in viā fābulam **suam** agunt. Illīc, in tabernae angulō, nōnnūllī virī paucae industriae āleās iēcērunt. Virī paucae industriae et paucae pecūniae semper multam pecūniam ob-
5 tinēre spērant, sed saepe (aut semper!) pecūniam **suam** āmittunt.

In viā nōnnūllī puerī pilā lūdunt et ad lūdum amīcōs **suōs** vōcant. Puellae rīdent et dē **suīs** amīcīs narrant. Ūna puella cum amīcā **suā** ambulat et clārē canat.

Servī dominōs **suōs** in lectīcīs portant. Ūnus servus magnam arcam **suī** dominī portat. Nōnnūllī aliī conservum **suum** servant. Ancillae post dominārum **suārum** lectīcās ambulant. Alia **suae** dominae passerem in caveā portat.
10 Fēminae quoque sūtōrēs, unguentāriōs, laniōs, argentāriōs, librāriōs, et multōs aliōs vīdērunt. Illī virī magnae industriae sunt et tōtam per diem in officīnīs **suīs** labōrant.

In aliā viae parte fullōnica est. Fullōnica est taberna ubi fullō tunicās, togās, et omnia alia vestīmenta ūrīnā pūrgat. Dum prope fullōnicam ambulant, fēminae nāsōs texērunt propter odōrem fortem ūrīnae ē fullōnicā. Fullō, vir natūrae laetae, eās salūtāvit, sed festīnāvērunt fēminae et mox īnsulam **suam** cōnspexērunt. Propter odōrem fullō vir paucōrum amīcōrum est.

Fēminae nāsōs texērunt

🔊 VERBA ŪTENDA

actōrēs actors
adiuvō (1) help
ālea, -ae f. die (singular of "dice")
alius, -a, -um other, another, aliī … aliī some … others
aliōs "other people"
amīca, -ae f. (girl) friend
āmittō, āmittere, āmīsī, āmissum lose
angulus, -ī m. corner
ante (+ acc.) ahead, before
arca, -ae f. chest
argentārius, -iī, m. banker
canō (1) sing
cavea, -ae f. cage
clārē clearly, loudly
conservus, -ī m. fellow slave
conspiciō, conspicere, conspexī, conspectum

catch sight of, look at, observe
diem day
dominus, -ī m. master
dum while, as long as
eās them (females)
fābula, -ae f. story, play
festīnō (1) hasten
fortem strong
fullō, -ōnis m. launderer
fullōnica, -ae f. laundry
hīc here, to this place
hominēs people
iaciō, iacere, iēcī to throw
illī they
illīc there
industria, -ae f. ambition
ingenium, -ī n. talent
insula, -ae f. island, apartment block

labōrō (1) work
lanius, -iī m. butcher
lectīca, -ae f. litter, sedan chair
librārius, -iī m. bookseller, book copier
mox soon
musicus, -ī m. musician
nasus, -ī m. nose
natūra, -ae f. nature, disposition
nōnnūllī, -ae, -a some, several
obtineō, obtinēre, obtinuī, obtentum hold, support, gain
occupāta busy
odōrem odor, scent
officīna, -ae f. (work)shop
omnia everything
parte part, piece

passerem sparrow
paucus, -a, -um few, little
pila, -ae f. ball
porrō further
propter (+ acc.) on account of
pūrgō (1) clean
rādō, rādere, rāsī shave
saltātōrēs dancers
spērō (1) hope
sūtōrēs cobblers, shoemakers
suus, -a, -um
   his/her/its/their own
tegō, tegere, tēxī cover
toga, -ae f. toga
tōtus, -a, -um entire, whole, all
tunica, -ae f. tunic
unguentārius, -iī m. perfume seller
ūrīna, -ae f. urine

POSTQUAM LĒGISTĪ

1. Where are the actors performing? What are the men doing in the corner of a shop?
2. What are the boys and girls doing in the street?
3. What are the various slaves doing?
4. What kinds of shops do Valeria and Licinia see?
5. Which shop do they dislike and why?
6. Describe the owner of this shop.
7. How does this street scene compare to a street in your hometown?

Grammatica B

Possessive and Reflexive Adjectives

"My" "your" "his" "her" "its" "our," and "their" are all examples of **possessive adjectives**. Can you see how these adjectives got their name? Here is an overview of Latin possessive adjectives. All of these words are *Verba Discenda*.

Hīc in viā sunt musicī et saltātōrēs.

PERSON	POSSESSIVE ADJECTIVES	TRANSLATION
Singular		
1st	**meus, -a, -um**	my
2nd	**tuus, -a, -um**	your
3rd	**suus, -a, -um** (reflexive)	his/her/its own
Plural		
1st	**noster, nostra, nostrum**	our
2nd	**vester, vestra, vestrum**	your
3rd	**suus, -a, -um** (reflexive)	their own

The 1st and 2nd person possessive adjectives are easy to translate.

Fēmina familiam **meam** *amat.*	The woman loves my family.
Fēmina familiam **nostram** *amat.*	The woman loves our family.
Fēmina familiam **tuam** *amat.*	The woman loves your family.
Fēmina familiam **vestram** *amat.*	The woman loves your family.

Suus, -a, -um, the 3rd person possessive, is more complicated because it is **reflexive**, that is, it must always refer back to (or "reflect") the subject of the sentence. In other words, *suus, -a, -um* means "the subject's own," and how we translate it depends on the subject. Notice how the translation of *suam* changes in each of the following sentences.

Vir familiam **suam** *amat.*	The man loves **his (own)** family.
Fēmina familiam **suam** *amat.*	The woman loves **her (own)** family.
Fēminae familiam **suam** *amant.*	The women love **their (own)** family.
Virī familiam **suam** *amant.*	The men love **their (own)** family.

In these sentences *suam* is a feminine singular adjective referring to *familiam,* but it is translated into English as "his own," "her own," or "their own" depending upon the subject of the sentence. In English translation the word "own" is optional.

Notā Bene: With body parts and personal artifacts like clothing, *suus, -a, -um* is not used; e.g., *Fēminae nāsōs texērunt propter odōrem fortem ūrīnae ē fullōnicā.* No *suōs* is needed here to tell you that the women cover their (own) noses!

EXERCEĀMUS!

9-4 Translating Reflexive Adjectives

Remember that the meaning of a reflexive adjective depends on the subject of the sentence, so the translation can change as the subject changes. Use the following sentences as models for translating the forms of *suus, -a, -um* accurately in this exercise.

→ Virī saepe pecūniam **suam** āmittunt.	Men often lose **their** money.
→ Vir saepe pecūniam **suam** āmittit.	The man often loses **his** money.
→ Fēminae saepe pecūniam **suam** āmittunt.	Women often lose **their** money.
→ Fēmina saepe pecūniam **suam** āmittit.	The woman often loses **her** money.

1. Actōrēs in viā fābulam suam agunt.   The actors perform their play in the street.
   Actor in viā fābulam suam agit.
   Fēminae in viā fābulam suam agunt.
   Flāvia in viā fābulam suam agit.

2. Puerī ad lūdum amīcōs suōs vōcant.   The boys call their friends to the game.
   Flāvia ad lūdum amīcōs suōs vōcat.
   Marcus ad lūdum amīcōs suōs vōcat.

3. Licinia cum amīcā suā ambulat.   Licinia walks with her girlfriend.
   Lūcius cum amīcā suā ambulat.
   Puerī cum amīcīs suīs ambulant.

4. Servus suī dominī magnam arcam portat.   The slave carries his master's chest.
   Servī suī dominī magnam arcam portant.
   Ancilla suī dominī magnam arcam portat.

5. Quisque in officīnā suā labōrat.   Each works in his own office.
   Virī in officīnā suā labōrant.
   Fēmina in officīnā suā labōrat.

Mōrēs Rōmānī

Fullōnica Rōmāna

A *fullōnica* or laundry was a place where clothes were cleaned. It was also sometimes a place to process cloth in other ways, like starching and dyeing. Such facilities were noted for the stench of sulphur and urine, both of which were used in the cleaning process. Such a laundry was probably not a very healthy place to work.

The simplest Roman laundry consisted of a one- or two-room establishment with work tables and one or two basins where clothes were soaked. They were then put in large terra cotta basins filled with detergents. Workers stomped on the clothes in these bowls to remove grease. The philosopher Seneca described this process as *saltus fullōnicus* or "the launderer's dance" (*Epistulae* 15.4). Urine, both animal and human, was used for bleaching. Some laundries were adjacent to public restrooms where urine was collected and piped into the laundry. Other laundries may simply have provided a large container outside the building to collect urine from passers-by. Burning sulphur was also used to clean the cloth. After the cleaning process, the cloth was soaked again in the basins in order to remove the cleaning agents. Then it was dried in the sun.

Here is a wall inscription from a laundry in Pompeii (CIL IV, 9131):

> *Fullōnēs ululamque canō nōn arma virumq(ue)*

The whole line is a pun on the first line of Vergil's *Aeneid*:
> *Arma virumque canō . . .*

Dea Minerva cum būbōne

The owl (*būbō, būbōnis* m.) was the bird of the goddess Minerva, the patroness of craftsmen like fullers.

🔊 VERBA ŪTENDA

arma (pl.) arms	*canō* (1) sing about	*fullōnēs* fullers, launderers	*ulula, -ae* f. screech owl

---

Latīna Hodierna

Latin in Modern Commerce

The Roman Empire was based as much on commerce as it was on Roman military might. Roman traders and merchants plied their wares all around the empire and beyond. As a result, Latin remains an important presence in the vocabulary and the philosophy of commerce in the modern world.

LATIN WORD	ENGLISH DERIVATIVE
commercium, -iī n. trade, commerce	commerce
merx, mercis f. merchandise, goods, wares	mercantile, mercantilism
mercātor, -ōris m. merchant	merchant
vendō, vendere sell	vend, vendor
redemptiō, -iōnis f. buying up; bribing, ransoming captives; tax farming	redeem, redemption
redemptor, -ōris m. buyer, contractor, independent tax gatherer; savior	redemptor
crēditus,-a, -um trusted	credit
dēbitus, -a, -um owed	debit
contrahō, contrahere, contraxī, contractum form an agreement	contract

And don't forget this Latin phrase, which expresses a basic principal of modern capitalism:

Caveat emptor "Let the buyer beware"

So the next time you make a major purchase, read the fine print and think about the Romans.

Orbis Terrārum Rōmānus

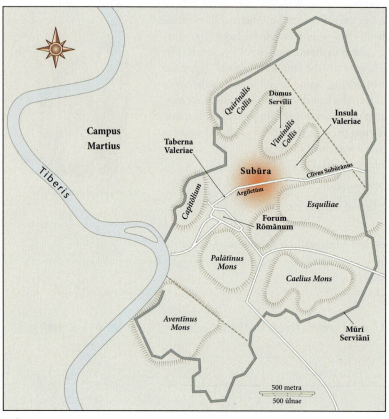

Subūra antīqua

Subūra

Valeria and her family live in the Subura (*Subūra, -ae* f.), a working-class neighborhood (*vīcus, -ī* m.) between the Viminal and Esquiline hills in Rome. Despite the Subura's reputation as a rough district in antiquity, the biographer Suetonius tells us, in his life of Julius Caesar (*Caes.* 46), that the future dictator grew up in this neighborhood. Many craftsmen worked in this part of the city, and there were many tenement houses (*insula, -ae* f.) here. The late 1st-century Roman satirist Juvenal described the neighborhood as *fervēns* ("teeming," XII.51). His contemporary Martial, who lived in Subura, called the area *clāmōsa* ("noisy," XII.18.2) and *sordida* ("filthy," V.22.5). The Argiletum (now known as Via Leonina and Via della Madonna dei Monti) was the main road from the Forum through the Subura. There are also references to a synagogue here in the 1st century B.C.

QUID PUTĀS?

1. What impressions of Rome do you get from the *lectiōnēs* in this chapter, especially the information about laundry techniques in *Mōrēs Rōmānī*?
2. Have you ever experienced a situation in which the expression *caveat emptor* would apply?
3. What does it suggest about Rome that there is still a neighborhood called "Suburra" there today?
4. Can you think of neighborhoods in modern large cities that are like the Subura? Why do people live there? How might this be the same for ancient Romans?

EXERCEĀMUS!

9-5 Scrībāmus

Look at the list of people and things Valeria and Licinia see on their walk through the Subura. Write a paragraph describing what they see. Keep it simple. All you need to do is link each phrase with *vident* (all the nouns are in the accusative case). For variety, you could also put some of the nouns in the nominative case and use the phrase *in viā est/sunt*. (Don't try to do this with nouns ending in *-em* or *-ēs*. These are 3rd declension nouns.) Occasionally link two phrases together with *et*. We have started the paragraph for you.

tonsōris tabernam	dominōs suōs in lecticīs	argentāriōs
actōrēs	dominī magnam arcam	librāriōs
virōs paucae pecūniae	passerem in caveā	virōs magnae industriae
puerōrum pilam	unguentāriōs	fullōnicam
puellārum pictūrās	laniōs	fullōnem natūrae laetae
sūtōrēs		
insulam suam		

Valeria et Licinia per viās eunt et populōs multōs et multa vident. Fēminae _____ vident. In viā sunt _____ . . . etc.

9-6   Colloquāmur

With a classmate, practice asking and answering questions based on the phrases in Exercise 9-5. In order to make it more challenging and fun, use the following list of people and items Valeria and Licinia do **not** see in the street. Mix these in with the phrases from 9-5, so the person you question has to think about the answer and reply *sīc* or *ita* (yes) or *nōn* (no). Follow the model. Use complete sentences.

sīmiam	Chīrōnis pictūram
Servīliam in lecticā	multam pecūniam
mē (in answer, use *tē* "you")	domum tuam
Chīrōnis discipulōs	paedagōgī saccum
Lūciī magistrum	poculum vīnī

Subūra hodierna

→ Videntne in viā Valeria et Licinia *sīmiam*?

   Nōn. Sīmiam nōn vident.

9-7   Verba Discenda

Answer the following questions about the *Verba Discenda*.

1. Write out the 3rd principal part of each verb (except *audeō*) in the *Verba Discenda*. Then translate this verb form into English.
2. Give the genitive singular of the two nouns in the *Verba Discenda*.
3. Find the two prepositions and indicate what case each takes.
4. Why do you think that the Romans used the word for "island" to refer to a block of apartments?
5. Give at least one additional English derivative for any five of the *Verba Discenda*.

Via in Subūrā hodierna

Gemma

audeō, audēre, ausus sum dare: The 3rd principal part of this verb is a special form. You will not be asked to use it until later.

🔊 VERBA DISCENDA

alius, -a, -um other, another [alienate]

āmittō, āmittere, āmīsī, āmissum lose

audeō, audēre, ausus sum dare [audacious]

audiō, audīre, audīvī, audītum hear [auditory, audible]

conspiciō, conspicere, conspexī, conspectum catch sight of, see, look at, observe [conspicuous]

festīnō (1) hasten

fābula, -ae f. story, play [fable, fabulous]

insula, -ae f. island, apartment block [insulate, insulin]

labōrō (1) work [laborious, laboratory]

mox soon

nōnnūllī, -ae, -a some, several

noster, nostra, nostrum our [nostrum, pater noster]

obtineō, obtinēre, obtinuī, obtentum hold, support, gain [obtain]

paucus, -a, -um few, little [paucity]

prō (+ abl.) before, in front of [project]

propter (+ acc.) on account of [post hoc, propter hoc]

spērō (1) hope

suus, -a, -um his/her/its/their own

Angulus Grammaticus

What Kind of Genitive Is That?
Genitives with Nouns and Adjectives

At first glance, the Latin genitive seemed straightforward and easy to translate, didn't it? All you had to do was put an "of" in front of the word. But the phrase *Servīliī fīlius* is most readily translated into English as "Servilius' son." In fact, only the genitive of possession can be translated with an **'s** or **s'** into English, and this is one way to know you have a genitive of possession. Compare these genitive phrases:

Valeriae taberna (the shop of Valeria)	genitive of possession
virī paucae pecūniæ (men of little money)	genitive of description
nēmō virōrum (no one of the men)	partitive genitive

Only the first of these can be translated with **'s**.

Some grammarians distinguish several other kinds of genitives:

- **Subjective genitive**, in which the noun in the genitive can be the subject of the action described. For example, *odor ūrīnae* means "the smell of urine." You could argue that this is a genitive of possession, but others might say that urine is the subject emitting the odor.
- **Objective genitive**, in which the noun in the genitive can be the object of the action described. For example, *amōr Valeriae* means "love for Valeria" rather than Valeria's love for someone else. A famous example of an objective genitive is the phrase *lacrimae rērum* (the tears of things) in Vergil's *Aeneid* (I.462), the better translation of which would be "here are things worth crying over."
- **Genitive with adjectives**, in which the noun in the genitive answers the question "how." This genitive is usually not translated with "of." For example, *sagāx lūdōrum* ("wise in games" or "wise in respect to games"), in which the genitive *lūdōrum* explains "how" the person is wise. This is a poetic expression you will not find very often.

These genitives are relatively rare, and you can usually get by with translating a genitive with "of."

10

Quantī Id Constat?

Lectiō Prīma

Antequam Legis

In this story Valeria negotiates the cost of several items she wants to buy. In Latin you use the **genitive case to ask how much something costs** and the **ablative case to give the price**. Here are some examples:

Quantī constat?   How much does it cost?
Quattuor dēnāriīs constat.   It costs four denarii.

The Dative Case

In this *lectiō* all the words marked in **bold** are in the **dative case**. It is one of the easiest cases to learn and is best translated by using **to** or **for**.

Valeriae sellam fabricāvī.   I made a chair **for Valeria**.
Virō pecūniam dedī.   I gave money **to the man**.

EXERCEĀMUS

10-1 **Dative Case**

As you read *Lectiō Prīma*, group all the words in the dative case (marked in **bold**) by similar endings. You will have an *-ae* group, an *-ō* group, and an *-īs* group.

Exemplar īnsulae Rōmānae

**LECTIŌNĒS:
ANTĪQUA ŌVA?
and
ASTROLOGUS**

Before going home, Valeria and Licinia do some shopping and consult a soothsayer about the baby Licinia is carrying.

🔊 ANTĪQUA ŌVA?

Tunc fēminae **macellō** appropinquāvērunt. Ecce—hominēs animāliaque ubīque sunt!
Mūlī, equī, et asinī hīc et illīc astant et aliquis **mūlīs, equīs**, et **asinīs** faenum dat.
Post macellum, prope lanium, canēs ossa edunt. Fēminae odōrem piscium et car-
nis et stercoris sensērunt. Hominum et animālium vōcēs fortēs audīvērunt. Sed
5 fēminae emere aliqua **cēnae** bona voluērunt et cibum in mensīs inspexērunt.
Holera et ōva et pōma spectāvērunt et dē cēnā cōgitāvērunt.

"Salvē!" inquit venditor.

"Et tū, salvē," inquit Valeria, "Quantī ista holera mala constant? Idonea
equīs sunt!"

10 "Mala holera? Quid dīcis!? Nōn mala sunt sed bona. **Augustō** idōnea!
Hodiē māne in agrō meō haec holera fuērunt! **Cēnae** bona sunt! Tribus assibus
constant."

Illa "Nimium pecūniae rogās," inquit. Venditor et Valeria longē arguērunt et
dēmum Valeria **virō** duōs nummōs dedit et venditor **Valeriae** holera dedit.

15 "Et, sī placet," inquit, "quantī constat ūnum ōvum? Ūnum ex istīs antīquīs ōvīs?"
"Antīqua ōva? Antīqua??!! Haec ōva hodiē sub gallīnā meā fuērunt. Haec ōva **aliīs** praes-
tant! Sex bona ōva tribus assibus bonīs constant. Aut quattuor ōva duōbus assibus."

Valeria et venditor iterum arguērunt et, dēmum venditor **Valeriae** concessit. Valeria **virō** duōs nummōs dedit et
venditor **Valeriae** quīnque ōva dedit. Ita Valeria quīnque ōva duōbus assibus ēmit.

Quantī constat ūnum ōvum?

🔊 VERBA ŪTENDA

ager, agrī m. field

aliīs others (other eggs)

aliqua some (things)

aliquis someone

animālium "of animals"

antīquus, -a, -um old,
    ancient

appropinquō (1) (+ dat.)
    to approach, come near

arguō, arguere, arguī to
    argue

asinus, -ī m. donkey

assibus asses (an "as" is
    a small Roman coin,
    like a penny)

astō, astāre, astitī stand (up)

bona good things

canēs dogs

carnis "of meat"

cēna, -ae f. dinner

***cōgitō* (1) think**

concēdō, concēdere,
    concessī (+ dat.)
    yield to

constō, constāre, con-
    ***stitī, constātum* to cost**

dēmum at last, finally

duōbus two

Ecce! Behold! Look!

equus, -ī m. horse

faenum, -ī n. hay

fortēs strong, loud

gallīna, -ae f. hen

haec these (eggs)

***hīc* here, in this place**

holera vegetables (nomi-
    native and accusative
    plural)

hominum of men,
    of people

idōnea suitable, fit

illa she

illīc there

inspiciō, inspicere,
    inspexī, inspectum
    look closely at

ista those

ita so, thus; yes

lanius, -iī m. butcher,
    butcher shop

longē for a long time

macellum, -ī n. grocery
    shop

mūlus, -ī m. mule

nimium too much

nummus, -ī m. coin

odōrem odor

omnibus all

ossa bones

***ōvum, -ī* n. egg** *ōva* =
    eggs (nominative
    and accusative plural)

***parvus, -a, -um* small**

piscium "of fish"

pōmum, -ī n. apple;
    pōma apples
    (accusative plural)

praestō, praestāre,
    praestitī, praestātum
    **(+ dat.) to be superior
    to; stand out from;
    surpass**

prōcēdō, prōcēdere,
    prōcessī, prōcessum
    to proceed

Quantī constat? How
    much does it cost?

***quantus, -a, um* how
    much**

***quattuor* four**

***quinque* five**

***rogō* (1) ask (for)**

sentiō, sentīre, sensī
    smell

***sex* six**

sī placet please

***spectō* (1) look at**

stercoris "of dung"

***super* (+ acc.) over**

***timeō, timēre, timuī* fear,
    be afraid**

tunc then

trēs, tribus three

ubīque everywhere

venditor merchant

vōcēs voices

POSTQUAM LĒGISTĪ

1. Describe the scene around the grocery store. How would it be different today?
2. How does the grocer respond when Valeria suggests the vegetables are not fresh? And what about his eggs?
3. What price does the grocer quote for eggs? How much does Valeria want to pay? How much does she pay in the end?
4. According to the grocer's first price quote, how much would two eggs cost? Three? Try to answer in Latin.

Haec ōva hodiē sub gallīnā meā fuērunt

Grammatica A

Genitive of Cost and Ablative of Price

In the *lectiō* Valeria asks:

> *Quantī ista holera constant?*   How much do these vegetables cost?

and the merchant responds:

> *Tribus assibus constant.*   They cost three asses.

Notice how the genitive case is used to indicate cost and the ablative to give the price. Here is how it works:

We say: "How much does that cost?" **Romans said:** "Of how much does it cost?"
                                        ***Quantī** constat?*
                                        Genitive of Cost

We say: "It costs five dollars." **Romans said:** "It costs at five denarii."
                                      *Quinque **dēnāriīs** constat.*
                                      Ablative of Price

Rules: "Genitive of cost..........ablative of price"

Cost = genitive. Price = ablative. Remember it!

Expressing price is easy because most numbers (like *quattuor*, *quīnque*, and *sex*) are indeclinable. Here are the ablative forms for the numbers 1, 2 and 3, which are declinable:

	M.	**F.**	**N.**
1	ūnō	ūnā	ūnō
2	duōbus	duābus	duōbus
3	tribus	tribus	tribus

(You will learn the other forms of these numbers later.)
So,

> ***Ūnō dēnāriō** constat.*   It costs one denarius.
> ***Duōbus dēnāriīs** constat.*   It costs two denarii.
> ***Tribus dēnāriīs** constat.*   It costs three denarii.

The Dative Case

Here is a chart for the 1st and 2nd declensions with the dative case added. This completes your chart of case endings for the 1st and 2nd declensions!

	1ST DECLENSION		2ND DECLENSION		
Singular					
Nominative	-a	fēmina	-us, -er, -ir	discipulus	vir	fīlius
Genitive	-ae	fēminae	-ī	discipulī	virī	fīliī
Dative	**-ae**	**fēminae**	**-ō**	**discipulō**	**virō**	**fīliō**
Accusative	-am	fēminam	-um	discipulum	virum	fīlium
Ablative	-ā	fēminā	-ō	discipulō	virō	fīliō
Vocative	-a	fēmina	-e, -ī, -r	discipule	vir	fīlī
Plural					
Nominative	-ae	fēminae	-ī	discipulī	virī	fīliī
Genitive	-ārum	fēminārum	-ōrum	discipulōrum	virōrum	fīliōrum
Dative	**-īs**	**fēminīs**	**-īs**	**discipulīs**	**virīs**	**fīliīs**
Accusative	-ās	fēminās	-ōs	discipulōs	virōs	fīliōs
Ablative	-īs	fēminīs	-īs	discipulīs	vīrīs	fīliīs
Vocative	-ae	fēminae	-ī	discipulī	virī	fīliī

Gemma

Words like *fēminae* can be genitive singular, dative singular, or nominative plural. *Virī* and *virō* can each be two different cases. Don't worry. Usage and word order make it hard to confuse them in a sentence. This is part of the beauty of Latin, that there is so little room for confusion and still a relative economy of endings.

Notā Bene:

- In any given declension, the dative and ablative plurals are **always** identical.
- In the 2nd declension, the dative and ablative singular are also identical.

Indirect Objects

The dative case is used to indicate someone or something **indirectly affected** by an action or a situation. A major use of the dative is the **indirect object**, which is very frequently used with the English verb "give" and the Latin verb *dō, dare*. In fact, the word "**dat**ive" comes from *dō, dare, dedi, *da**t**um*.

Compare these two sentences in which the accusative *sīmiam* is the direct object and the dative *fīliae* is the indirect object:

> *Valeria **Liciniae** sīmiam dedit.*
> *Valeria sīmiam **Liciniae** dedit.*

We can translate either sentence into English in two ways:

> Valeria gave the monkey **to Licinia**.
> Valeria gave **Licinia** the monkey.

Gemma

Mihi and *tibi* are two datives you have already seen. ***Mihi** sīmiam dedit*. He gave me a monkey. ***Tibi** sīmiam dedit*. He gave you a monkey.

Usually the indirect object comes before the direct object in Latin, but note that reversing the order of these objects does not change the meaning of the Latin sentence as long as the case endings remain the same. In English, however, reversing the order of the direct and indirect objects can change the meaning in unintended ways:

> Valeria gave **Licinia** a monkey.
> Valeria gave a monkey **Licinia**.

Which sentence doesn't work?

Dative with Compound Verbs

Latin is very fond of compound verbs, i.e., verbs that are prefixed with a preposition to change their meaning slightly. Many of these verbs take a dative where we would expect an accusative direct object in English. Watch for datives especially if the compound is formed with one of the following prepositions: *ad, ante, circum, con* (from *cum*), *in, inter, ob, post, prae, sub,* or *super*.

Here are the compound verbs you saw in *Lectiō Prīma*. Note the datives (marked in **bold**) in the phrases that accompany them.

- *ad* (to) + *propinquāre* (to draw near) ⟶ *appropinquāre* (to draw near to, approach)

Nunc fēminae **macellō** *appropinquāvērunt.*	Now the women approached the grocery store. Now the women drew near to the grocery store.

Notā Bene: Notice how "grocery store" is the object of the verb "approached" in English. But if you remember that *appropinquō* also means "draw near **to**," it is easier to understand the dative in Latin.

- *con* (very) + *cēdere* (to yield, give way) ⟶ *concēdere* (to yield to, give in to, to concede)

Venditor **Valeriae** *concessit.*	The grocer gave in to Valeria.

- *prae* (before) + *stāre* (to stand) ⟶ *praestāre* (to stand before, surpass)

Haec ōva **omnibus aliīs** *praestant!*	These eggs surpass all others!

- *ad* (to) + *esse* (to be) ⟶ *adesse* (to be present for, to be there for someone, to support, to help)

Fēminīs *adesse voluit.*	He wanted to help the women. He wanted to be there for the women.

Such verbs will have a notation in the vocabulary that reads "(+ dat)."
HINT: Pay attention to the way the preposition changes the spelling of the forms. More on this in *Angulus Grammaticus*.

Dative with Adjectives

The dative is also used with certain adjectives:

Augustō *idōneum*	fit **for Augustus**
bona **mihi**	good **to/for me**
via tūta **fēminīs**	a road safe **for women**

Note again that the English adjective also suggests the dative: "good **for**" and "safe **for**."

EXERCEĀMUS!

10-2 Datives

Find the dative in each sentence and translate it. Follow the model.

⟶ Venditor Valeriae holera dedit.   *Valeriae*   (to) Valeria

1. Valeria ōva tria familiae emit.
2. Fēminae emere aliqua cēnae bona voluērunt.
3. Valeria ūnum ōvum virīs emit.
4. Nunc fēminae macellō appropinquāvērunt.
5. Venditor mihi quattuor ōva dedit.
6. Valeria tibi duōs nummōs dedit.

Chaldaea: Rome was filled with people who came from far and wide to make their fortune at the center of the known world. The astrologer is from Chaldea. Can you find Chaldea on the map? What country would it be called today?

Maximus hērōs Graecus Perseus

Lectiō Secunda

Antequam Legis

Neuter Nouns

You have already learned the following *Verba Discenda:*

> *forum, -ī* forum
> *ōvum, -ī* egg
> *vīnum, -ī* wine

It is time you learned why they have nominative singulars ending in *-um*. The *-um* ending tells you that these second declension nouns are neuter rather than masculine.

Watch for neuter nouns in *Lectiō Secunda*. They are marked in **bold**. Note that nominative and accusative plural neuter nouns end in *-a*; e.g., *fora*, *ōva*, and *vīna*. We will talk more about these neuter nouns after you read the *lectiō*.

EXERCEĀMUS!

10-3   **Neuter Nouns**

Make a line-by-line list of all the neuter nouns marked in **bold** in *Lectio Secunda*. Then determine the case from the context of the sentence. Remember that subjects need to agree with the main verb in number. So, for example, a neuter noun ending in *-a* is plural and cannot be the subject of a singular verb. Then give the meaning of the neuter word. Follow the model.

Line	Neuter Word	Number	Case	Reason	Meaning
→ 1	holera	plural	acc.	object of *ēmit*	vegetables

🔊 ASTROLOGUS

Valeria **holera** et **ōva** et **vīnum** ēmit. Tunc domum fēminae prōcessērunt.

Domus in insulā magnā fuit et sōlum duās cellās parvās continuit. In duābus cellīs quīnque hominēs habitant—Valeria, Licinia, Aelius (Liciniae vir), Plōtia (Valeriae māter) et ancilla Flāvia—et mox infans!

5 Priusquam fēminae insulam suam intrāvērunt, **dēlūbrum** Iūnōnis Lūcīnae vīdērunt.

Valeria "Offerāmus aliquid deae," inquit. "Gravidae fēminae aliquid deae Iūnōnī dare dēbent." Ūnum **ōvum** in **dēlūbrō** prō infante futūrō relīquērunt. Iuxtā **dēlūbrum** astrologus Chaldaeus sēdit. Chaldaea terra antīqua in Mesopotamiā fuit et
10 multī Chaldaeī astrologī fuērunt. Astrologus fēminās salūtāvit:

"Salvēte!" inquit. "Vultisne dē infante tuō aliquid scīre?"

"Certē!" clāmāvērunt. Astrologō nummōs paucōs dedērunt et silenter stetērunt.

Astrologus **oleum** super aquam effūdit. **Oleum** lentē in aquam diffūdit et formās figūrāsque variās fēcit. Formās figūrāsque inspexit et diū nihil dīxit. Dēnique **praedictum** astrologus Liciniae dīxit:

15 "Ecce! Infans tuus puer est. **Fātum** bonum est. Sānus est hodiē et sānus crās erit. Puerī **fātum** iam omnibus virīs praestat. Fortis puer erit et **magna opera** faciet. Nōlī timēre, **omnia bona** sunt. Fīlius tam fortis quam pater suus erit. Tam fortis quam maximus hērōs Graecus Perseus erit!"

Oleum formās figūrāsque variās fēcit

🔊 VERBA ŪTENDA

aliquid something
astrologus, -ī m. astrologer
cella, -ae f. room
certē certainly
Chaldaeus, -a, -um Chaldaean, an inhabitant of Mesopotamia
contineō, continere, continuī contain, hold
dea, -ae f. goddess
dēlūbrum, -ī n. shrine
diffundō, diffundere, diffūdī spread out
Ecce! Behold! Look!
erit "he will be"
diū for a long time
effundō, effundere, effūdī pour out
faciet "he will do"
fātum, -ī n. fate, destiny

figūra, -ae f. shape, figure
forma, -ae f. shape, form
fortis strong
futūrus, -a, -um future, coming
gravidus, -a, -um pregnant
habitō (1) live in
hērōs hero
holera vegetables
infans m./f. infant; *infante* (abl.)
inspiciō, inspicere, inspexī, inspectum look closely at
Iūnō, Iūnōnis f. Juno, queen of the gods; *Iūnōnī* "to Juno"
iuxtā (+ acc.) near

lentē slowly
māter mother
maximus very great
Mesopotamia, -ae f. Mesopotamia, the land between the Tigris and Euphrates rivers
nummus, -ī m. coin
offerāmus "let us offer"
oleum, -ī n. oil
omnia everything
opera works, deeds
ōvum, -ī n. egg
parvus, -a, -um small
pater father
Perseus Perseus, Greek hero who decapitated Medusa
praedictum, -ī n. prophecy, prediction

praestō, praestāre, praestitī, praestātum (+ dat.) be superior to; stand out from; surpass
priusquam before
quam than
relīnquō, relīnquere, relīquī leave
sānus, -a, -um healthy
sciō, scīre, sciī / scīvī know
silenter silently
super (+ acc.) over
tam . . . quam as . . . as . . .
timeō, timēre, timuī fear, be afraid
varius, -a, -um mixed, varied

POSTQUAM LĒGISTĪ

1. Describe Valeria's home. What does this residence tell you about the family's social status?
2. Where do the women stop as they near their apartment house? Why?
3. Describe some of the religious practices which occur in this *lectiō*. Do they have any modern parallels?
4. What is the fate predicted for the child?
5. How do Licinia's efforts to learn about her child's future compare to the things parents do in various modern cultures?

Grammatica B

Neuter Nouns

Did you have any trouble understanding the following sentences in *Lectiō Prīma* and *Secunda*?

Quantī ista holera mala constant?   How much are these rotten vegetables?

Quantī constat ūnum ex istīs antīquīs ōvīs?   How much is one of these old eggs?

If you remember that Latin uses the genitive to ask about cost, you will recognize that *quantī* is a genitive and not a nominative plural. Then it is clear from the context and word order that *holera* is actually the subject even

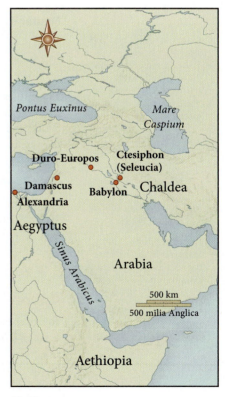

Chaldea

though it ends in *-a*. Since the verb ends in *-nt*, you also have a hint that *holera* is, in fact, neuter plural.

In the 2nd declension, neuter nouns have the same endings as masculine nouns, with three exceptions. Look at the chart first, find the exceptions, then learn the three "neuter rules" listed below.

	1ST DECLENSION		2ND DECLENSION
	Singular		
	Feminine	**Masculine**	**Neuter**
Nominative	fēmina	discipulus	**vīnum** ←
Genitive	fēminae	discipulī	vīnī
Dative	fēminae	discipulō	vīnō
Accusative	fēminam	discipulum	vīnum
Ablative	fēminā	discipulō	vīnō
	Plural		
Nominative	fēminae	discipulī	**vīna** ←
Genitive	fēminārum	discipulōrum	vīnōrum
Dative	fēminīs	discipulīs	vīnīs
Accusative	fēminās	discipulōs	**vīna** ←
Ablative	fēminīs	discipulīs	vīnīs

Neuter Rules:

- The nominative and accusative of every neuter noun are identical.
- The nominative neuter singular always ends in *-um* in the 2nd declension.
- Neuter nominative and accusative plurals end in *-a*.

These rules are true not only in the 2nd declension but in other declensions you will learn later. In fact, *holera* is a 3rd declension noun, but you can recognize its case and number because it is neuter and all neuter nominative and accusative plurals end in *-a*, no matter what declension they are in.

Notā Bene:

- If what seems to be the subject ends in *a* but the verb is plural, you probably have a neuter noun. Check to be sure.
- If a subject seems to end in *-um*, check to see if it is a 2nd declension neuter.
- There are no neuter nouns in the first declension.

A Word on Adjectives

You may have noticed that we have been listing adjectives with three forms, as in *magnus, -a, -um*. This is the standard dictionary entry for such words. These forms are used to help adjectives "agree" with their nouns. The *-us, -a, -um* endings for all adjectives are listed in the *Verba Ūtenda*. These three forms are masculine (*-us*), feminine (*-a*), and neuter (*-um*). These three classifications represent the **gender** of the adjectival form. Study the following chart.

GENDER	MASCULINE 2ND DECLENSION	FEMININE 1ST DECLENSION	NEUTER 2ND DECLENSION
Singular			
Nominative	magn**us**	magn**a**	magn**um**
Genitive	magn**ī**	magn**ae**	magn**ī**
Dative	magn**ō**	magn**ae**	magn**ō**
Accusative	magn**um**	magn**am**	magn**um**
Ablative	magn**ō**	magn**ā**	magn**ō**
Vocative	magn**e**	magn**a**	magn**um**
Plural			
Nominative	magn**ī**	magn**ae**	magn**a**
Genitive	magn**ōrum**	magn**ārum**	magn**ōrum**
Dative	magn**īs**	magn**īs**	magn**īs**
Accusative	magn**ōs**	magn**ās**	magn**a**
Ablative	magn**īs**	magn**īs**	magn**īs**
Vocative	magn**ī**	magn**ae**	magn**a**

EXERCEĀMUS!

10-4 **Declining 2nd Declension Masculines and Neuters**

Use *discipulus* (m.) and *vīnum* (n.) as guides to decline *servus* (m.) and *ōvum* (n.). Underline those masculine and neuter endings that are different from each other.

Mōrēs Rōmānī

Monēta Rōmāna

The Latin word for money is *pecūnia, -ae* (f.), and is actually related to *pecus* (cattle), since wealth was once measured in livestock. But because Roman coins were minted in the Temple of Juno Moneta on the Capitoline Hill in Rome, the Latin word for "coinage" is *monēta, -ae* (f.). Here is a list of major Roman coin denominations. To help put it into context, consider that a Roman legionary in the time of Augustus earned 225 *dēnāriī* a year. An *astrologus* like the one in the story earned much less.

NAME OF COIN	MATERIAL	VALUE
uncia	bronze	½₂ as
quadrans		¼ as
dupondius	bronze or copper	2 asses
sestertius	metal alloy	4 asses
dēnārius	silver alloy *argentum, -ī* n.	16 asses
aureus	gold *aurum, -ī* n.	400 asses

The emperor Vespasian (69–79 A.D.) was known for his caustic wit. Once, when his son Titus criticized him for introducing a tax on the urine collected in public toilets for use by fullers and others, the emperor is said to have held a coin up to Titus and to have asked him if he was offended by the odor. When Titus replied "no," Vespasian, suggesting to his son that any tax revenue was good revenue, said:

> *Atquī ē lōtiō est.*
> Suetonius, *Vesp.* 23

Vespasian's comment about money is better known today in this form:

> *Pecūnia nōn olet.*

Did F. Scott Fitzgerald know his Suetonius? He may be referencing Vespasian's words in *The Great Gatsby* (1925) when he refers to cities "built . . . out of non-olfactory money."

Here is the inscription around the edge of the coin issued by the emperor Vespasian and depicted at left:

> IMPCAESARVESPASIANAUGPMTRPPPCOSIII

Once the abbreviations are expanded, you see:

> *Imp(erātor) Caesar Vespāsiān(us) Aug(ustus) P(ontifex) M(aximus)*
> *Tr(ibūniciā) P(otestāte) P(ater) P(atriae) Co(n)s(ul) III*

Many of these imperial titles began with Augustus, the emperor at the time of our story, and were routinely held by later emperors. Each office carried not only a certain prestige, but also some actual power.

Monēta Vespāsiānī

🔊 VERBA ŪTENDA

atquī yet	*lōtium, -ī* n. urine	*potestāte* f. with the power, authority
consul m. consul	*maximus, -a, -um* chief	
imperātor m. commander, general	*oleō, olēre* smell, stink	*pontifex* m. priest
	pater m. father	*tribūnicius, -a, -um* m. belonging to a tribune
III = three times	*patria, -ae* f. country	

Latīna Hodierna

Roman Money Today

Look at how several Latin words dealing with money have become part of four modern languages:

LATIN	ENGLISH	FRENCH	SPANISH	ITALIAN
pecūnia, -ae (f.) money	impecunious (broke)	*impécunieux* (broke); *impécuniosité* (state of being broke)		
monēta, -ae (f.) coin	money	*la monnaie* (money, small change)	*la moneda* (money)	*la moneta* (money)
argentum, -ī (n.) silver	argent Argentina argentine	*l'argent* (money)		
dēnārius, -iī (n.)	denary (tenfold)		*el dinero* (money)	*il denaro* (money)

Orbis Terrārum Rōmānus

Aedēs in Capitōliō

Two important temples stood on the Arx (*arx, arcis* n. summit) of the Capitoline Hill. The one known as the Temple of Juno Moneta (*Aedēs Iūnōnis Monētae*) was built by L. Furius Camillus in 344 B.C. to fulfill a vow. By tradition, this was the spot where Juno's sacred geese warned the Romans of danger during a siege by the Gauls in 390 B.C. Juno's epithet *Monēta* (related to the verb *moneō*, warn) seems to refer to this event and to the goddess' protective role in Roman so-

ciety. A workshop for minting coins built near this temple came to be known as the *Monēta* (the Mint), leading to the derivation of the English word "money." The remains of the Temple of Juno Moneta lie within and under the Church of Santa Maria in Aracolei (*Ara Coelī* "Altar of Heaven") on the Capitoline Hill. (See photo below.)

The coin below, depicting the goddess Juno, is a silver denarius issued in honor of Faustina, the wife of the emperor Septimius Severus (193–211 A.D.). On the obverse the head of the empress is surrounded by the words FAUSTINA AUGUSTA. On the reverse is an image of Juno standing with a peacock at her feet. Around the edge of the reverse is the word IUNO.

Capitōlium

The second temple was the Capitolium or Temple of Jupiter Optimus Maximus (*Aedēs Iovis Optimī Maximī Capitōlīnī*). Here Jupiter was worshipped together with the goddesses Juno and Minerva. For this reason, the temple is also called the Capitoline Triad. Each deity had a separate room in the temple. Traditionally, this temple is said to have been built in the 6th century B.C. by Tarquin the Proud, the last king of Rome. Excavations begun in 1998 in the Roman Garden inside the Palazzo dei Conservatori of the Capitoline Museums have uncovered some of the foundations of the Temple of Capitoline Jupiter.

Many cities throughout the Roman Empire had Capitolia in their fora.

Templum Iūnōnis Monētae hodiē

Iūno dea

QUID PUTĀS?

1. Explain to a friend what the emperor Vespasian meant when he said that "the money doesn't stink."
2. Look at what the Romans chose to put on their coins. Compare this with the American penny in order to get a sense of each society's numismatic propaganda. How are they alike or different?
3. Why would Christians have built a church dedicated to Mary the mother of Jesus on the site of the Temple of Juno Moneta?
4. What modern country or countries comprise the area of ancient Chaldea?

EXERCEĀMUS!

10-5 Scrībāmus

So far you have learned the numbers I–VI in Latin: *ūnum* (I); *duo* (II); *tria* (III); *quattuor* (IV); *quinque* (V); and *sex* (VI). Using the model below, create additional problems based on these numbers. (Be sure your answers don't go higher than six!)

⟶ *Ūnum et ūnum sunt: duo*

10-6 Colloquāmur

Each member of the class has six tokens. One person poses in Latin one of the mathematical problems in Exercise 10-5 to another member of the class. If the person responds correctly in Latin, the questioner gives the responder a token. If not, the responder gives the questioner a token. Change partners after each question. The first person to get ten tokens wins.

10-7 Verba Discenda

Use the meaning of the *Verba Discenda* to explain the meaning of each of the following English derivatives. If you need help, consult an English dictionary.

⟶ antiquarian   *someone who studies or deals with old artifacts, especially books*

1. ovary	5. sextuplet	9. parvovirus
2. processional	6. supernumerary	10. quaternary
3. quantify	7. timid	11. timidity
4. interrogatory	8. figuration	

🔊 VERBA DISCENDA

antīquus, -a, -um old, ancient [antique]

cōgitō (1) think [cogitation]

constō, constāre, constitī, constātum to cost

figūra, -ae f. shape, figure [configure]

hīc here, in this place

inspiciō, inspicere, inspexī, inspectum look closely at [inspect]

ōvum, -ī n. egg [ovulate]

parvus, -a, -um small [parvovirus]

praestō, prāestare, praestitī, praestātum be superior to; surpass

prōcēdō, prōcēdere, prōcessī, prōcessum to proceed [procession]

quam than

quantus, -a, -um how much [quantum physics]

quattuor four

quinque five [quinquennial]

rogō (1) ask (for) [interrogate]

sex six [sextet]

spectō (1) look at [spectator]

super (+ acc.) over [supernatural]

timeō, timēre, timuī fear, be afraid [timid]

Angulus Grammaticus

Forming Compound Verbs

Note the spelling changes that occur in compound verbs:

> *ad- + fuī = affuī*
> *cum- + cēdō = concēdō*
> *ob- + ferō = offerō*

These changes are called **assimilation**. Typically the prepositional prefix changes to be more similar in sound to the verb form. Here are some rules for assimilation that apply to nouns, verbs, adjectives, etc.:

- **ad:** when added to a word beginning with a vowel, *ad-* remains the same; e.g., *adesse.*

When added to a word beginning with a consonant, the "d" usually changes to match the consonant at the beginning of the verb; e.g., *appropinquāre* and *affuī.*

- **cum:** usually becomes *con-* as a prefix; e.g., *concēdō.* But before a word beginning with "m," the "n" becomes "m"; *committō*

Note that English follows the Latin pattern here: "concede," "commit."

- **in:** before a vowel, is unchanged. Before other letters, such as "m," it becomes "m." e.g., *immittō.*

- **ob:** unchanged before a vowel, doubles before a consonant. Thus, *offerō.*

Knowing about compound verbs may save you many unnecessary trips to the dictionary. Note how the assimilation can change if the principal parts of the verb change:

> **ad**sum, **ad**esse, **af**fuī
> **af**ferō, **af**ferre, **at**tulī, **al**lātum

Also, you can determine the general meaning of the compound verb by combining the meaning of the verb with the meaning of the prepositional prefix.

> **ad**sum = *sum* (I am) + *ad* (to, at) = "I am at"

If you look this word up in the dictionary, it means "I am present."

> **off**erō = *ferō* (I carry) + *ob* (for) = "I carry for" or "I bring before"

Cavē canem.

GRAMMATICA
Three Kinds of Infinitive
More on the Perfect

MŌRĒS RŌMĀNĪ
Iūno Dea

LATĪNA HODIERNA
Vēnī, Vīdī, Vīcī

ORBIS TERRĀRUM RŌMĀNUS
Gallia Est Omnis Dīvīsa in Partēs Trēs?

ANGULUS GRAMMATICUS
The "Present Perfect" and the "Inchoate Suffix" -scō

LECTIŌNĒS:
LATRŌNĒS
and
QUID ACCIDIT HODIĒ?

The Valeria and Servilia families arrive home.

Domum

Lectiō Prīma

Antequam Legis

In *Lectiō Prīma* Valeria and Licinia are mugged as they approach their *insula*. As you read about how the women escape from the muggers, you will learn more about infinitives.

Watch for Infinitives

Earlier you saw how Latin uses complementary infinitives with verbs like *possum* and *volō* in phrases such as:

Vīnum potāre possum.	I can drink wine. / I am able to drink wine.
Vīnum potāre volō.	I want to drink wine.

In this chapter, you will see other ways Latin uses infinitives, including:

Vīnum potāre dēbeō.	I ought to drink wine.
Vīnum potāre Marcum iubeō.	I order Marcus to drink wine.
Vīnum potāre bonum est.	Drinking wine is good.

In *Lectiō Prīma* words which introduce infinitives are marked in **bold** and the infinitives themselves are marked in ***bold italics***.

EXERCEĀMUS!

11-1 **Skimming for Comprehension**

Before you read the *lectiō,* scan it and try to find the answers to these questions. This will help you translate. We give you a line range within which to find your answer. Follow the model.

Lines 1–4

→ Why are Licinia and Valeria happy?
Because of what the astrologer said about the baby

1. Why is Flavia happy?

2. Why is Socrates happy?

Lines 5–7

   3. Whom do the ladies see as they approach their *insula*?

   4. Where is he and what is he doing?

Lines 8–11

   5. How does Socrates try to defend the women from
      the muggers?

   6. How does Aelius do the same? With what?

Lines 12–16

   7. What do the muggers see that scares them off?

Gemma

Grātiās ēgērunt: This phrase is an idiomatic use of the verb *agō, agere*. It literally means "to do thanks." If you want to say "thank you" in Latin, say *grātiās tibi agō* or *grātiās vōbīs agō*. "I do you thanks."

Gemma

The Latin word *musculum* is the origin of the English word "muscle." Literally, in Latin it means "little mouse" (*mūs*).

🔊 LATRŌNĒS

Licinia et Valeria laetae fuērunt propter verba bona astrologī dē īnfante et grātiās maximās et deae et astrologō ēgērunt. Flāvia quoque laeta fuit quod nunc īnsula nōn longinqua fuit. Flāvia quoque fessa fuit quod saccum (et Sōcratem!) longē per viās *portāre* **dēbuit**. Et Sōcratēs laetus fuit quod iēiūnus fuit et cibus domī
5 fuit.

    Dum fēminae īnsulae suae appropinquāvērunt, Aeliī fabricam vīdērunt. Aelius prō fabricā suā stetit et labōrāvit. Licinia laeta virum suum *salūtāre* et virō suō omnia dē verbīs astrologī *narrāre* **voluit**.

    Sed subitō trēs latrōnēs ex angiportō saluērunt. Saccum fēminārum *rapere* **voluērunt** et fēm-
10 inae territae fuērunt. Trēs fēminae fortiter clāmāvērunt. Sōcratēs quoque clāmāvit et ad terram saluit. Sōcratēs etiam ūnum latrōnem momordit! Nunc latrō quoque fortiter clāmāvit!

    Aelius vōcēs in viā audīvit. Fēminās vīdit et in latrōnēs magnā cum īrā cucurrit. Malleum magnum tenuit. Fēminīs *adesse* **voluit**. Aelius latrōnēs *currere* **vetuit**. Sed, dum virīs malīs appropinquat, latrōnēs et malleum et musculōs Aeliī vīdērunt. Aelium *pugnāre* **nōluērunt**. Aeliō
15 *concēdere* **māluērunt** et celeriter sine saccō fūgērunt.

    Sīc semper est. Viae Rōmānae, praesertim in Subūrā, fēminīs (atque virīs!) tūtae nōn sunt. *Vīvere* Rōmae valdē **difficile est!**

Aelius malleum magnum tenuit

🔊 VERBA ŪTENDA

adsum, adesse, afuī (+ dat.) to be present, be "there for" someone, be of assistance, help, aid

angiportum, -ī n. alley

angustiae, -ārum f. pl. trouble, difficulty

appropinquō (1) (+ dat.) approach, come near to

atque and, and also, and even

celeriter quickly

concēdō, concēdere, concessī go away, withdraw

dea, -ae f. goddess

difficile hard, difficult

domī at home

etiam and also, too

fabrica, -ae f. workshop

fortiter loudly

fugiō, fugere, fūgī flee

in (+ acc.) against

īnfante infant

īra, -ae, f. anger

iēiūnus, -a, -um hungry

latrō, latrōnis m. thief, robber

longē a long distance, far off

longinquus, -a, -um far away

malleus, -ī m. hammer

maximus, -a, -um greatest

mordeō, mordēre, momordī bite

musculus, -ī m. muscle

narrō (1) tell, seek

omnia everything

portō (1) carry

praesertim especially

pugnō (1) fight

rapiō, rapere, rapuī snatch, seize

Rōma, -ae f. Rome; *Rōmae* at Rome

Rōmānus, -a, -um Roman

saccus, -ī m. wallet, sack, bag, pocketbook

saliō, salīre, saliī/saluī, saltum leap, jump

sīc thus, in this way; yes

subitō suddenly

teneō, tenēre, tenuī hold

territus, -a, -um scared, terrified

tūtus, -a, -um safe

valdē very, a lot

verbum, -ī n. word

vetō, vetāre, vetuī forbid

vīvō, vīvere, vīxī live

vōcēs voices

POSTQUAM LĒGISTĪ

1. How does this scene compare with life in a modern American city?
2. Does this scene remind you of any episodes in movies you have seen? How?
3. Have you or someone you know ever been in a similar situation? How was the situation the same? How was it different?

Grammatica A

Three Kinds of Infinitive

Grammarians divide infinitives into three types: **complementary, subjective,** and **objective**. Here are some sentences with infinitives from the story you just read. The infinitives are in **bold**.

> *Licinia laeta virum suum* **salūtāre** *voluit.*
> *Aelius fēminīs* **adesse** *voluit.*
> *Flāvia saccum longē per viās* **portāre** *dēbuit.*

All of these sentences contain **complementary infinitives**. A complementary infinitive is used to complete the action of certain verbs, like *volō, nōlō, mālō, possum,* and *dēbeō.* Generally it is easy to recognize and translate complementary infinitives because these verbs work the same way in Latin and in English.

scrībere volō	I want to write.
scrībere nōlō	I do not want to write.
scrībere mālō	I prefer to write.
scrībere possum	I am able to write. I can write.
scrībere dēbeō	I ought to write.

Remember that, as a **verbal noun**, an infinitive is a verb that functions like a noun in the sentence. This will help you understand two other kinds of infinitive.

An **objective infinitive** is used as the direct object of certain verbs, like *cupiō* (I wish), *doceō* (I teach), *vetō* (I forbid) and *iubeō* (I order). Just as you can want an apple, you can want someone to do something. Consider these examples:

Valeria Flāviam saccum **portāre** *iussit.*	Valeria ordered Flavia to carry the sack.
Valeria Flāviam saccum **portāre** *cupit.*	Valeria wishes Flavia to carry the sack.
Valeria Flāviam saccum **portāre** *vetat.*	Valeria forbids Flavia to carry the sack.

Why all the accusatives? Even though you can easily translate the sentences above, you might ask why *Flāviam* and *saccum* are both accusative. Here are the basics.

- The object of the main verb (*iussit, cupit, vetat*) is actually the infinitive, *portāre.* The subject is ordering/wanting/forbidding the "carrying." Remember that an infinitive is a **verbal noun**.
- You know that the subject of a conjugated verb is nominative, but in Latin, the subject of an **infinitive** is always in the accusative case. That is why *Flāviam* is accusative in each sentence.
- But the "verbal" part of the infinitive can also take a direct object: that is, Flavia is carrying **something**. This too has to be in the accusative, and in these sentences, that word is *saccum.*
- In situations like this, where you have two accusatives in a row with an infinitive, the **first one is the subject** of the infinitive and the **second one is the object** of the infinitive. Word order makes a difference here! Compare these two sentences:

Flāviam sīmiam portāre iubeō.	I order Flavia to carry the monkey.
Sīmiam Flāviam portāre iubeō.	I order the monkey to carry Flavia.

Latin also sometimes uses an infinitive as the subject of a sentence. As you might guess, this is called the **subjective infinitive**. In such cases, the infinitive is commonly accompanied by a form of *est* and, as a verbal noun, is neuter singular. English more commonly uses a gerund ending in "-ing" to translate a Latin subjective infinitive.

*Pecūniam **rapere** malum est.*	To steal money is bad.
Errāre hūmānum est.	To err is human.

EXERCEĀMUS!

11-2 Infinitives

Find the infinitive in each of the following sentences and indicate whether it is complementary, subjective, or objective. HINT: Look for verbs like *volō* and *possum* for complementary infinitives, *est* for subjective infinitives, and *cupiō* for objective infinitives. Follow the model.

→ **Vīvere** Rōmae difficile est!   *Vīvere is a subjective infinitive because it is the subject of **est***.

1. Latrōnēs saccum rapere volunt.

2. Latrōnēs Aelium pugnāre nōluērunt.

3. Amīcōs salūtāre bonum est!

4. Fēminae Sōcratem clāmāre cupīvērunt.

5. Licinia Aeliō verba astrologī narrāre cupīvit.

6. Licinia verba astrologī narrāre potest.

7. Verba astrologī narrāre difficile est.

8. Paedagōgus sīmiam fugere vetat.

Lectiō Secunda

Antequam Legis

Perfect Tense—All Persons

You already know the 3rd person perfect active endings: *-it* and *-ērunt,* as in *vēn**it*** and *vēn**ērunt***.

In *Lectiō Secunda* Lucius tells his mother what happened today at school and you are introduced to the remaining perfect active endings. Before you read, be sure to do Exercise 11-3, as it will teach you the other forms of the perfect tense.

EXERCEĀMUS!

11-3 Recognizing the 1st and 2nd Person Perfect Forms

This exercise is designed to let you discover the endings for the 1st (I, we) and 2nd (you, y'all) persons of the perfect tense. The following chart lists the stems of all the verbs in *Lectiō Secunda* with 1st or 2nd person perfect active endings. These words are marked in **bold** in the reading. Your job is to supply the endings from the readings and to use hints and context from the *lectiō* to translate the words in the correct person. Here are some clues to finding the endings in the text.

- All the endings you seek begin with the letter *-i.*
- When you see the pronoun *ego* you can expect a 1st person singular verb.
- The 1st person plural ending looks a lot like the 1st person plural present.
- Look for 2nd person verb endings with vocatives.

Fill out the following chart as you read.

PERFECT ACTIVE		
Person	**Singular**	**Plural**
1st person	audīv-	audīv-
	fodicāv-	rīs-
	vīd-	vīd-
2nd person	cucurr-	audīv-
	nōv-	vīd-
	vīd-	

Cavē!! Be very attentive to the tenses of the verbs in this reading. Lucius is a young lad and, like many younger speakers, he switches tenses at the drop of a hat, especially when he is excited.

🔊 QUID ACCIDIT HODIĒ?

Lūcius, Servīlia, et Hermēs ad domum Servīliī adveniunt.
Canem familiae salūtant. Nōmen canī Albus est. (Nōmen
iocōsum est quod Albus niger, nōn albus est.) Caecilia Metella et Marcus vōcēs Lūciī et Servīliae audiunt, ad ianuam adve-
5 niunt, et in ātriō stant.

Lūcius ē lectīcā surgit et in domum currit. "Marce!
Mātercula!" clamat, "**audīvistis**ne dē sīmiā in Forō? Crēdite
mihi—iocōsum fuit!!"

Māter respondet: "Fīlī, nōn **audīvī**. Quid accidit? Cūr
10 **cucurristī**? Cūr tam agitātus es?"

"Et ego nōn **audīvī**, mī frāter," addit Marcus, "Dīc mihi!
Quid **vīdistī**?"

"In lūdō ego et aliī puerī sumus. Chīrōn librum legit—ut semper! Fessī sumus et amīcus meus, Iūlius, dormit (ut semper!). Sed
15 Chīrōn eum nōn videt. Neque magister dīcit "Cūr dormīs, Iūlī?"
neque virgam tollit. Ego Iūliī latus **fodicāvī** et ille oculōs aperuit.

"Subitō clāmōrem magnam **audīvimus**. Ecce! Prīmum
sīmiam **vīdī**. Tunc paedagōgum in viā **vīdimus**. Hermēs et
sīmia cucurrērunt per viam. Paedagōgus permaximē clāmāvit
20 et post sīmiam cucurrit. Sīmia saccum paedagōgī habuit. Fortasse hunc sīmiam **nōvistī**? Valeriae sīmia est. Valeria tabernam
illam iuxtā Forum habet. Hermēs, valdē īrātus, clāmāvit et
sīmiam capere voluit. Paedagōgus sīmiae appropinquāvit
sed eum nōn capere potuit. Dēnique sīmia in āram Dīvī
25 Iūliī saluit. **Rīsimus**! Marce māterque, sīmiam umquam
vīdistīs in Forō? Sīmiam in ārā vidēre rīdiculōsum est!"

Caecilia in ātriō stat

🔊 VERBA ŪTENDA

accidō, accidere, accidī
  happen
addō, addere, addidī add
advenio, advenīre,
  advēnī, adventum
  arrive at, come to
albus, -a, -um white
aperiō, aperīre, aperuī
  open
appropinquō (1)
  (+ dat.) approach
  come near to
ātrium, -iī n. atrium, public
  greeting room of a
  Roman house
canī "of the dog"

clāmōrem shout
crēdō, crēdere, crēdidī believe
cūr why
dēnique finally, at last
dormiō, dormīre, dormīvī
  sleep
erat "it was"
eum him
fodicō (1) poke; *latus*
  fodicāre poke in the ribs
fortasse perhaps
frāter brother
hunc "this" (refers to
  sīmiam)
ianua, -ae f. door
illam (adj.) that

iocōsus, -a, -um funny
iuxtā (+ acc.) near to
latus side, ribs
legō, legere, lēgī read
liber, librī m. book
māter mother
mātercula, -ae f. dear
  mother, mommy
mī my (vocative)
neque. . . neque neither . . .
  nor
niger, nigra, nigrum black
noscō, noscere, nōvī,
  nōtum know, get to
  know; *nōvisti* "you
  know" (See *Angulus*

Grammaticus for
  explanation)
oculus, -ī m. eye
permaximē very loudly
prīmum first, at first
saccus, -ī m. wallet, sack,
  bag, pocketbook
saliō, salīre, saliī/saluī,
  saltum leap, jump
subitō suddenly
surgō, surgere, surrēxī get
  up, rise
umquam at any time, ever
ut as
valdē very, a lot
virga, -ae f. rod

POSTQUAM LĒGISTĪ

1. What is the name of the dog of the Servilius family? Why is this name a joke? Do you know any pets with similarly funny names? Explain.
2. With what event does Lucius begin as he describes his day to his mother and brother?
3. What event is the highlight of his day? What did Lucius like about this event?

Grammatica B

More on the Perfect

The chart you filled in as you read *Lectiō Prīma* should have given you the following new endings (marked with an asterisk) for the **perfect tense**. You now know the full perfect. Note the perfect infinitive form, also.

	SINGULAR		PLURAL	
1st person*	vēn**ī**	I came	vēn**imus**	we came
2nd person*	vēn**istī**	you came	vēn**istis**	you all came
3rd person	vēn**it**	he/she/it came	vēn**ērunt**	they came
Infinitive	vēn**isse**	to have come		

Notā Bene:

- All the personal endings in the perfect active begin with *-i-* except the 3rd person plural, which begins with *-ē-*.

Gemma

- Note *ad domum* in line 1. *Domum* without a preposition means "home" as in "I am going home." Sometimes, as here, a preposition is used when the word *domus* just meant "house."
- Lucius calls his mother *mātercula* instead of *māter* as a term of endearment. Add *-culus, -a, -um* to a Latin word to make it smaller or dearer. You already saw this with *musculum* (little mouse).

- The present and perfect share some common endings. This means that, with some verbs, the only difference between a present and a perfect may be a long vowel. So a macron can make quite a difference:

  *Ille ignāvus hodiē **fugit** sīcut semper **fūgit**.*
  That coward is fleeing today just as he always has fled.

- Some verbs, like *accidō*, have identical present and perfect stems. These can be troublesome to translate, but let context help you.

- Don't worry about the perfect infinitive now. You will not see it used in Latin for many chapters. For now, just be aware of its existence.

Here are some more present and perfect forms that appear very similar to each other and require that you pay careful attention to the stems:

Present	**vs.**	**Perfect**
habēmus	vs.	*habuimus*
habet	vs.	*habuit*
videt	vs.	*vīdit*
dīcit	vs.	*dīxit*
venit	vs.	*vēnit*

EXERCEĀMUS!

11-4 Presents and Perfects

Match the Latin form in column A with the best translation from column B.

	A		B
_____	1. audīvimus	A.	he can
_____	2. audīmus	B.	he shouted
_____	3. vīdistis	C.	he shouts
_____	4. vidētis	D.	he wished
_____	5. cucurrit	E.	she could
_____	6. currit	F.	she ran
_____	7. clāmāvit	G.	she runs
_____	8. clāmat	H.	she wishes
_____	9. voluit	I.	we hear
_____	10. vult	J.	we heard
_____	11. potuit	K.	you have seen
_____	12. potest	L.	you see

Mōrēs Rōmānī

Iūno Dea

You met *Iūnō Monēta* in Chapter 10, but the Roman goddess Juno was best known as the wife of the sky god Jupiter and as queen of the gods. For this reason the Romans often depicted her wearing a crown and carrying a scepter as on the coin at left. Her sacred bird was the peacock. Many of the myths associated with her emphasized the jealousy she displayed toward her husband's numerous lovers, including Danae (mother of Perseus), Semele (mother of Dionysus), and especially Alcmena (mother of Hercules).

The goddess was also a major divine force of the Romans. Along with Jupiter and Minerva, Juno was one of the Capitoline Triad worshipped by the Romans on the Capitoline Hill.

For pregnant women like Licinia, Juno was most important as *Iūnō Lūcīna*, or "she who brings to light (*lux*)." In other words, Juno was the goddess of childbirth.

Iūnō Rēgīna

On March 1st the Romans celebrated the *Mātrōnālia*, the anniversary of the founding of Juno's temple on the Esquiline Hill. On this feast day, Roman wives were honored by their husbands with gifts. In *Lectiō Secunda* Licinia and Valeria visited a small roadside shrine dedicated to Juno Lucina, rather than a major temple. On the Roman coin to the right Juno is depicted as Lucina. You can read the last part of the word "Lucina" around the rim. The SC on either side of standing Juno mean "by decree of the Senate."

Iūnō Lūcīna

Gemma

In 1843, or so the story goes, a British general named Napier annexed an area of Pakistan that was then called Sinde (alternatively Sindh or Sind). With a flair for the theatrical, Napier dispatched the news of his victory to the British government in Latin: *Peccāvī!* This is translated as "I have sinned," and was a pun for "I have Sinde," that is," I have taken the area of Sinde."

Regrettably, the story appears to have been published first in the magazine Punch as a joke. But it does demonstrate the power of a good Latin-based education.

Latīna Hodierna

Vēnī, Vīdī, Vīcī

Now that you have seen all the forms of the perfect active you can better appreciate Julius Caesar's famous phrase *Vēnī, Vīdī, Vīcī*, which was used to describe his lightning victory over king Pharnaces II of Pontus in 47 B.C. at the battle of Zela in what is now Turkey. The brevity of the statement is telling. The lack of conjunctions (like *et*), the avoidance of detailed description, and the quick succession of verbs were intended to emphasize not only the speed of Caesar's victory but also his decisiveness. Also note the assonance of the phrase, i.e., the repetition of the sounds *v* and *ī*.

Caesar's use of the perfect tense is significant here and further demonstrates his boastfulness. Compare these possible variations of Caesar's statement:

I came. I saw. I conquered.

I have come. I have seen. I have conquered.

I did come. I did see. I did conquer.

When I came (to Pontus), I saw (the situation) and I conquered (Pharnaces).

Which of these four English translations do you think comes closest to expressing the simplicity of Caesar's three simple words?

Watch for Caecilia, the wife of Servilius, to use a variation of this famous phrase in the next chapter. This phrase quickly became proverbial, so it is no surprise that a woman like Caecilia would use it in everyday conversation.

Julius Caesar's phrase *Vēnī, Vīdī, Vīcī* has become part of our modern culture, and you will find it used in many unexpected places. For example, the token depicted below, from the 1975 Mardi Gras in New Orleans, is modeled on an ancient coin with Caesar's famous saying.

Several other sayings by Caesar are sometimes quoted in Latin today. Use the *Verba Ūtenda* to translate any unfamiliar phrases.

🔊 **VERBA ŪTENDA**

ālea, -ae f. die (singular of dice)

iactus, -a, -um thrown, cast

- *Ālea iacta est.* By tradition, Caesar said this as he crossed the Rubicon River and entered Italy with his army in 49 B.C. By law Caesar was not supposed to bring his army into Italy without the permission of the Senate. By saying *Ālea iacta est*, Caesar was suggesting that there was no turning back and war was inevitable.

- *Et tū Brute?* "Even you, Brutus?" According to the Greek historian Plutarch, Caesar actually spoke his dying words in Greek, not Latin. Brutus has been one of Caesar's closest friends, so Brutus' involvement in the assassination came as a great surprise to Caesar.

"Vēnī, Vīdī, Vīcī" hodiē

🔊 **VERBA ŪTENDA**

dīvīsus, -a, -um divided
Gallia omnis "all of Gaul,"
the Roman province now
known as France
partēs parts

- *Gallia est omnis dīvīsa in partēs trēs.* These are the famous first words in Caesar's *Dē Bellō Gallicō* (*On the Gallic War*). His succinct style is reflected in this short but memorable beginning.

The following two famous expressions associated with Caesar are not used in Latin:

- Once, when rumor had implicated his wife in a religious scandal that also involved adultery, Caesar divorced her even though she might be innocent. Caesar is supposed to have said that "Caesar's wife must be above suspicion." In other words, people associated with a person of prominence must avoid scandal.

- And then there is the famous "Beware of the Ides of March." Caesar was assassinated on the Ides of March (March 15th) in 44 B.C. The words are from Act I, Scene ii, of Shakespeare's *Julius Caesar*, where they were spoken, to no avail, to Caesar by a soothsayer.

Orbis Terrārum Rōmānus

Gallia Est Omnis Dīvīsa in Partēs Trēs?

For the Romans *Gallia* (the land of the Gauls) encompassed not only modern France, but also Belgium, parts of Switzerland, and even northern Italy. The Gauls had been a constant threat to Rome over many centuries. The Gauls invaded Rome around 390 B.C., and the Roman defenders on the Capitoline Hill were saved only by the honking of Juno's sacred geese. In the Second Punic War (218–201 B.C.) the Gauls in northern Italy sided with the Carthaginian invader, Hannibal. At one point there were three provinces of Gaul:

- *Gallia Cisalpīna* (Gaul on this side of the Alps)
- *Gallia Transalpīna* (Gaul on the other side of the Alps), what is now southern France
- *Gallia Narbōnensis*, named after the city of *Narbō* (modern Narbonne). Because the Romans often referred to this province simply as *Prōvincia Nostra* or simply *Prōvincia* (the Province), this region of France is known today as Provence.

It was as governor of *Gallia Narbōnensis* that Julius Caesar began the conquest of the rest of Gaul in 58 B.C. This long and brutal war ended only in 52 B.C. with the defeat of the Gallic chieftain, Vercingetorix, at the battle of Alesia. About one fourth of the inhabitants of Gaul died during Caesar's campaign and many more were enslaved. Over the next centuries, Gaul became fully Romanized, and the Celtic language was replaced by Latin (and eventually by its descendant, modern French).

Templum Nemausī

Aquaeductus Rōmānus hodiē

When Julius Caesar began his history of the wars in Gaul (*Dē Bellō Gallicō*) with the words *Gallia est omnis dīvīsa in partēs trēs,* he was talking about the non-Roman regions of *Gallia Transalpīna.* These were *Belgica* (approximately modern Belgium), *Aquitānia* (approximately the French region of Aquitaine) and *Celtica* (most of France).

In imperial times there were seven Gallic provinces:

- *Aquitānia*
- *Gallia Lugdunensis,* with a capital at *Lugdunum* (modern Lyon)
- *Belgica*
- *Gallia Narbōnensis,* with its major city *Massilia* (modern Marseille)
- and three small provinces around the Alps (*Alpēs, -ium* f.): *Alpēs Maritimae, Alpēs Penninae,* and *Alpēs Cottiae*

Paris, the capital of modern France, was only a minor town (*Lutetia*) in Roman times.

One of the best preserved Roman temples is in Nemausus (modern Nîmes). Built by Agrippa in 19–16 B.C., it is known today as the Maison Carrée. One of the best preserved Roman aqueducts was built in the 1st century A.D. to carry water to Nemausus. It is known today as the Pont du Gard. Both structures are depicted at the bottom of page 136.

QUID PUTĀS?

1. Use the Internet to find a 1942 statement of General Douglas MacArthur that is just as famous and just as pithy as *Vēnī, Vīdī, Vīcī.*
2. Why do you think Juno was called Lūcīna ("she who brings light") as goddess of childbirth?
3. Do you think that Caesar's statement that "Caesar's wife must be above suspicion" applies to prominent people today? Is the statement also sexist, implying that the men could get away with anything?
4. What do you think is the modern French attitude toward Julius Caesar and his conquest of Gaul? Why?

EXERCEĀMUS!

11-5 Scrībāmus

Retell the following episode from Chapter 6 in the perfect tense. In order to do this, you need to change the words marked in **bold** from present to perfect tense. You have already seen all of these words as *Verba Discenda*, so if you do not remember the perfect stem, look it up! If you are really ambitious, try adding a bit more to the story in your own words. We have started the retelling for you.

> Chīrōn īrātus prō Lūciō **stat**. Omnēs puerī et puellae **rident** et, in viā, Hermēs quoque **rīdet**. Sōlus Chīrōn nōn **rīdet**, sed virgam **capit** et Lūciō **appropinquat**. Lūcius **sedet** sub virgā magistrī et valdē **timet**. Chīrōn virgam altē **tollit** sed tunc Hermēs paedagōgus magnā vōce **clāmat**. Chīrōn paulīsper **cōgitat**. Chīrōn Lūcium verberāre **vult**, sed Chīrōn Servīlium, patrem Lūciī, irrītāre nōn **vult**.

 *Chīrōn īrātus prō Lūciō **stetit**.*

11-6 Colloquāmur

Now ask your classmate a "Who?" question based on the narrative you rewrote for Exercise 11-5. In order to do this, simply replace a singular subject with *quis* or a plural subject with *quī*. Follow the model.

 Chīrōn īrātus prō Lūciō **stetit**. → Quis prō Lūciō stetit?
Chīrōn prō Lūciō stetit.

11-7 Verba Discenda

Find the following in the *Verba Discenda*: five verbs, seven adverbs, four nouns, one interjection, and one adjective.

> **VERBA DISCENDA**
>
> ***adveniō, advenīre, advēnī, adventum*** arrive at, come to [advent, adventure]
> ***appropinquō* (1) (+ dat.)** approach, come near to [propinquity]
> ***cūr*** why
> ***dea, -ae* f.** goddess [deify]
> ***Ecce!*** Behold! Look!
> ***fortasse*** perhaps
>
> ***longē*** far off, far, a long distance
> ***nōscō, nōscere, nōvī, nōtum*** know, get to know [notation]
> ***Rōma, -ae* f.** Rome
> ***Rōmānus, -a, -um*** Roman
> ***saccus, -ī* m.** wallet, sack, bag, pocketbook
>
> ***saliō, salīre, saliī/saluī, saltum*** leap, jump [salient]
> ***sīc*** thus, in this way; yes
> ***subitō*** suddenly
> ***tam*** so, so much (as)
> ***tollō, tollere, sustulī, sublātum*** lift, raise
> ***valdē*** very, a lot
> ***verbum, -ī* n.** word [verbose]

Angulus Grammaticus

The "Present Perfect" and the "Inchoate Suffix" -scō

The normal use of the perfect tense is to indicate a single act that was finished some time in the past: "I painted the house," "We have gone there before," and the like. But in Latin, the perfect tense can also have a sense that the thing that was done has an effect on the present. Consider these sentences:

> I have come to save you!   (I am here to save you)
> I've learned *that* lesson!   (I'm too smart for that now)

This concept will be important for some grammatical concepts you will learn later on. For now, however, it affects your understanding of some very special verbs. The most common one that you have encountered is **nōvī**, which, though perfect tense, is always translated in the present.

> *Nōvistīne eum?*   *Ita, eum nōvī.*
> Do you know him?   Yes, I know him.

How did this happen? The full verb is *noscō, noscere, nōvī, nōtum* which, in the present tense, means "to come to know something." Thus, *nōvī*, the perfect of *noscō*, means "I have come to know something," and, if you have come to know something, then you do in fact know it.

There is another verb that is perfect tense in form, but is translated as a present tense:

ōdī is perfect in form but is translated in the present tense: "I hate"

In his famous poem #85, Catullus says *Ōdī et amō* (I hate and I love)—both at the same time—and thus captures the essence of many love affairs.

Note the *-sc-* in the 1st principal part of the verb *noscō*. This suffix is added to Latin verbs to show that the action is just starting or beginning. That is why *noscō* is translated as "begin to know, get to know." Verbs with this verbal suffix are sometimes called **inchoatives**, from the Latin verb *inchoō* (1) "to begin."

You will find this inchoate suffix in several English derivatives. See if you can figure out how each of the following Latin verbs indicates the beginning of an action. We have done the first one for you.

LATIN WORD	VERB MEANING	ENGLISH DERIVATIVE	"BEGINNING TO ..."
adulēscō	grow up, mature	adolescent	beginning to grow, be an adult
crēscō	grow	crescent	
nāscor	be born	nascent	
quiēscō	be quiet	quiescent	

Noscō is a common verb and is found in a lot of Latin compound verbs:

agnoscō   to recognize
cognoscō   to get to know someone
ignoscō   to pardon, excuse (literally, "getting not to know any more;" i.e., "to forget")

Ātrium

LECTIŌNĒS:
HERMĒS ET SĪMIA
and
DOMUS SERVĪLIĪ

Lucius finishes telling his family about his day, and the Servilius family is described.

12

In Domō Magnā

Lectiō Prīma

Antequam Legis

At the Home of the Servilii

In this chapter you will visit the home of the wealthy and upwardly mobile Servilii, who share the events of their day. As you read, you should look for the following:

- new uses of the dative
- impersonal verbs
- adverbs

Dative with Special Verbs

Watch in the readings for **special verbs** like *noceō, nocēre* (to harm), which take dative rather than accusative objects. Don't worry right now about why these verbs take the dative rather than the accusative. You can easily understand what they mean; for example, in *Lectiō Prīma*, Hermes tells his family:

*Sīmiae **nocēre** nōn potuī.*   I was not able **to harm** the monkey.

The words marked in **bold** in *Lectiō Prīma* are special verbs, so just look for a dative object when you see one.

Impersonal Verbs and Expressions

"It is going to rain." Easily understood in English, but hard to define grammatically. What is the subject of the verb? "It." Such verbs are called **impersonal** because no "person" is the subject, just a sort of vague "it." Latin has the same construction. Consider these sentences in which the <u>underlined</u> infinitive is the subject of the impersonal verb.

Paedagōgum sīmiam <u>capere</u> oportet!	It is fitting for the tutor to catch the monkey.
	The tutor ought to catch the monkey.
Paedagōgō sīmiam <u>capere</u> necesse est!	It is necessary for the tutor to catch the monkey.
	The tutor has to catch the monkey.

All of the impersonal expressions in *Lectiō Prīma* are marked in ***bold italics***. When you see them, remember to make the subject "it" and look for an infinitive to serve as the subject of the impersonal expression.

Adverbs

The part of speech introduced in this chapter is the **adverb**, a word that describes a verb, an adjective, or another adverb. Many English adverbs are made by adding **-ly** to an adjective.

Adjective	**Adverb**
angry	angri**ly**
timid	timid**ly**

Latin can make adverbs in a similar way, by adding *-ē* to an adjective's stem.

Adjective	**Adverb**
īrātus	*īrāt**ē***
timidus	*timid**ē***

Watch for these and other adverbs ending in *-ē* (sometimes *-e*) as you read *Lectiō Prīma*.

EXERCEĀMUS!

12-1   Impersonal Expressions and Datives with Special Verbs

As you read *Lectiō Prīma*, make two line-by-line lists. In the first, list the ***impersonal expressions*** (marked in ***bold italics***) and the infinitives that are their subjects. In the second, list the **special verbs** (marked in **bold**) and their dative objects. Finally, translate the two words together. Follow the model.

Impersonal Expressions

	Line	Verb	Infinitive Subject	Translation
→	1	placet	audīre	it is pleasing to hear

Special Verbs

	Line	Verb	Dative Direct Object	Translation
→	5	crēde	mihi	believe me

HERMĒS ET SĪMIA

Fābulam audīre dē sīmiā in Forō Marcō *placet*. Marcus rīdet et Hermem rogat, "Cūr tam valdē īrātus fuistī, ō paedagōge? Cūr tam strēnuē cucurristī?"

"Ah, domine," Marcō respondit, "Sīmia malus furtīvē saccum meum cēpit et ad Forum fūgit. Illa pecūnia patris tuī est et mihi saccum custōdīre *necesse est*. Nōn
5 sīmiīs pecūniam habēre *licet*! Hōc officium meum est. Sīmiam cēpī, sed mihi *crēde*— sīmiae nōn *nocuī*, sed *ignōvī*!"

"Quōmodo sīmiam capere potuistī?"

"Sīmiae *imperāvī* sed semper cucurrit. Tōtum per Forum longē cu- currimus, sed eum capere nōn potuī. Dēmum, sīmia fessus fuit et ad āram
10 Dīvī Iūliī cucurrit ubī sēdit, tremuit, et timidē clāmāvit. Eum tunc īrātē cēpī sed sīmiae *nocēre* nōn potuī. In illō locō sacrō et sīmiīs *parcere* *oportet*."

"Euge!!" Caecilia clāmāvit, "Bene factum!!! Sīmiam cēpistī. Vēnistī. Vīdistī. Vīcistī!"

15 "Ita vērō," Marcus inquit, "Nōn iam paedagōgus es, sed bestiārius! Ille sīmia malus in mūneribus in amphitheātrō pugnāre dēbet! Animal perīculōsum est!"

Paedagōgus Marcō respondit: "Sī tibi *placeat*, domine, nōlī mē irrīdēre! Territus fuī! Sī pecūniam patris tuī āmīsī…"

"Sed pecūniam nōn āmīsistī!" Caecilia confirmāvit. "Omnia salva sunt. Nunc cēnāre *necesse est*. Lūcī et Marce,
20 vōs cēnae parāte. Servīlia, tē mihi *adesse* *oportet*."

In illō locō sacrō et sīmiīs parcere oportet.

VERBA ŪTENDA

adsum, adesse, adfuī (+ dat.) be near, be present; be "there for" someone, be of assistance, help, aid

āmittō, āmittere, āmīsī lose

bestiārius, -iī m. animal fighter

cēna, -ae f. dinner

cēnō (1) dine

confirmō (1) reassure

crēdō, crēdere, crēdidī (+ dat) believe

custōdiō, custōdīre, custōdīvī / custōdiī guard, watch

dēmum at last

dominus, -ī m. master, lord

et here, "even"

euge! Good! Great!

eum him

factum "done"

fugiō, fugere, fūgī, fugitum flee

furtivē secretly

ignoscō, ignoscere, ignōvī (+ dat.) forgive, pardon

illa and *ille* that

imperō (1) (+ dat.) command

implōrō (1) plead, beg

īrātē angrily

irrīdeō, irrīdēre, irrīsī laugh at

ita yes

licet (+ dat.) it is permitted

locus, -ī m. place

longē far

mūneribus games

necesse est (+ dat. + inf.) it is necessary to

nōs us

noceō, nocēre, nocuī, nocitum (+ dat.) harm, do injury to

officium, -iī n. duty, task, job

omnia everything

oportet, oportuit (+ inf.) one ought

parcō, parcere, pepercī / parsī / parcuī, parsūrus (+ dat.) spare, pardon, show mercy to

parō (1) prepare, make ready

perīculōsus, -a, -um dangerous

placeō, placēre, placuit, placitum (+ dat.) please, be pleasing to;

sī placet (+ inf.) = "please"; "it is pleasing to"

pugnō (1) fight

quōmodo how

sacer, sacra, sacrum holy, sacred

salvus, -a, -um safe

strēnuē vigorously

timidus, -a, -um timid

tōtus, -a, -um the whole

tremō, tremere, tremuī tremble

tuus, -a, -um your

vērō indeed

vincō, vincere, vīcī, victum conquer

vōs yourselves

POSTQUAM LĒGISTĪ

Answer these questions in both Latin and English. Follow the model.

→ Why does Marcus laugh at the beginning of the *lectiō*?
  Fabūla Lūciī Marcō placet. Lucius' story pleases Marcus.

1. What part of his job does Hermes emphasize in the story about the monkey?

2. Why does Hermes say that he did not harm the monkey?

3. What words of Caecilia are a paraphrase of a famous saying by Julius Caesar? How are her words different from Caesar's?

4. What joke does Marcus make about Hermes and the monkey?

Gemma

In the phrase *et sīmiīs* (line 11) the word *et* does not mean "and." It means "even." Translate *et* in this way when two things are not being connected.

Grammatica A

Dative with Special Verbs

Read the following sentence from *Lectiō Prīma*:

*In illō locō sacrō et **sīmiīs** parcere oportet.*

In this sencence, ***sīmiīs*** is the dative object of the verb *parcere* (to spare). In English we simply consider "monkeys" to be the object of "spare." So we might expect Latin to use an accusative case, but it doesn't. Instead *sīmiīs* is in the dative case. The rule is that Latin has a number of verbs that take a dative object instead of an accusative one. These special verbs include the following *Verba Discenda*:

Gemma

Note that Latin indicates that, as a "student," you are supposed to be "eager" and "devoted" to your learning process!

noceō, nocēre, nocuī, nocitum (+ dat.)	harm, injure, do injury to
parcō, parcere, pepercī, parsūrus (+ dat.)	spare, show mercy toward
placeō, placēre, placuī, placitum (+ dat.)	please, be pleasing to
studeō, studēre, studuī (+ dat.)	be eager to, devote oneself to, study
respondeō, respondēre, respondī, responsum (+ dat.)	respond to, answer

Such verbs are always marked in the dictionary by (+ dat.). Notice how English translations of these verbs often include prepositions, indicating, for example, that the action is happening "to" or "toward" someone. So

Sīmiae parcere oportet.

can be translated two ways:

One ought to spare the monkey.
One ought to show mercy **toward** the monkey.

EXERCEĀMUS!

12-2 **Translating More Than One Way**

Retranslate each of the following sentences to include the word "to" or "toward." Follow the model. HINT: Use the translations provided in the list of special verbs that take the dative.

→ *Sīmiae parcit.*   He spares the monkey.
        He shows mercy **toward** the monkey.

1. *Cēna mihi placet.*   Dinner pleases me.

2. *Fīliō crēdō.*   I believe my son.

3. *Ancillīs ignoscimus.*   We pardon the maid servants.

4. *Servō imperāvit.*   He commanded the slave.

5. *Num amīcō nocēs?*   You are not harming your friend, are you?

Impersonal Verbs and Expressions

Impersonal verbs do not have "persons" as subjects. These verbs are often translated in English with "it," as in "it is necessary that," and they commonly have special constructions, especially infinitives, associated with them. In all of the following examples, the subject of the impersonal expression is the infinitive *facere*. Some use the dative to show the person affected by the verb, some do not. Compare the following:

IMPERSONAL EXPRESSION	EXAMPLE	TRANSLATION	NOTES
necesse est	*Discipulīs opus facere necesse est.*	The students have to do their work.	necessity implied, dative
oportet	*Discipulōs opus facere oportet.*	The students ought to do their work.	less forceful, no dative
placet	*Discipulīs opus facere placet.*	It is pleasing for the students to do their work.	dative
licet	*Discipulīs opus facere licet.*	The students are allowed to do their work.	dative

Notā Bene:

- The dative *discipulīs* tells you to whom it is pleasing, while the accusative *opus* is the direct object of the infinitive *facere*.
- Look for another impersonal verb, *decet* (it is fitting), in the next reading.

Saying Please in Latin

Did you notice the impersonal expression *sī tibi placeat* in *Lectiō Prīma*? Literally, it means "if it might be pleasing to you." This is a very polite way of saying "please" in Latin. Here are some other ways to say "please":

sī placet	if it is pleasing
sī tibi placet	if it is pleasing to you
sī placeat	if it might be pleasing (more polite)

If you are speaking to more than one person, use *vōbīs*:

sī vōbīs placet	if it is pleasing to (all of) you

Adverbs

Here are some of the adverbs used in *Lectiō Prīma*:

Cūr tam **strēnuē** cucurristī?	Why did you run so **vigorously**?
Sīmia **timidē** clāmāvit.	The monkey cried **timidly**.
Eum tunc **īrātē** cēpī.	Then I seized him **angrily**.

All of these adverbs were made by adding *-ē* to the stem of an adjective ending in *-us, -a, -um*.

īrātus, -a, -um angry	*īrātē* angri**ly**
strēnuus, -a, -um strong	*strēnuē* strong**ly**
timidus, -a, -um fearful, timid	*timidē* fearful**ly**, timid**ly**

Unlike adjectives, adverbs have no gender, number, or case, so the ending is always the same. Sometimes the stem changes in the process of making an adverb:

bonus, -a, -um good	*bene* well (from *bon-* + *-e*)
validus, -a, -um strong	*valdē* very (contracted from *val(i)dē*)

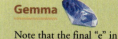

Gemma

Note that the final "e" in *bene* is short.

Lectiō Secunda

Antequam Legis

The family of Valeria does not have much money and lives in a small, crowded apartment. The Servilii, on the other hand, are patricians (members of established families) and live high on a hill in an expensive house, spacious enough for the entire household, which includes many slaves. In this *lectiō* you read about many of the people who live in this house.

Adjective Agreement

As you read, look closely at the **adjectives**. Adjectives agree with the nouns they modify in gender, number, and case (**GNC**). Often this means that they have the same endings (*multam pecūniam*) **but not always**! Sometimes an adjective has a different ending from the noun but still agrees with it in GNC. As you read *Lectiō Secunda*, look for the adjectives and nouns marked in **bold**. These are noun/adjective pairs that do not have identical endings but still agree. After you read, we will explain how adjective agreement works.

EXERCEĀMUS!

12-3 **Adjective Agreement**

Using the words marked in **bold** as a guide, answer the following questions as you scan *Lectiō Secunda*. Then translate each noun/adjective pair. Follow the model. HINT: Use the *Verba Ūtenda* if you do not know the meaning of a word.

→ Line 1	What word describes *domus*?	***magna***	the large house
1. Line 4	What word describes *avus*?		
2. Line 7	What word describes *uxor*?		
3. Line 7	Now find another word describing *uxor*.		
4. Line 10	What word describes *frāter*?		
5. Line 13	What word describes *parte*?		
6. Line 13	What word describes *domī*?		

🔊 DOMUS SERVĪLIĪ

Domus Servīliī valdē **magna** est quod Servīlius multam pecūniam habet. In Vīminālī multī Rōmānī aedificia magna fabricāvērunt. Hīc multae familiae in aedificiīs magnīs habitant. **Domus antīqua** Servīliī quoque magnum spatium habet et plūs quam quindecim conclāvia—et parva et magna—continet. Hīc habitant Servīlius, **cara uxor**, Caecilia Metella, et trēs līberī Servīliī. Pater Servīliī quoque hīc habitat, sed rārē ē cubiculō exit, quod **avus aeger** est
5 et octōgintā duōs annōs **nātus** est.

Servīlius pater familiās est. **Vir** quadrāgintā quīnque annōs **nātus** est. Caecilia Metella, Servīliī uxor, trīgintā octō annōs nāta est. Caecilia Servīliī **uxor secunda** est. Cornelia **uxor prīma** fuit, sed Servīlius Corneliam dīmīserat abhinc duodecim annōs.

Caecilia Metella māter Lūciī est. **Puer**, Chīrōnis discipulus, decem annōs **nātus** est.
10 Cornēlia māter Marcī et Servīliae est. Servīlia sēdecim annōs nāta est, sed nōndum virum habet. **Frāter** ūnum et vīgintī annōs **nātus** est et rhētoricae studet.

Domus quoque servōs multōs habet. Hermēs hīc habitat et, quamquam servus est, paedagōgō cubiculum proprium habēre decet. Aliī servī—ancillae, coquī, lectīcāriī, custōdēs, iānitor inter aliōs—in **aliā parte domī magnae** habitant ubi multī in cubiculō ūnō dormiunt.

🔊 VERBA ŪTENDA

abhinc duodecim annōs "twelve years ago"
aedificium, -iī n. building
aeger, -gra, -grum sick, ill
annus, -ī m. year
avus, -ī m. grandfather
cārus, -a, -um dear
Chīrōnis of Chiron
conclāvia rooms
contineō, continēre contain
coquus, -ī m. cook
cubiculum, -ī n. bedroom
custōdēs guards
decet, decēre, decuit (+ dat.) it is fitting

decem ten
dīmīserat (he) had divorced
duodecim twelve
exit leaves
fabricō (1) build
habitō (1) live in, inhabit
iānitor doorkeeper
inter (+ acc.) among
lectīcārius, -iī m. litter bearer
līberī, -ōrum m. pl. children
māter f. mother
nam for
***nātus, -a, -um* born, xx annōs; *nātus est* = is xx years old**

nōmine "by name"
nōndum not yet
octō eight
octōgintā eighty
parte part
pater m. father
pater familiās m. head of the family
plūs more
prīmus, -a, -um first
proprius, -a, -um one's own
quadrāgintā forty
quamquam although
quindecim fifteen

rārus, -a, -um rare
secundus, -a, -um second
sēdecim sixteen
spatium, -iī n. space
***studeō, studēre, studuī* (+ dat.) to devote oneself to, be eager for, to study**
trīgintā thirty
uxor f. wife
vīgintī twenty
Vīminālis the Viminal Hill
virum husband

POSTQUAM LĒGISTĪ

Wherever possible, answer these questions in both Latin and English.

1. Describe the neighborhood in which the *familia Servīliī* live. How does it compare to your neighborhood?

2. Identify the people who live in this house. Would this be considered a large household today?

3. Describe the kinds of household slaves in the house. Compare these workers to the kind of staff in a wealthy house today. What would the modern equivalent of a *lectīcārius* be?

Grammatica B

Adjective Agreement

You probably had no trouble translating the title of this chapter, *In Domō Magnā*, even though endings of *domō* and *magnā* are not the same. In *Lectiō Secunda* you saw a variety of other examples of noun/adjective pairs which do not match in endings: *vir nātus, puer nātus, uxor prīma, pater nātus*, etc.

Adjectives must agree with the noun they describe in gender, number, and case. As shorthand, we say they "GNC" (pronounced "ga-nick"). Technically, this is called **grammatical agreement**. You have mostly seen noun/adjective pairs where the endings mirror each other, as in *fēmina bona* or *ōvum malum*. It would be nice if this were always the case, but it is not.

Nouns and adjectives belong to certain declensions and use the endings that are reserved for that declension. Adjectives like *bonus, bona, bonum* or *noster, nostra, nostrum* are sometimes called **2-1-2 adjectives**, because they use endings from those declensions. Adjectives cannot change the declension endings they use. 2-1-2 adjectives use 2nd declension endings for the masculine and neuter forms and 1st declension for the feminine.

So adjectives and nouns must GNC, but they do not necessarily have to have the same endings. Consider these pairs. *Sīmia* is 1st declension but can be either masculine or feminine. *Domus* is second declension but is feminine.

Notice how the endings do not match, but the words GNC. Can you continue the declension of both words into the plural?

Nom.	sīmia bonus	domus bona
Gen.	sīmiae bonī	domī bonae
Dat.	sīmiae bonō	domō bonae
Acc.	sīmiam bonum	domum bonam
Abl.	sīmiā bonō	domō bonā

For more on 1st declension masculine nouns see the *Angulus Grammaticus*.

In the reading you also saw pairs with non-identical endings like *uxor prīma* and *frāter nātus*. Here a 2-1-2 adjective is modifying a 3rd declension noun. You will learn these nouns in the next chapter.

Summary

- Nouns and adjectives must GNC.
- But they must use the endings from the declension to which they belong.

All you do is choose the appropriate ending from the 2-1-2 columns based on which GNC you need.

EXERCEĀMUS!

12-4 Adjective Agreement

The 2-1-2 adjectives are marked in **bold** in the following sentences. Identify the nouns they modify and use the 2-1-2 adjective to determine the gender, number, and case of these nouns. Follow the model. In some examples, the nouns are 3rd declension, but you should be able to figure them out from the adjectival endings.

	Noun	Gender	Number	Case
→ Hermēs **bonus** intrat.	Hermēs	m.	sing.	nom.

1. Domus **magna** Servīliī in colle Vīminālī est.
2. Caecilia Servīliī uxor **secunda** est.
3. Aliī servī in **aliā** parte domī habitant.
4. Chīrōn **īrātus** est.
5. In pictūrā vir **malus** nāsum longum habet.
6. Lūcius patrem **bonum** videt.
7. Hermēs sīmiae **malō** vīnum dat.
8. Fabūla dē sīmiā **malō** iocōsa est.
9. Nōmen sīmiae **malō** Sōcratēs est.
10. Familia sīmiae **malī** bona est.
11. Sīmiae **malī** pecūniam cēpērunt.

Mōrēs Rōmānī

Domī Rōmānae

The house of the Servilii is a more modest version of an upwardly-mobile Roman's residence, both in the city and throughout Italy. (The best examples survive in the city of Pompeii.) The façade of this building would have little ostentation. Indeed the house would look little different from storefronts, warehouses, and apartments in the same block. Romans put their money and effort into decorating the inside of the dwelling. Sometimes shops were built into the front wall of the house and rented out for income or used in a family business. Two such shops are at the front of the house of the Servilii.

The front door was large, heavy, and strongly bolted. A prosperous family like the Servilii would have a *iānitor*, a slave who guarded the door and controlled access to the home. Some of these "janitors" were even chained to the spot and not allowed to leave. Just inside the door was a passageway called the *vestibulum*, originally a place to hang one's cloak (*vestis*). The *vestibulum* is also sometimes called the *faucēs* (jaws) or *ostium* (mouth). This leads into the *ātrium*, the main public room of the house where guests were greeted. In the center of the atrium was the *impluvium*, a pool intended to catch water from the *compluvium*, a hole in the roof directly above the *impluvium*. The *compluvium* let in light and allowed the household to collect drinking water in a cistern. By the time of the first century B.C., however, most of the *impluvia* were merely decoration and the rainwater ran out through a channel into the street.

The rooms on either side of the *ātrium* often served as *cubicula* or bedrooms. Sometimes a small shrine to the household gods was located in the corner of the atrium, near the front door. The Servilii had such a shrine in their house, and as you will see later, exhibited the death masks of their ancestors in the *ātrium*. All of this was done partly out of piety and partly to remind visitors that the Servilii came from good stock.

Beyond the *ātrium* was the *tablīnum* or office where the head of the house conducted business. It often had screens that could be drawn to close it off from the *ātrium* (and from

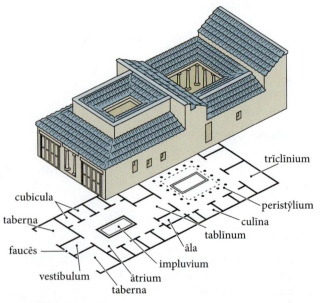

triclīnium
peristȳlium
culīna
tablīnum
āla
impluvium
ātrium
cubicula
taberna
faucēs
vestibulum
taberna

Domus Rōmāna

the *peristȳlium* behind). Two *alae* (wings) were small rooms flanking the *ātrium*. They may have been used to receive guests. The *peristȳlium* was a garden toward the back of the house. It usually had a colonnaded area along the outer perimeter and an unroofed area in the center, where the garden was located. A Roman family would spend much of its time in the peristyle, where only good friends would be welcome and where, in very hot weather, meals could even be served. Along the side of the peristyle are one or more *trīclīnia* or dining rooms. The *culīna* or kitchen was often located along the peristyle also.

Especially in city houses, there might also be a second story of rooms, and Servilia will put this area to good use during a party that you will read about.

Wealthy and ambitious Romans like Servilius acquired houses to advance their careers and reputations. Cicero, for example, owned a prominent house on the Palatine Hill. In his philosophical work *Dē Officiīs* (*On Duty*, I.138), however, Cicero preaches caution in this area.

> *Ornāta enim est dignitās domō, nōn ex domō tōta quaesīta, nec domō dominus, sed ā dominō domus honestāta est.*

In *Odēs* II.14 the poet Horace includes *domus et placens uxor* among the joys lost as we grow old and die.

In *Carmina* (*Poems*, XXIII.436) Apollinaris Sidonius, a 5th-century A.D. bishop and poet from Gaul, sings *ō dulcis domus, ō piī penātēs*, reminiscent of our "Home sweet home." In fact, *Dulce Dōmum* is the Latin title of Chapter 5 of Kenneth Graham's *Wind in the Willows*. Later on you will learn enough to understand that these words are actually rather bad Latin.

🔊 VERBA ŪTENDA

dignitās f. dignity (subject of *est*)	*ornāta* decorated	*quaesīta* sought
dulcis sweet	*penātēs* household gods	*tōta* entirely
honestāta honored	*pius, -a, -um* pious	*uxor* wife
	placens pleasing	

Latīna Hodierna

The Vocabulary of the Roman House in English

Did you notice how many terms related to a Roman house are used in English today? Sometimes the meanings are the same. Sometimes they have changed significantly.

LATIN WORD	MEANING	ENGLISH WORD	MEANING
*dom**us***	house	**dom**icile	place of residence
ātrium	greeting room	**atrium**	a large open area within a building
*vestibul**um***	corridor leading from the front door into the atrium	**vestibul**e	entry area of a building
iānitor	slave guarding the front door	**janitor**	someone who cleans and maintains a large office or residential building
peristȳlium	a colonnaded courtyard	**peristyl**e	a colonnade
culīna	kitchen	**culina**ry	pertaining to food

Orbis Terrārum Rōmānus

Pompēiī et Herculāneum

Our best knowledge of Roman houses and furnishings comes from the archaeological excavations at Pompeii and Herculaneum, two cities destroyed in the eruption of Mt. Vesuvius in 79 A.D. Preserved in the ash and lava of the volcanic eruption were not only many homes but also wall paintings and various household artifacts, including mosaics, sculpture, and even wooden bedframes, chairs, and chests.

But keep in mind that the houses in these two resort cities are not typical everyday dwellings.

Sinus Cūmānus

Pompēiī et Vesuvius hodiē

Peristŷlium Pompēiīs

QUID PUTĀS?

1. Do you think that most Americans agree with Cicero that the reputation of the owner brings prominence to the house, not vice versa? What does Cicero's statement suggest about Roman attitudes toward home and career?
2. What do you think it would be like to live in a house like that of the Servilii? Would this architecture be practical in your hometown? Why or why not?
3. The architecture of a Roman house has been called "inward," since it presents a blank face to passersby. Why might the Romans have chosen to do this?
4. How might the architecture of a Roman house reflect the climate of the area?

EXERCEĀMUS!

12-5 Scrībāmus: Answering Questions—Perfect Tense

Use the *lectiōnēs* in this chapter to write a response in Latin for each of these questions, using the perfect tense. In your reply, you should respond *Ita/Sīc* or *Nōn*, followed by a complete sentence. Follow the model.

→ Fuitne Hermēs valdē īrātus?
   Ita, valdē īrātus fuit.

1. Cucurrēruntne Hermēs et sīmia strēnuē?
2. Cēpitne sīmia Valeriae saccum furtīvē?
3. Cucurrēruntne Hermēs et sīmia tōtum per Forum longē?
4. Fuitne domus Servīliī valdē magna?
5. Habuitne Hermēs cubiculum proprium in domō Servīliā?
6. Fuitne Servīlia nāta decem annōs?
7. Habuitne Servīlia virum?
8. Habitāvitne Lūcius in aedificiō magnō in Vīminālī?

12-6 **Colloquāmur**

Ask a classmate any one of the questions in Exercise 12-5. The classmate should respond *Ita/Sīc* or *Nōn*, followed by a complete sentence.

12-7 **Verba Discenda**

Use the *Verba Discenda* to answer the following questions.

1. Give the first principal part of these verb forms: *fūgimus, studuit, vīcistis, dormīvit*.

2. Find the four numbers in the *Verba Discenda* and give their English equivalents. Remember that these numbers are indeclinable—this means that they do not show case or gender.

3. Make a list of the four *Verba Discenda* that are special verbs that take the dative. Then use the 1st principal part in a short Latin sentence illustrating this use of the dative. Finally, translate the Latin sentence into English.

4. Make a list of the three *Verba Discenda* that are impersonal verbs. Add an infinitive to this impersonal verb. Then translate this Latin phrase into English.

🔊 VERBA DISCENDA

annus, -ī m. year [annual]
cēna, -ae f. dinner
cēnō (1) dine
cubiculum, -ī n. bedroom [cubicle]
decem ten [December]
dormiō, dormīre, dormīvī / dormiī, dormītum sleep [dormant, dormitory]
duodecim twelve
fugiō, fugere, fūgī, fugitum flee [fugitive]

habitō (1) live in, inhabit [habitat]
nātus, -a, -um born, *xx, annōs; natus est* = is xx years old [natal]
necesse est (+ inf.) it is necessary to
noceō, nocēre, nocuī, nocitum (+ dat.) harm, do injury to [noxious, innocent]
octō eight [octave, October]

oportet, oportuit (+ inf.) one ought; it is necessary, proper to
parcō, parcere, pepercī / parsī / parcuī, parsūrus (+ dat.) spare, pardon, show mercy to
parō (1) prepare, make ready [preparation]
placet, placēre, placuit, placitum (+ dat.) please, be pleasing to;

placet (+ inf.) "it is pleasing to" [placebo]
pugnō (1) fight [pugnacious]
studeō, studēre, studuī (+ dat.) to devote oneself to, be eager for [studious]
vīgintī twenty
vincō, vincere, vīcī, victum conquer [invincible]

Angulus Grammaticus

Natural vs. Grammatical Gender

We have already talked about how gender in Latin is more grammatical than natural. So most 1st declension nouns are feminine and most 2nd declension nouns are masculine or neuter. But there are exceptions.

- The first declension has **some** masculine nouns.

The more common ones are sometimes called the **PAINS** words.

P	*poēta* (poet), *pīrāta* (pirate)
A	*agricola* (farmer)
I	*incola* (inhabitant)
N	*nauta* (sailor)
S	*scrība* (scribe)

Notice how most of these tend to be naturally masculine (at least from an ancient Roman point of view). Some can be either masculine or feminine:

advena, -ae	foreigner, stranger
convīva, -ae	dining partner, guest
sīmia, -ae	monkey

Such words are often said to have "common" gender.

- **The second declension has some feminine nouns** including *domus, -i* f. house. Also, most trees are feminine in Latin (they were associated with nymphs), and thus most second declension trees are feminine.

fraxinus, fraxinī	ash tree
mālus, mālī	apple tree
pīnus, pīnī	pine tree
ficus, ficī	fig tree

Gemma

Trees may be feminine but the gender of their fruit can vary. The figs Valeria sells are feminine but apples (*pŏma* or *māla*) are neuter.

Now see how this works with agreement of adjectives:

agricola Rōmānus
poētae bonī
nautās territōs
mālus mala (= a bad apple tree! Note the macron.)

Māter et Fīlia
The J. Paul Getty Museum/Getty Villa Museum

GRAMMATICA
The 3rd Declension
3rd Declension Nouns and 2-1-2 Adjectives

MŌRĒS RŌMĀNĪ
Echoes of Catullus

LATĪNA HODIERNA
Latin in Modern Families

ORBIS TERRĀRUM RŌMĀNUS
Vērōna

ANGULUS GRAMMATICUS
How Multi-Faceted a Word *Quam* Is!

**LECTIŌNĒS:
FESTĪNĀ LENTĒ!
and
NĒMŌ MĒ INTELLEGIT!**

Servilia tries to tell her mother about a young man she has seen.

13

Māter et Fīlia

Lectiō Prīma

Antequam Legis

Watching for a New Declension

In *Lectiō Prīma,* Servilia tries to tell her family about her day and, especially, about her feelings for a young man named Cordus, but she finds her brothers and mother unreceptive.

In this reading we want you to look out for nouns in a new declension. You have seen some of these words before, but now we will formally introduce the **3rd declension** endings to you.

EXERCEĀMUS!

13-1 **Recognizing 3rd Declension Nouns**

In *Lectiō Prīma* all the 3rd declension nouns are marked in **bold**. As you read, make a line-by-line list of these words and indicate the case and number of each word, based on how the word is used in the sentence. You should be able to find at least one word used in each case and number (except the vocative plural). Follow the models.

Line	Word	Case	Number
→ 1	*māter*	vocative	singular
→ 3	*frātrem*	accusative	singular

Once you finish this list, see if you can make a declension chart for *frāter*.

CASE	SINGULAR	PLURAL
Nominative		
Genitive		
Dative		
Accusative	frātrem	
Ablative		
Vocative	frāter (1)	

GAIUS
VALERIUS
CATULLUS

87 AC–54 AC

FESTĪNĀ LENTĒ!

"Sed, ō **māter** cāra," clāmāvit Servīlia, "dē meō amīcō novō nōndum dīximus! Hodiē amīcam meam Naeviam visitāvī et **frātrem** eius vīdī. **Nōmen frātrī** Quīntus Naevius Cordus est, et . . ."

In culīnā fratrēs placentās petīvērunt.

5 "Festīnā lentē, filia!" respondet **māter**. "Dē amīcīs post cēnam dīcere possumus. Mox **pater** domum revenit et nōs parātae esse dēbēmus. Nunc est **tempus** quiescere et dē cēnā cōgitāre."

Lūcius "Heus! Moxne cēnāmus?" rogāvit. "Iēiūnus sum.
10 Paene mortuus sum quod multās hōrās nihil nōn ēdī! Dē amīcō **sorōris** . . ."

Marcus manum super **ōs** Lūciī posuit et "Eho, frātercule, tacē," mōnuit. "**Soror** et **māter** occupātae sunt. Venī mēcum. Aliquid cibī in culīnā invenīre possumus. **Frāter** meus mortuus esse nōn dēbet!" Duo **frātrēs** abeunt et cibum quaerunt. Caecilia post **frātrēs** clāmāvit: "Tū, Lūcī, tē lavā! Sordidus es!"

15 In culīnā **frātrēs** placentās ā coquō petīvērunt. Coquus, **nōmine** Sicō, **frātribus** duōbus placentās dedit et rīsit: "Lūcī, grātiās **frātrī** tuō agere dēbēs! **Frātrēs** māiōrēs semper **custōdēs frātrum** minōrum sunt!"

VERBA ŪTENDA

aliquid some
amīca, -ae f. (female) **friend, girlfriend**
atque and, and also, and even
cārus, -a, -um dear, expensive
cēnō (1) dine
custōs, custōdis m. guardian, protector
coquus, -ī m. cook
culīna, -ae f. kitchen
eho! here you! hey! (often followed by *tū* or a vocative)
eius her, his

eum him
festīnō (1) hasten, hurry
frāter, frātris m. brother
frāterculus, -ī m. dear brother, little brother
grātiās agere to give thanks (to), to thank
heus! hey! you there! (to draw attention)
iēiūnus, -a, -um hungry
inveniō, invenīre, invēnī find, discover
lavō, lavāre, lāvī wash
lentē slowly
māior older

manum hand
māter, mātris f. mother
minōris younger (gen.)
mortuus, -a, -um dead
nōndum not yet
nōs we
occupātus, -a, -um busy
ōs, ōris n. mouth, face
paene almost
pater, patris m. father
placenta, -ae f. cake (Roman cakes looked more like pancakes)
quaerō, quaerere, quaesīvī / quaesiī seek, look for, ask for

quiescō, quiescere, quiēvī rest
reveniō, revenīre, revēnī come back, return
Sicō, Sicōnis m. Sico, a man's name
sordidus, -a, -um filthy
soror, sorōris f. sister
spīrō (1) breathe
taceō, tacēre, tacuī, tacitum be quiet, be silent
tē yourself
tempus, temporis n. time, season
visitō (1) visit

POSTQUAM LĒGISTĪ

Answer in Latin. The clues are in the *lectiō*.

1. What does Servilia want to talk about?
2. When does Caecilia say they will talk about Cordus?
3. What is Lucius worried about?
4. Why does Marcus tell Lucius to be quiet?
5. Where do the brothers go at the end of the *lectiō*?
6. Who is Sico?

Gemma

"*Nihil nōn ēdī*" cries the always hungry Lucius. In Latin double negatives are acceptable to show emphasis.

Grammatica A

The 3rd Declension

Third declension words are marked by the genitive singular ending *-is*. Their nominative singular forms vary widely.

Finding the stem: Remember that the stem of a noun is identified by dropping the ending of the genitive singular. This is especially important in the 3rd declension. Consider the range of stems in these 3rd declension nouns:

Nominative	Genitive	Stem
homō	*hominis*	*homin-*
frāter	*frātris*	*frātr-*
nōmen	*nōminis*	*nōmin-*

Notā Bene: English words derived from 3rd declension nouns often include the stem, not the nominative form: e.g, "hominid" from *homō, hominis*; "nominal" from *nōmen*, and "fratricide" from *frāter*. The rule is not universal, however, as you can see in "homicide," "fraternity," and "nomenclature."

Gender: All three genders appear in the 3rd declension. There are no hard and fast rules about this, but here are some general tendencies:

- Sometimes the genders are logical to us, like the genders of *pater* (m.), *māter* (f.), *frāter* (m.), and *soror* (f.).

- Words that indicate ideas or concepts often end in *-tās* and *-tūdō* and are feminine: *antīquitās, antīquitātis* (antiquity), *lībertās, lībertātis* (freedom, liberty); *longitūdō, longitūdinis* (length), and *fortitūdō, fortitūdinis* (strength, bravery).

- But the majority of words in the 3rd declension follow no easily discernable pattern. Just pay attention to the entry for the word in the vocabulary or dictionary.

Endings: Now see how the list you compiled of the 3rd declension endings in Exercise 13-1 compares to this chart.

3RD DECLENSION		
Singular	**Feminine**	**Neuter**
Nominative	soror	nōmen
Genitive	sorōr**is**	nōmin**is**
Dative	sorōr**ī**	nōmin**ī**
Accusative	sorōr**em**	nōmen
Ablative	sorōr**e**	nōmin**e**
Vocative	soror	nōmen
Plural		
Nominative	sorōr**ēs**	nōmin**a**
Genitive	sorōr**um**	nōmin**um**
Dative	sorōr**ibus**	nōmin**ibus**
Accusative	sorōr**ēs**	nōmin**a**
Ablative	sorōr**ibus**	nōmin**ibus**
Vocative	sorōr**ēs**	nōmin**a**

Notā Bene: The following statements are generally true of all declensions:

- **For all nouns**

  Within a given declension, the dative and ablative plurals are identical.
  The genitive plurals end in *-um* (puellā**rum**, virō**rum**, frātr**um**).

- **For masculine and feminine nouns**

  The accusative singular ends in *-m* (puella**m**, viru**m**, frātre**m**).
  The accusative plural ends in *-s* (puellā**s**, virō**s**, frātrē**s**).

- **For neuter nouns**

  The accusative always is identical to its nominative, singular or plural.
  All neuter nominative and accusative plurals, end in *-a* (for**a**, nōmin**a**).

In general, these rules apply to pronouns and adjectives as well as nouns, with some exceptions that you will meet later.

EXERCEĀMUS!

13-2 Substitutions: 3rd Declension

Replace the underlined 1st or 2nd declension word with the correct form of the 3rd declension word in parentheses. Follow the model.

→ Illa pēcūnia <u>fīliī</u> tuī est. (pater, patris m.)
  Illa pēcūnia <u>patris</u> tuī est.

1. Mox <u>dominus</u> domum revenit. (pater, patris m.)
2. <u>Fēminae</u> emere cēnam voluērunt. (māter, mātris f.)
3. Hodiē <u>amīcam</u> meam Naeviam visitāvī. (soror, sorōris f.)
4. Vēnditor <u>Valeriae</u> holera dedit. (māter, mātris f.)
5. Nunc fēminae <u>virō</u> appropinquāvērunt. (homō, hominis m./f.)
6. <u>Fēminārum</u> vōcēs fortēs audīvīmus. (homō, hominis m./f.)
7. Virī dē <u>cēnā</u> cogitāvērunt. (tempus, temporis n.)
8. Dē <u>amīcīs</u> post cēnam dīcere possumus. (frāter, frātris m.)
9. Caput hominis ūnum <u>nāsum</u> habet. (ōs, ōris n.)

Lectiō Secunda

Antequam Legis

More on Adjective Agreement

Now that you are more familiar with 3rd declension nouns, look for them modified by 2-1-2 adjectives in *Lectiō Secunda*. These noun adjective pairs are marked in **bold**. Think about what you learned in the last chapter about adjective agreement and see if you can see how it works with the 3rd declension.

EXERCEĀMUS!

13-3 GNC'ing with 3rd Declension Nouns

Remember that adjectives GNC with nouns. So a 2-1-2 adjective agreeing with a 3rd declension noun does not use 3rd declension endings. It stays 2-1-2 and agrees with the noun in gender, number, and case. Before you read, make a line-by-line list of the noun/adjective pairs marked in **bold** in *Lectiō Secunda*. Determine the GNC for each pair. Then translate the two words into English. Follow the model.

Line	Noun	Adjective	Gender	Number	Case	Translation
→ 1	frātrēs	iēiūnī	m.	pl.	nominative	the hungry brothers

🔊 NĒMŌ MĒ INTELLEGIT!

Postquam **frātrēs iēiūnī** abiērunt, Servīlia dīxit. "**Māter cāra**," clāmāvit fīlia, "Sī tibi placeat, audī mē dē Cordō! Ego et Naevia in peristȳliō fuimus et Cordus intrāvit. Expalluī! Spīrāre nōn potuī! Sonitus magnus in **auribus meīs** fuit!! Dīcere nōn potuī! Et tunc Cordus . . ."

Caecilia "Pāx! Tacē, mea fīlia!" inquit. "Sērius! Sērius dē Cordō cum **patre tuō** dīcere tempus est! Nunc mē in 5 culīnam īre et cum Sicōne, coquō nostrō, dē cēnā dīcere oportet." Et abiit.

Servīlia, in ātriō sōla stetit et effūsē lacrimāvit. "Nēmō mē intellegit!" clāmāvit, "Nēmō dē vītā meā cūrat! Ō mī Corde! Quam fōrmōsus es! Quam pulcher! Quam **homō rōbustus** atque nōbilis! Quam vehementer tē amō!" Sīc dīxit et ad cubiculum suum cucurrit.

In cubiculō, Servīlia librum Catullī tollit et legit. Paulō post, Servīlia 10 susurrat et dīcit,

    Cordus mihi pār deō esse vidētur
    Cordus, sī fās est, superāre deōs vidētur,
    Cordum dulciter rīdentem vīdī et omnēs sēnsūs
    ā mē fūgērunt. Nam simul atque tē aspexī,
15   Corde, mihi superest **nūlla vōx** in **ōre meō**.
    Audiō **nōmen tuum** et lingua mea torpet
    et tenuis flamma per **corpus meum** movet!
    Aurēs meae sonitū suō tintinnant!
    Et nox oculōs meōs tegit!
20 Tum Servīlia sē super lectum iēcit et rursus effūsē lacrimāvit.

Servīlia librum Catullī legit.

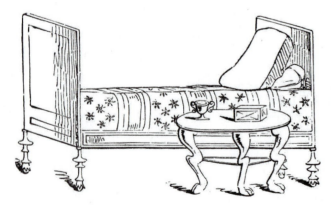

Lectus in cubiculō

Lectus antīquus

🔊 VERBA ŪTENDA

amō (1) love
aspiciō, aspicere, aspexī
    look at
ātrium, -iī n. atrium, public
    greeting room of a
    Roman house
auris, auris f. ear
cārus, -a, -um dear,
    expensive
coquus, -ī m. cook
corpus, corporis n. body
cubiculum, -ī n. bedroom
culīna, -ae f. kitchen
cūrō (1) care for
deus, -ī m. god
dulciter sweetly
effūsē a lot
expallescō, expallescere,
    expalluī turn very pale
fās est it is right

flamma, -ae, f. flame
formōsus, -a, -um
    handsome, pretty
frāter, frātris m. brother
homō, hominis m./f.
    person, human being,
    man
iaciō, -ere, iēcī throw
iēiūnus, -a, -um hungry
intellegō, intellegere,
    intellēxī, intellectum
    understand
lacrimō (1) cry, shed tears
lectus, -ī m. bed
lingua, -ae f. tongue
māter, mātris f. mother
moveō, movēre, mōvī move,
    affect
nēmō, nēminis m./f. nobody
nōbilis, -e noble

nox, noctis f. night
nullus, -a, -um no
ōs, ōris, n. mouth
pār equal
pater, patris m. father
pāx! quiet! enough!
peristȳlium, -iī n. peristyle,
    colonnaded garden
postquam after
pulcher, pulchra,
    pulchrum pretty,
    handsome
rōbustus, -a, -um strong
quam! how!
rīdentem laughing
rursus again
sē herself
sensūs senses (nom. pl.)
sērius later, too late
simul atque as soon as

sonitū suō with their own
    sound
spīrō (1) breathe
superō (1) surpass, conquer
supersum, superesse,
    superfuī be left
susurrō (1) whisper, mutter
taceō, tacēre, tacuī, taci-
    tum be quiet, be silent
tegō, tegere, texī hide, cover
tempus, temporis n. time,
    season
tenuis thin (modifies flame)
tintin(n)ō (1) ring
torpeō, torpēre, torpuī grow
    numb
ut as
vidētur (he) seems
vīta, -ae f. life
vox, vōcis f. voice

POSTQUAM LĒGISTĪ

1. Do you think that Servilia is right that no one understands her? Why?
2. What physical effect does seeing Cordus have on Servilia?
3. What does Caecilia want Servilia to do instead of talking about Cordus?
4. Does Servilia do what her mother wants her to do?
5. Where does Servilia go at the end of the *lectiō*? Where would you go under similar circumstances?
6. What does Servilia mean when she says "night covers her eyes"?
7. Are Servilia's symptoms of love sickness ever found today?

Grammatica B

3rd Declension Nouns and 2-1-2 Adjectives

Do you remember **GNC** from the last chapter? Adjectives agree with their nouns in **G**ender, **N**umber, and **C**ase. You will be especially aware of this when you see adjectives from one declension modifying nouns from another, as you did in these pairs from the last reading:

> *frātrēs iēiūnī*   *māter cāra*   *auribus meīs*

In all three phrases, a 2-1-2 adjective is describing a 3rd declension noun. Notice how the noun/adjective combination can help you determine case and number. For example, *frātrēs* can be nominative or accusative plural, but *frātrēs iēiūnī* can only be nominative. The accusative would be *frātrēs iēiūnōs*. An adjective is often the difference between a right and a wrong translation!

Here is a declension chart to help demonstrate this fact to you.

NOUN-ADJECTIVE AGREEMENT			
Singular	**Feminine**	**Masculine**	**Neuter**
Nominative	māter me**a**	pater me**us**	nōmen me**um**
Genitive	mātr**is** me**ae**	patr**is** me**ī**	nōmin**is** me**ī**
Dative	mātr**ī** me**ae**	patr**ī** me**ō**	nōmin**ī** me**ō**
Accusative	mātr**em** me**am**	patr**em** me**um**	nōmen me**um**
Ablative	mātr**e** me**ā**	patr**e** me**ō**	nōmin**e** me**ō**
Vocative	māter me**a**	pater m**ī**	nōmen me**um**
Plural			
Nominative	mātr**ēs** me**ae**	patr**ēs** me**ī**	nōmin**a** me**a**
Genitive	mātr**um** me**ārum**	patr**um** me**ōrum**	nōmin**um** me**ōrum**
Dative	mātr**ibus** me**īs**	patr**ibus** me**īs**	nōmin**ibus** me**īs**
Accusative	mātr**ēs** me**ās**	patr**ēs** me**ōs**	nōmin**a** me**a**
Ablative	mātr**ibus** me**īs**	patr**ibus** me**īs**	nōmin**ibus** me**īs**
Vocative	mātr**ēs** me**ae**	patr**ēs** me**ī**	nōmin**a** me**a**

Since the gender of a 3rd declension noun is often difficult to predict and requires memorization, it is helpful to learn a 3rd declension noun with a 2-1-2 adjective; i.e., if you learn *nōmen meum* you know right away that *nōmen* is neuter.

EXERCEĀMUS!

13-4 Adjective Agreement

Use the adjective to help you determine the GNC of the following phrases with 3rd declension nouns. Follow the model.

HINT: Those marked with an asterisk have two possibilities.

	Gender	Number	Case
→ *homō novus*	*masculine*	*singular*	*nominative*

1. mātris tuae
2. sorōrī tuae
3. fullōnēs Rōmānī
4. latrōnēs Rōmānōs
5. actōribus īrātīs*

6. tonsōrum bonōrum
7. nōmen longum*
8. frātrī parvō
9. operum perīculōsōrum
10. temporī necessāriō

11. pater fessus
12. opus perīculōsum*
13. vōce magnā
14. senātōrēs agitātī
15. opera perīculōsa*

Mōrēs Rōmānī

Echoes of Catullus

In *Lectiō Secunda* Servilia echoes the love poet Catullus, a contemporary of Caesar. She recites one of his most famous poems, specifically the one where Catullus describes the first time he laid eyes on Lesbia, his future lover.

Before you read, you might also want to think about your own experiences. If you have ever been in the presence of someone you love or with whom you are falling in love, how many of Catullus' symptoms did you experience? Catullus died about 45 years before the time of our story. Yet his description was perfect for Servilia, and aptly describes lovers today.

We have modified the original poem a bit to help you read it. We have also used combinations of boldfacing and italics to show you which words go together. With this help, in addition to the *Verba Ūtenda* below, you should be able to understand the poem.

> Ille (vir) mihi pār deō esse vidētur,
> ille, sī fās est, superāre deōs (vidētur),
> (ille) quī sedēns adversus, tē
>   identidem spectat et audit
>
> 5 *(tē)* dulciter ***rīdentem,*** quod **omnēs sēnsūs**
> ā *mē miserō* ēripit: nam simul atque, Lesbia,
> tē aspexī, mihi superest nihil
>   vōcis in ōre
>
> Sed lingua (mea) torpet, **tenuis flamma**
> 10 sub **artūs (meōs)** dēmānat, *sonitū suō*
> tintinant aurēs (meae), *gemīnā nocte*
>   oculī (meī) teguntur.

Catullus 51.1–12

🔊 VERBA ŪTENDA

adversus (+ acc.) opposite (*tē* is object)
artūs limbs (acc.)
aspiciō, aspicere, aspexī, aspectum look at
auris, auris f. ear
dēmānō (1) flow out, spread out
deus, -ī m. god
dīvus, -a, -um divine
dulce sweetly
ēripiō, -ere, ēripuī snatch
et even

fās right, proper
flamma, -ae f. flame
geminus, -a, um twin;
identidem again and again
ille he
lingua, -ae f. tongue
lūmen, lūminis n. light; "lights" = "eyes"
mihi to me
miser, misera, miserum wretched
nox, noctis f. night

ōs, ōris n. mouth
pār equal
prius formerly, in the past
quod a fact that, something which
rīdentem laughing
sedēns sitting
sēnsūs feelings (acc. pl.)
simul atque as soon as
sonitū suō with their own sound
spectō (1) look at

superō (1) conquer
supersum, superesse, superfuī be left
tenuis thin
tintin(n)ō (1) ring
torpeō, torpēre, torpuī grow numb
vidētur seems
vox, vōcis f. voice; goes with *nihil;* "nothing of voice" = "no voice"

Catullus 51 is actually a loose translation of a famous poem by the Greek poet Sappho of Lesbos. In his poem, Catullus does not mention this. He assumes that his Latin readers will recognize and appreciate how he has used Sappho's poem. In today's world, what Catullus did might be considered plagiarism or stealing someone else's literary property. In the ancient world such imitation was the highest form of praise. For example, the Roman poet Vergil used Homer's *Iliad* and *Odyssey* as close models for his long epic poem, the *Aeneid*. In the *Divine Comedy* Italian national poet Dante Alighieri (1265–1321) borrowed from the *Aeneid* many scenes and characters (including Vergil himself). Several of Shakespeare's plays are retellings of plays of Plautus and the Roman playwrights Plautus and Terence themselves modeled their comedies on earlier Greek works. In their prologues, in fact, they often tell their audiences what Greek plays they are "translating."

Although we are much more cautious about copying the work of others today, the writings of the ancient Romans are certainly past the statute of limitations for modern copyright laws. So their works and sayings have often been used and reused, worked and reworked by modern authors. To take an ancient author's works and to imitate them or to incorporate parts of them into one's own work remains a very high compliment and lends the luster of classical erudition to the modern author!

Latīna Hodierna

Latin in Modern Families

Although English words for family members like "father," "mother," "brother," and "sister" are all native English words derived from Anglo-Saxon sources, Latin words related to the family are widely used in English.

We can begin with the word "family" itself, which comes from the Latin word *familia, -ae* f. Both the Latin and English words have a wide range of meanings. Consider:

familia, -ae **f.**

In English, a "family" can refer to a household of people living together. It can also refer to all the members of the "clan" that are related to each other. Biologically, it can refer to a grouping of organisms. But the Roman word is more legal than biological in meaning. A Roman could use this word to refer to a "household," to all individuals under the legal control of a *pater familias* (father of the family), including relatives and even slaves. Some Roman wives were never legally members of their husband's family, and many Roman children were members of a family by adoption rather than birth.

Now consider how words for specific family members come into English.

LATIN WORD	MEANING	ENGLISH DERIVATIVES
pater, patris m.	father	**pater**nal, **pater**nity, **patri**cide
māter, mātris f.	mother	**mater**nal, **mater**nity, **matri**cide
fīlius, -ī m.	son	af**filia**te, af**filia**tion, **fili**al,
fīlia, -ae f.	daughter	**fili**ation
soror, sorōris f.	sister	**soror**al, **soror**ity, **soror**icide
frāter, frātris m.	brother	**frater**nal, **frater**nity, **fratri**cide
avunculus, -ī m.	mother's brother	**uncl**e, **avuncul**ar
patruus, -ī m.	father's brother	
nepos, nepōtis m.	grandson, descendant	**nepot**ism, **nep**hew
neptis, neptis f.	granddaughter	

Note that Latin had separate words for mother's brother and father's brother. The relationship between a Roman and these men is indicated by the fact that *pātruus* could also mean "a severe critic" in Latin whereas an *avunculus* was considered more loving and caring. *Nepos* means both "nephew" and "grandson" so Latin often simply said *fīlius/fīlia frātris* (brother's son/daughter) or *fīlius/fīlia sorōris* (sister's son/daughter).

Marriage was an important legal event in a woman's life. Before marriage, she was under the father's *patria potestās* (authority). After marriage, she often went under the authority of her husband and earned the status of *mātrōna*, i.e., a "married woman." There were certain political and religious activities that only married women could perform. Note that the English word "matron" has a much more limited use today.

Orbis Terrārum Rōmānus

Vērōna

The poet Catullus and the family of Valeria were all from Verona. Catullus was probably born in c. 84 B.C., when the city was part of the Roman province of *Gallia Cisalpīna* (which we visited in the *Orbis Terrārum Rōmānus* in Chapter 11). His father was said to have been a friend of Julius Caesar, who was governor of the province in 58–49 B.C. Catullus mentions Caesar, not always favorably, in some of his poems.

Vērōna in Galliā Cisalpīnā

Vērōna hodiē

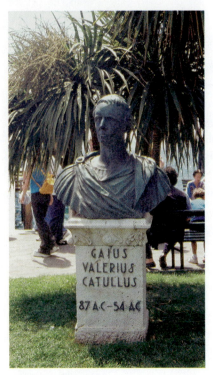

C. Valerius Catullus

Located at major crossroads in northern Italy, Verona was an important transportation center. The city became a Roman colony in 89 B.C. Residents of the city were granted Roman citizenship in 59 B.C. and ten years later the city was raised to the status of *mūnicipium* (a town subject to Rome but governed by its own laws).

By the time Valeria and her family left Verona for Rome, Augustus had changed the status of *Gallia Cisalpīna* from a province to a part of Italy.

An amphitheater, which could hold at least 20,000 spectators, was built in Verona in 70–80 A.D. This structure (now known as Arena di Verona) is one of the best preserved Roman amphitheaters and is still used today for opera performances.

QUID PUTĀS?

1. How well do you think Catullus describes the emotion of being in love?
2. Do you think modern attitudes toward copying and plagiarism have changed from the ancient Roman view, or do today's poets and authors do much the same thing?
3. The English word "matron" comes from the Latin *mātrōna* (wife, matron). Would you call your mother or wife a matron? When would you use the word "matron" in English? How is the word used in England?
4. Relate the English word "nepotism" to the meaning of the Latin word *nepos, -ōtis* m. grandson.
5. List two modern literary works based directly on the work of an ancient Roman author.

EXERCEĀMUS!

13-5 Colloquāmur

Pick a partner. Take turns describing your family to each other. Use the following questions to get started. Follow the model. Don't worry about making mistakes. Just try to communicate! Additional vocabulary you may need:

grandfather	*avus, -ī* m.
grandmother	*avia, -ae* f.
stepbrother	*vītricī fīlius* (acc. *vītricī fīlium*)
stepfather	*vītricus, -ī* m.
stepmother	*noverca, -ae* f.
stepsister	*novercae fīlia*
twin	*geminus, -ī* m.

→ Habēsne frātrem in familiā tuā?   *Ita, trēs frātrēs habeō!*   *Frātrēs nōn habeō.*

1. Habēsne frātrem minōrem (younger)?
2. Habēsne frātrem māiōrem (older)?
3. Habēsne sorōrem in familiā tuā?
4. Habēsne sorōrem minōrem?
5. Habēsne sorōrem maiōrem?
6. Suntne geminī in familiā tuā?
7. Estne avus aut avia in familiā tuā?
8. Habēsne cubiculum tuum in domō?
9. Estne soror aut frāter in cubiculō tuō?

13-6 Scrībāmus

Write a short paragraph in Latin that describes your family. You can use phrases from the previous exercise and from the readings in this chapter. You could also refer back to the description of the Servilian family in *Lectiō Secunda* of Chapter 12. When you need to refer to numbers you do not know (but that you will learn soon) feel free simply to write the number as a number—use Roman numerals if you know how! We have begun a sample paragraph for you.

→ In meā familiā sumus ego, pater meus, māter mea, I (ūnus) frāter et III (trēs) sorōrēs. Meus frāter XIII annōs nātus est et mea soror VIII annōs nāta est. In familiā ūna avia et duo avī sunt. Mea māter trēs frātrēs sed sorōrem nōn habet . . .

13-7 Verba Discenda

Use an English dictionary, if necessary, to find at least one additional English derivative for ten of the *Verba Discenda*. See if you can use the meaning of the Latin word to define each English derivative.

Here is one to get you started:

amorous, from *amō* "pertaining to **love**"

Gemma

Why do you think Jules Verne named the main character in *Two Thousand Leagues Under the Sea* Captain Nemo?

🔊 VERBA DISCENDA

amīca, -ae f. friend, girlfriend [amicable]

amō (1) love [amity]

cārus, -a, -um dear, expensive

cūrō (1) care for [curative]

frāter, frātris m. brother [fraternal]

homō, hominis m./f. person, human being, man [hominid]

iēiūnus, -a, -um hungry [jejune]

intellegō, intellegere, intellexī, intellectum understand [intellect]

māter, mātris f. mother [maternal]

nēmō, nēminis m./f. nobody

ōs, ōris n. mouth, face [oral]

pater, patris m. father [paternal, paternity]

pulcher, pulchra, pulchrum pretty, handsome [pulchritude]

quam! how!

soror, sorōris f. sister [sorority]

taceō, tacēre, tacuī, tacitum be quiet, be silent [tacit]

tempus, temporis n. time, season [temporal]

vīta, -ae f. life [vital, vitality]

Angulus Grammaticus

How Multi-Faceted a Word *Quam* Is!

Quam is one of a number of Latin words that can have widely different meanings depending on context. In this chapter you have seen how *quam* is used in Latin to introduce the exclamation "How!" in phrases like the following:

Quam formōsus est!
Quam pulcher!
Quam nōbilis atque rōbustus!
Quam vehementer tē amō!

In all of these cases, *quam* is an adverb modifiying an adjective or an adverb to create expressions like "How handsome!" or "How strongly!"

Until now you have mostly seen *quam* used to mean "than" in expressions like:

> *Sīmia mē amat magis* **quam** *puer.*
> *Sedēre in lectīcā melius est* **quam** *ambulāre in viā.*

In this case, *quam* is used to express a comparison, i.e., to show that something is more "X" than something else.

Finally, you have seen *quam* used with *tam* to mean "as X as."

> *Puer tam fortis* **quam** *pater suus est.*

Later on, you will find out that *quam* can also mean "whom" or "which." It can also mean "as X as possible" with a superlative adjective or adverb, like *quam fortissimus* (as strong as possible) or *quam fortissimē* (as strongly as possible).

So, how can you know how to translate *quam* when you see it? Well, your best guide is to pay attention to *quam*'s surroundings. For example, if *quam* is at the beginning of a sentence ending in an exclamation point, it probably means "How!" If *quam* is used with a comparative like *magis* or *melius* it probably means "than."

English does the same sort of thing even more frequently than Latin does. For example, think of all the ways the word "iron" can be used in English. As a noun, the word "iron" can refer to an element, a household tool, and a golf club. And it can also be a verb meaning "to iron clothing" or "to iron out a problem." Or it can be an adjective as in the phrase "an iron rod." How do we know what "iron" means in English? The same way we do in Latin. By context!

14

Dē Perseō

Acrisius, Danaēque Perseus Infansque et Arca
Attic red-figured hydria, attributed to the Gallatin
Painter, from Gela, ca. 490 B.C. H: 0.417 m, D: 0.27 m.
Francis Bartlett Fund. Courtesy, Museum of Fine Arts,
Boston

Lectiō Prīma

Antequam Legis

The astrologer told Licinia that her child would be a new Perseus, the Greek hero who decapitated the Gorgon Medusa and rescued the Ethiopian princess Andromeda from a sea monster. In this reading you will learn about Perseus' birth and his early adventures. Acrisius, king of the Argives, had heard that any son of his daughter, Danaë, would overthrow him. So he shut her up in a bronze chamber. But this was no impediment to Jupiter, who visited Danaë in the form of a golden rain shower. Danaë tried to keep hidden the resulting child, Perseus, but to no avail. Our story picks up when Acrisius is planning to do away with Perseus.

2nd Declension Nouns and Adjectives in *-er*

As you read the story of Perseus and his mother, watch out for 2nd declension words like *liber, librī* (book) and *ager, agrī* (field). They are 2nd declension words with nominative singulars in *-er* instead of *-us*. All the other endings are the same 2nd declension endings you already know. Look for more of these 2nd declension *-er* words (*puer* "boy" and *pulcher* "pretty") marked in **bold**.

Substantives

Also look in the *lectiō* for adjectives that stand by themselves and are not associated with any expressed noun. These words, which act as if they are nouns, are called **substantives**. In order to translate substantives, determine their gender and number and add "man/men," "woman/women," "one/ones/people," or "thing/things" accordingly. Thus, in *Lectiō Prīma* you have:

multa	= many things
omnia	= all things
parvus	= the small one
territōs	= the terrifed ones/people
quīdam	= certain people

We have marked all the substantives in the *lectiō* in ***bold italics***.

LECTIŌNĒS:
PERSEUS INFANS
and
DANAĒ ET DICTYS

Here you read about Perseus, the Greek hero to whom Licinia's unborn child was compared in Chapter 10.

EXERCEĀMUS!

14-1   Derivatives

Before you read the story about Perseus, use the English words in parentheses to help you match the Latin word in column A with its meaning in column B. This will help with the vocabulary you will see in the chapter.

	A		B
_____	1. *arcā* (ark)	A.	sleep
_____	2. *dormit* (dormitory)	B.	afraid
_____	3. *inclūdunt* (enclose)	C.	mother
_____	4. *ligneam* (ligneous)	D.	storm
_____	5. *mare* (marine)	E.	wooden
_____	6. *māter* (maternal)	F.	greatest
_____	7. *maximus* (maximum)	G.	chest, box
_____	8. *narrant* (narrate)	H.	sea
_____	9. *tempestās* (tempest)	I.	tell
_____	10. *territōs* (terrified)	J.	shut in

Watch for these words in the following story about the Greek hero Perseus.

PERSEUS INFANS

Astrologus **bona** Liciniae dīxit: "Infans tuus tam fortis quam maximus hērōs Graecus Perseus erit!" Poētae Rōmānī **multa** dē Perseō in **librīs** narrant. Perseus fīlius Iovis, rēgis deōrum, fuit; avus eius, Acrisius nōmine, rex Argōrum in Graeciā fuit.

Acrisius **puerum** interficere cupit; servī Acrisiī igitur arcam ligneam faciunt. Perseum parvum capiunt et in arcā cum mātre **pulchrā** includunt. Tum arcam in mare coniciunt. Danaē, Perseī māter, magnopere territa est; enim
5   tempestās magna mare turbat. **Parvus** autem in mātris cārae brācchiīs dormit. Quid futūrum infanti est?

Iuppiter tamen **omnia** videt, et fīlium suum servāre cupit. Igitur mare tranquillum facit et arcam ad insulam Serīphum perdūcit. Postquam arca ad lītus advenit, Danaē infansque in harēnā quiescunt. Post breve tempus **quīdam** mātrem et infantem inveniunt et **territōs** per **agrōs** ad rēgis frātrem addūcunt. (Nōmen frātrī Dictys est.)

VERBA ŪTENDA

addūcō, addūcere, addūxī
  bring in, lead to
ager, agrī m. field
arca, -ae f. chest
Argī, Argōrum m. pl. the
  people of Argos, a city in
  Greece; Argives
autem however
avus, -ī m. grandfather
brāc(c)hium, -iī n. arm
brevis, breve short
coniciō, conicere, coniēcī
  hurl, cast
Danaē, Danaēs f., Danaë,
  Perseus' mother
**deus, -ī m. god; dī
  (alternate nom. pl.)**

Dictys, -yos m. Dictys,
  brother of the king of
  Seriphos
eius his
enim for
erit (he) will be
futūrum, -ī n. future
harēna, -ae f. sand
igitur therefore
inclūdō, inclūdere, inclūsī
  shut in, enclose
infans, infantis m./f. infant
insula, -ae f. translate as "island" here, referring to
  Seriphos
**interficiō, interficere,
  interfēcī, interfectum kill**

**inveniō, invenīre, invēnī,
  inventum find, discover**
Iuppiter, Iovis m. Jupiter,
  king of the gods
liber, librī m. book
ligneus, -a, -um wooden
lītus, lītoris n. shore
magnopere greatly
mare, maris n. sea
maximus, -a, -um
  very great
narrō (1) say, tell
omnia "all things," everything
perdūcō, perdūcere, perdūxī
  conduct, bring through
Perseus, -eī m. Perseus

poēta, -ae m. poet
Polydectes, -is m.
  Polydectes, king of
  Seriphos
postquam after
quīdam some men
**quiescō, quiescere, quiēvī,
  quiētum rest**
rex, rēgis m. king
servō (1) save, protect
tamen nevertheless
tempestās, tempestātis f.
  storm
territus -a, -um afraid
tranquillus, -a, -um still,
  peaceful
turbō (1) disturb

POSTQUAM LĒGISTĪ

Try to answer these questions in both Latin and English.

1. What is Perseus' relationship with each of the following: Jupiter, Acrisius, and Danaë?
2. How does Acrisius try to kill Perseus?
3. Why is Perseus not afraid?
4. Who finds Perseus and his mother? Who gives them sanctuary?
5. What happens to Perseus and Danaë at the end of *Lectiō Prīma*?

Gemma

Notice the unusual genitive endings for *Danaē* and *Dictys*. These names are Greek and retain Greek genitive endings in Latin.

Grammatica A

2nd Declension Nouns in *-er*

Some masculine words of the second declension have a nominative singular ending in *-er* instead of *-us*. These include the following *Verba Discenda*:

> *ager, agrī* m. field   *liber, librī* m. book   *puer, puerī* m. boy

Notā Bene:

- Sometimes the stem loses the "e" as in *liber, librī* and *ager, agrī*.
- Other stems retain the "e" as in *puer, puerī*.
- English derivatives can help you know whether the "e" stays or drops out: "library," "puerile," and "agriculture." You do not, after all, go to the liberary to read a book on "agericulture"!
- The other endings of the declension remain unchanged.
- The vocative is the same as the nominative.

	SINGULAR		PLURAL	
Nominative	liber	puer	librī	puerī
Genitive	librī	puerī	librōrum	puerōrum
Dative	librō	puerō	librīs	puerīs
Accusative	librum	puerum	librōs	puerōs
Ablative	librō	puerō	librīs	puerīs
Vocative	liber	puer	librī	puerī

2nd Declension Adjectives in *-er*

Some 2-1-2 adjectives work the same way. Consider these *Verba Discenda*:

> **līber, lībera, līberum free**
> **pulcher, pulchra, pulchrum pretty, handsome**

"What is going on with the stem of *pulcher*?" you may ask. Is it *pulcher* or *pulchr-*? It is the latter. But the stem of *līber* is *līber-*. **You find the stem of an adjective by dropping the ending from the nominative singular feminine form.** That is why vocabularies and lexicons give you the entire nominative singular as an entry. Thus:

pulcher, pulchra, pulchrum ⟶ stem *pulchr-*
līber, lībera, līberum ⟶ stem *līber-* (not to be confused with the short *-i* noun
                                          libr-, book)

Notā Bene:

- English helps once more. Consider: "If you doubt my spelling of **pulchr**itude, you are at **liber**ty to look it up in the **libr**ary!"
- *līberī, -ōrum* (m. pl. substantive) means "children"—the non-adults in the house who were "the free ones." The others, of course, were slaves.

Substantives

Look closely at the words in bold in these sentences:

Poētae **multa** *dē Perseō narrant.*	The poets tell **many things** about Perseus.
Iuppiter **omnia** *vīdit.*	Jupiter saw **all things**.
Multa varia *vīdērunt.*	They saw **many different things**.
Astrologī **multa** *dē* **multīs** *dīcunt.*	Astrologers say **many things** (much) about **many things**.

All of the words in bold are examples of **substantives** or adjectives being used as nouns. Another way to explain this is to say that the adjective agrees with the gender, number, and case of a noun understood but not expressed. When we translate Latin substantives into English, we usually need to supply the understood noun. So in the sentence

Virī circumstant et **multa** *dīcunt.*

multa is neuter accusative plural with "things" understood.

Here are some other examples where the understood noun is very clear:

Bonus venit.	The good man is coming.
Bona venit.	The good woman is coming.
Bonum venit.	A good thing is coming.
Bonī veniunt.	Good men are coming.
Bonae veniunt.	Good women are coming.
Bona veniunt.	Good things are coming.

Sometimes you can only tell from context how to translate a substantive. For example, in the sentence

Virī dē bonīs dīcunt.

the substantive *bonīs* can be translated as "good men," "good women," or "good things" depending on the context and what went before.

Sometimes the verb helps you sort things out. Compare the following two sentences. The verb in each sentence tells us how to translate *mala* the way we do.

*Mala celeriter adveni**t**.*	The bad woman is approaching quickly.
*Mala celeriter adveniu**nt**.*	Bad things are approaching quickly.

Now let's see some substantives in action. Democritus was a fifth-century pre-Socratic philosopher who theorized that the essential elements of matter were indivisable elements called, in Greek, *atomī* (literally, "those things that cannot be cut"). Cicero uses a series of neuter plural accusative substantives in this description of the extent of Democritus' wisdom. These substantitives are all marked in **bold**:

> Democritus lūminibus āmissīs **alba** discernere et **ātra** nōn poterat, at vērō **bona mala, aequa, inīqua, honesta, turpia, ūtilia, inūtilia, magna, parva** poterat.

Cicero. *Tusculan Disputations.* V.114

🔊 **VERBA ŪTENDA**

aequa "fair things"
alba "white things"
at = sed
ātra "black things" (from *āter, ātra, ātrum*)
bona "good things"
discernō, discernere distinguish

honesta "decent things"
inīqua "unfair things"
inūtilia "useless things"
lūminibus āmissīs "after he lost his lights (eyes)," i.e., when he became blind

magna "great things"
mala "bad things"
poterat he was able
turpia "vile things"
ūtilia "useful things"
vērō indeed, truly

EXERCEĀMUS!

14-2   Substantives

Choose the correct translation of the substantive underlined in each of the following sentences. Remember to translate a neuter as "thing/things," a feminine as "woman/women," and a masculine as "man/men."

1. <u>Multī</u> dē theātrō dīcunt. (many men, many things, many women)

2. Valeria <u>bona</u> videt. (a good woman, good things, a good thing)

3. Puerī <u>pauca</u> dē theātrō dīcunt. (few men, few things, few women)

4. Paedagōgus <u>multa</u> audit. (many women, many things, many men)

5. Dē <u>bonō</u> māter dīcit. (a good thing, a good woman, good men)

6. Marcus <u>pulchram</u> vidēre vult. (the pretty woman, the pretty women, pretty things)

Lectiō Secunda

Antequam Legis

In *Lectiō Secunda* Danaë retells in the perfect tense the story told in the present tense in *Lectiō Prīma*. This will give you practice working with both tenses. Also note that *Lectiō Prīma* was in the 3rd person whereas *Lectiō Secunda* is mostly in the 1st person.

   This reading also introduces you to a special group of 3rd declension words called **i-stems** because an *-i-* is sometimes added to or substituted for the regular 3rd declension ending. Such words are marked in **bold** in *Lectiō Secunda*. See if you can use what you know about the 3rd declension and the context to determine how they are used.

EXERCEĀMUS!

14-3   Recognizing 3rd Declension i-Stems

Before you read *Lectiō Secunda* make a line-by-line list of all the words marked in bold. These are all 3rd declension i-stems. Indicate the case, number, and meaning of each word. Follow the model. Can you identify the ending that has an *-i-* added?

Line	Word	Case	Number	Meaning
→ 7	*mare*	accusative	singular	sea

DANAĒ ET DICTYS

Poētae multa alia dē Perseō in librīs narrant:

Dictys, ubi fēminam infantemque vīdit, "Quis es?" inquit. "Et unde tū et puer tuus vēnistis?" Danaē respondit et frātrī rēgis suam fābulam dīxit: "Nōmen mihi Danaē est. Fīlia lībera rēgis Acrisiī sum. Ūnā **nocte** Iuppiter

5 ad mē in nimbō aureō vēnit et decem post **mēnsēs** fīlium deī, Perseum nōmine, peperī. Pater meus, avus infantis, eum interficere voluit. Ergō nōs in arcā posuit et in **mare** iēcit. Sed tūtī hūc vēnimus. Virī tuī nōs invēnērunt et per agrōs apud tē addūxērunt. Simul atque tē vīdī, tē benignum esse invēnī. Cupimus, fīlius meus et ego, domum tūtam. Concēde nōbīs, quaesō, nōmen

10 hospitum et nōn **hostium**. Nōn **hostēs** sed hospitēs sumus. Parce nōbīs et concēde nōbīs **ignem** et aquam. In insulā tuā concēde **sēdem** tūtam."

Ubi Dictys mātrem et parvum benignē excēpit, Danaē respondit: "Mihi filiōque **sēdem** tūtam in **fīnibus** tuīs dedistī. Hoc dōnum libenter accipiō." Sīc Danaē laeta prō tantō beneficiō hominī bonō et deīs grātiās ēgit. Ergō

15 māter filiusque multōs annōs ibi habitāvērunt et multōs annōs Perseus cum mātre cārā vītam beātam ēgit.

Perseus et Danaē

VERBA ŪTENDA

accipiō, accipere, accēpī accept, receive
addūcō, adducere, addūxī lead to
ager, agrī m. field
alia other "things"
apud tē "to your house"
aureus, -a, -um golden
avus, -ī m. grandfather
beātus, -a, -um blessed, happy
benignē kindly
benignus, -a, -um kind
beneficium, -ī n. favor, benefit

concēdō, concēdere, concessī grant
cum when
deus, -ī m. god; ***dī*** (alternate nom. pl.)
dōnum, -ī n. gift
eram "I was"
eum him
excipiō, excipere, excēpī receive
fīnis, fīnis m. end; pl. country, territory
grātiās agere to thank
hoc this
hospes, hospitis m./f. guest, stranger

hostis, hostis m./f. stranger, foreigner, enemy; pl. the enemy
hūc to this place
iaciō, iacere, iēcī throw
ibi there
ignis, ignis m. fire
infans, infantis m./f. infant
interficiō, interficere, interfēcī, interfectum kill
inveniō, invenīre, invēnī, inventum find, discover
libenter freely, willingly
liber, librī m. book
līber, lībera, līberum free
mare, maris n. sea
mensis, mensis f. month

nimbus, -ī m. cloud
nōbīs to us
nox, noctis f. night
pariō, parere, peperī give birth to
poēta, -ae m. poet
posteā afterward, then
quaesō, -ere, quaesivī / quaesiī ask, beg
rex, rēgis m. king
sēdēs, sēdis f. seat, home, residence
simul atque as soon as
tantus, -a, -um so great a
territus -a, -um afraid
tūtus, -a, -um safe
unde from where

POSTQUAM LĒGISTĪ

Try to answer these questions in both Latin and English.

1. What questions does Dictys ask when he sees Danaë?
2. What new details does Danaë add to the story you read in *Lectiō Prīma* about what happened in Argos?

3. Why does Danaë mention *hostēs* in line 10?
4. What do you think happens next in the story?

Grammatica B

3rd Declension i-Stems

You have just seen how there is a special group of 2nd declension nouns with nominative singulars ending in *-er*. In the 3rd declension there is a special group of nouns that are notable for the presence of an *-i* in certain endings. These are called **3rd declension i-stems**. You saw several of these words in *Lectiō Secunda*. All of them are *Verba Discenda*.

> *fīnis, fīnis* m. end
> *hostis, hostis* m./f. enemy
> *mare, maris* n. sea
> *nox, noctis* f. night
> *sēdēs, sēdis* f. seat, home

As the following chart shows, i-stems differ in only a few spots from the "regular" 3rd declension endings. We have marked the different endings with an asterisk.

	3RD REGULAR	MASC./FEM. I-STEM	NEUTER I-STEM
Singular			
Nominative	homō	ignis	mare
Genitive	homin**is**	ign**is**	mar**is**
Dative	homin**ī**	ign**ī**	mar**ī**
Accusative	homin**em**	ign**em**	mare
Ablative	homin**e**	ign**e** or ign**ī***	mar**ī***
Plural			
Nominative	homin**ēs**	ign**ēs** or ign**īs***	mar**ia***
Genitive	homin**um**	ign**ium***	mar**ium***
Dative	homin**ibus**	ign**ibus**	mar**ibus**
Accusative	homin**ēs**	ign**ēs** or ign**īs***	mar**ia***
Ablative	homin**ibus**	ign**ibus**	mar**ibus**

Generally you do not need to know which nouns are i-stems, as long as you recognize *-ium* as an alternative genitive plural ending and *-ī* and *-ia* an alternative neuter endings. But here are some rules to determine whether a 3rd declension noun is an i-stem:

Masculine and Feminine

1. **Parisyllabic rule:** if the nominative ends in *-is* or *-ēs* and the genitive singular has the same number of syllables as the nominative:

> *aedēs, aedis* f. building, temple
> *hostis, hostis* m./f. enemy
> *mensis, mensis*, f. month

2. **Double consonant rule:** if the stem of the noun ends in two consonants:

mens, mentis f. mind
mons, montis m. mountain
nox, noctis f. night

3. **Neuters:** If the neuter nominative singular ends in *-e, -al,* or *-ar*:

animal, -ālis n. animal
exemplar, -āris n. example
mare, maris n. sea

Notā Bene:

- There are notable exceptions to the rules. For example, *canis, canis* m./f. "dog", *infans, infantis* m./f., and *iuvenis, -is* "youth, young man" should act like i-stems but do not.
- The ablative singular of masculine and feminine i-stems varies between *-e* and *-ī*. Be on the lookout for either. Neuter *-i* stems almost always have the *-ī*. Thus, *animalī*.
- Some older words in the language had an *-i* in every case ending. Sometimes these are called "pure" i-stems. Thus you will encounter forms like *Tiberim* (accusative singular for the river Tiber) and *tussīs* (nom./acc. pl.) "cough." In context, these will not cause much of a problem.

Summary

- I-stems are only found in the 3rd declension.
- I-stem endings only differ from regular 3rd declension endings in the following instances:

All genders	i-stems → gen. pl.	*-ium*
Masc. and fem.	abl. sing.	sometimes *-ī*
	nom./acc. pl.	sometimes *-īs*
Neuter i-stems →	abl. sing	*-ī* (almost always)
	nom./acc. pl	*-ia*

EXERCEĀMUS!

14-4 i-Stems

Make the nominative and genitive plural forms of each of the following i-stem nouns.
HINT: Remember how the special *-ium* and *-ia* endings are used.

1. hostis, hostis m./f.
2. nox, noctis f.
3. sēdēs, sēdis f.
4. mare, maris n.
5. animal, animālis n.
6. mons, montis m.
7. ignis, ignis m.
8. aedēs, aedis f.

Deceptive Pairs—Agreement Review

Now consider the following phrases from the *lectiōnēs*:

tempestās magna   a great storm
pater meus   my father
hominī bonō   to the good man

Notice that in each case the adjective does not have the same ending as the word it modifies. Nevertheless, the adjective agrees (GNCs) with its noun in gender, number, and case. Thus

tempestās magna   feminine singular nominative
pater meus   masculine singular nominative
hominī bonō   masculine singular dative

Latīna Hodierna

Liberty and Libraries

English has two words that mean basically the same thing: "freedom" (an Anglo-Saxon–based word) and "liberty," which finds its origin in the Latin adjective *līber* (free). In Latin, the equivalent of "liberty" is *lībertās, lībertātis* f.

Compare these cognates of *lībertās, lībertātis* f. in some Romance languages:

liberté	French
libertad	Spanish
libertà	Italian
liberdade	Portuguese

Now consider how many other English words are related to the Latin word *līber*.

liberal	liberate	libertarian
liberalism	liberation	libertine
liberality	Liberia	libertinism
liberalize		

Can you see the "freedom" in each of those words?

Now consider why the words "library" and "librarian" were not included in that list. This is because these two words are derived from *liber, librī* m. (book) rather than *līber, lībera, līberum* (free). It is easy to distinguish them if you remember that *libr-* is the Latin stem for "book" whereas *liber-* is the Latin stem for "free."

Finally, look at these Latin words dealing with books:

librārius, -a, -um related to books
librārius, -iī m. someone who copies books (keep in mind that all ancient
     books were "manuscripts," i.e., they were written by hand)
librārium, -iī n. a bookcase
taberna librāria a book store
bibliothēca, -ae f. a book collection, a library (a Latin word borrowing from
     the Greek, meaning "book repository")

Notice how both English and Romance languages have borrowed from these Latin words. (But note that Latin borrowed *bibliothēca* from Greek.)

Latin	*librārium, -iī* n. a bookcase	*bibliothēca, -ae* f. a library
English	library	bibliotheca (a book collection)
French	librairie (bookstore)	bibliothèque
Italian	libreria (bookstore or bookcase)	biblioteca
Spanish	librería (bookstore or bookcase)	biblioteca

Librī

Mōrēs Rōmānī

Romans and Greek Myth

Although Perseus was a Greek hero, he was well known by Romans who liked to hear his story or see it depicted in art. The Roman poet Ovid, for example, described the hero's adventures, including his conception by Zeus in a shower of gold, in the *Metamorphoses* (*Changes of Shape*). All of the stories in this poem deal with humans and gods changing their shape. The disguise Zeus used in his encounter with Danaë is an example of such a metamorphosis.

The Romans were fond of linking tales about Greek heroes with their own legends. For example, they could easily compare Acrisius' attempt to kill his grandson with a similar effort by king Numitor to dispose of his daughter's twin sons, Romulus and Remus, who eventually founded the city of Rome. Both grandfathers set their grandsons adrift on water, Perseus in the chest and Romulus and Remus in a reed basket on the bank of the Tiber River, where they were nursed by a she-wolf and discovered by a shepherd named Faustulus. The nursing wolf became an important symbol of Rome, and images of Romulus, Remus, and the she-wolf are proudly displayed in Rome to this day.

Here is a simplified version of the story of Romulus and Remus as told by the historian Livy in book one of *Ab Urbe Conditā* (*From the Founding of the City*):

Lupa in Capitōliō

Sed fāta statuērunt, ut opīnor, orīginem tantae urbis et principium maximī imperiī. Vestālis geminum partum ēdidit et Martem incertae stirpis patrem nuncupāvit. Sed nec dī nec hominēs aut ipsam aut stirpem ā crūdēlitate rēgis, patris suī, vindicāvērunt. Rex iussit fēminam in custōdiam darī et puerōs in aquam pōnī. Servī puerum in alveō in aquā exposuērunt, sed tenuis aqua alveum in siccō destituit. Tunc lupa sitiens ē montibus quī circā erant ad vāgītum puerōrum vēnit et infantibus mammās dedit. Magister pecoris—cui Faustulus nōmen erat—lupam puerōs linguā lambentem invēnit. Faustulus puerōs ad stabula portāvit et Larentiae uxōrī dedit. Faustulus et Larentia puerōs ut suōs ēdūxērunt.

🔊 VERBA ŪTENDA

alveus, -eī m. tub, basin
circā round about
crūdēlitās, -tātis f. cruelty
cui to whom
custōdia, -ae f. custody
darī to be given
destituō, destituere, destituī leave
deus, -ī m. god; dī (alternate nom. pl.)
ēdō, ēdere, ēdidī beget
ēdūcō, ēdūcere, ēdūxī rear, raise
erant were

expositus, -a, -um exposed
fātum, -ī n. fate
geminus, -a, -um twin
imperium, -ī n. rule, empire
incertus, -a, -um uncertain, illegitimate
infans, infantis m./f. infant
inveniō, invenīre, invēnī, inventum find, discover
ipsam herself
iubeō, iubēre, iussī order
lambentem licking
lingua, -ae f. tongue
lupa, -ae f. she-wolf

mamma, -ae f. breast
Mars, Martis m. Mars, god of war
maximus, -a, -um greatest
mons, montis m. mountain
nuncupō (1) name
opīnor I believe; the subject is Livy
orīgō, -ginis f. origin
partum birth
pecus, pecoris n. herd
principium, -ī n. beginning
quī which
rex, rēgis m. king

siccum, -ī n. dry land
sitiens thirsty
stabulum, -ī n. stable
statuō, statuere, statuī decree
stirps, stirpis f. offspring, children
tantus -a, -um so great
tenuis mild
urbs, urbis f. city (Rome)
ut as
uxor, uxōris f. wife
vāgītum crying
Vestālis, Vestālis f. Vestal virgin
vindicō (1) protect

Orbis Terrārum Rōmānus

Palātium

The story of Romulus and Remus is especially associated with the Palatine Hill (*Palātium, -ī* n.), which you already know is one of the most important of the seven hills of Rome. In fact, it was on this hill that the emperors built their palaces. Even more important in Roman history and tradition is the association of the Palatine with Romulus and Remus, and thus with the early history of Rome and Roman religion. The life-sized bronze statue of a she-wolf (depicted above), now in the Capitoline Museum in Rome, has traditionally been dated to the 5th century B.C. while the bronze figures of the infants Romulus and Remus were added in the Renaissance.

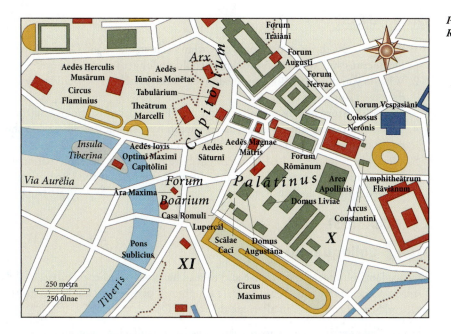

Potesne invenīre Casa Romulī in Palātiō?

The Romans revered the *Casa Romulī* ("Hut of Romulus") on the Palatine Hill. Ancient sources tell us that this hut, considered a sacred shrine, was rebuilt in a traditional oval shape every time the old one was destroyed by fire or fell into permanent disrepair. Several Iron Age (8th century B.C.) circular houses have been found near this spot.

By tradition the Lupercal (*Lupercal, -ālis* n.) or the cave of the she-wolf who nursed Romulus and Remus, was also located on the Palatine Hill, but no physical evidence for this shrine was known until 2007, when archaeologists uncovered, deep in the hill, a vaulted structure decorated with marble, mosaics, and shells, which may have been the sacred place.

Every February at the Lupercal on the Palatine, the Romans celebrated the Lupercalia (*Lupercālia, -ōrum* n. pl.), a religious festival directed by Luperci (*Lupercus, -ī* m.), or priests dressed in goatskins, who sacrificed goats on an altar at the Lupercal, smeared goat's blood on their foreheads, cut thongs from the skins of the sacrificed animals, and then, running naked around the Palatine Hill, struck female by-standers with the straps. Women struck by the straps were believed to be granted fertility and an easy childbirth. Animal sacrifice, by the way, was an important feature of Roman ritual. The association of Lupercal with fertility is carried down in the celebration of Valentine's Day at the same time of year today.

① Forum Rōmānum ② Palātium

Forum Rōmānum (ā sinistrā) et Palātium (ā dextrā)

Domus antīquissima Palātiī

QUID PUTĀS?

1. What do you think is the point of Cicero's statement about Democritus? What could Democritus still know even though he could no longer see with his eyes?
2. Why do you think the Romans liked to tell Greek myths? Why would they want to model their own stories on Greek ones?
3. How is the story of Moses similar to those of Perseus or of Romulus and Remus?
4. If someone from France or Spain asked you, in English, for the "library" in the mall, what might they actually be looking for? How did they make their error?
5. What places in the United States might have been given the same national respect and state-sponsored preservation that the Hut of Romulus and the Lupercal on the Palatine enjoyed from the ancient Romans?

EXERCEĀMUS!

14-5 Colloquāmur

One student volunteers to be Danaë and to read her story to other members of the class. After Danaë tells her story, you should prepare (in groups, perhaps) to ask her follow-up questions in Latin. Several students can alternate the role of Danaë.

Here is Danaë's script. (Dont' worry about the bold boldfacing right now.)

> Fīlia rēgis Acrisiī **sum**. Ūnā nocte in torō **eram**, cum Iuppiter ad mē in nimbō aureō vēnit. In uterō meō deī fīlium **tulī** et decem post mensēs puerum pulchrum, Perseum nōmine, **peperī**, sed infantem **celāvī** quod avus infantis eum interficere voluit. Sed in arcā ligneā hūc **vēnimus**. Domum tūtam **cupīvī**. Cum fīliō meō multōs annōs ibi **habitāvī**.

Here is one sample follow-up question.

> ⟶ Quid nōmen patrī est?

14-6 Scrībāmus

Now rewrite the script from Exercise 14-5 to retell this narrative as if you are talking **about** Danaë to Polydectes. In other words,

- Change all the 1st person verbs marked in **boldface** into 3rd person.
- Change all the 1st person pronouns and adjectives to 3rd person.
- HINT: "her" (direct object) = *eam*; "her" (adjective) = *suus, -a, -um*.

Here is a sample sentence to use as a model:

> ⟶ In uterō **meō** deī fīlium **tulī** et decem post mensēs puerum pulchrum, Perseum nōmine, **peperī** . . .

becomes

> ⟶ In uterō **suō** deī fīlium **tulit** et decem post mensēs puerum pulchrum, Perseum nōmine, **peperit** . . .

14-7 Verba Discenda

Most of these *Verba Discenda* are nouns. Make three columns and list each noun (nominative and genitive) by declension. Mark 2nd declension -*er* nouns and 3rd declension i-stems with asterisks. Follow the model.

1st Declension	2nd Declension	3rd Declension
	ager, agrī*	

🔊 VERBA DISCENDA

ager, agrī m. field
  [agriculture]
brāc(c)hium, -iī n. arm
  [brachiation]
deus, -ī m. god; **dī** (nom.
  pl.) [deify]
fīnis, fīnis m. end; pl.
  country, territory
  [finite, infinite]
futūrum, -ī n. future
  [future]

hostis, hostis m./f. stranger,
  foreigner, enemy; pl. the
  enemy [hostile]
infans, infantis m./f. infant
  [infantile]
**interficiō, interficere,
  interfēcī,
  interfectum** kill
**inveniō, invenīre,
  invēnī, inventum**
  find, discover [invention]

liber, librī m. book
  [library]
liber, lībera, līberum free
  [liberty]
mare, maris n. sea [marine]
mensis, mensis m. month
  [menstruation]
narrō (1) say, tell
  [narration]
nox, noctis f. night
  [nocturnal]

poēta, -ae m. poet
  [poetic]
**quiescō, quiescere, quiēvī,
  quiētum** rest
  [quiescent]
rex, rēgis m. king
  [regal]
sēdēs, sēdis f. seat, home,
  residence
territus, -a, -um afraid
tūtus, -a, -um safe

Angulus Grammaticus

Latin Homonyms and Homophones

Homonyms are words that have the same spelling and different meanings, like "refuse" (n.) / "refuse" (v.). **Homophones** are words that have the same sound but different meanings, like "to" / "two" / "too." Here are two pairs of Latin homonyms. Which pair are also homophones?

> *liber līber*   the free book   *līberī līberī*   the free children

Now compare these Latin homophones, distinguished only by gender:

> *mālus, -ī m.*   pole, ship's mast   *mālus, -ī f.*   apple tree

which also share this homonym:

> *malus, -a, -um*   bad

So consider these pairs where the gender of the adjective indicates the meaning of the noun:

> *mālus mala*   *mālus malus*
> the bad apple tree   the bad mast

To make matters worse, you can add the verb *mālō* (I prefer) as another homonym, and create the following Latin oddity, probably the work of bored schoolboys (who took a bit of liberty with formal grammar rules):

> *Mālō mālō mālō mālō.*
> I prefer (to be in) an apple tree than to be on a bad mast.

Benjamin Britten interpreted the last *mālō* slightly differently when he wrote his libretto for the 1954 opera *The Turn of the Screw:*

> Malo: I would rather be
> Malo: in an apple-tree
> Malo: than a naughty boy
> Malo: in adversity.

What other translations are possible, if you write it as the Romans would, without long marks?

Iuvenis Rōmāna
Picture Desk, Inc./Kobal Collection/Dagli Orti (A)

LECTIŌNĒS:
LACRIMAE IN CUBICULŌ
and
CORDUS

Marcus and Servilia talk about her
infatuation with Naevius Cordus.

15

Frāter et Soror

Lectiō Prīma

Antequam Legis

The *lectiōnēs* in this chapter continue the family conversations in the house of Servilius. In *Lectiō Prīma* Marcus has a private conversation with his sister Servilia.

3rd Declension Adjectives

In this chapter you are introduced formally to 3rd declension adjectives. You have seen some of these adjectives before. For example, in Chapter 7 Hermes used the 3rd declension adjective *omnis* (each, every; all):

> *Habeō saccum meum et **omnem** pecūniam meam.*

The astrologer used the 3rd declension adjective *fortis* (brave, strong) to describe the hero Perseus in Chapter 10:

> ***fortis** quam maximus hērōs Graecus Perseus erit!*

And Servilia used *nōbilis* (noble, notable) to describe Cordus in Chapter 13:

> *Quam homō rōbustus atque **nōbilis!***

Notice how all three adjectives have the same nominative ending (*-is*) as 3rd declension i-stem nouns like *fīnis* and *hostis*. This is because **3rd declension adjectives use i-stem endings.** Watch for these adjectives as you read *Lectiō Prīma*.

EXERCEĀMUS!

15-1 **Pre-Reading Vocabulary**

For each of the 3rd declension adjectives in column A find an English meaning and derivative in column B. Watch for some of these adjectives marked in **bold** in *Lectiō Prīma*.

	A		B
_____	1. *celer*	a.	clever, smart (an **intelligent** idea)
_____	2. *crūdēlis*	b.	exalted (a **nobl**e goal)
_____	3. *difficilis*	c.	each, all (an **omni**bus tax bill)
_____	4. *facilis*	d.	easy (a **facile** argument)
_____	5. *fortis*	e.	harsh (the **cruel** fact)
_____	6. *gravis*	f.	heavy, serious (a **grav**e situation)
_____	7. *intellegens*	g.	not easy, hard (a **diffi**cult task)
_____	8. *nōbilis*	h.	powerful (a **pot**ent medication)
_____	9. *omnis*	i.	strong (**fort**itude)
_____	10. *potens*	j.	swift (an ac**celer**ant for fire)
_____	11. *tristis*	k.	unhappy, sad (Chopin's *Valse **Triste***)

Dum ambulat in peristȳliō, librum legit.

🔊 LACRIMAE IN CUBICULŌ

Servīlia **tristis** et īrāta in cubiculō suō sedet. Marcus sorōrem suam audit et in cubiculum intrat. Marcus quoque **tristis** est quod Servīliae lacrimās vīdet et sorōrem suam valdē amat. Servīliae appropinquat et "Cūr lacrimās, soror?" rogat, "Quōmodo tē adiuvāre possum?"

"Nēmō mē," respondet Servīlia, "adiuvāre potest. Vīta tam **crūdēlis** est! Amō iuvenem
5 formōsum et **intellegentem**, Naevium Cordum nōmine, et nēmō nec dē Cordō nec dē mē cūrat!"

"Vēra nōn dīcis, soror. Ego multum cūrō. Dīc mihi **omnia** dē iuvene. Hic Cordus—nōnne frāter **māior** amīcae tuae, Naeviae, est?"

"Rectē dīcis. Hodiē Cordum in domō meae amīcae Naeviae vīdī. Adulescentem in peristȳliō vīdī et corpus **forte** et formam **nōbilem** habuit. Dum ambulat, librum lēgit et verba **potentia** ōrātiōnis Cicerōnis, optimī ōrātōris, prōnun-
10 tiāvit. Cum clāmāvit 'Quam diū etiam furor iste tuus nōs ēlūdet?' cor meum palpitāvit. Vox Cordī praeclāra et **gravis** est et iuvenis quoque praeclārus est!"

"Et ego Cordum nōvī," inquit Marcus, "amīcus meus est. Ego et Cordus artī **difficilī** rhētoricae studēmus. Et vēra dīcis—adulescens bonus est et in studiō rhētoricō perītus. In gymnasiō quoque **fortis** et **celer** est."

🔊 VERBA ŪTENDA

adiuvō, adiuvāre, adiūvī help
adulescens, -entis m./f. **youth**
ars, artis f. art, skill
celer, celeris, celere fast, swift
cor, cordis n. heart
corpus, corporis n. **body**
crūdēlis, crūdēle harsh, cruel
cum when
difficilis, difficile hard, difficult
diū long, for a long time
ēlūdet "will mock"
etiam also, even
forma, -ae f. beauty

formōsus, -a, -um handsome
fortis, forte strong, brave
furor, furōris m. fury, rage
gravis, grave heavy, serious
gymnasium, -iī n. gymnasium, open area for training
hic this
intellegens, intellegentis smart, intelligent
iste tuus "that ___ of yours"
iuvenis, iuvenis m./f. youth
lacrima, -ae f. tear
lacrimō (1) cry, shed tears

legō, legere, lēgī, lectum read, gather, choose
māior, māius greater, larger, older; m. pl. **ancestors, elders**
multum a lot
nec and not; nec…nec… neither. . .nor. . .
nōbilis, nōbile notable, noble
omnis, omne each, every; pl. all
optimus, -a, -um best
ōrātiō, -iōnis f. speech
ōrātor, -ōris m. speaker, orator

palpitō (1) beat, throb
peristȳlium, -iī n. peristyle
perītus, -a, -um experienced, skillful
potens, potentis powerful
praeclārus, -a, -um very clear, noble, excellent
prōnuntiō (1) recite, report
quōmodo how
rhētoricus, -a, -um rhetorical
tristis, triste sad
vox, vōcis f. **voice**

POSTQUAM LĒGISTĪ

Try to answer these questions in both Latin and English.

1. Describe Servilia's feelings as the *lectiō* begins. Why does she feel this way?
2. Why does Marcus come to talk to her?
3. What does this suggest to you about their relationship as brother and sister? How does this compare to brother-sister relationships you have known?
4. Servilia tries to explain her feelings to her brother. Summarize what she says.
5. Does Marcus agree with what her sister says? Why or why not?
6. Where did Servilia see Cordus and what was he doing?
7. Would an American girl typically admire a boy for doing what Cordus was doing?
8. How does Marcus know Cordus? What is his opinion of him?

Grammatica A

3rd Declension Adjectives

Latin has two major groups of adjectives:

1. 2-1-2 adjectives using endings of the 1st and 2nd declension, like:

    bonus, -a, -um   *līber, lībera, līberum*   *pulcher, pulchra, pulchrum*

2. 3rd declension adjectives using endings of the 3rd declension

    celer, celeris, celere   *fortis, forte*   *potens*

Third declension adjectives are declined like 3rd declension i-stem nouns with one exception. Try to spot it in the following chart, where we have put all the i-stem endings in **bold**. Locate the one place where the adjective differs from the pattern in the nouns.

3RD DECLENSION				
	i-Stem Nouns		**Adjectives**	
Gender	**Masc./Fem.**	**Neuter**	**Masc./Fem.**	**Neuter**
Singular				
Nominative	hostis	mare	fortis	forte
Genitive	hostis	maris	fortis	fortis
Dative	hostī	marī	fortī	fortī
Accusative	hostem	mare	fortem	forte
Ablative	hoste	marī	fortī/e	fortī
Vocative	hostis	mare	fortis	forte
Plural				
Nominative	hostēs	mar**ia**	fortēs	fort**ia**
Genitive	host**ium**	mar**ium**	fort**ium**	fort**ium**
Dative	hostibus	maribus	fortibus	fortibus
Accusative	hostēs	mar**ia**	fortēs	fort**ia**
Ablative	hostibus	maribus	fortibus	fortibus
Vocative	hostēs	mar**ia**	fortēs	fort**ia**

Notā Bene:

i-Stem Similarities

- Genitive plurals end in *-ium*
- Neuter nominative and accusative plurals end in *-ia*
- **BUT** ablative singulars can end in *-ī* for all genders (not just neuter). Note that some authors use an *-e* ending here as well.
- The dative and ablative singular of 3rd declension adjectives are identical, but you have seen the same ending serve two cases before (e.g., all dative and ablative plurals), and you know that context and the endings of the nouns and adjectives can help you sort it out:

> *Ego et Cordus **fēminae potentī** appropinquāmus.*

The word *potentī* could be dative or ablative, but the ending on the 1st declension noun tells you that it must be dative.

The 3rd declension adjectives appear in your vocabularies and dictionaries in one of three ways. Note how each of the following would be listed in a dictionary:

celer, celeris, celere	adj.	swift, quick
fortis, forte	adj.	strong
potens, potentis	adj.	powerful

Types of 3rd Declension Adjectives

Celer is a **three termination adjective**, so named because it has three distinct endings in the nominative singular—masculine, feminine, and neuter. In adjectives like this, the masculine and feminine have identical endings everywhere **but** in the nominative singular. Remember that the stem of an adjective comes from dropping the ending from the nominative feminine singular: *celer* ➔ *celer-*. Thus:

> *Virum **celerem** videō.*
> *Fēminam **celerem** videō.*
> *Animal **celere** videō.*

Celer is the only three termination adjective you will learn right now.

Fortis, forte is a **two termination adjective**. In such words, the first form is masculine and feminine and the third form is neuter. You get the stem from the first form in such an instance: *fortis* ➔ *fort-*. Thus:

> *Virum **fortem** videō.*
> *Fēminam **fortem** videō.*
> *Animal **forte** videō.*

Potens, potentis is a **one termination adjective**. In this case, the first form listed in a dictionary is masculine, feminine, and neuter nominative singular. The second form is genitive singular and is used to determine the stem of the adjective: *potentis* ➔ *potent-*. Thus:

> *Virum **potentem** videō.*
> *Fēminam **potentem** videō.*
> *Animal **potens** videō.*

This sort of adjective can be a bit confusing if you do not remember the neuter rule that the neuter nominative = the neuter accusative. But context generally helps.

Here are several common **two termination** 3rd declension adjectives. The ones marked in **bold** are *Verba Discenda* in this chapter.

crūdēlis, crūdēle cruel

difficilis, difficile not easy, harsh, difficult

dulcis, dulce sweet

facilis, facile easy

gravis, grave heavy, serious

nōbilis, nōbile dignified, noble

omnis, omne each, every (sing.); all (plural)

tristis, triste sad

Common **one-termination** 3rd declension adjectives include the following:

dīves, dīvitis rich, wealthy   *fēlix, fēlīcis* happy, fortunate   **intellegens, intellegentis clever, smart**

EXERCEĀMUS!

15-2 3rd Declension Adjectives

Identify all the possible GNCs for each of the following 3rd declension adjective forms. Note: Some words have more than one possibility. This is an important exercise because as you read along in Latin, your brain often has to decide between such options on the fly. Follow the model. Then give the meanings.

	Adjective	Gender	Number	Case	Meaning
→	intellegens	MFN	singular	nominative (MFN) accusative (N)	intelligent

1. omnēs
2. difficilia
3. tristibus
4. nōbilium

Lectiō Secunda

Antequam Legis

As you continue reading the conversation between Marcus and Servilia about Cordus in *Lectiō Secunda*, consider the following features of 3rd declension adjectives.

GNC'ing and Agreement

Now that you have learned a bit about 3rd declension adjectives, pay attention in the next reading to their **GNC**, i.e., to their agreement in gender, number, and case, especially with nouns in the 1st and 2nd declensions. Consider the phrase *Servīlia miserābilis* (miserable Servilia) in line 1 of *Lectiō Secunda*. Note how the 3rd declension adjective *miserābilis* agrees with the 1st declension noun *Servīlia*. All 3rd declension adjectives are marked in **bold** in this *lectiō*.

Substantives

Also look in *Lectiō Secunda* for some of 3rd declension adjectives used as substantives, like *omnia* (all things, everything). These are **<u>bold and underlined</u>** in the *lectiā*

Adverbs

Finally, look for **adverbs** formed from 3rd declension adjectives marked in ***bold italics*** in this reading. HINT: They end in *-iter* or *-ter* as in ***fortiter*** (strongly) from *fortis*.

EXERCEĀMUS!

15-3 More on 3rd Declension Adjectives

As you read, create a list based on the one below that shows nouns modified by 3rd declension adjectives marked in **bold** in *Lectiō Secunda*. Follow the models.

Line	Noun/Adjective	GNC	Translation
→ 1	Servīlia miserābilis	fem. nom. s.	miserable Servilia
→ 1	frātrem māiōrem	masc. acc. s.	older brother

🔊 CORDUS

Nunc Servīlia **miserābilis** frātrem **māiōrem** dē Cordō interrogat: "Et nōnne pater Cordī Naeviaeque vir **dīves potens**que est?"

"Vērē, dīcis," respondet Marcus. "Pater Augustī amīcus est et Cordus in domō imperātōris mox laborāre cupit. Quid Cordus tibi dīxit?"

5   Servīlia "Nōlī nūgās dīcere!" inquit. "Sōlum procul Cordum vīdī et audīvī. Cordum bene noscere cupiō sed hoc *faciliter* facere nōn possum!"

Frāter respondet: "Nōnne semper legis carmina poētae bonī et **intellegentis** Catullī? In carminibus Catullī multa verba apta dē amōre et **dulcī** et **trīstī** sunt! Sī Cordum nōn nōvistī, sī eum sōlum vīdistī, quōmodo eum amāre potes?"

10   "Sed Cordum noscere cupiō! Adulescens **fortis** et pulcher est! Fortasse Cordum hodiē nōn amō sed amāre volō! Potesne, fortasse, crās ad Cordum mēcum īre? Fortasse . . ."

"Et fortasse parentēs nostrī virum **nōbilem** alium tibi iam ēlēgērunt! Sīcut māter nostra semper dīcit–'Festīnā lentē!', mea soror! Pater et māter tibi vītam **fēlīcem** et optimam cupiunt. Parentēs **nōbilēs** Rōmānī marītōs filiābus suīs semper ēligunt. Sīc est mōs **māiōrum**, noster mōs Rōmānus! Quod parentēs volunt, hoc nōs facere debēmus! Et

15 Catullus tuus **omnēs** dē perīculīs **gravibus** amōris monet. Festīnā lentē!"

"Sed **difficile** est!" Servīlia clāmat *miserābiliter*.

Marcus **tristis** "Ita, vērō," inquit. "Sērius, post cēnam, patrī dē Cordō tuō dīcam. Crēde mihi, nōs **omnēs**—ego, māter, pater, Lūcius—vērē tē **fēlicem** esse cupimus."

Lūcius, quī post iānuam stetit et **omnia** audīvit, "Sed ego," inquit, "ego cibum cupiō. Cēna parāta est. Eāmus

20 *celeriter*!"

Nōnne semper legis carmina Catullī?

🔊 VERBA ŪTENDA

adulescens, -entis m./f. **youth**
amor, amōris m. **love**
aptus, -a, -um fit, suitable
carmen, carminis n. poem
celer, celeris, celere fast, swift
celeriter swiftly, quickly
crēdō, crēdere, crēdidī (+ dat.) believe, trust
dīcam "I will speak"
difficilis, difficile hard, difficult
dīves, dīvitis rich
dulcis, dulce sweet
eāmus "let's go!"
ēligō, ēligere, ēlēgī pick out, choose

faciliter easily
fēlix, fēlīcis happy
fortis, forte strong, brave
gravis, grave heavy, serious
hoc this
iānua, -ae f. door
intellegens, intellegentis smart, intelligent
interrogō (1) ask, question
ita so, thus; yes
legō, legere, lēgī, lectum gather, choose; read
lentē slowly
māior, māius greater, larger, older; m. pl. ancestors, elders
marītus, -ī m. husband
mēcum with me

miserābilis, miserābile miserable
miserābiliter miserably
mōs, mōris m. **custom; pl. character**; mōs māiōrum the custom of our ancestors.
nec and not; nec ... nec ... neither ... nor ...
nōbilis, nōbile notable, noble
nūgae, -ārum f. pl. trifle, nonsense
omnis, omne each, every; pl. all
optimus, -a, -um best
parātus, -a,-um ready, prepared

parens, parentis m./f. **parent**
perīculum -ī n. danger
potens, potentis powerful
princeps, -cipis m. head, leader, chief. One of Augustus' titles.
procul from far away
quī who
quod that which
quōmodo how
sērius later
tristis, triste sad
vērē truly
vērō indeed
vērus, -a, -um true

POSTQUAM LĒGISTĪ

Answer these questions in both Latin and English if the question is followed by (L). Otherwise, just respond in English.

1. What information do you learn about Cordus and his family in this *lectiō* (L)?
2. Why does Marcus tell Servilia about the poet Catullus?
3. Describe Servilia's relationship with Cordus at this point. Have the two met, spoken, etc.?
4. What do you learn about Roman customs regarding engagement and marriage in this reading? Who makes the decisions?
5. Why is Marcus sad in line 17? (L)
6. Where was Lucius and what does he want? (L)

Grammatica B

3rd Declension Adjectives: Agreement and Substantives

In previous chapters we have talked about adjective agreement (**GNC**), especially in terms of noun/adjective combinations in which the endings agree but are not the same. For example, *bonus puer*, *magnus poēta*, and *magna māter*. 3rd declension adjectives work the same way and create phrases like *fortis puer*, *celer poēta*, and *fēlix māter*. Here are some examples you saw in *Lectiō Secunda*:

homō **dīves**	masculine nominative singular	"rich person"
(dē) amōre **dulcī**	masculine ablative singular	"about sweet love"
nōbilēs marītōs	masculine accusative plural	"noble husbands"

Notice how GNC works in all these phrases.

Here is how *fortis, forte* works with 1st and 2nd declension nouns:

	1ST DECLENSION		2ND DECLENSION			
Gender	**Feminine**		**Masculine**		**Neuter**	
Singular						
Nominative	fēmina	fortis	discipulus	fortis	vīnum	forte
Genitive	fēminae	fortis	discipulī	fortis	vīnī	fortis
Dative	fēminae	fortī	discipulō	fortī	vīnō	fortī
Accusative	fēminam	fortem	discipulum	fortem	vīnum	forte
Ablative	fēminā	fortī	discipulō	fortī	vīnō	fortī
Vocative	fēmina	fortis	discipule	fortis	vīnum	forte
Plural						
Nominative	fēminae	fortēs	discipulī	fortēs	vīna	fortia
Genitive	fēminārum	fortium	discipulōrum	fortium	vīnōrum	fortium
Dative	fēminīs	fortibus	discipulīs	fortibus	vīnīs	fortibus
Accusative	fēminās	fortēs	discipulōs	fortēs	vīna	fortia
Ablative	fēminīs	fortibus	discipulīs	fortibus	vīnīs	fortibus
Vocative	fēminae	fortēs	discipulī	fortēs	vīna	fortia

Like 2-1-2 adjectives, 3rd declension adjectives can also serve as **substantives**. The two examples in the reading were *omnia* (all things, everything) and *māiōrum* (of those older, of elders, ancestors).

Here are some examples from *Lectiō Secunda*

Catullus **omnēs** *admonet.*	*omnēs* = all people, everyone
Lūcius **omnia** *audīvit.*	*omnia* = all things, everything

3rd Declension Adverbs

Most 3rd declension adjectives form adverbs by adding *-iter* or *-ter* to the stem. These adverbs are easy to recognize. You don't need to worry too much about when Latin adds *-iter* and when it adds *-ter,* but here are some simple guidelines:

- Most 3rd declension adjectives form adverbs with *-iter*; e.g., *facil**iter***
- Some 3rd declension adjectives add *-ter*; e.g., *audac**ter***
- If the stem already ends in *-t,* just add *-er*; e.g., *potent**er*** or *intellegent**er***

Here are some phrases from *Lectiō Secunda* with adverbs formed from 3rd declension adjectives:

Hoc **faciliter** *facere nōn possum.*	I cannot do this **easily**.
Servīlia clāmat **miserābiliter**.	Servilia shouts **miserably**.
Eāmus **celeriter***!*	Let's go **quickly**!

EXERCEĀMUS!

15-4 **3rd Declension Adverbs**

Fill in the blanks to identify the stem of each adjective. Then form the adverb and indicate its meaning. Do the best you can, since the rules for forming these adverbs are fairly flexible. Follow the models.

Adjective	Stem	Adverb	Meaning
→ facilis, facile	facil-	facil**iter**	easi**ly**
→ intellegens, intellegentis	intellegent-	intellegent**er**	clever**ly**

1. fortis, forte

2. gravis, grave

3. potens, potentis

4. dulcis, dulce

5. celer, celeris, celere

Mōrēs Rōmānī

Mōs Māiōrum

Mōs māiōrum ("the custom of our ancestors") was the unwritten code of behavior by which Romans were taught to live. It emphasized tradition, respect for authority, both divine and civic, and obedience to one's elders. Good Romans were expected to place their own needs second to the needs of family and the state. They were expected to show *disciplīna* (an ordered life), *industria* (diligence) *frūgālitās* (economy), *gravitās* (seriousness), *officium* (a sense of obligation), and *virtūs* (manliness, excellence, virtue).

Above all, they were to have *pietās* (dutifulness) to their fathers (*patrēs*), to their *patria* (fatherland), and to their gods, especially to Jupiter, whose very name contains a root meaning "father" (*-piter*). A common example for *pietās* was Aeneas, the Trojan hero who escaped from burning Troy with his elderly father Anchises on his shoulders and with the household gods of Troy in Anchises' arms. He appears on the silver denarius depicted at right. This coin was issued by Julius Caesar from an African mint in 47–46 B.C. On the obverve is the image of the goddess Venus, Caesar's maternal ancestor. On the reverse is an image of Venus' son Aeneas with his father Archises.

Aenēās et Pater

🔊 **VERBA ŪTENDA**

abūtēre (+abl.) you will
    abuse
audācia, -ae f. daring
effrēnātus, -a, -um unbridled
ēlūdet will escape
etiam also, too, even now
fīnis, -is m. end
furor, -ōris m. fury, rage
iactābit will hurl, throw
iste, ista, istud that _____ of
    yours
patientia, -ae f. patience
quam diū for how long
quem ad fīnem to what
    end?
quōusque how long
tandem at last, at length,
    finally

Both Marcus and Servilia were raised on the *mōs māiōrum* and are aware of its obligations. For Servilia this means that she will have to accept the husband chosen for her by her father, even if she likes Cordus better.

The speech Servilia hears Cordus reciting as part of his rhetorical training is Cicero's first speech against Catiline (*In Catilīnam*). There were four of these speeches, which Cicero gave in the Senate in 63 B.C. while he was consul. Servilia's grandfather (whom you will meet later in the story) would have been in his prime during this period.

In these speeches Cicero describes the plot of Catiline and his followers to overthrow the Roman government. He begins the first speech against Catiline with a series of three blistering questions addressed directly to Catiline, who was present in the senate when this speech was given.

Pay attention to the verbs in the future tense (which are glossed in the *Verba Ūtenda*). We will learn the future in the next chapter.

> *Quōusque tandem abūtēre, Catilīna, patientiā nostrā? Quam diū etiam furor iste tuus nōs ēlūdet? Quem ad fīnem sē effrēnāta iactābit audācia?*

Cicero does not really expect Catiline to answer these questions. Rather he uses them for dramatic effect upon his audience. These kinds of questions are called **rhetorical questions** and must have produced quite a response in the senate house. Notice how the *furor* and *audācia* which Cicero associates with Catiline contrast with traditional Roman virtues.

This speech was well known and admired even in Cicero's lifetime and was long practiced by young men studying rhetoric.

Latīna Hodierna

Virtūtēs Rōmānae Hodiē

"Duty, Honor, Country" is the motto of the U.S. Military Academy at West Point. This motto also appears on the academy's coat of arms. In many ways these words celebrate the same ideals honored in the Roman concept of *mōs māiōrum*. Indeed, the Puritan virtues that were the foundational principles of American society were similar to Roman ones. Now look at these Roman virtues and the English derivatives. Notice how the meanings of the Latin words and of their English derivatives are not always the same.

LATIN WORD	ENGLISH MEANING	DERIVATIVES
virtūs, virtūtis f.	manliness, excellence, worth	virtue virtuous
disciplīna, -ae f.	training, education, an ordered life based upon such training	discipline disciplinary
frūgālitās, -tātis f.	economy	frugal frugality
gravitās, -tātis f.	weight, heaviness, seriousness, authority	grave gravity
industria, -ae f.	diligence, hard work	industry industrious
officium, -iī n.	duty, obligation, service, business	office officious officiousness
pietās, pietātis f.	dutifulness	piety pious

Orbis Terrārum Rōmānus

Ītalia Cicerōnis

For Cicero, home was Rome, and there was no place he would rather have been. When he served as governor of Cicilia (in modern Turkey) or when he was sent into exile, he was miserable and could not wait to return to the city. But Cicero had strong connections with several places outside the city:

Ītalia Cicerōnis

Arpinum (*Arpīnum, -ī* n.; modern Arpino), his birthplace in the Alban Hills of Latium in central Italy. Arpinum was originally a Volscian and Samnite settlement, but its residents were granted Roman citizenship in 188 B.C. Cicero kept his family estate in Arpinum and visited it occasionally. The city also boasted as native sons C. Marius (Julius Caesar's uncle) and M. Vipsanius Agrippa (Augustus' advisor and son-in-law). You will meet Agrippa later in the narrative.

Tusculum (*Tusculum, -ī* n.), an ancient town of Latium. Tusculum accepted Roman control in 381 B.C, and its citizens were granted Roman suffrage in the same year. Marcus Porcius Cato (Cato the Elder) was born here in 234 B.C. The city was considered a health spa and was a popular place for wealthy Romans to own villas. Cicero owned a favorite villa here where he wrote a famous philosophical treatise called *Tusculānae Disputātiōnēs* (*Tusculan Disputations*).

Formiae (*Formiae, -iārum* f. pl.; modern Formia). Cicero owned a seaside villa in this popular resort town on the Appian Way in Latium. It was here that he was killed by Marc Antony's troops in 43 B.C. A structure called the tomb of Cicero is shown to tourists to this day.

Arpīnum

QUID PUTĀS?

1. What speeches in American history would be as famous as Cicero's speeches about Catiline were in ancient Rome? What lines can you recite from memory?
2. Give an example of a rhetorical question you might address to a friend.
3. How many of the traditional Roman virtues do you think are admired in modern American society? How many are actually followed?

EXERCEĀMUS!

15-5 Scrībāmus

Transform each of the following Latin sentences into questions by putting the verb at the beginning of the sentence and adding -ne. Then answer the question with either sīc/ita or nōn and a complete sentence. Follow the model.

→ Servīlia fēlix in cubiculō suō sedet.

　　Quaestiō:　　Sedetne Servīlia fēlix in cubiculō suō?
　　Responsum:　　Nōn, Servīlia nōn fēlix est.

1. Tristis Servīliae vīta est.
   Quaestiō:
   Responsum:

2. Cordus pater Marcī est.
   Quaestiō:
   Responsum:

3. Servīlia Cordum in domō suā vīdit.
   Quaestiō:
   Responsum:

4. Vōx Cordī crūdēlis fuit!
   Quaestiō:
   Responsum:

15-6 Colloquāmur

Now ask another member of your class one of the questions you made in Exercise 15-5. Your classmate will respond with an appropriate response from the same exercise. Follow the model.

→ Sedetne Servīlia fēlix in cubiculō suō?
　　Nōn. Servīlia nōn fēlix est.

15-7 Verba Discenda Count Down!

Use the *Verba Discenda* to find the information required.

Decem. Find ten adjectives in this list.
Novem. Find nine 3rd declension adjectives.
Octo. Find an additional English derivative for any eight different words on this list.
Septem. Find seven neuter nominative singular adjective forms.
Sex. Find six two-termination 3rd declension adjectives.
Quinque. Find five nouns.
Quattuor. Find four 3rd declension nouns.
Tria. Find three adjectives that could describe a hero.
Duo. Find two one-termination 3rd declension adjectives.
Unum. Find one three-termination 3rd declension adjective.

🔊 VERBA DISCENDA

adulescens, -entis m./f. youth [adolescent]

amor, amōris m. love [amorous]

celer, celeris, celere fast, swift [accelerate]

corpus, corporis n. body [incorporate]

cum when

difficilis, difficile hard, difficult [difficulty]

fortis, forte strong, brave [fortitude]

gravis, grave heavy, serious [gravity]

intellegens, intellegentis smart, intelligent [intelligentsia]

iuvenis, iuvenis m./f. youth [juvenile]

legō, legere, lēgī, lectum gather, choose; read [legible, lecture]

māior, māius greater, larger, older; m. pl. ancestors, elders [majority]

mōs, mōris m. custom; pl. character [mores]

nec and not; nec . . . nec . . . neither . . . nor . . .

nōbilis, nōbile notable, noble [nobility]

omnis, omne each, every; pl. all [omnipotent]

potens, potentis powerful [potential]

tristis, triste sad

vērē truly

vērus, -a, -um true [verify]

vox, vōcis f. voice [vocal]

Angulus Grammaticus

Much, Many, Each, and Every

Sometimes you will see dictionary entries like this:

> *multus,-a, -um* much; (pl.) many
> *omnis, omne* each, every; (pl.) all

This means that the word has one translation in the singular and another in the plural. So when you see these adjectives in a sentence you need to think a bit more before you translate them. Pay attention especially to the number of the noun, which determines how the adjective is translated. Here are some examples:

omnis puer	every boy	*omnēs puerī*	all (the) boys
multum vīnum	much wine	*multa vīna*	many wines

Notā Bene: In English derivatives, "mult(i)-" commonly means "many" and "omn(i)-" can mean "every" or "all." Here are some examples:

multidisciplinary "having many areas of study"
multiethnic "having many ethnic groups"
multifaceted "many-sided"
multilingual "having many languages"
multipolar "having many centers of power"
multivalent "having many meanings or values"

omnidirectional "moving in all directions" or "moving in every direction"
omnipotent "having all powers" or "having every power"
omnipresent "being present in all places" or "being present in every place"
omniscient "knowing all things" or "knowing everything"
omnivorous "eating all things" or "eating everything"

16

In Cēnā

Cēna Rōmāna

GRAMMATICA

The Future Tense

The Future of *Sum, Eō,* and Other Irregular Verbs

MŌRĒS RŌMĀNĪ

Rhetoric and Oratory

LATĪNA HODIERNA

Latin in the New World

ORBIS TERRĀRUM RŌMĀNUS

Latium

ANGULUS GRAMMATICUS

Reading Backward in Latin

LECTIŌNĒS:
IN TRĪCLĪNIŌ
and
PATER ET FĪLIA

At dinner the family discuss their day. The boys talk about school. Servilia tells her father about Cordus. Her father responds with some news his daughter does not want to hear.

Lectiō Prīma

Antequam Legis

The family of Servilius is now sitting down for dinner and discussing their day. Lucius and Marcus both talk about events at school, and their father looks toward their future careers. As you read, pay attention to how the Romans ate their meals. It is rather different from our customs.

Looking Into the Future

In this chapter we introduce you to the **future tense**. It is easy to recognize, but like the present tense, the future tense of the 1st and 2nd conjugations is formed differently than the 3rd and 4th conjugations.

Future				
1st and 2nd Conjugations	Present Stem +	-bō	-bimus	
		-bis	-bitis	
		-bit	-bunt	
3rd and 4th Conjugations	Short Present Stem +	-am	-ēmus	
		-ēs	-ētis	
		-et	-ent	
Remember:	Present Stem	= 2nd principal part, drop *-re*		
	Short Present Stem	= 1st principal part, drop *-ō*		

Translate the future just like the English future, by using the helping verb "will."

EXERCEĀMUS!

16-1 Future Tense

We have put all the future tenses in *Lectiō Prīma* in **bold**. Before you read, make a list of these forms and use the preceding rule to indicate whether each is a 1st/2nd conjugation future or a 3rd/4th conjugation verb. Then identify the actual conjugation it is (you may have to check your vocabulary for this). Follow the models.

	Line	Verb	Type	Conjugation
→	4	portābunt	1st/2nd	1st
→	6	scrībēs	3rd/4th	3rd

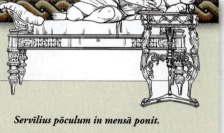

Servīlius pōculum in mensā ponit.

🔊 IN TRĪCLĪNIŌ

In trīclīniō tōta familia recumbit et cēnam exspectat. Servīlius et Marcus et Lūcius in lectīs recumbunt. Et Caecilia et Servīlia in sellīs sedent. (Fēminīs in lectīs recumbere nōn decet.) Mox aliī servī cibum vīnumque ad mensās **portābunt** et aliī post lectōs **stābunt** et familiam **adiuvābunt**.

5   Lūcius parentibus multum dē sīmiā nārrat et omnēs rīdent. Pater "Eugae, Lūcī!" inquit. "Fābulās bene nārrās. Fortasse, sīcut Horātius noster, fābulās aut saturās aliquandō **scrībēs** et, praeclārus poēta, fāmam et glōriam **capiēs**!" Caecilia rīdet et "Fīlius noster" inquit, "praeclārus iam est! Lucius tantum cibum quantum Herculēs dēvorat! Mox familia nullum cibum in culīnā **habēbit**!"

Marcus dē Valgiō Rufō rhētore suō dīcit et "Valgius Rufus," inquit, "nōbīs nimium labōris rursus hodiē dedit.
10 suāsōriam scrībere dēbuimus–*Caesar dēlīberat an Antōniō clēmentiam offerre necesse sit.* Heu mē! Difficile est bonam suāsōriam scrībere et nihil Valgiō placet! Ars rhētorica difficilis est! Crās rursus nimium labōris **habēbimus**!"

Servīlius pōculum in mensā ponit. Rīdet et "Marce," inquit, "labor strēnuus numquam nēminem necāvit. Scrībere ōrātiōnēs bonās difficile est, sed quoque necesse est! Mox ōrātiōnēs multās **habēbis**—et in Forō et in Senātū—et eō tempore disciplīna Valgiī tibi **placēbit**. Ōrātiōnēs bonae tē hominem fortūnātum atque praeclārum in
15 Senātū **facient**. Tunc tū et amīcī tuī Valgiō grātiās maximās **agētis**!"

🔊 VERBA ŪTENDA

adiuvō, adiuvāre, adiūvī,
  adiūtum help
aliī servī . . . aliī some
  slaves . . . other
  (slaves)
aliquandō someday
an whether
***ars, artis* f. art, skill**
atque and, and also
clēmentia, -ae f. mercy,
  clemency
decet it is fitting
dēlīberō (1) debate,
  deliberate
dēvorō (1) devour,
  consume

disciplīna, -ae f. instruction,
  knowledge
eugae! terrific! bravo!
***exspectō* (1) await, wait for**
fortūnātus, -a, -um lucky,
  fortunate
Heu mē! Oh, my!
***labor, labōris,* m. work,**
  labor
lectus, -ī m. dining couch
***mensa, -ae* f. table**
***multum* a lot, much**
necō (1) kill, slay
***nimium* too much**
numquam never
offerō, offerre, obtulī offer

***ōrātiō, ōrātiōnis* f. speech**
ōrātiōnem habēre to
  deliver a speech
***parens, parentis* m./f.**
  parent
***praeclārus, -a, -um* very**
  clear, famous, noble,
  excellent, beautiful
quantum See *tantum.*
recumbō, recumbere,
  recubuī recline, lie down
***rhētor, rhētoris* m.**
  teacher of rhetoric
  (public speaking)
rhētoricus, -a, -um
  rhetorical

rursus again
satura, -ae f. satire
sella, -ae f. chair, seat
senātū senate (ablative
  sing.)
sit "might be"
strēnuus, -a, -um hard,
  strenuous
suāsōria, -ae f. persuasive
  speech
tantum . . . quantum as
  much . . . as
tōtus, -a, -um whole,
  entire
trīclīnium, -iī n. dining
  room

POSTQUAM LĒGISTĪ

Answer these questions in both Latin and English if the question is followed by (L). Otherwise, just respond in English.

1. List the Latin words that tell you what kinds of furniture the family uses to dine.
2. Who else is in the room, and what they are doing?
3. What does Lucius talk about? How do his parents respond? (L)
4. What does Marcus talk about? (L)
5. Why does Servilius laugh after Marcus finishes talking?
6. What plans does Servilius have for his two sons?
7. How does this family meal compare to a meal in your house?
8. Are there any rules for dining today that are based on gender, similar to those of Rome?

Grammatica A

The Future Tense

The future tense is quite regular in English. All we need to do is put "will" between pronoun and verb and we are in the future.

he will work   they will drive   it will happen

1st and 2nd Conjugation Future

To form the future: present stem (2nd principle part minus the *-re*) + *-bō, -bis, -bit, -bimus, -bitis, -bunt*.

FUTURE	
vocā**bō**	I **will** call
vocā**bis**	you **will** call
vocā**bit**	he/she/it **will** call
vocā**bimus**	we **will** call
vocā**bitis**	you **will** call
vocā**bunt**	they **will** call

Notā Bene:

- The future uses the same personal endings as the present in the 1st and 2nd conjugations: *-ō, -s, -t, -mus, -tis, -nt*.
- Note the vowel pattern before the personal endings in the future: (*ō, i, i, i, i, u*). You have already seen that pattern in the present tense of 3rd and 4th conjugation verbs.

3rd Conjugation Future

To form the future: short present stem (1st principal part minus the *-ō*) + *-am, -ēs, -et, -ēmus, -ētis, -ent*.

FUTURE	
scrībam	I **will** write
scrībēs	you **will** write
scrībet	he/she/it **will** write
scrībēmus	we **will** write
scrībētis	you **will** write
scrībent	they **will** write

3rd -io and 4th Conjugation Future

To form the future: short present stem (1st principal part minus the -ō) + -am, -ēs, -et, -ēmus, -ētis, -ent.

FUTURE			
capiam	I **will** seize	audiam	I **will** hear
capiēs	you **will** seize	audiēs	you **will** hear
capiet	he/she/it **will** seize	audiet	he/she/it **will** hear
capiēmus	we **will** seize	audiēmus	we **will** hear
capiētis	you **will** seize	audiētis	you **will** hear
capient	they **will** seize	audient	they **will** hear

Notā Bene:

- The 3rd -io future is formed exactly like the 4th conjugation future.
- Note the -m ending in the first person singular future and remember:

  MOST MUST ISN'T!

Possible Sources of Confusion

The -e in verb endings can be confusing. If you do not know that *vidēmus* comes from a 2nd conjugation verb, you might think that it is a 3rd conjugation future. So if you were to come upon a verb you did not know, as in a form like *merētis*, you would not know if it were from a 2nd conjugation verb *mereō, -ēre* or a 3rd conjugation verb *merō, -ere*. You might even guess it means "to earn" (which it does) but you would not know whether to translate it "you earn" or "you will earn."

The verb is, in fact, 2nd conjugation, once more showing the economy of Latin endings, but there is little confusion as long as you know the conjugation. So here is your new mantra: **When in doubt, look it up!**

EXERCEĀMUS!

16-2 Present vs. Future

Indicate whether each of the following verbs is present or future.

1. habent

2. habēbimus

3. dūcitis

4. dūcam

5. ambulābimus

6. ambulat

7. capiet

8. capīmus

9. vocābō

10. dīcent

Lectiō Secunda

Antequam Legis

Finally Servilia has an opportunity to tell her parents about Cordus but her father has some unexpected news for her. He has already chosen a husband for her and his name is Iullus Antonius.

Iullus Antonius

Iullus Antonius, the man chosen as Servilia's spouse by her father, is a historical figure, although we have taken certain liberties with the course of his life. He would have been just the sort of husband Servilius would seek for his daughter, since he was the son of Marc Antony and was connected closely by marriage with the family of Augustus. In fact, his story is indicative of the way marriages became political during this period.

The Future of *Sum* and *Eō*

In this *lectiō* you are introduced to the future forms of the irregular verbs *sum* and *eō*. The future of *sum* uses personal endings you are familiar with:

erō	I will be	*erimus*	we will be
eris	you will be	*eritis*	you will be
erit	he/she/it will be	*erunt*	they will be

Once you know this you also know the future of *possum*. If you remember that its stem is *pot-*, you will easily understand its future forms like *poterō* (*pot+erō*).

The future of *eō* is also easily recognized:

ībō	I will go	*ībimus*	we will go
ībis	you will go	*ībitis*	you will go
ībit	he/she/it will go	*ībunt*	they will go

Remember that *eō* is found in many compounds. So you should be on the lookout for forms like *adībis*.

The futures of all these verbs are marked in **bold** in the *lectiō*.

EXERCEĀMUS!

16-3   **Pre-Reading Questions**

These are questions to answer as you read this *lectiō* for the first time. If you keep these questions in mind, they will help you translate more quickly and accurately.

Line 9: What is the object of *nārrāvit*?

Line 13: What is the subject of *ambulābunt*?

Line 15: What word requires *parentibus* to be in the dative case?

Line 18: *Lēgī* can mean "I read" or "I chose." Which makes better sense here?

Line 21: To whom does *virō* refer?

🔊 PATER ET FĪLIA

Pater "Et tū, Servīlia," inquit. "Quid agit apud amīcam tuam Naeviam? Nōnne Fortūna Naeviae et familiae omnī favet?"

Servīlia "Omnis familia bene agit," inquit. "Nūper Naevia et māter adiērunt ad templum Fortūnae Prīmigeniae et familiam Praenestīnam
5 visitāvērunt. Hodiē mihi multa narrāvit dē templō praeclārō in monte et dē tessellātīs Nīlōticīs in templō. **Poterimusne** aliquandō illūc iter facere?"

Servīlius "Fortasse, fīlia," inquit. "mox cum matre **adībis**."

Tunc Servīlia parentibus omnia dē Cordō narrāvit. Diū dīxit et, tandem, "Crās, cum Marcō, rursus ad Naeviam **ībō**! Cordus et ego in hortōs
10 Maecēnātis **ībimus** et circumambulābimus. Nōlīte anxiī esse, mī parentēs, ancillae meae **aderunt** et nōbīscum ambulābunt!! Omnia salva **erunt**, pater, nam Marcus quoque nōbīscum **erit**."

Pater! Nōlī frontem contrahere!

Fīliae verba parentibus nūllō modō placent et diū Servīlius et Caecilia nihil dīcunt. Silentium tōtum trīclīnium tenet. Tandem pater, haud laetus, "Ecce mē, fīliola," inquit. "cum Cordō īre in hortōs Maecēnātis nōn **poteris**. Cum
15 Cordō nōn **ībis**. Rē vērā, cum Cordō numquam **eris**. Iam marītum tibi lēgī. Bonus vir est, dē familiā nōbilī, et mox apud Augustum labōrāre **poterit**."

Servīlia "Ēheu! Quid dīcis?" susurrāvit. "Sed quis marītus meus **erit**?"

"Nōmen," pater respondit, "virō Iullus Antōnius est et fīlius Marcī Antōniī et Fulviae est. Ego et Iullus Antōnius multa prō rē pūblicā efficere **poterimus**! Iam amīcī sumus, sed post nuptiās affīnēs **erimus**! Iullus Antōnius marītus
20 tuus **erit**. Mox **eris** mātrōna! Et fortasse nepōtēs **erunt**. . . ."

Pater multum magis dīcit sed fīlia nōn audit . . .

Intrā sē puella "Nōn," inquit "Iullī sed Cordī uxor **erō**! Sed, quōmodo **poterō**?"

🔊 VERBA ŪTENDA

adsum, adesse, affuī be present
affīnēs related by marriage
aliquandō sometime, some day
anxius, -a, -um uneasy, anxious
apud (+ acc.) at the house of, with, at _____'s
circumambulō (1) walk around
diū for a long time
ēheu! alas! oh no!
faveō, favēre, fāvī (+ dat.) favor
fīliola, -ae f. dear daughter

fortūna, -ae f. fortune, luck, chance
haud by no means
hortus, -ī m. garden
illūc (to) there
intrā sē to herself
Maecēnās, Maecēnātis m. G. Clinius Maecenas (70–8 B.C.)
magis more, rather
marītus, -ī m. husband
mātrōna, -ae f. married woman
mons, montis m. mountain
multum a lot, much

nepōs, nepōtis m. grandchild
Nīlōticus, -a, -um of the Nile (river)
nōbīscum with us
nūllus, -a, -um not any, non
nūper recently, not long ago
nūptiae, -ārum f. pl. marriage
parens, parentis m./f. parent
praeclārus, -a, -um very clear, famous, noble, excellent, beautiful
Praenestīnus, -a, -um of Praeneste, a town in Latium
prīmigenius, -a, -um original

quōmodo how
rēs pūblica, reī pūblicae f. republic
rē vērā in fact
rursus again
salvus, -a, -um alright, safe, well
silentium, -(i)ī n. silence
susurrō (1) whisper
tandem at last, finally
tessellāta, -ōrum n. mosaic
tōtus, -a, -um whole, entire
trīclīnium, -iī n. dining room
uxor, uxōris f. wife
vīsitō (1) visit

POSTQUAM LĒGISTĪ

Answer these questions in both Latin and English if the question is followed by (L). Otherwise, just respond in English.

1. What trip did Naevia and her mother recently make? What did they see there? (L)
2. What does Servilia ask her parents about this trip? What is the answer? (L)
3. Why does Servilia think her parents are anxious about her plans to see Cordus? How does she try to reassure them? Would modern American parents have similar concerns?
4. Why is Servilius not happy? What news does he have for his daughter? How does he try to make her happier about this news? (L)
5. What does this conversation between Servilia and her parents tell you about the relationship between Roman parents and their daughters?
6. Why do you think Caecilia is not a more active participant in this conversation?

Grammatica B

The Future of *Sum, Eō,* and Other Irregular Verbs

Compare the present and future forms of *sum*:

SUM			
Present		**Future**	
sum	I am	*erō*	I will be
es	you are	*eris*	you will be
est	he/she/it is	*erit*	he/she/it will be
sumus	we are	*erimus*	we will be
estis	you are	*eritis*	you will be
sunt	they are	*erunt*	they will be

Once you know the future of *sum* you can make the future of compounds like *adsum* (I am present): *aderō* (I will be present). You can also use the future of *sum* to make the future of *possum*. Just add these forms to the stem *pot-*:

pot**erō**	I will be able	pot**erimus**	we will be able
pot**eris**	you will be able	pot**eritis**	you will be able
pot**erit**	he/she/it will be able	pot**erunt**	they will be able

The irregular verbs *volō, nōlō,* and *mālō* are quite regular in the future with 3rd conjugation future endings:

volam	nōlam	mālam
volēs	nōlēs	mālēs
volet	nōlet	mālet
volēmus	nōlēmus	mālēmus
volētis	nōlētis	mālētis
volent	nōlent	mālent

How would you translate these words?

The verb *eō, īre, īvī/iī* (go) is an exception. Although its infinitive shows that it is a 4th conjugation verb, it uses the 1st and 2nd conjugation *-bō, -bis* endings:

ībō	I will go	*ībimus*	we will go
ībis	you will go	*ībitis*	you will go
ībit	he/she/it will go	*ībunt*	they will go

EXERCEĀMUS!

16-4 Irregular Verb Review

Select the form of *sum, eō, volō, nōlō,* or *mālō* that best represents the underlined English words in the sentence. Be careful of tense!

_____	1. <u>I will be</u> there at 5 P.M.	A.	abīmus
_____	2. Where <u>is he going</u>?	B.	aderunt
_____	3. <u>Will he be able</u> to help us?	C.	erō
_____	4. Trust me, <u>you will not want</u> to see that movie.	D.	es
_____	5. Charlie? <u>He was</u> here, but he left.	E.	fuit
_____	6. He scratched our car, but <u>we preferred</u> not to prosecute.	F.	ībis
_____	7. <u>Will you be going</u> to see the new movie?	G.	it
_____	8. <u>You are</u> so right!	H.	māluimus
_____	9. Tell me, <u>will they be present</u> too?	I.	nōn volēs
_____	10. <u>We will leave</u> at 6 A.M.	J.	poterit

Mōrēs Rōmānī

Rhetoric and Oratory

The importance of public speaking in Roman society is illustrated by the impact of Cicero's speeches against Catiline, discussed in the previous chapter. Young Roman men from prominent or ambitious families were expected to follow their study of literature under a *grammaticus* with an intense rhetorical education under a *rhētor*. This education consisted of declamation and practice in public speaking, such as Cordus' recitation of Cicero that Servilia overhears, as well as speech writing. In *Lectiō Prīma* Marcus refers to these written exercises, which are often called either *suāsōriae* (persuasive speeches) or *contrōversiae* (fictional law cases and legal arguments). Following his time with the *rhētor*, a young man from a wealthy family might go off to southern Italy or Greece to study under a master rhetorician or philosopher. Marcus is about to make such a journey.

Marcus' rhetoric teacher, Valgius Rufus, is based on a real person of that name. A close friend of Horace, Augustus, and his "minister of culture" Maecenas, Rufus wrote poetry but also may have written some works on rhetoric. We have made him a *rhētor* for the sake of the plot.

Rufus asks Marcus to write a *suāsōria* addressed to Julius Caesar on the necessity of clemency. This sort of historical topic was very popular in Greek and Roman rhetorical schools. Some examples of both *suāsōriae* and *contrōversiae* survive in the works of that name by the Spaniard Seneca the Elder (54 B.C.–39 A.D.). Here are some topics for *suāsōriae* mentioned by Seneca. (We have simplified the Latin for you. The *Verba Ūtenda* will also help.)

> *Dēliberat Alexander an Ōceanum nāviget.*
> *Trēcentī Laconēs contrā Xerxen missī dēliberant an fugiant.*
> *Dēliberat Agamemnōn an Īphigenīam immolet.*
> *Dēliberat Cicerō an Antōnium dēprecētur.*

Such themes from mythology, Greek history, and current Roman events were very popular in schools of rhetoric.

🔊 VERBA ŪTENDA

Agamemnōn, -nonis m. Agamemnon, king of Mycenae; note the Greek nom. sing.

Alexander, -ī m. Alexander (the Great), king of Macedonia

an whether

contrā (+ acc.) against

dēlīberō (1) deliberate, debate

dēprecētur (+ dat.) "he should seek pardon from"

fugiant "they should flee"

immolet "he should sacrifice"

Īphigenīa, -ae f. Iphigenia, daughter of Agamemnon

Lacō, Laconis m. Laconian, Spartan

missus, -a, -um sent

nāviget "he should sail"

trēcentī 300

Xerxen Xerxes, king of Persia; note the Greek acc. sing.

Latīna Hodierna

Latin in the New World

We can never understimate the lasting influence of Latin. When the Spaniards came to the New World, they brought with them the Latin language and Roman culture, Here, for example, is some advice on table manners written in the margin of a text of Ovid's *Tristia* published in Mexico in 1577. You might imagine Caecilia giving her sons much the same advice as they sit down to the family's evening meal. (We have simplified and shortened the passage.)

Beginning in line 3, each line contains an imperative. Can you find the verb in the future tense?

Ad Iuventūtem

Nēmō quī haec documenta spernit, cibum capiet:
Dum mensae accumbitis:
Vultum hilarem habē!
Sāl cultellō cape!
5   Rixās et murmur fuge!
Membrīs rectīs sedē.
Mappam mundam tenē.
Nōlī scalpere!
Aliīs partem oblatōrum da!
10   Modicum (sī crēbrō) bibe
Grātiās deō semper age!

🔊 VERBA ŪTENDA

accumbō, accumbere, accubuī
(+ dat.) recline at table
aliīs to others
crēbrō frequently
cultellus, -ī m. knife
documentum, -ī n. instruction, warning
fuge! avoid!
Grātiās age! "Give thanks!"
haec these
hilaris, hilare cheerful
iuventūs, -tūtis f. youth

mappa, -ae f.
table napkin
membrum, -ī n. limbs
(arms and legs)
modicum moderately
mundus, -a, -um clean
murmur, murmuris
n. whispering,
murmuring
oblāta, -ōrum n. pl. "that
which has been served"
pars, partis f. part, piece

quī who
quid what
rectus, -a, -um straight
rixa, -ae f. violent
quarrel
sāl, salis m./n. salt
scalpō, scalpere
scratch
spernō, spernere, sprēvī
reject, scorn
vultum m. face

Orbis Terrārum Rōmānus

Latium

The region around Rome was called Latium (*Latium, -ī* n., modern Lazio), i.e., the land of the Latins or the Latin-speaking people. Originally the region consisted of a number of independent towns that organized in the seventh century B.C. into the Latin League, under the leadership of the town of Alba Longa. Rome was not originally part of this league, which was

Latium Antīquum

intended as a defensive coalition against powerful Etruscan cities in Etruria and other non-Latin peoples. It took Rome several centuries to bring Latium fully under its control, and in 90 B.C., by the *Lex Iulia*, all the Latin peoples gained full Roman citizenship.

The towns of Arpinum, Tusculum, and Formiae described in the last chapter are all in Latium. Another prominent town is Praeneste (modern Palestrina), located about 23 miles east of Rome. In the imperial period, Praeneste became a fashionable resort town and was especially known for its oracle and imposing temple of *Fortūna Prīmigenia* (Original Fortune) which Servilia's friend Naevia and her mother recently visited.

Tessellāta Nīlōtica Praenestīna

Praeneste hodiē

QUID PUTĀS?

1. If *suāsōriae* and *contrōversiae* were written today what might some of the topics be?
2. What does the career of Iullus Antonius tell you about this period in Roman history? Can you compare his career to that of any famous Americans?
3. How do the table manners described in the poem from Mexico compare to the manners you were taught as a child?
4. How would you describe Rome's relationship with the cities of Latium?

EXERCEĀMUS!

16-5 Scrībāmus

To practice your new knowledge of the future of regular and irregular verbs, we return to the story of Valeria and the thieves from Chapter 11. Replace all the words marked in **bold** with appropriate future forms. Follow the model.

→ Licinia et Valeria ab Iūnōne deā beneficia **petent** . . .

Licinia et Valeria ab Iūnōne deā beneficia **petīvērunt** et grātiās maximās astrologō **ēgērunt**. Fēminae laetae **fuērunt** propter verba bona dē īnfante. Flāvia quoque laeta **fuit** quod nunc īnsula nōn longinqua est. Flāvia fessa **fuit** quod saccum (et Sōcratem!) longē per viās portāre dēbuit. Et Sōcratēs laetus **fuit** quod iēiūnus est et cibus domī **fuit**.

Subitō trēs latrōnēs ex angiportō **saluērunt**. Saccum rapere **voluērunt** et fēminae perterritae **fuērunt**. Fēminae fortiter **clāmāvērunt**.

Aelius vōcēs in viā **audīvit**. Fēminās in angustiīs **vīdit** et in latrōnēs magnā cum īrā **cucurrit**. Malleum magnum **tenuit**. Latrōnēs et malleum et musculōs Aeliī **vīdērunt**. Aelium pugnāre **nōluērunt**. Aeliō concēdere **māluērunt** et celeriter sine saccō **fūgērunt**.

16-6 Colloquāmur

Now use the narrative in Exercise 16-5 to ask and answer questions with a classmate using perfect or future tense verbs randomly. See how many answers you can make, using interrogative words like *-ne, quid, quis,* etc. Follow the models.

Based on line 1, you could ask

→ *Quid Licinia et Valeria ab Iūnōne deā petivērunt?*
→ *Quid Licinia et Valeria ab Iūnōne deā petent?*

The appropriate responses would be

→ *Licinia et Valeria ab Iūnōne deā beneficia petivērunt.*
→ *Licinia et Valeria ab Iūnōne deā beneficia petent.*

16-7 Verba Discenda

Use the *Verba Discenda* to find the following:

1. the 3rd principal part of *exspectō*

2. a preposition that takes the accusative

3. a 2nd declension noun

4. the feminine equivalent of *praeclārus*

5. a 3rd declension noun that is both masculine and feminine

6. an interjection

7. the genitive singular of *labor*

8. a 1st declension noun

🔊 **VERBA DISCENDA**

adiuvō, adiuvāre, adiūvī,
  adiūtum **help**
  [adjutant]
apud **(+ acc.) at the**
  house of, with,
  at _____'s
ars, artis **f. art, skill**
  [artistic]
diū **for a long time**
ēheu! **alas! oh no!**
exspectō **(1) await, wait**
  for [expectation]

haud **by no means**
labor, labōris
  m. work, labor [laborious]
magis **more, rather**
  [magiscule]
marītus, -ī **m. husband**
  [marital]
mensa, -ae **f. table**
multum **a lot, much**
nimium **too much**
ōrātiō, ōrātiōnis
  f. speech [oration]

parens, parentis **m./f.**
  parent [parental]
praeclārus, -a, -um **very**
  clear, famous, noble,
  excellent, beautiful
rhētor, rhētoris **m.**
  teacher of rhetoric
  (public speaking)
  [rhetorician]
rhētoricus, -a, -um
  rhetorical
rursus **again**

Angulus Grammaticus

Reading Backward in Latin

When you learn Latin, you are, in a way, rewiring your brain to process word elements in an order that is the reverse of English.

In English we have phrases like: "she will work" and "we will have." The pronoun comes first, then the "will," which tells us the tense we are dealing with, and finally, we get to the sense of the verb.

Pronoun	Tense	Meaning
she	will	work

But where is it written that this is the only way a language can work? The Latin verb reads from front to back. For example,

Verb Meaning	Tense	Pronoun
labōrā	*bi*	*t*
work	will	he/she/it
habē	*bi*	*mus*
have	will	we
disc	*ē*	*tis*
learn	will	you

This is true not just for the future but for other verb tenses as well. Here are some examples from the perfect:

labōrāv	*it*
worked	he/she/it
habu	*imus*
had	we
didic	*istis*
learned	you

So the Latin verbs are rather like Yoda-speak. Just don't translate this way!

17

Dē Amōre et Lūdīs

Lesbia Passerque

Lectiō Prīma

Antequam Legis

This *lectiō* shows us a distraught Servilia in her room, consoling herself with her pet sparrow named Lesbia.

Present Participles

In this chapter you are introduced to a new verb form called the **participle**. A participle is a **verbal adjective**. In English we make present participles by adding **-ing** to a verb. So "work" becomes "working." In the sentences

The man **working** in the kitchen is old.   I saw the man **working**.

the word "working" is a participle describing the man. Here are the same sentences in Latin:

*Vir **labōrāns** in culīnā senex est.*   *Virum **labōrantem** vīdī.*

For now, as you read, do the following:

- Translate any participle (in **bold**) with the verb form ending in "-ing."
- Watch for the case endings and just translate them accordingly.
- Ask who is performing the action of the participle, i.e., "who is —ing?"

All the participles are marked in **bold** in the *lectiō*.

EXERCEĀMUS!

17-1   Participles

Find the words that ten participles marked in **bold** in the *lectiō* modify (GNC). With the help of this word and what you already know about case endings, identify the case and number of each participle. Then translate the word together with its participle. Follow the model.

Line	Participle	Word	Case	Number	English Translation
→ 1	lacrimāns	Servīlia	nom.	sing.	Servīlia

> **LECTIŌNĒS:**
> **SERVĪLIA MAESTA**
> **and**
> **DĒ MŪNERIBUS**
> After a difficult conversation with her parents, Servilia consoles herself by petting Lesbia, her pet sparrow. Meanwhile her brothers look forward to tomorrow's games in the amphitheater.

SERVĪLIA MAESTA

Post cēnam Servīlia sōla in cubiculō **lacrimāns** sedet. Puella, sōlāciolum suī dolōris **petēns**, passerem **sedentem** in
gremiō tenet. Passer lūdit et puella tristis lacrimat. Nōmen
passerī Lesbia est. Lesbia praeclāra est quod poēta Catullus
5 eam amāvit et, sīcut omnēs poetae **amantēs**, dē eā multa
carmina amātōria scrīpsit. Lesbia quoque passerem habuit
et Catullus carmen fāmōsum dē morte illīus passeris scripsit.
Omnēs amantēs carmina Catullī legere dēbent!

Servīlia, hoc carmen in mente **habēns**, passerī
10 **pīpiantī** plōrāvit: "Quid facere necesse est, dēliciae meae?
Quōmodo vītam meam dūcam cum hōc virō ignōtō? Iullus Antonius vetus est! Plūs quam trīgintā quinque annōs
nātus est! In domō istīus senis numquam habitābō! Cor meum vīrō senī numquam dabō! Cor meum Naeviō adules-
centī iam dedī! Nūllī aliī virō cor numquam meum dabō. Fortasse neutrī cor meum dabō et neuter mē in
mātrimōnium dūcet! Fortasse ego **habitāns** sōla numquam nūbam!

15 "Ōh, quid facere necesse est, dēliciae meae? Nōn istum Iullum nōvī! Iullum in viā **ambulantem** numquam vīdī!
Numquam vōcem Iullī **dīcentis** audīvī. Vae mē! Nōlō tālem ignōtum nūbere. Cordum nūbere volō! Eum in peristȳliō
ambulantem vīdī! Vōcem Cordī **dīcentis** audīvī. Cūr pater illī ignōtō mē dat? Cūr parentēs meī Cordum **ignōrantēs**
mē nōn auscultant? Nōn Iullum sed alterum amō! Vae mē! Tōta vīta mea miserābilis erit."

Passer **circumsiliēns** et **pīpiāns** nihil puellae **lacrimantī** dīcit. Servīlia passerī prīmum digitum dat et avis digi-
20 tum puellae **lacrimantis** rostrō mordet. Avis sīc cūrās tristēs puellae levat. Servīlia, etiam misera, rīdet per lacrimās
cadentēs et "Passer," inquit puella, "amīcus meus fidēlis es."

Puella passerem in gremiō tenet.

VERBA ŪTENDA

alter, altera, alterum **the**
other (of two)
amātōrius, -a -um amatory,
love
auscultō (1) listen to
avis, avis f. bird
cadō, cadere, cecidī fall
carmen, carminis n. **song,**
poem
circumsiliō, circumsilīre,
circumsiluī leap around,
hop
cor, cordis n. **heart**
cūra, -ae f. care, concern
dēliciae, -ārum f. pl. delight,
pet
digitus, -ī m. finger (see
prīmum)

dolor, dolōris n. pain, grief;
suī dolōris is gen., but
translate "for her sorrow."
dūcere in mātrimōnium marry
etiam still, and also, even
now
fidēlis, -e faithful
gremium, -iī n. lap
hoc/hōc this
ignōrō (1) be ignorant of
ignōtus, -a, -um unknown
ille, illa, illud he, she, it;
they; that, those; *illīus*
of that; *illī* to that
is, ea, id he, she, it; they
iste, ista, istud that one
(derogatory); *istīus* of
that

lacrimō (1) **cry, shed tears**
levō (1) lift, lighten
maestus, -a, -um sad
mens, mentis f. mind
miser, misera, miserum
wretched, miserable
miserābilis, -e miserable
mordeō, mordēre,
momordī bite
neuter, neutra, neutrum
neither; *neutrī* "to
neither"
nūbō, nūbere, nupsī marry
nūllus, -a, -um no, not any,
none; *nūllī aliī* to no other
numquam never
ōh oh! (used to express
surprise, joy, pain, etc.)

passer, passeris m. sparrow
petō, petere, petīvī/petiī
seek, look for
pīpiō (1) chirp
plōrō (1) weep, cry
plūs more
prīmum digitum the tip of
her finger
quōmodo how
rostrum, -ī n. beak
senex, senis m. old man
sōlāciolum, -ī n. relief,
comfort
tālis, -e such
tōtus, -a, -um whole, all
trīgintā thirty
vae woe! (in pain or dread)
vetus, veteris old

POSTQUAM LĒGISTĪ

Answer in English or Latin (L) as directed.

1. (L) Where and when does *Lectiō Prīma* take place?
2. (L) What is Servilia doing as the *lectiō* begins?
3. What is the name of Servilia's pet bird? Why does it have this name?
4. Why is Servilia upset?
5. How do Servilia's situation and feelings compare to those of a modern American teenage girl in similar circumstances?
6. Why does Servilia laugh at the end of the *lectiō*?

Grammatica A

Forming the Present Participle

As verbal adjectives, participles have grammatical features of both parts of speech.

- **As verbs,** they express actions, can take objects, and have tense and voice.
- **As adjectives**, they agree with nouns in gender, number, and case (GNC).

The participles you are learning right now are **present** tense and are translated by adding -ing to the verb; e.g., *vōcans* (calling). There are also participles in other tenses you will learn later.

Here are the complete forms of the present active participle *vocāns*:

SINGULAR		CASE	PLURAL	
Masculine/ Feminine	**Neuter**		**Masculine/ Feminine**	**Neuter**
vocā**ns**	vocā**ns**	Nominative	voca**ntēs**	voca**ntia**
voca**ntis**	voca**ntis**	Genitive	voca**ntium**	voca**ntium**
voca**ntī**	voca**ntī**	Dative	voca**ntibus**	voca**ntibus**
voca**ntem**	vocā**ns**	Accusative	voca**ntēs**	voca**ntia**
voca**ntī** / voca**nte**	voca**ntī** / voca**nte**	Ablative	voca**ntibus**	voca**ntibus**

Reminder: The neuter differs from the masculine/feminine forms in only a few places. Find them.

Notā Bene:

- Present participles generally use the same endings as 3ʳᵈ declension adjectives.
- The ablative singular normally ends in -*ntī*. You will learn later when the -*nte* ending is used.

Forming participles from other conjugations is just a matter of getting the connecting vowel(s) right:

1ˢᵗ Conjugation	2ⁿᵈ Conjugation	3ʳᵈ Conjugation	3ʳᵈ -*iō* Conjugation	4ᵗʰ Conjugation
*vocā**ns***	*hab**ēns***	*dūc**ēns***	*cap**iēns***	*aud**iēns***
calling	having	leading	taking	hearing

While you were doing Exercise 17-1, you probably noticed that most of the participles were marked by -*ēns*/-*ent*-. The -*e*- is of limited help in determining the conjugation of the participle. The only sure way to confirm the conjugation is to look up the verb in a dictionary.

EXERCEĀMUS!

17-2 Identifying Participles

Use the declension of *vocāns* to identify the correct case and number of each of the following participles.

1. dūcentis: a. genitive singular; b. genitive plural; c. accusative plural; d. ablative plural

2. audientem: a. nominative singular; b. genitive singular; c. dative singular; d. accusative singular

3. capientēs: a. accusative singular; b. genitive plural; c. nominative plural; d. ablative plural

4. habentibus: a. nominative singular; b. genitive plural; c. accusative plural; d. dative plural

5. ambulantium: a. ablative plural; b. accusative singular; c. genitive plural; d. nominative singular

6. dūcentī: a. accusative singular; b. ablative singular; c. nominative singular; d. genitive singular

7. audiēns: a. nominative singular; b. nominative plural; c. ablative singular; d. genitive singular

8. capientibus: a. accusative singular; b. genitive plural; c. nominative plural; d. ablative plural

Using Participles

Participles as Substantives

As adjectives, participles describe people and things and therefore have gender, number, and case. So, as you noticed when you did Exercise 17-1, whenever you see a participle in a Latin sentence you must ask yourself what this participle is describing or modifying.

Sometimes, however, participles have no noun to describe but are **substantives**, i.e., they are adjectives acting like nouns.

Here is an example of a participle used as a substantive, from *Lectiō Prīma:*

> *Omnēs **amantēs** carmina Catullī legere dēbent.*
> All those loving ought to read the poems of Catullus.
> All people loving ought to read the poems of Catullus.
> All people who are in love ought to read the poems of Catullus.
> All lovers ought to read the poems of Catullus.

Notice how many ways we can translate ***amantēs*** into English to show that it is plural. Here are a few more examples based on sentences from *Lectiō Prīma.*

*Post cēnam in cubiculō **lacrimāns** sedet.*	**lacrimāns** = the person crying
*Post cēnam sōla in cubiculō **lacrimāns** sedet.*	**lacrimāns** = the crying girl
*In vīā **ambulantem** numquam vīdī.*	**ambulantem** = a person walking
*In vīā **ambulantēs** numquam vīdī.*	**ambulantēs** = people walking

How many other ways can you translate these participles into English?

Relative Time in Participles

The tense of a participle does not show real time, but relative time. This means that the participle has no time of its own but rather shows a relationship with the time of the main verb. This takes some consideration to understand, and you will learn a lot more about relative time as you continue your study of Latin. The **present participle** indicates that the "time" of the participle is the **same time as the main verb**.

Compare these sentences:

Servīliam lacrimantem videō.	I see Servilia crying.
Servīliam lacrimantem vīdī.	I saw Servilia crying.
Servīliam lacrimantem vidēbō.	I will see Servilia crying.

In each case, the present participle indicates that the crying is, was, or will be simultaneous with the main verb.

EXERCEĀMUS!

17-3 Translating Participles

Translate these sentences, which show various cases of the participle. Three are substantives. The participles are underlined.

1. Passer puellae <u>lacrimantis</u> in gremiō sedet.
2. Nōmen <u>lacrimantī</u> Servīlia est.
3. Marcus sorōrem <u>lacrimantem</u> valdē amat.
4. Cor <u>amantis</u> saepe triste est.
5. Catullus <u>amantēs</u> bene intellegit.

Lectiō Secunda

Antequam Legis

In this *lectiō* Marcus and Lucius talk about the upcoming gladiatorial games. As you read about these games, watch for examples of a special group of adjectives and pronouns.

-īus/-ī Adjectives

Consider the following sentences from *Lectiō Prīma*:

*In domō **istīus** senis numquam habitābō!* (line 12)
***Nūllī aliī** virō cor umquam meum dabō!* (line 13)
Fortasse **neutrī** cor meum dabō. (line 13)

These words marked in bold are part of a group of adjectives and pronouns that have normal 2-1-2 adjective endings, **except in two places**:

- m./f./n. gen. sing. **-īus**   *nūllīus, neutrīus, istīus, alīus*
- m./f./n. dative sing. **-ī**   *nūllī, neutrī, istī, aliī*

You should have no trouble translating these words, once you recognize their special genitive and dative singular endings. Watch for more of these words in *Lectiō Secunda*, where they are marked in **bold**.

EXERCEĀMUS!

17-4 -īus/-ī Adjectives

Find ten *-īus/-ī* adjectives marked in **bold** in *Lectiō Secunda*. List the number, case, and meaning of each word. Remember that *-īus* is genitive singular and *-ī* is dative singular. Follow the models.

Line	*-ius/-ī* Adjective	Number	Case	Meaning
1	aliā	sing.	abl.	other
2	ipse	sing.	nom.	himself

🔊 DĒ MŪNERIBUS

Sedentēs in **aliā** parte domī Servīlius, Marcus et Lūcius dē mūneribus dīcunt. Crās Imperātor Augustus **ipse** magna mūnera in amphitheātrō dabit.

"Marce et Lūcī, spectābitisne mūnera?" Servīlius rogat.

5   "Certē, pater," respondet Marcus. "Haec mūnera magnifica erunt! Sed quid vidēbimus in amphitheātrō sedentēs?"

"Vidēbitis," respondet pater, "gladiātōrēs cum **aliīs** gladiātōribus pugnantēs. **Aliī** gladiīs pugnābunt, **aliī** tridentibus et rētibus. In **ūnā** pugnā duō gladiātōrēs pugnābunt—**ūnus** gladiō et **alter** tridente

10 pugnābit. Fortasse **neuter** vīvus ex amphitheātrō exībit."

Lūcius rogat: "Eruntne animālia in mūneribus? Quālia animālia?"

Leō ferox damnātum in harēnā interficit.

Pater "Sīc, fīlī," inquit. "**Nōnnūllī** gladiātōrēs et multī damnātī cum animālibus exōticīs **tōtīus** Āfricae pugnābunt. Vidēbitis leōnēs et panthērās et elephantēs. Et harēnam cruentam quoque vidēbitis—cruōrem et

15 animālium et hominum!"

"Euax! Quandō," poscit Lūcius, "ad amphitheātrum ībimus?"

"Māne," respondet **alter** frāter, "īre dēbēbimus, sī **ulla** animālia vidēre poterimus. Multī māne surgentēs ad amphitheātrum venient et **illī** adveniēntēs māne optimum prospectum habēbunt." Sed tū, pater, ībisne nōbīscum?"

Servīlius "Nōn vōbīscum," inquit, "īre possum. Crās **nūlla** mūnera vidēbō quod multa negōtia mihi erunt. Sed

20 **illa** mūnera nōn **ūnīus** diēī sed trium diērum sunt et fortasse sērius ea vidēbō.

🔊 VERBA ŪTENDA

Āfrica, -ae f. the Roman province of Africa (modern Tunisia and Algeria)
aliī . . . aliī some . . . others . . .
alter, altera, alterum the other (of two)
amphitheātrum, -ī n. amphitheater
animal, -ālis n. animal
certē certainly
cruentus, -a, -um bloody
cruor, cruōris m. gore, blood
damnātus condemned criminal
diēs, diēī m. day

ea them
elephās, -antis m. elephant
euax! hurray!
exōticus, -a, -um strange, exotic
ferox, ferōcis fierce
gladiātor, -ōris m. gladiator
gladius, -iī m. sword
haec these
harēna, -ae f. sand
ille, illa, illud he, she, it; they; that, those
imperātor, -tōris m. emperor
ipse, ipsa, ipsum he, she, it; they; himself, herself,

itself, themselves (emphatic)
is, ea, id he, she, it, they
leō, leōnis m. lion
magnificus, -a, -um noble, elegant, magnificent
mūnus, -eris, n. function, duty; gift; pl. games, public shows, spectacles
neuter, neutra, neutrum neither
nōbīscum with us
nōnnūllī some, several
nūllus, -a, -um no, not any, none
optimus, -a, -um best

panthēra, -ae f. leopard
pars, partis f. part, piece
prospectum m. view
pugna, -ae f. fight
quālis, quāle? what kind of? what sort of?
quandō when
rēte, rētis n. net
sērius later, too late
surgō, surgere, surrēxī rise, get up
tōtus, -a, -um whole, all
tridens, tridentis m. trident
ūllus, -a, -um any
vīvus, -a, -um living
vōbīs dat./abl. you (all); *vōbīscum* "with you"

POSTQUAM LĒGISTĪ

Answer in English or Latin (L) as directed.

1. What characters are holding a conversation in *Lectiō Secunda*? Where are they?
2. What kinds of gladiatorial contests are mentioned in this conversation?

3. When will these gladiatorial contests take place? Who is sponsoring them?
4. (L) Answer Lucius' questions in lines 11-12: *Eruntne animālia in mūneribus? Quālia animālia?*
5. At what other times in European or American history have condemned criminals been a source of sport or entertainment for the general public?
6. (L) Why is Servilius unable to go to these games?
7. How does this form of entertainment compare to those in the United States today?

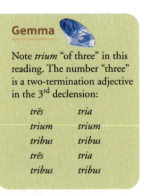

Gemma

Note *trium* "of three" in this reading. The number "three" is a two-termination adjective in the 3rd declension:

trēs	*tria*
trium	*trium*
tribus	*tribus*
trēs	*tria*
tribus	*tribus*

Grammatica B

Special Adjectives: UNUS NAUTA

A number of Latin 2-1-2 adjectives have -*īus* genitive singular endings and -*ī* dative singular endings. The phrase UNUS NAUTA forms an acronym to help you remember most of these words.

Ūllus, -a, -um any
Nūllus, -a, -um no, none
Ūnus, -a, -um one
Sōlus, -a, -um alone, only

Neuter, neutra, neutrum neither
Alter, altera, alterum the other (of two)
Uter, utra, utrum either, which (of two)
Tōtus, -a, -um whole, entire
Alius, -a, -ud another, other

Gemma

Criminals were often condemned (*damnātī*) to die in the arena in ancient Rome.

Notā Bene:

- Most of these adjectives have masculine singulars ending in -*us*, but *uter* and *neuter* have -*er* endings and have stems like *pulcher, pulchra, pulchrum*; *alter* has a stem like *līber, lībera, līberum*.
- The rest of the endings for these words are regular.

Gemma

UNUS NAUTA is also a great way to remember that, although *nauta* is in the 1st declension, it is nevertheless masculine.

Here is the full declension of *sōlus* with the unusual endings in **bold**.

SINGULAR			CASE	PLURAL		
Masculine	**Feminine**	**Neuter**		**Masculine**	**Feminine**	**Neuter**
sōlus	sōla	sōlum	Nominative	sōlī	sōlae	sōla
sōlīus	**sōlīus**	**sōlīus**	Genitive	sōlōrum	sōlārum	sōlōrum
sōlī	**sōlī**	**sōlī**	Dative	sōlīs	sōlīs	sōlīs
sōlum	sōlam	sōlum	Accusative	sōlōs	sōlās	sōla
sōlō	sōlā	sōlō	Ablative	sōlīs	sōlīs	sōlīs

The endings of these words can cause some confusion. For example, *ūllī* can be masculine nominative plural or dative singular, any gender. But often the accompanying words will help you identify what GNC the pair represents.

ūllī fēminae dative singular (*ūllī* cannot be masculine here because it is GNC'ing with a feminine word)

ūllī virī nominative plural (**virī** can be genitive singular or nominative plural, but **ūllī** can only be nominative plural)

ūllīus virī genitive singular

ūllī virō dative singular

Is, Ea, Id

These pronouns are declined similarly to the UNUS NAUTA words. They are most common-ly used as **3rd person personal pronouns**, i.e., to indicate "he," "she," "it," and "they." You al-ready learned some forms of *is, ea, id*. Now look at the entire declension and take special note of the genitive and dative singular forms in **bold**.

SINGULAR			CASE	PLURAL		
Masculine	**Feminine**	**Neuter**		**Masculine**	**Feminine**	**Neuter**
is	ea	id	Nominative	eī	eae	ea
eius	**eius**	**eius**	Genitive	eōrum	eārum	eōrum
eī	**eī**	**eī**	Dative	eīs	eīs	eīs
eum	eam	id	Accusative	eōs	eās	ea
eō	eā	eō	Ablative	eīs	eīs	eīs

Notā Bene:

- The plural forms are entirely regular 2-1-2 adjectives, with the stem *e-*.
- Note *eius* vs. *sōlīus*, i.e., the short rather than long *-i-*.
- Unlike the English "they," the forms of *is, ea, id* can distinguish the gender in the 3rd person plural:

Vocant.	They call.
Eī vocant.	They (men) call.
Eae vocant.	They (women) call.

Demonstrative Pronouns and Adjectives

Three demonstrative pronouns and adjectives also have the same endings as the UNUS NAUTA words and *is, ea, id*. **Demonstratives** are words used to point out (*demonstrō, demon-strāre*) or emphasize the nouns to which they refer. Some English demonstratives are "this," "that," "these," and "those."

Your job is just to remember what they mean and not to forget the endings you already know, especially *-īus* in the genitive singular and *-ī* in the dative singular.

ipse, ipsa, ipsum	one's self (emphatic)
iste, ista, istud	that man (of yours), that woman, that thing
ille, illa, illud	that man, that woman, that thing

Notā Bene:

- *Iste* is generally not well intentioned. So *iste amīcus tuus* often means "that so-and-so friend of yours."
- *Ipse* is translated depending on what it modifies or refers to. Compare:

*Fēmina **ipsa** id fēcit.*	The woman **herself** did it.
*Ego **ipse** id fēcī.*	I **myself** did it.
*Nōs **ipsī** id fēcimus.*	We **ourselves** did it.

- The forms of *ille* can be either pronouns or adjectives. Compare:

ille	he	*ille vir*	that man
illa	she	*illa fēmina*	that woman
illud	it	*illud carmen*	that song

EXERCEĀMUS!

17-5 **GNC'ing**

Identify the GNCs of these word pairs. Then translate the pairs accordingly.

1. alīus puellae
2. neutrō homine
3. nūllī hominī
4. sōlōrum animālium

5. ūllae sorōrēs
6. aliī ancillae
7. virī ipsīus
8. iste adulescens

9. tōtā familiā
10. illīus fēminae

Mōrēs Rōmānī

Roman Attitudes Toward Animals

Romans had a more practical view of animals than we do today. For the most part, domesticated animals were kept for specific purposes. They provided food (sheep, goats); labor (oxen, horses, mules); raw material (wax, horn, pelts, fibers); and entertainment (the exotic animals at the games). Dogs were kept for guarding or hunting. Cats were ratters, and you will soon meet a cat that earns its keep in the Subura. Socrates the pet monkey served as entertainment for the customers at Licinia's *taberna* and is modeled on actual depictions of such animals in Roman life.

The animals Romans kept also varied according to their social status, wealth, and living accommodations. Dogs were commonly employed in the city as watchdogs, but in the country they would guard herds and flocks. Other dogs were used for hunting. A lap dog indicated that the owner could afford an animal that served no useful purpose. This definition of a "pet" fits Servilia's sparrow nicely.

Here is a simplified version of Catullus 2, the poem about Lesbia's sparrow. This poem served as an inspiration for the scene with Servilia and her pet sparrow. See how many echoes of this poem you can find in *Lectiō Prīma*.

> Passer, dēliciae meae puellae,
> quīcum lūdere solet
> quem in sinū tenēre solet
> cui prīmum digitum dare appetentī solet
> 5 et cui acrīs morsūs incitāre solet,
> cum libet dēsīderiō meō iocārī,
> et sōlāciolum suī dolōris invenīre
> ut tum ardor gravis acquiescat:
> tēcum lūdere sīcut ipsa
> 10 et cūrās tristēs animī levāre possem!

🔊 VERBA ŪTENDA

acquiescō (1) quiet down, subside
acer, acris, acre sharp; *acrīs = acrēs*
aliquid something
animus, -ī m. mind
appetō, appetere, appetīvī / appetiī seek, grasp for
ardor, ardōris m. fire, flame
cui to whom

cūra, ae f. worry, concern, care, anxiety
dēliciae, -ārum f. pl. delight, favorite, pet
dēsīderium, -iī n. desire, wish
digitus, -ī m. finger
dolor, dolōris m. pain, grief
incitō (1) incite; spur on
iocārī to joke
ipse, ipsa, ipsum he, she, it; they; himself, herself,

itself, themselves (emphatic)
levō (1) lift, lighten
libet imp. (+ dat.) it is pleasing (to someone)
lūdō, lūdere, lūsī play, tease
morsūs bites, nibbles (acc. pl.)
passer, passeris m. sparrow
possem "I wish I were able"
prīmum digitum fingertip

quem whom
quīcum with whom
quid = aliquid some
sinū lap
sōlāciolum, -ī n. relief, comfort
soleō, solēre be accustomed (to)
tum then
ut so that, in order that

Latīna Hodierna

Opposites in Latin and English

Thinking in terms of opposites not only helps you learn Latin vocabulary but will increase your English vocabulary. Here are some examples:

magnus, -a, -um	large	**magn**ify, **magn**ificent
parvus, -a, -um	small	**parv**ovirus
longus, -a, -um	long	**long**itude, e**long**ate, pro**long**
brevis, -e	short	**brief**, **brev**ity, **brev**iary
immānis, immāne	huge, vast	**immen**se
exiguus, -a, -um	scanty, very small	**exigu**ous, **exigu**ity
celer, celeris, celere	swift, fast	**celer**ity, ac**celer**ate, de**celer**ate
tardus, -a, -um	slow	**tard**y, **tard**iness

Orbis Terrārum Rōmānus

Prōvinciae Āfricānae

The Romans used the word *Āfrica* to refer in general to the entire continent as far as it was known to them; however, the word most commonly referred to the province located in what is now modern Tunisia and Algeria, bordering on the Mediterranean. This area came under Roman control after 146 B.C. with the final defeat of Carthage in the Third Punic War.

By the time of Augustus, both Numidia and Mauritania had also come under direct Roman control and the original province became known as *Āfrica prōconsulāris* (Proconsular Africa), *Āfrica Vetus* (Old Africa), or *Āfrica Propria* (Africa Proper). The entire region became

Prōvinciae Āfricānae

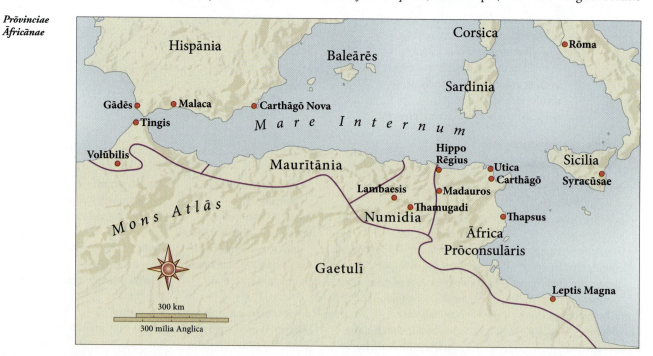

very urbanized with important cities like Carthage, Leptis Magna, Thapsus, and Utica. During the Empire, the entire Mediterranean coast of Africa was an important agricultural and commercial region as well as an important source for wild beasts for the games in the arena. Many army veterans were also settled in colonies at Thamugadi (modern Timgad, Algeria) and Lambaesis (also in Algeria).

Some important Romans from the provinces of Africa included:

Basilica Septimiī Sevērī Leptis Magnae

- **Apuleius** (ca. 123/125–ca. 180 A.D.), the author of *Metamorphōsēs* (*The Metamorphoses*) or *Aureus Asinus* (*The Golden Ass*), was born in Madaurus (now M'Daourouch, Algeria) in Numidia.

- **Septimius Sevērus** (145–211 A.D.), emperor from 193 until 211, was born in Leptis Magna (now in Libya). As emperor he beautified and enriched his hometown. The remains of the Severan basilica in Leptis Magna illustrate the magnificence of his gifts.

- **Augustine** (354–430 A.D.), was a major theologian and Father of the Christian Church. He was born in Hippo Regius, where he later served as bishop. He was also the author of an autobiography called *Confessiōnēs* (*The Confessions*).

QUID PUTĀS?

1. How do you think Roman attitudes toward animals compare to modern American attitudes?
2. How do the boundaries of the Roman provinces in African compare to national boundaries today?
3. Servilia takes solace in the poetry of Catullus. Where might a modern American go for similar comfort today?
4. Use Latin to explain the relationship between the English words "immense" and "exiguous."

EXERCEĀMUS!

17-6 Scrībāmus

Use the *lectiōnēs* to answer the following questions in Latin. Base your answers on the story (not on the Catullus poem) and answer in complete Latin sentences. Follow the model.

→ Quis sōlāciolum suī dolōris petēns rīdet?
    Servīlia, sōlāciolum petēns, rīdet.

1. Quis passerem sedentem in gremiō tenet?

2. Quis Iullum ambulantem in viā numquam vīdit?

3. Quis circumsiliēns et pīpiāns nihil dīcit?

4. Quis circumsilientī passerī dīcit?

5. Quis digitum puellae lacrimantis mordet?

17-7 Colloquāmur

Use the questions and answers in Exercise 17-6 to practice asking and answering questions with a classmate.

Gemma

Since **neuter, neutra, neutrum** = **neither**, "neuter" gender is "neither" masculine nor feminine!

17-8   Verba Discenda

Use the *Verba Discenda* to answer the questions below.

1. List the UNUS NAUTA words included in this *Verba Discenda*. What do they mean?

2. Find at least three words directly related to the Roman games. What do they mean?

3. What is the 3rd principal part of *lacrimō*?

4. What Latin word is the plural equivalent of *tibi*?

5. Which Latin pronoun in the *Verba Discenda* would you use to refer to someone you do not like?

6. *Passerēs, leōnēs, panthērae,* and *elephantēs* are examples of this *Verbum Discendum*.

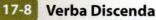 **VERBA DISCENDA**

alter, altera, alterum the other (of two) [alteration]

amphitheātrum, -ī n. amphitheater

animal, -ālis n. animal

carmen, carminis n. song, poem

cor, cordis n. heart [cordial]

etiam still, and also, even now

gladiātor, -ōris m. gladiator

gladius, -iī m. sword [gladiola]

ille, illa, illud he, she, it; they; that, those

ipse, ipsa, ipsum he, she, it; they; himself, herself, itself, themselves (emphatic)

is, ea, id he, she, it; they [id]

iste, ista, istud that one (derogatory)

lacrimō (1) cry, shed tears [lacrimose]

mūnus, -eris, n. function, duty; gift; pl. games, public shows, spectacles [munificence]

neuter, neutra, neutrum neither [neutral]

nūllus, -a, -um no, not any, none [nullify]

numquam never

quōmodo how

sērius later, too late

tōtus, -a, -um whole, all [totality]

ūllus, -a, -um any

vōbīs dat./abl. you (all)

Angulus Grammaticus

Gender

English, like Latin, knows about grammatical gender. What do we mean by that? Well, in English we can show gender by means of pronouns like "he," "she," and "it" and with words like "his," "her," and "its." Sometimes we can distinguish male and female by changing suffixes; for example, "-ess" in "seamster"/"seamstress," "poet"/"poetess," "master"/"mistress".

English has also borrowed from Latin another suffix that can make English nouns feminine instead of masculine: "-trix," as in "mediator"/"mediatrix," "aviator"/"aviatrix," and "testator"/"testatrix". But these gender indicators began dying out in English as gender equality became more and more important in American society.

Latin, on the other hand, uses the concept of gender more rigorously, since every noun bears a **grammatical gender**. So words like *pecūnia* (money), *virtūs* (virtue, manliness), and *mālus* (apple tree) are always feminine, while *mālus* (ship's mast), *lūdus* (game, school), *amor* (love), and *annus* (year) are always masculine. This makes little sense to an English speaker for whom all these words are things and therefore neuter. Modern European languages like French, Spanish, Italian, and German, however, employ gender in much the same way that Latin does. So studying Latin can help you understand how those languages work.

18

Fugitīvus!

Lectiō Prīma

Antequam Legis

Here we get to see a glimpse of life inside an *insula*. We meet Mendax the beggar, his cat Felix, and an unexpected visitor. Amid all this you will also meet the **imperfect tense**.

The Imperfect Tense

The imperfect tense of regular verbs:

- has the tense marker *-ba-* before the normal personal endings. Thus: *-bam, -bās, -bat, -bāmus, -bātis, -bant.*

- Translate it by using the English "used to" or "was/were 'verb'ing". Thus, *vocābāmus* is translated "we used to call" or "we were calling."

The imperfect tense of *sum* and *possum*:

- Do you remember that the stem of *sum* for the future was *er-* as in *erō, eris, erit*, etc.?

- The imperfect of *sum* uses the same *er-* stem but with a different vowel pattern: *eram, erās, erat*, etc. Translate as a simple "was/were" or "used to be."

- The imperfect of *possum*, whose stem is *pot-* is easy: *poteram, poterās, poterat*, etc. Translate as "was/were able" or "could."

  That is all you need to know in order to translate the next section. To help you, all the imperfect tense verbs are in **bold** in the *Lectiō Prīma*.

Pistrīnum Pompeiīs

Fēlix Fēlēs Murēs Multōs Capit.

EXERCEĀMUS!

18-1 Identifying Imperfects

Before you read *Lectiō Prīma*, make a line-by-line list of all the imperfect verbs (marked in **bold**). Determine their person and number. Then use the *Verba Ūtenda* to translate them. Follow the model.

	Line	Verb	Person	Number	English Translation
→	2	adveniēbant	3rd	plural	they were arriving at

MENDAX

Dum Marcus et Lūcius in Vīminālī dē mūneribus dīcunt, in Subūrā Licinia, Valeria, et Flāvia ad insulam suam **adveniēbant**. Multī habitantēs in insulā egēnī sunt et nūllam pecūniam habent. Ūnus ex eīs Mendax est. Ōlim, cum in pistrīnō **labōrābat**, nōmen eī "Quintus" **erat** sed labor

5 strēnuus **erat** et mox Quintus, aegrescēns, nōn **labōrābat**. Rōmam **veniēbat** sed aeger labōrem invenīre nōn **poterat**.

Ut Mendāx dīcit: "Egēnus **eram** et famem magnam **habēbam**. Ergō, pecūniam ab hominibus in viā ambulantibus poscere **incipiēbam**. Quid aliud facere **poteram**?"

10 Mox Quintus nōmen novum **habēbat**—Mendax. Cūr? Quod mendīcus est vir pecūniam ab aliīs poscēns et talēs hominēs rārō vērum dīcunt.

Mendax prō paucīs nummīs nōn cellam propriam sed parvum spatium sub scālīs habēre **poterat**. Hoc spatium parvum et fētidum, sed siccum est, et hīc nōn sōlum Mendax sed etiam fēlēs sua, Fēlix nōmine,

15 trēs annōs habitant. Fēlix illud nōmen habet quod Mendax eam aegram et paene mortuam in viā invēnit. Omnēs Fēlīcem amant quod iam dūdum mūrēs multōs in insulā capit—et in Subūrā multī mūrēs sunt!

Valeria in insulam intrāns Mendācem salūtat. "Salvē, Mendax," inquit Valeria, "quid tū et Fēlix agitis? Quid fortūnae hodiē **capiēbātis**?"

20 "Bonum nōbīs est," respondet Mendax. "Hodiē ego multōs nummōs et Fēlix quinque mūrēs cēpimus. Mea fēlēs fortis in amphitheātrō pugnāre dēbet!"

Subitō, vir territus in insulam rūpit. Sē ad terram iēcit et, "Mē adiuvāte!!" clāmāvit.

Valeria et aliī attonitī sunt quod homō territus servus est. Collāre in collō habet et collāre inscriptiōnem habet. Prīmae magnae litterae sunt "TMQF" et hae litterae significant "Tenē mē quia fūgī." Ecce, servus fugiēns!

Hīc habitat Familia Valeriae—omnēs in duābus cellīs!

Ōlim Mendax in pistrīnō labōrābat.

🔊 VERBA ŪTENDA

aeger, aegra, aegrum sick
aegrescō, aegrescere
   grow sick
attonitus, -a, -um
   astonished
cella, -ae f. room
collāre, collāris n. collar
collum, -ī n. neck
dūdum See *iam.*
egēnus, -a, -um destitute,
   poverty stricken
famēs, -is f. hunger
fēlēs, fēlis f. cat
**fēlix, fēlīcis lucky,
   fortunate**
fētidus, -a, -um foul
   smelling
hae these
iaciō, iacere, iēcī hurl,
   throw

iam dūdum for a long time
   now (used with
   present tense)
**incipiō, incipere, incēpī,
   inceptum begin**
inscriptiō, -iōnis f.
   inscription
intrō (1) enter
littera, -ae f. letter of the
   alphabet
mendax, mendācis
   untruthful; *Mendax* "Liar"
mendīcus, -ī m. beggar
mortuus, -a, -um dead
mūs, mūris m. mouse
nōn sōlum ... sed etiam
   not only ... but also
nummus, -ī m. coin
ōlim once, formerly
paene almost

pistrīnum, -ī n. mill
prīmus, -a, -um first
proprius, -a, -um one's own
quia since
rārō rarely
Rōmam "to Rome"
rumpō, rumpere, rūpī burst,
   break open
scālae, -ārum f. pl. stairs,
   staircase
siccus, -a, -um dry
significō (1) mean
spatium, -iī n. space
strēnuus, -a, -um hard,
   strenuous
tālis, tāle such, of such a
   sort
vērus, -a, um true; *vērum* is a
   substantive, so translate
   here as "the truth"

POSTQUAM LĒGISTĪ

1. What was the beggar Mendax's original name? Where did he work formerly?
2. How did he become a beggar? And how did he get the name *Mendax*?
3. Why do the residents of this apartment building like Felix?
4. Who appears suddenly at the end of the story? How is his identity known?

Grammatica A

Forming the Imperfect Tense

The imperfect tense is the third and last tense in what is called the **present system**, which also includes the present and future tenses. The following chart shows you how to form the imperfect.

FORMING THE IMPERFECT							
1st / 2nd **Conjugations**				3rd / 4th **Conjugations**			
Present Stem + (2nd principal part – *-re*)				**Short Present Stem** + (1st principal part – *-ō*)			
		-bam	-bāmus			-ēbam	-ēbāmus
		-bās	-bātis			-ēbās	-ēbātis
		-bat	-bant			-ēbat	-ēbant

Thus:

IMPERFECT ENDINGS	1ST CONJUGATION	2ND CONJUGATION	3RD CONJUGATION	3RD-iō CONJUGATION	4TH CONJUGATION
-bam	vocābam	monēbam	dūcēbam	capiēbam	audiēbam
-bās	vocābās	monēbās	dūcēbās	capiēbās	audiēbās
-bat	vocābat	monēbat	dūcēbat	capiēbat	audiēbat
-bāmus	vocābāmus	monēbāmus	dūcēbāmus	capiēbāmus	audiēbāmus
-bātis	vocābātis	monēbātis	dūcēbātis	capiēbātis	audiēbātis
-bant	vocābant	monēbant	dūcēbant	capiēbant	audiēbant

Notā Bene:

- 3rd -io and 4th conjugation verbs have *-ie-* before *-ba-*.
- *Sum* and *possum* use familiar endings but have an irregular stem for the imperfect:

SUM	POSSUM
eram	poteram
erās	poterās
erat	poterat
erāmus	poterāmus
erātis	poterātis
erant	poterant

Aspect of the Imperfect and Perfect

Why does Latin need both an imperfect and a perfect tense? The answer is something grammarians call **aspect**. The perfect tense indicates that the action of the verb is simple, i.e., it happened only once in the past. (Think of a photograph.) The imperfect tense indicates that the action of the verb is a continuing action in the past. (Think of a video recording.) Consider this English sentence:

We were watching television when the lights went out.

"We were watching television" is the equivalent of the Latin imperfect. It shows that the action continued in the past for a period of time. "The lights went out" is the equivalent of the Latin perfect. It indicates that the action happened only once.

Note: Latin and English tenses do not always match on a one-to-one basis. For example, Latin uses the **present tense** to indicate a continuous action that started in the past but continues in the present, in an expression like:

*Hīc Mendax et fēlēs sua, Fēlix nōmine, trēs annōs **habitant**.*
Here Mendax and his cat, Felix by name, have lived for three years.

In this case English prefers the perfect tense (have lived) while Latin uses the present tense (*habitant*). Likewise, whereas English says "While we were walking ..." Latin says *Dum ambulāmus ...* literally, "While we walk." This is always the case, even if the surrounding verbs are in the past tenses.

Compare this example of **continuous time with the conjunction *dum*** in a sentence from *Lectiō Prīma*:

***Dum** Marcus et Lūcius dē mūneribus **dīcunt**, in Subūrā Licinia, Valeria, et Flāvia ad insulam suam adveniēbant.*
While Marcus and Lucius were talking about the games, in the Subura Licinia, Valeria, and Flavia were arriving at their apartment house.

18-2 **Tense Substitution**

Change each of the following present tense verbs to the imperfect without changing person and number. Then translate both verbs. Follow the model.

	Present	Translation	Imperfect	Translation
→	dīcunt	they say	dīcēbant	they were saying

1. habitant
2. advenis
3. habent
4. est
5. labōrō

6. venītis
7. potest
8. incipiunt
9. possumus
10. invenit

11. intrāmus
12. estis
13. amātis
14. capit

Lectiō Secunda

Antequam Legis

The inhabitants of the *insula* are in a bind. Helping a runaway slave was a serious crime and their instincts fight with their sense of self-preservation. As they do so, they use a lot of what Latin students have called "all those Q-words."

Interrogative and Relative Pronouns and Adjectives

The "Q-words" tend to look alike and be used in several ways. In English they are the "W-words" as in "who, what, which" and their various forms.

Here is what you need to know to read the following passage:

- *Quī, quae, quod* can mean "who," "which," or even "that."
- *Quis, quid?* are always interrogative and mean "who?" or "what?"
- *Cuius, quōrum, quārum* can mean "whose," of "whom," or "of which."
- Some forms, like *quō* and *quārum*, use 2-1-2 declension endings.
- Other forms, like *cuius* and *cui*, have genitive and dative singular endings like those in *is* and *ille*.

As you read the *lectiō* use these hints to translate the "Q-words." But keep your eyes peeled. Sometimes the "Q-word" is used alone and sometimes it modifies a noun. At other times it asks a question.

18-3 **Identifying Relative and Interrogative Pronouns**

As you read *Lectiō Secunda* make a line-by-line list of all Q-words marked in **bold**. Use the endings and the guidelines above to identify the case and number of each. Then translate the word into English. Use a question mark where appropriate. Follow the model.

	Line	Pronoun	Case	Number	Translation
→	1	quis	nom.	sing.	who?

🔊 TENĒ MĒ QUIA FŪGĪ

Servus, tremēns, oculōs ad terram tenēbat. Valeria eum rogāvit, "**Quis** es, aut, rectius, **cuius** es? **Cui** labōrās? A **quō** fūgistī? Ad **quem** locum fugis?"

Servus nihil dīxit, sed digitō trementī collāre monstrāvit. Valeria litterās **quae** in collārī erant lēgit: "TMQF. Revocā mē dominō meō Publiō Nonniō Zēthō, Ostiensī. Praemium accipiēs."

5   Brevī tempore silentium erat. Perīculōsum est servō fugientī auxilium dare. Cīvēs Rōmānī servīs **quī** fūgērunt nūllum auxilium dare dēbent.

Sed Valeria alma servō iterum dīxit: "Publiī Nonnī es. Hoc sciō. Sed **quis** est ille Publius Nonnius? **Quem** aut **quid** quaeris?"

Vox servī trementis dēbilis erat: "Zēthus pistor est et Ostiae pistrīnum habet. In pistrīnō
10 istō ego labōrābam dōnec dominus meus, iste Zēthus, uxōrem meam **quā**cum labōrābam āmīsit. Dominus crūdēlis est et ergō fūgī."

Mendax et Valeria cicātrīcēs, **quae** in dorsō servī sunt, aspexērunt. Valeria servum adiuvāre volēbat, sed nōn audēbat. Cibum, **quem** in macellō ēmit, eī dedit, et maesta, nihil dīcēns, ad cellās suās ascendit. Flāvia, **quae** ipsa serva est, quoque maesta erat sed nihil agere aut dīcere potu-
15 it. Illa quoque ascendit.

Nunc Mendax, quia omnēs pistōrēs ōdit, servum adiuvāre volēbat. Sed quōmodo?

Subitō vōcem virī clāmantis in viā audīvērunt: "Quaerō servum **quī** herī ā mē fūgit. Aliquisne eum vīdit?"

Mendax servum sub pannīs fētidīs, **quī** prō lectō sunt, abdit. Rōmānus obēsus **quī**
20 fustem in manū tenēbat, in insulam rumpēbat.

Servus tremēns oculōs ad terram tenēbat

🔊 VERBA ŪTENDA

abdō, abdere, abdidī hide
aliquis, aliquid **someone, something**
almus, -a, -um **nourishing, kind, dear**
ascendō, ascendere, ascendī climb
aspiciō, aspicere, aspexī look at
auxilium, -ī n. help, aid
brevis, breve **short**
cella, -ae f. **room**
cicātrīx, cicātrīcis f. scar
cīvis, cīvis m./f. citizen
crūdēlis, crūdēle **cruel**
dēbilis, dēbile weak
difficultās, -tātis f. difficulty
digitus, -ī m. finger

dominus, -ī m. **master**
dōnec until
emō, emere, ēmī, emptum **buy**
fētidus, -a, -um filthy
fugitīvus, -ī m. runaway, fugitive
fustis, fustis m. staff, club
hoc "this (thing)"
lectus, -ī m. **couch, bed**
littera, -ae f. letter of the alphabet
locus, -ī m. place
macellum, -ī n. market
maestus, -a, -um **sad, gloomy**
monstrō (1) point out, show

nōn sōlum ... sed etiam ... **not only ... but also ...**
obēsus, -a, -um fat
oculus, -ī m. eye
ōdī, ōdisse hate
Ostia, -ae f. Ostia, the harbor of Rome; *Ostiae* "at Ostia"
Ostiensis, -e pertaining to Ostia, Rome's port, Ostian
pannus, -ī m. cloth, garment, rag
perīculōsus, -a, -um dangerous
pistor, pistōris m. miller
pistrīnum, -ī n. mill, bakery
praemium, -iī n. reward

prō lectō sunt "served as his bed"
quaerō, quaerere, quaesīvī / quaesiī, quaesītum **ask, seek, look for**
quī, quae, quod **who, which**
quia **since, because**
quis, quid **who? what?**
rectius "more correctly"
revocō (1) bring back, return
rumpō, rumpere, rūpī burst, break open
silentium, -iī n. silence
tremō, tremere, tremuī tremble
uxor, uxōris f. **wife**

POSTQUAM LĒGISTĪ

1. What is written on the slave's collar?
2. Where did the slave work?
3. (L) Why did he run away?
4. What does Valeria give the slave? Why doesn't she help him more?
5. Why does Mendax help the slave? Where does he hide him?
6. Who do you think the fat Roman is and what does he want?

Gemma

***Ostiae* = in Ostia**: Note how Latin expresses location in a city with a special ending (*-ae*) and no preposition. You have seen this already with *Rōmae* "at Rome." This is called the **locative** case. You will learn more about it later.

Grammatica B

Relative and Interrogative Pronouns and Adjectives

First of all, what do we mean by interrogatives and relatives?

- A **relative pronoun** connects or relates two pieces of information about the same person. "I know the person **who** ate your cake." That is it "relates" one part of a sentence to another.

- An **interrogative pronoun** asks a question; for example, "**Who** ate my piece of cake?"

- An **interrogative adjective** modifies a noun and asks "which?" as in "which person did that?"

- Notice that, in English, the interrogative and relative words are exactly the same.

Here are some examples of interrogative and relative pronouns in English:

Interrogative Pronouns

CASE	SINGULAR		PLURAL	
	Masc./Fem. **Who**	**Neuter** **Which**	**Masc./Fem.** **Who**	**Neuter** **Which**
Nominative	**quī/quis**	**quod/quid**	quī	quae
Genitive	cuius	cuius	quōrum	quōrum
Dative	cui	cui	quibus	quibus
Accusative	quem	**quod/quid**	quōs	quae
Ablative	quō	quō	quibus	quibus

Gemma

quācum: "with whom": Note that the preposition *cum* follows the ablatives *quō, quā,* and *quibus*: *quōcum, quācum, quibuscum*

Relative Pronouns and Interrogative Adjectives

CASE	SINGULAR			PLURAL		
	Masculine **Who**	**Feminine** **Who**	**Neuter** **Which**	**Masculine** **Who**	**Feminine** **Who**	**Neuter** **Which**
Nominative	quī	quae	quod	quī	quae	quae
Genitive	cuius	cuius	cuius	quōrum	quārum	quōrum
Dative	cui	cui	cui	quibus	quibus	quibus
Accusative	quem	quam	quod	quōs	quās	quae
Ablative	quō	quā	quō	quibus	quibus	quibus

Gemma

You may have already seen some of these Latin interrogative and relative pronouns in English in phrases like:

- cui bono (*cui bonō*?) "to what good?"
- quid pro quo (*quid prō quō*) "what for what?"
- sine qua non (*sine quā nōn*) "without which not"

We have given you the literal translations of the Latin phrases. What do they mean in English?

Notā Bene:

- The neuter plural nominative and accusative do not end in "-*a*."
- The genitive and dative singular endings remind you of the *UNUS NAUTA* declension.
- So ... what four GNC's can the form *quae* be?
- You might want to compare the two charts and circle the forms that are different from one chart to the other. You will see that there are very few.
- Relative pronouns and interrogative adjectives are the same in Latin but not in English.

Relative Pronoun	**Interrogative Adjectives**
Quaerō servum **qui** *ā mē fugīt.*	**Qui** *servus ā mē fūgit?*
I seek the slave **who** fled from me.	**Which** slave fled from me?

- Don't worry about the Latin forms that look alike. Context will always make it clear whether the word is a relative or an interrogative.
- There is nothing here you have not seen before. It is just an amalgam of endings from different declension patterns.

EXERCEĀMUS!

18-4 Forms of *Quī, Quae, Quod*

Answer the following questions.

1. Find the forms in the chart that are the same as the 1st and 2nd declensions.

2. Find the forms that look like 3rd declension endings.

3. Find the forms that use UNUS NAUTA endings that were first introduced to you in *is, ea, id* and *ille, illa, illud.*

Using Interrogatives and Relatives

Interrogatives

You can usually recognize an interrogative because of the question mark at the end of the sentence.

Quis *es?*	Who are you?
Cuius *es?*	Whose (slave) are you?
Cui *labōrās?*	For whom do you work?
Ad **quem** *locum fugis?*	To what place are you fleeing?

Relatives

A relative pronoun "relates" one part of a sentence to another. It is used to avoid choppy sentences. Consider this English.

Licinia works in the snack shop. Licinia is Valeria's daughter.
Licinia, **who** is Valeria's daughter, works in the snack shop.

Notā Bene:

- Two sentences have been made into one, with the second sentence becoming a **relative clause** introduced by the word "who."
- In the second sentence, "who" refers back to Licinia but it also is the subject of the clause set off by commas.
- The relative pronoun can be in any case but still refer back to the same noun. Consider:

Licinia, whose husband is Aelius, works in the snack shop. (genitive)
Licinia, to whom I gave a present, is Valeria's daughter. (dative)
Licinia, with whom I walked home, has a jealous husband. (ablative)

The concepts are the same in Latin as in English, but, of course, there are endings to consider. A relative pronoun has **gender**, **number**, and **case (GNC)**. Here are two important rule:

- A relative pronoun takes its **gender and number from the antecedent**.
- But it takes its **case from the function it performs in its own clause**.

Let's try this in English first.

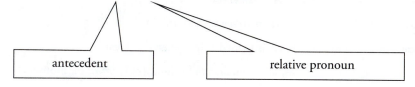

- The **who** refers to "slave," so it must be masculine and singular.
- But in the clause **who** is the nominative subject of "fled."
- So the Latin form for **who** would be masculine, singular, nominative: *quī*.

Determining the gender and number is always fairly simple, but sometimes it is difficult to determine the case of a relative pronoun. To determine the case, break the long sentence into two short ones.

I seek the slave <u>who</u> ran away from me yesterday.
I seek a slave.
　　The slave ran away from me yesterday.

Notā Bene: Interrogatives don't have antecedents. They simply ask a question.

Relative:　　　*Quaerō servum <u>quī</u> herī ā mē fūgit.* (antecedent is *servum*)
　　　　　　　I seek the slave who fled from me yesterday.

Interrogative:　*Quis herī ā mē fūgit?* (antecedent is unknown)
　　　　　　　Who fled from me yesterday?
　　　　　　　Quī servus herī ā mē fugit?
　　　　　　　What slave fled from me yesterday?

Summary and Simplification

WHEN YOU SEE	CASE	TRANSLATE
quī, quae, quod	nominative	who/which/that
cuius, quōrum, quārum	genitive	whose/of whom/of which
cui, quibus	dative	to whom/to which
quem, quam, quōs, quās, quae	accusative	whom/which
quō, quā, quibus	ablative	BWIOF whom/which

EXERCEĀMUS!

18-5 GNC'ing Relative Pronouns

What would be the GNC of the underlined relative pronoun if the sentence were in Latin? Follow the model.

> → Valeria, <u>whom</u> I saw yesterday, owns the snack shop.
>   fem. s. (refers to Valeria), acc. (direct object of clause)

1. Aelius, <u>whose</u> wife is Licinia, is a very strong man.

2. Servilia, <u>for whom</u> a husband has been chosen, is very unhappy.

3. Lucius, <u>who</u> is always hungry, wants to see the games.

4. The cat, <u>who</u> catches many mice, is named Felix. (*fēlēs, fēlis* f. cat)

5. The mice, <u>which</u> Felix catches, don't much care for him. (*mūs, mūris* m. mouse)

18-6 Forming Relative Pronouns

Now go back and, using the declension chart of *quī, quae, quod*, determine what the relative pronoun would be in Latin for the sentences in Exercise 18-5.

> → fem. acc. s. → *quam*

Mōrēs Rōmānī

Roman Slavery

Slavery was always part of Roman life, and few in antiquity questioned its cruelty or inhumanity. As the Roman Empire grew, especially following the conquest of Greece and Carthage in the second century B.C., many slaves flooded into Italy. A good number of these were captives of war. Slavery was a major factor in the growth of large rural estates called *lātifundia* owned by wealthy Romans who lived in the city and left the management of these estates to managers (who were often themselves slaves or former slaves).

The possibility of runaway slaves was a major concern for Roman society and law. Romans were expected to return runaway slaves to their masters, and it was illegal to assist a runaway. To discourage flight, slaves were sometimes branded or collared with identifying tags like the one on the fugitive in the story.

Slave revolts occasionally occurred and were brutally suppressed. The most famous of these was led by Spartacus, a Thracian gladiator slave whose brilliant successes against the superior Roman army made him a folk hero. Perhaps you have seen Kirk Douglas starring as Spartacus in Stanley Kubrick's 1960 film or a more modern television series on Spartacus. Behind all the romanticism of these portrayals stands a real historical figure and the brutal reality of Roman slavery. Spartacus died in battle, and 6,600 of his followers were crucified along the Appian Way from Rome to Brundisium after their defeat by the Roman general M. Licinius Crassus in 71 B.C.

Slaves were considered property, not people. In a farming manual entitled *Dē Rē Rusticā* (*On Country Matters*) Marcus Terentius Varro (116–27 B.C.) considers slaves no more than *instrūmentī genus vōcāle* (a talking sort of tool). Here is Varro's quote in context, modified just a bit to help you read it. (Note all the relative pronouns marked in **bold**! Can you find their antecedents?)

Kirk Douglas, Spartacus Americānus

Dē fundī quattuor partibus, **quae** cum solō haerent, et dē alterīs quattuor, **quae** extrā fundum sunt et ad cultūram pertinent, dīxī. Nunc dīcam, dē rēbus **quibus** agrōs colunt. Hās rēs aliī dīvidunt in duās partēs, in hominēs et instrumenta hominum, sine **quibus** colere nōn possunt; aliī in trēs partēs, in-
5 strūmentī genus vōcāle et sēmivōcāle et mūtum—vōcāle, in **quō** sunt servī; et semivōcāle, in **quō** sunt bovēs; et mūtum, in **quō** sunt plaustra.

Dē Rē Rusticā 1.17.1

🔊 VERBA ŪTENDA

ager, agrī m. field
aliī ... aliī ... some ... others ...
bōs, bovis m./f. bull, cow
colō, colere, coluī look after, care for
cultūra, -ae f. agriculture
extrā (+ acc.) beyond, outside of
fundus, -ī m. farm

genus, generis n. type
haerent are connected with
instrūmentum, -ī n. tool
mūtus, -a, -um speechless, mute
pars, partis f. part
pertineō, pertinēre, pertinuī belong to

plaustrum, -ī n. wagon
dē rēbus quibus "about those things by means of which"
sēmi- prefix, "half"
solum, solī n. earth, soil
vōcālis, vōcāle speaking, vocal

Latīna Hodierna

Slaves, Slavs, and Serfs

Would you see any connection between the words "slave," "Slav," and "serf"? They are actually connected through the Latin word *servus, -ī* m. slave. In medieval times, so many people of Slavic background came to be enslaved that *sclavus*, a Latin word for "Slav," came to be used for "slave." At the same time, the meaning of the word *servus* shifted to mean someone bound to the land or a "serf." Here is how these two words come into some modern languages:

	SERVUS (SLAVE)	*SCLAVUS (SLAV)*
Italian	servo della gleba	schiavo/a
Spanish	siervo	esclavo
French	serf	esclave
English	serf	slave

Orbis Terrārum Rōmānus

Ostia

The fugitive slave escaped from his master in Ostia the port of Rome. Ostia is located about sixteen miles east of the capital city, at the mouth (*ōs, ōris* n.) of the river Tiber (*Tiberis, Tiberis* m.). This area was an important source of salt, which Romans exported from earliest times, and was Rome's first colony (*colōnia, -ae* f.).

Ostia was a major source of imported essentials and luxuries for Rome. Large ships could not sail up the Tiber, so cargoes had to be unloaded at Ostia and stored in large warehouses until the merchandise could be taken in smaller sail or tow boats up the river to Rome.

In the mid first century A.D. the emperor Claudius built a major new harbor for Ostia a few miles north of the city. This harbor was expanded by later emperors, especially by Trajan in the early second century.

Ostiā Rōmam

Horrea Ostiae

Insula Ostiae

The area around Ostia silted up over the centuries and the ancient city, which has been excavated by archaeologists, is no longer on the sea. Its warehouses (*horrea, -ōrum* n. pl) and large *insulae* or apartment houses (like the one Valeria and her family live in) are important evidence for similar architecture that did not survive in Rome.

QUID PUTĀS?

1. Varro lists three categories of things without which fields cannot be taken care of. Can you list these three categories and one example from each?
2. What effect do you think slavery had on Roman society?
3. In what ways do you think the institution of slavery was similar and different in American and Roman societies?
4. Do you think that ancient Romans would have romanticized the story of Spartacus the way Hollywood has? Why or why not?
5. To which American cities could you compare Ostia? How?

EXERCEĀMUS!

18-7   Scrībāmus

Use *Lectiō Secunda* to answer each of the following questions in Latin. Follow the model.

 Quid servus in collō habet? *Collāre habet.*

1. Quis tremēns oculōs ad terram tenēbat?
2. Cuius est fugitīvus?
3. Quid Valeria in servī collārī lēgit?
4. Quōcum fugitīvus in pistrīnō labōrābat?
5. Quis est Publius Zēthus?
6. Quem Publius Zēthus āmīsit?
7. Quid Mendax et Valeria in dorsō fugitīvī aspiciunt?
8. Cui Valeria cibum dat?
9. Quid Rōmānus obēsus quaerit?
10. Sub quibus Mendax celeriter servum abdit?

18-8 Colloquāmur

This exercise is like a spelling bee. All the students in the class stand up and the teacher asks each student one of the questions from Exercise 18-7. Students responding correctly in Latin remain standing for the next round. Students responding incorrectly sit down and do not continue to the next round. The teacher continues to ask questions until only one student remains standing and is the victor.

HINT: Students may prepare more questions to use prior to the activity. Use the questions randomly and the same questions can be used more than once.

18-9 Verba Discenda

Use the *Verba Discenda* to answer the questions that follow. All of the answers are in the *Verba Discenda*.

1. What is the nominative neuter singular form of *crūdēlis*?
2. Give an English expression employing a form of the word *almus, -a, -um*. It is mostly associated with colleges and universities. What does it mean in common usage? How is it translated literally?
3. Which form of *maestus, -a, -um* would be used with *uxor*?
4. If the pen- in the English word "peninsula" comes from *paene*, what does "peninsula" literally mean?
5. What is the feminine form of *aliquis, aliquid*?
6. What is the neuter nominative singular form of *fēlix*?
7. What is the alternate form for *quaesiī*?

VERBA DISCENDA

aliquis, aliquid someone, something
almus, -a, -um nourishing, kind, dear [alma mater]
brevis, breve short [brevity]
cella, -ae f. room [cell]
crūdēlis, crūdēle cruel

dominus, -ī m. lord, master [dominate, dominion]
emō, emere, ēmī, emptum buy
fēlix, fēlīcis lucky, fortunate [felicity]
incipiō, incipere, incēpī, inceptum

begin [incipient, inception]
lectus, -ī m. couch, bed
maestus, -a, -um sad
nōn sōlum . . . sed etiam . . . not only . . . but also . . .
paene almost [peninsula]
prīmus, -a, -um first [primary]

quaerō, quaerere, quaesīvī / quaesiī, quaesītum ask, seek, look for [question]
quī, quae, quod who, which
quia since
quis, quid who? what?
uxor, uxōris f. wife [uxorious]

Angulus Grammaticus

Building Your Latin Vocabulary

You can increase your Latin (and English) vocabulary by paying attention to the way Latin uses prefixes and suffixes to form words. Look at some examples in the following charts. Combine the meaning of the stem with the meaning of the suffixes (and prefixes) to determine the general meaning of the word. For example,

dictātor   "one who speaks"

Look the word up in a Latin dictionary for more precise meanings. Do you recognize any English words in this list?

dict- say

PREFIX	STEM	SUFFIX	LATIN WORD	
	dict- say	*-or* "one"	*dictātor, -ōris* m.	one who speaks
	dict- say	*-iō* "the act of"	*dictiō, -iōnis* f.	act of speaking
contrā "against"	*dict-* say	*-iō* "the act of"	*contrā**dictiō***, *-iōnis* f.	act of speaking against

fac- make, do

PREFIX	STEM	SUFFIX	LATIN WORD	
	fac- make, do	*-ilis* "able to"	*facilis*	able to do
dis- "not"	*fac-* make, do	*-ilis* "able to"	*difficilis*	not able to do
	fac- make, do	*-iō* "the act of"	*factiō, -iōnis* f.	act of doing

pot- be able

PREFIX	STEM	SUFFIX	LATIN WORD	
	pot- be able	*-ens* "-ing"	*potens*	being able
in- "not"	*pot-* be able	*-ens* "-ing"	*impotens*	not being able
	pot- be able	*-ia* "state of"	*potentia, -ae* f.	state of being able
in- "not"	*pot-* be able	*-ia* "state of"	*impotentia*	state of not being able
	pot- be able	*-tās* "the act of"	*potestās, -tātis* f.	act of being able

pōt- drink

PREFIX	STEM	SUFFIX	LATIN WORD	
	pōt- drink	*-or* "one who"	*pōtor*	one who drinks
	pōt- drink	*-rix* "she who"	*pōtrix*	she who drinks
	pōt- drink	*-iō* "act of"	*pōtātiō, pōtātiōnis* f.	act of drinking
	pōt- drink	*-iō* "act of"	*pōtiō, pōtiōnis* f.	act of drinking, a drink

19

Vēnātiō

Opus Mūlō nōn Virō Aptum
Wikipedia Commons/Foto Musei Vaticani

Lectiō Prīma

Antequam Legis

Work in a Mill

In this *lectiō* the runaway slave describes his work in the bakery/mill. His job was to turn enormously heavy millstones around all day long, pushing on a beam that was inserted into the square hole. Life in a mill was one of the worst fates a slave could endure, and slaves were often sent to work there as punishment.

The Pluperfect Tense

As you read the story, you will learn the **pluperfect tense**. This tense, represented in English by the helping verb "had," indicates a completed action that preceded another action in the past; for example, "I had seen" or "you had run."

For now, when you see a form with the endings marked in **bold** below, translate the verb using the helping verb "had."

-eram	-erāmus
-erās	-erātis
-erat	-erant

Note that these endings are identical to the imperfect forms of the verb *sum, esse.*

mans**erat**	**he had** remained
labōrāv**erāmus**	**we had** worked

LECTIŌNĒS:
IN NOCTEM
and
MŪNERA

Mendax sends the owner of the fugitive slave off on the wrong track. The next morning the games begin.

231

Hic, haec, hoc

Other words to look for in this *lectiō* are forms of *hic, haec, hoc* (this/these). This demonstrative pronoun/adjective is the counterpart to *ille, illa, illud* (that/those) and it, too, is one of the words with a genitive in *-ius*. Pay attention to the forms, marked in ***bold italics*** in the *lectiō*. Note especially the following substantives where the adjective is used as a noun:

- Dative singular forms: *huic* (to this man/woman/thing)
- Accusative singular forms: *hunc, hanc, hoc* (this man/woman/thing)
- Neuter nominative and accusative plural forms: *haec* (these things)

EXERCEĀMUS!

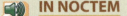 **19-1**   *Hic, haec, hoc*

Create a line-by-line list of all the phrases with *hic, haec, hoc* in *Lectiō Prīma*. Before you read, use the phrases to help you identify the GNC of the *hic, haec, hoc* forms. When in doubt, check out the context of the phrase in the *lectiō*. Watch out for substantives. Follow the model.

→ hunc servum (line 3): *masc. sing. acc.*

🔊 IN NOCTEM

Zēthus in insulam irrūpit et Mendācī appropinquāvit. "Cīvis," inquit, "quaerō servum quī herī ā mē fūgit. Num **hunc** servum vīdistī?"

P. Nonius Zēthus

Wikipedia Commons/ Foto Musei Vaticani

Mendax rīdēns, "Nēminem," inquit, "in **hāc** insulā
5 vīdī. Fortasse **hic** servus in cloācā sē abdidit aut fortasse in Forum ad āram Caesaris fūgit. **Hoc** sōlum certē dīcere possum—nōn adest."

Zēthus circumspectāvit et locum in quō servus latēbat inspectāvit, sed pannōs fētidōs tangere nōluit. Fustem quatiēns et fortiter clāmāns abiit.

10 Servus territus quī sub pannīs **quiētus manserat** diūtius mansit et tunc exiit. "Abestne Zēthus?" rogāvit.

"Ita, vērō" respondit Mendax, "abest. Nunc dīc mihi dē **hāc** difficultāte tuā."

"Ut scīs, nōs in pistrīnō **huius** Zēthī multōs annōs **labōrāverāmus** cum subitō dominus uxōrem āmīsit. Uxor pānem in furnō torrēbat et ego molās cotīdiē prōpellēbam—opus mūlō nōn virō aptum."

Mendax quī quoque in pistrīnō **labōrāverat** cachinnāvit et **huic** servō exclāmāvit: "Rectē dīxistī, amīce. **Hī**
15 Rōmānī quibus labōrāvistis vōs servōs 'animālia loquentia' aut 'instrūmenta vōcālia' nominant. Tū et uxor, laetīne **fuerātis?**"

Servus dīxit: "Aliquid pecūniae **servāverāmus** quā lībertātem nostram emere spērābāmus. Sed dominus nōbīs dīxit: 'Aliud pistrīnum in Calabriā habeō, sed pānis illīus pistrīnī malus est. Uxōrem tuam quae pānem optimum torret ad illum pistrīnum crās mittam.'"

20 "Abhinc quattuor diēs uxor mea abiit et quattuor diēs miser sum. Sine uxōre meā, servus **huius** malī dominī nōn erō! Propter **haec**, herī ab **hōc** malō dominō fūgī. Perīculōsum est, sed uxōrem quam valdē amō invenīre necesse est. Ōlim antehāc **fūgeram** et ergō mihi **hoc** collāre dominus **dederat**. Et nunc iterum fugitīvus sum. Grātiās tibi permaximās agō, sed nunc abeō. Uxōrem meam invenīre dēbeō."

Tālia dīcēns in noctem abiit.

🔊 VERBA ŪTENDA

abdō, abdere, abdidī,
  abditum **hide, conceal**

abhinc ago

absum, abesse, āfuī **be**
  absent, gone

adsum, adesse, adfuī **be**
  near, be present here,
  be there for, help

antehāc before this time

aptus, -a, -um fit, suitable

āra, -ae **f. altar**

cachinnō (1) laugh
  loudly

Calabria, -ae f. region in the
  heel of Italy

certē certainly

circumspectō (1) look
  around

cīvis, cīvis m./f. citizen

cloāca, -ae f. sewer

collāre, collāris n. collar

cotīdiē **daily**

cum when

difficultās, -ātis f.
  difficulty

diūtius (comparative) for a
  bit longer

exeō, exīre, exiī go out

fētidus, -a, -um filthy

fugitīvus, -ī m. fugitive

furnus, -ī m. oven,
  bakehouse

fustis, fustis m. club, stick

grātia, -ae **f. grace; favor;**
  pl. thanks; *grātiās*
  agere **to thank**
  someone

herī **yesterday**

hic, haec, hoc **this**

inspectō (1) **look**
  closely at

instrūmentum, -ī n. tool

irrumpō, irrumpere, irrūpī
  burst

ita so, thus; yes

lībertās, -tātis f. freedom

locus, -ī **m. place**

loquentia "talking"

maneō, manēre, mansī stay,
  remain

miser, misera, miserum
  wretched, miserable

mittō, mittere, mīsī send

molae, -ārum f. pl. mill

mūlus, -ī m. mule

nōbīs to us

nōminō (1) name

nōs we, us

ōlim **once, formerly**

optimus, -a, -um best

opus, operis n. work

pānis, pānis m. bread

pannus, -ī m. cloth, rags

perīculōsus, -a, -um
  dangerous

permaximus, -a, -um very
  great

pistrīnum, -ī n. bakery

prōpellō, prōpellere,
  prōpulī drive, push
  forward

quatiō, -ere, quassī shake,
  wave about

quiētus, -a, -um quiet

servō (1) save

spērō (1) hope

tālis, tāle such

tangō, tangere, tetigī
  touch

torreō, torrēre, torruī
  bake

ut as

vōcālis, -e speaking

POSTQUAM LĒGISTĪ

Answer these questions in English. If the question is followed by (L), also answer in Latin.

1. Where does Mendax suggest the runaway slave is hiding? Where is he really hiding? (L)
2. Why does Mendax laugh when he learns that the runaway slave worked in a mill? (L)
3. What plans did the runaway slave and his wife have?
4. Why was the wife sent to Calabria? (L)

Grammatica A

The Pluperfect Tense

The pluperfect tense is the second member of the perfect system you have met. The first was the perfect tense. Here are the "formulas" for forming these two tenses:

			-ī	-imus
Perfect	◆ Perfect Stem	+	-istī	-istis
	Perfect stem = 3rd principal part minus the -ī		-it	-ērunt
Pluperfect	◆ Perfect Stem	+	-eram	-erāmus
			-erās	-erātis
			-erat	-erant

Gemma

P. Nonius Zethus was a real baker and priest of Augustus in Ostia. A marble block intended to hold the cinerary urns of Nonius, a fellow freedwoman and his wife, is illustrated in *Lectiō Prīma*. Here is a transcription of the inscription on the front:

P. NONIUS ZETHUS
AUG(USTALIS)
FECIT SIBI ET
NONIAE HILARAE
CONLIBERTAE
NONIAE P. L(IBERTAE)
PELAGIAE CONIUGI
P. NONIUS HERACLIO

Here is the conjugation of *vocō* in the perfect and pluperfect. Notice how easy it is to form the pluperfect from the perfect by using endings identical to the imperfect of *sum*.

PERFECT		PLUPERFECT	
vocāvī	I have called	vocāv**eram**	I had called
vocāvistī	you have called	vocāv**erās**	you had called
vocāvit	he/she/it has called	vocāv**erat**	he/she/it had called
vocāvimus	we have called	vocāv**erāmus**	we had called
vocāvistis	you have called	vocāv**erātis**	you had called
vocāvērunt	they have called	vocāv**erant**	they had called

Notā Bene:

- The plu- in "pluperfect" comes from the Latin word *plūs* "more." So the tense is literally "more than perfect."
- The **pluperfect** is sometimes called the "past perfect" because it refers to a time prior to the perfect.

Marcus dormīvit postquam cēnāverat.
Marcus **slept** after he **had dined**.

EXERCEĀMUS!

19-2 **Using the Pluperfect**

Take each pair of Latin sentences and combine them into one sentence beginning with *postquam* (after). Put the sentence with the verb marked in **bold** after *postquam*, and put that verb into the pluperfect tense. Follow the model.

→ Zēthus ex insulā **abiit**. Servus in noctem fūgit.
Postquam Zēthus ex insulā abierat, servus in noctem fūgit.

1. Publius Zēthus in insulam **rūpit**. Zēthus Mendācī appropinquāvit.

2. Servus ā Zēthō **fūgit**. Zēthus fugitīvum quaesīvit.

3. Mendax fugitīvum in pannīs fētidīs **abdidit**. Zēthus locum in quō servus latēbat inspectāvit.

4. Zēthus fustem quatiēns et fortiter clāmāns **abiit**. Servus ē pannīs exiit.

5. Servus et uxor in pistrīnō Zēthī multōs annōs **labōrābant**. Dominus uxōrem āmīsit.

6. Servus et uxor aliquid pecūniae **servāvērunt**. Dominus uxōrem ad alterum pistrīnum mīsit.

7. Dominus servō collāre **dedit**. Servus ab hōc malō dominō fūgit.

8. Fugitīvus Mendācī grātiās **ēgit**. In noctem abiit.

Gemma

Do not confuse *eram*, which is imperfect, with *fueram*, which uses the perfect stem and is pluperfect.

The Demonstrative *hic, haec, hoc*

Here is the full declension of *hic, haec, hoc* (this, these):

	MASCULINE	FEMININE	NEUTER
Singular			
Nominative	hic	haec	hoc
Genitive	huius	huius	huius
Dative	huic	huic	huic
Accusative	hunc	hanc	hoc
Ablative	hōc	hāc	hōc
Plural			
Nominative	hī	hae	haec
Genitive	hōrum	hārum	hōrum
Dative	hīs	hīs	hīs
Accusative	hōs	hās	haec
Ablative	hīs	hīs	hīs

All the singular forms of this word are translated "this" in English. All the plurals are "these." *Hic, haec, hoc* refers to someone or something close by or recently mentioned whereas *ille, illa, illud* (that, those) refers to someone or something farther away or mentioned earlier.

Notā Bene:

- Note the *-ius* ending in the genitive singular. Where have you seen this ending before?
- The ending *-c* means "here" and follows familiar endings: *hui-* like *cui* (dative singular) and the ablative singular 2-1-2 endings *-ō, -ā, -ō; hum + c → hunc* and *ham + c → hanc*.
- Compare *hoc* and *hōc*. How does the macron change the meaning of this word?
- All the plural forms except the neuter nominative and accusative have regular 2-1-2 endings.
- The feminine nominative singular and the neuter nominative and accusative plural forms also have the *-c* (here) ending. Note that *haec* can thus mean "this woman," "these things" (subject), or "these things" (object).

Hic, haec, hoc is used as a demonstrative (pointing out) adjective, so remember that it GNCs:

| *hic vir* | this man | *haec fēmina* | this woman | *hoc dōnum* | this gift |
| *hī virī* | these men | *hae fēminae* | these women | *haec dōna* | these gifts |

Lectiō Secunda

Antequam Legis

In this *lectiō* we get a glimpse of the world of the Roman gladiatorial games. You will practice the pluperfect a bit more and learn how to express comparisons in Latin.

Comparisons

"More," "better," "less," "happier ..." All these words are what grammarians call **comparatives**, and they all seem to require the word "than." "X is bigger *than* Y." "A is happier *than* B." Note that the simplest way to make a comparative in English is to add **-er** to the adjective. Sometimes, English uses "more" instead, for example, "more beautiful," "more careful."

The words marked in **bold** in *Lectiō Secunda* are comparatives. The ones that are regular add some form of the ending *-ior* to the basic stem of the adjective. Thus, you will have no trouble in seeing that *longior* means "longer/taller" and *brevior* "shorter."

Other words are irregular (e.g., *melior* "better") and will have to be looked up and/or memorized. Most languages, including English, tend to have some irregular comparatives. Think of "good, better, best," for example.

Whether regular or irregular, all comparatives use the endings of regular 3rd declension nouns, so there is nothing new to learn!

You have already seen how *quam* is used in Latin to mean "than," but "than" can also be expressed in Latin in another way. We have put all the "than" expressions in *italics* in *Lectiō Secunda*. Try to figure out from context the other way that the Romans expressed "than."

EXERCEĀMUS!

19-3   Translating Comparatives

All of the words in column A are comparative adjectives marked in **bold** in *Lectiō Secunda*. Use the reading and English derivatives to match each adjective with its English meaning in column B.

	A	**B**
_____	1. difficiliōra	A. better
_____	2. ferociōra	B. bigger
_____	3. iuvenior	C. fiercer
_____	4. māior	D. harder
_____	5. meliōra	E. higher
_____	6. minor	F. more
_____	7. pēiora	G. smaller
_____	8. plūs	H. worse
_____	9. superiōre	I. younger

Vēnātor et Leō Pugnantēs in Arēnā

MŪNERA

Amphitheātrum plēnum hominibus est quod hodiē Imperātor mūnera magna populīs Rōmānīs dat. In variīs locīs aliī alia agunt.

Hīc, ēditor lūdōrum et Fabius, vir quī animālia Rōmam mūneribus portāvit, in ūnā parte amphitheātrī stant. Ēditor "Fabī," inquit, "anteā, multa bona animālia Rōmam ab Āfricā 5 portāvistī, sed haec animālia quae nūper tulistī **meliōra** atque **ferociōra** *quam* illa omnia alia animālia sunt!"

Illīc, in aliō locō fīliī Servīliī colloquuntur. "Lūcī," Marcus rogat, "timēsne mūnera et animālia ferōcia?"

"Nūllō modō!" respondet Lūcius īrātus. "Ōlim, ubi **iuvenior** et **minor** eram, strepitum et cruōrem timēbam, sed nunc aetāte **māior** sum et nōn iam timeō. **Plūs** sanguinis et cruōris **melius** est!"

10   In parte **superiōre** amphitheātrī nōnnūllī spectātōrēs dē mūneribus dīcunt.

Ūnus rogat: "Vīdistīne mūnera quae ōlim Pompeius Magnus dedit? Haec mūnera certē bona erunt, sed illa **meliōra** erant."

Alibī paucī gladiātōrēs pauca verba dīcunt sed **plūrēs** silentium tenent. Ūnus gladiātor "Ille Thrax" intrā sē inquit "multō **māior** *aliīs* est. Contrā hunc pugnāre nōn volō!" Et Thrax: "Ille gladiātor quī prope mūrum stat" intrā sē inquit "ille 15 multō **minor** *mē* est. Contrā hunc pugnāre volō. Fortasse in fīne mūnerum vīvus erō!" Sīc omnēs stant, aliī alia cōgitantēs.

Duo aliī gladiātōrēs quī amīcī sunt inter sē dīcunt. Ūnus "Haec," inquit, "animālia in Urbe nunc **difficiliōra** et **māiōra** sunt *quam* illa **pēiōra** animālia quae tunc in prōvinciīs pugnābāmus."

In aliō locō ūnus bestiārius vestem Herculis trahēns sōlus et maestus stat. Hodiē contrā multōs leōnēs pugnābit sīcut ōlim Herculēs contrā leōnem pugnāvit. Nōn gladiō sed fūste pugnābit, sīcut Herculēs. Hodiē hic bestiārius certē 20 in terrā iacēbit.

🔊 VERBA ŪTENDA

aetās, aetātis f. age, period

Āfrica, -ae f. the Roman province of Africa (modern Tunisia)

alibī elswhere, in other places

aliī alia agunt "Some were doing some things while others were doing others."

anteā previously

atque and, and also

bestiārius, -iī m. animal fighter

certē certainly

colloquuntur "(they) are speaking"

contrā (+ acc.) against, opposite (to)

cruor, cruōris m. gore, blood

cum when

ēditor, -ōris m. organizer; *ēditor lūdōrum* public official in charge of the games

ferōx, ferōcis fierce

fustis, fustis m. staff, club

gerō, gerere, gessī, bear, carry, wear

hic, haec, hoc this

hīc here

iaceō, iacēre, iacuī lie

illīc there

imperātor, imperātōris m. general, commander, emperor

intrā sē "to himself"

iuvenis young; *iuvenior,* younger

leō, leōnis m. lion

locus, -ī m. place

maestus, -a, -um sad

māior, māius greater, larger, older; m. pl. ancestors, elders

melior, melius better

minor, minus smaller

mīrābilis, mīrābile amazing, wonderous

modus, -ī m. way, manner

mūrus, -ī m. wall

nōn iam no longer

nūper recently

ōlim once, formerly

pars, partis f. part, piece

pēior, pēius worse

plēnus, -a, -um (+ abl.) full of, filled with

plūrēs, plūra more (in number)

plūs more (in amount)

prior, prius former

priusquam before

Rōmam "to Rome"

sanguis, sanguinis m. blood

silentium, -iī n. silence

spectātor, -ōris m. spectator

strepitum m. noise

superior, superius higher

Thrax, Thrācis m. Thracian; a fighter with lighter armor, including a helmet and greaves on both legs

urbs, urbis f. city, esp. the city of Rome

varius, -a, -um varied, mixed

vestis, vestis f. garments, clothing

vīvus, -a, -um living

POSTQUAM LĒGISTĪ

Answer these questions in both Latin and English if the question is followed by (L). Otherwise, just respond in English.

1. What job does the *ēditor lūdōrum* do and what does he think about the animals acquired for today's games?
2. How has Lucius' attitude toward the games changed over the years?
3. What did people think about the games sponsored by Pompey the Great? (L)
4. What weapon does the bestiarius dressed like Hercules carry? What will he fight in the arena? (L)
5. What would your reaction be if you witnessed such games today? Why?

Grammatica B

Forming Comparatives in Latin

Most regular comparative adjectives are formed by adding *-ior* (masc. and fem.) and *-ius* (neuter) to the stem, followed by regular 3rd declension endings. It does not matter whether the simple (positive) form of the adjective uses 2-1-2 or 3rd declension endings. Here is how it works:

vērus, -a, -um   *vēr- + -ior, -ius = vērior, -ius* truer, rather true, fairly true

pulcher, pulchra, pulchrum   *pulchr- + -ior, -ius = pulchrior, -ius* more beautiful

fortis, forte   *fort- + -ior, -ius = fortior, -ius* braver

Now see how the other forms are made. Comparative adjectives are two-termination 3rd declension adjectives.

	MASCULINE / FEMININE	NEUTER	MASCULINE / FEMININE	NEUTER
Singular				
Nominative	pulchrior	pulchrius	fortior	fortius
Genitive	pulchriōris	pulchriōris	fortiōris	fortiōris
Dative	pulchriōrī	pulchriōrī	fortiōrī	fortiōrī
Accusative	pulchriōrem	pulchrius	fortiōrem	fortius
Ablative	pulchriōre	pulchriōre	fortiōre	fortiōre
Plural				
Nominative	pulchriōrēs	pulchriōra	fortiōrēs	fortiōra
Genitive	pulchriōrum	pulchriōrum	fortiōrum	fortiōrum
Dative	pulchriōribus	pulchriōribus	fortiōribus	fortiōribus
Accusative	pulchriōrēs	pulchriōra	fortiōrēs	fortiōra
Ablative	pulchriōribus	pulchriōribus	fortiōribus	fortiōribus

Notā Bene:

- Comparative adjectives use regular 3rd declension, not i-stem, endings. Thus, you find the genitive plural *fortiōrum* (not *fortiōrium*) and neuter nominative and accusative plural *fortiōra* (not *fortiōria*).
- The neuter nominative and accusative singular forms are the only ones not formed from the *-ior* stem. To create these forms, drop the *-or* and add *-us*, as in *pulchrius* and *fortius*.

Some Latin adjectives form their comparatives by changing their stems. This happens in English too:

good   better
bad   worse

Latin does the same thing with these words:

| *bonus, -a, -um* | ***melior, melius*** | better |
| *malus, -a, -um* | ***pēior, pēius*** | worse |

The following adjectives have regular comparatives in English but irregular ones in Latin. Remember that the words marked in bold are *Verba Discenda*.

magnus, -a, -um	***māior, māius***	greater, older
multus, -a, -um	**(no masc./fem.), *plūs***	more (in amount)
multī, -ae, -a	***plūrēs, plūra***	more (in number)
parvus, -a, -um	***minor, minus***	smaller, younger

The Latin **comparative adverb** is identical in form to the neuter nominative comparative adjective. Compare these sentences:

***Melius** vīnum videō.*   I see a better wine.
***Melius** nunc videō.*   I see better now.

In the first sentence *melius* is an adjective modifying *vīnum*. In the second it is an adverb describing the verbal action. How can you tell the difference between a comparative adjective and a comparative adverb? If there is no singular neuter noun in the sentence, try the adverb first. In other words, let context be your guide, just as in English, where the two uses of "better" rarely confuse us.

Using Comparatives in Latin

Typically, a comparative is comparing two people or things. If both elements are expressed, they are joined in Latin by the word *quam* and in English by the word "than":

*Hic **melior quam** ille est.*	This person is **better than** that one.
*Haec **intelligentior quam** hic est.*	This woman is **more intelligent than** this man.
*Haec **celerius quam** hic currit.*	She runs **faster than** he does.

When you read *Lectiō Secunda*, did you notice the other way that Latin can express a comparison? Here are some examples:

*Ille Thrax multō **māior aliīs** est.*	That Thracian is much bigger than the others.
*Ille multō **minor mē** est.*	That guy is much smaller than I am.

In these sentences Latin has used the ablative case instead of *quam*. This is called the **ablative of comparison**.

Translating Comparatives

If comparatives can be translated "more," "rather," and "too," how do you know which to choose? If no explicit comparison is being made in the sentence, it may make more sense to translate the comparative as a simple (positive) adjective with "rather" or "too."

*Haec **melior** est.*	"She is better." or "She is rather good." or "She is too good."
*Hic **intelligentior** est.*	"He is more intelligent." or "He is rather intelligent." or "He is too intelligent."

In general, pick the translation that makes the best sense in context! It is useful to know that, in order of frequency, the translations are: "more," then "rather," and finally "too."

> **Gemma**
>
> Notice the use of *multō* with comparative adjectives: *multō māior* = much older Literally this means "older by much" in Latin. *Multō* is in the ablative case and this use of the ablative is called **ablative of degree of difference**.

EXERCEĀMUS!

19-4 **Comparatives**

Choose the word in parentheses with which the comparative adjective in bold agrees in GNC. Then translate the sentence two ways, if the sentence allows it. Follow the model.

→ Haec (bursae, animālia, virī) **meliōra** sunt.	*Haec animālia meliōra sunt.* These animals are rather good. These animals are better.

1. (Fēminae, virīs, animālia) **meliōrēs** sunt.

2. (Fēmina, virōs, animālia) **ferōciōra** invēnērunt?

3. (Puer, Animal, Puellae) **pēior** est.

4. (Gladiī, Forum, Insula) **mīrābiliōrēs** sunt.

5. (Mūnera, Puella, Gladiātōrēs) **grandiōra** quam illa vīderāmus!

6. **Plūrēs** (spectātōrēs, animālia, gladiātōribus) mūnera vident.

Mōrēs Rōmānī

Mūnera Rōmāna

Mūnera, or games like the ones described in this chapter, were a regular feature of Roman life from early times. The earliest ones were probably funeral games held in honor of important men.

Over time, games became more and more elaborate and were organized around religious festivals and other public occasions. *Aedīlēs,* elected magistrates in charge of public works, were responsible for these games, which they were expected to pay for out of their own pockets. Ambitious politicians like Julius Caesar went deeply into debt as aediles to organize very expensive games in order to curry favor with the public.

These games often included gladiators, or fighters with a *gladius* (sword). Most gladiators were prisoners of war, slaves, or indentured free citizens. Some were even condemned criminals.

There were different kinds of gladiators, distinguished by their weaponry and armor.

- ***Samnīs, Samnītis*** m. Samnite. A heavily armed and armored fighter, equipped with helmet (*galea, -ae* f.), oblong shield (*scūtum, -ī* n.), sword (*gladius, -iī* m.), wide leather belt (*balteus, -ī* m.), and metal greave (*ocrea, -ae* f.) on one leg only.

- ***Mirmillō, -ōnis*** m. Mirmillo. Armed like a Samnite, but with a special, fish-shaped helmet.

- ***Rētiārius, -iī*** m. Netter. This fighter was protected only with a shoulder guard (on his left side). For attacking, he carried a trident and a net and was often pitted against a Samnite or a Mirmillo.

- ***Thrax, Thrācis*** n. Thracian. A fighter with lighter armor, including a helmet and greaves on both legs. With a bare torso and an arm guard (*manica, -ae* f.) on his right arm, he carried a small shield (*parmula, -ae* f.) in one hand and a short sword (*sīca, -ae* f.) in the other.

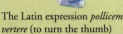
In addition to these gladiators, other performers in the games included the animal fighter (*bestiārius, iī* m.) and hunter (*vēnātor, -ōris* m.), both of whom specialized in battling exotic animals like elephants, lions, bears, and leopards.

Roman spectators especially enjoyed unusual pairings of contestants, not only human vs. human, but even human vs. wild animal. Despite its many historical inaccuracies, Ridley Scott's film *Gladiator* (2000) captures the exotic and bloody nature of such contests.

Gladiators were the sports superstars of ancient Rome and were often celebrated out of the arena. Here is an excerpt from a poem by Martial (V, 24), in which the many great qualities of a gladiator named Hermes are listed. There is no main verb in this poem. In each line, understand Hermes as the subject of *est* (Hermes is . . .). See the *Verba Ūtenda* and you should be able to translate this fairly easily.

> Hermēs Martia saeculī voluptās,
> Hermēs omnibus ērudītus armīs,
> Hermēs et gladiātor et magister,
> Hermēs, vincere nec ferīre doctus,
> Hermēs cūra labōrque lūdiārum.

Notice Hermes' great reputation among the women. This was apparently not unusual. Here are two pieces of graffiti from the walls of Pompeii to illustrate this appeal:

> Suspīrium puellārum Celadus Thrax.

> *Corpus Inscriptiōnum Latīnārum* (C.I.L.) IV, 4397

> Crescens rētiārius pupārum nocturnārum

> C.I.L. 4. 4356

Pollice Verso, *pictūra (1872) ā Jean-Léon Gérôme (1824–1904)*

🔊 VERBA ŪTENDA

arma, armōrum n. pl. arms, weapons

Avē! Hail!

cūra, ae f. worry, concern, care, anxiety

doctus, -a, -um learned

ērudītus, -a, -um skilled

feriō, ferīre hit, kill, slay

lūdia, -ae f. a gladiator's girl, "girl of the *lūdus*," a sort of groupie!

Martius, -a, -um of Mars, martial

nocturnus, -a, -um nocturnal, of the night

pūpa, -ae f. doll, girl

rētiārius, -iī m. netter

saeculum, -ī n. age, era

suspīrium, -iī n. sigh, heartthrob

Latīna Hodierna

Latin Comparative Adjectives in English

Latin comparatives have resulted in a number of English derivatives. Knowing the meaning of the Latin word makes it easier to understand what these English words mean:

Latin Comparative	English Meaning	Derivative
melior, melius	better	ameliorate
pēior, pēius	worse	pejorative
māior, māius	greater, older	majority
(no masc./fem.), *plūs*	more (in amount)	plus
plūrēs, plūra	more (in number)	plurality
minor, minus	smaller, younger	minus, minority
posterior, posterius	later; inferior	posterior
priōr, prius	former	priority
superior, superius	higher	superiority

Notā Bene:

- Remember the birth of "J" illustrated in words like "pejorative" and "majority."
- In mathematics the words *plūs* (+) and *minus* (-) are used to refer to arithmetic functions.

Lawyers, for example, talk about arguments a fortiori (from the stronger), in which one claim is proven or supported by another stronger argument. For example, one can argue a fortiori that, if it is illegal to steal $10, then it is also illegal to steal $50.

Philosophers talk about a priori (from the former) and a posteriori (from the later) proofs or knowledge. For example, we know a priori that all Romans spoke Latin but we know a posteriori that some Romans also spoke Greek. Note the *-ī* alternate ending for the ablative singular.

The motto of the International Olympic Committee consists of three comparative Latin adverbs:

Citius! Altius! Fortius! "Faster! Higher! Stronger!"

Watch for a character to use the Olympic motto in an upcoming *lectiō.*

The motto of the State of New York is the comparative adjective *Excelsior!* (Higher!).

Finally, don't forget the following expression inscribed on the Great Seal of the United States of America (to the right):

Ē plūribus ūnum "Out of many, one"

Can you find this expression on the detail of a dollar bill at right? Although we have used the traditional translation of this expression, "many" does not accurately translate *plūribus*, does it? This is another good reason to study Latin!

Ē Plūribus Ūnum

Orbis Terrārum Rōmānus

Amphitheātrum Flāviānum

The earliest gladiatorial contests were informal affairs fought in temporary facilities in open areas like the Roman Forum. The first stone amphitheater was built in Rome in 29 B.C. and was destroyed in the great fire in 64 A.D. during the reign of Nero.

Work on a new stone amphitheater began in 70–72 A.D. under the reign of Vespasian, but the building was not completed until 80 A.D., under Titus, with spectacular games commemorated in the poetry of Martial. The original name of this building was the Flavian Amphitheater (*Amphitheātrum Flāviānum*).

This amphitheater was the largest such structure ever built by the Romans. Because of its size and because of the Colossus, a giant statue of Nero located nearby, the amphitheater eventually became known as the Colosseum, the name by which we know it today.

The structure, a masterpiece of Roman engineering, was built of concrete and stone with a marble façade. The amphitheater was capable of holding about 50,000 spectators and had awnings that could be drawn to protect these crowds from the elements. So the Colosseum was in many ways comparable to one of our modern domed stadiums.

Adjacent to the Flavian Amphitheater and connected via an underground passage way was the *Lūdus Magnus*, a gladiatorial school with its own practice arena in the same elliptical shape as that of the amphitheater.

The Colosseum remained intact and was used for games and entertainment until the medieval period. Unfortunately, in subsequent years the building was used as a quarry for building materials.

Amphitheātrum Flāviānum, Lūdus Magnus et Colossus Nerōnis

① **Colossus Nerōnis**   ② **Amphiteātrum Flāviānun**   ③ **Lūdus Magnus**

Amphitheātrum Flāviānum Hodiē

Lūdus Magnus et Amphitheātrum Flāviānum

QUID PUTĀS?

1. Compare the gladiator Hermes described by Martial to a modern American athlete. Be sure to explain why you chose that particular athlete.

2. Why do you think the Romans had so many different types of gladiators?

3. In a contest between a retiarius and a Samnite, which do you think would have the advantage and why?

4. What modern building or monument would have a reputation comparable to that of the Colosseum in Rome? Why?

5. Why do you think the expression "e pluribus unum" was chosen as the motto of the United States? Why do you think that the Founding Fathers chose to say this in Latin instead of English?

1 Forum Rōmānum   **2** Amphitheātrum Flāviānum

Amphitheātrum Flāviānum et Forum Rōmānum dē Caelō

EXERCEĀMUS!

19-5 Scrībāmus

Retell events from *Lectiō Prīma* in the present tense by changing the form of every verb marked in **bold** in the following sentences. HINT: You may have to consult the *Verb Ūtenda* following *Lectiō Prīma* for help with principal parts.

1. Zēthus in insulam **rūpit** et Mendācī **appropinquāvit**.

2. Zēthus **circumspectāvit** et locum, in quō servus **latēbat**, **inspectāvit**, sed pannōs fētidōs tangere **nōluit**.

3. Fustem quatiēns et fortiter clāmāns **abiit**.

4. Servus sub pannīs diūtius **mānsit** et tunc **exiit**.

5. Mendax dē difficultāte servī audīre **voluit**.

6. Tunc servus dē difficultātibus suīs **dīxit**.

7. In pistrīnō huius Zēthī cum uxōre **labōrāveram**.

8. Uxor pānem in furnō **torrēbat** et ego molās cotīdiē **prōpellēbam.**

9. Talia dīcēns, servus in noctem **abiit**.

19-6 Colloquāmur

For this class exercise you will need some items found in any classroom. Here are some suggestions: two writing utensils (*stilus, -ī* n.), two books (*liber, librī* m.), two sheets of paper (*charta, -ae* f.), two wristwatches (*hōrologium, -iī* n.), and two coins (*nummus, -ī* m.). Pile these objects in two groups in different parts of the classroom. Then make commands following the models.

Point to the book in the far pile and say to one classmate

→ *Da mihi, sī tibi placet,* **illum librum**.

Now point to the book in the pile near you and say to more than one classmate

→ *Date mihi, sī vōbīs placet,* **hunc librum**.

Continue asking for other objects using similar patterns.

19-7   Verba Discenda

Use the *Verba Discenda* to form the comparative adjective for each Latin adjective listed below. Then give the meaning of each and an English derivative for the comparative form. Follow the model.

Adjective	Meaning	Comparative	Meaning	Derivative
→ *bonus, -a, -um*	good	melior, melius	better	ameliorate

1. *malus, -a, -um*; 2. *multus, -a, um*; 3. *multī, -ae, -a*; 4. *parvus, -a, -um*; 5. *superus, -a, -um*

VERBA DISCENDA

abdo, abdere, abdidī, abditum hide, conceal
absum, abesse, āfuī be absent, gone
adsum, adesse, adfuī be near, be present or here, be there for, help
āra, -ae f. altar

contrā (+ acc.) against, facing [contradict]
grātia, -ae f. grace; favor; pl. thanks; **grātiās agere** to thank someone
herī yesterday
hic, haec, hoc this [ad hoc]
inspectō (1) look closely at [inspector]
locus, -ī m. place [locality]

māior, māius greater, larger, older; m. pl. ancestors, elders
melior, melius better [amelioration]
minor, minus smaller [minority]
ōlim once, formerly
pars, partis f. part, piece [partition]

pēior, pēius worse [pejorative]
plūrēs, plūra more (in number) [plurality]
plūs more (in amount)
prior, prius former [priority]
priusquam before
superior, superius higher [superiority]

Angulus Grammaticus

"This Here" Deictic Enclitic *-c(e)*

The forms of *hic, haec, hoc* make more sense if you know that Latin can add a *-c(e)* at the end of a word to mean "here" or "there." The technical term for this is a **deictic enclitic**, i.e., a word ending that points out or shows something, especially direction. In earlier Latin authors like Plautus, there are forms like *illīc* (that man there) and *illaec* (that woman there). This type of expression is not that far from some dialectical forms of American English where we can still hear "this here one" and "that one yonder."

The genitive singular of *hic, haec, hoc* is *huius,* but, occasionally, Romans used *huiusce,* as in the expression *huiusce modī* (of this type here). The *-c(e)* was not regularly used with *huius,* but now look back at the declension of *hic, haec, hoc* and point out the forms where this *-c(e)* was always used.

The *-c(e)* is visible is in other Latin words, such as *Ecce!* (Look here!), and is useful for understanding the following Latin adverbs:

hīc	at this place here	*illīc*	at that place over there
hūc	to this place here	*illūc*	to that place over there
hinc	from this place here	*illinc*	from that place over there
hāc	by this path here	*illāc*	by that path over there

Now compare these adverbs with those formed from *iste, ista, istud:*

illīc	at that place over there	*istīc*	at that place of yours, where you are
illūc	to that place over there	*istūc*	to that place of yours, to where you are
illinc	from that place over there	*istinc*	from that place of yours, from where you are
illāc	by that path over there	*istāc*	by that path of yours

By comparison, adverbs formed from *is, ea, id* do not have this deictic emphasis:

ibi	there	*eō*	to that place	*eā*	that way, by that path

If you can recognize the fine distinctions in meaning among all these words, you know you are really beginning to think like a Roman.

20

Nōn Perseus sed Herculēs!

Herculēs Infans cum Serpente

Lectiō Prīma

Antequam Legis

In *Lectiō Prīma* Aelius and Licinia talk together about their unborn child. Their decision to compare him to the hero Hercules instead of Perseus leads Aelius to tell his wife the story of baby Hercules and the snakes.

Hercules

Hercules was the son of Jupiter and Alcmena, a mortal Greek woman, who was already pregnant by her mortal husband, Amphitryon, when Jupiter visited her. You will hear about all these events again soon, when the two families attend a play of Plautus based on this story. Alcmena bore twins, Hercules (son of Jupiter) and his mortal half brother, Iphicles (son of Amphitryon). Juno, Jupiter's sister and jealous wife, was furious and tried to eliminate Hercules. This is the point in the story where *Lectiō Prīma* starts.

Superlatives

In Chapter 19 you learned about comparatives (e.g., bigger, better). There is a third degree of adjective, called the **superlative**. In English we form these by using the word "most" or by adding "-est" to the adjective, but there are irregular forms as well.

POSITIVE	COMPARATIVE	SUPERLATIVE
angry	angrier more angry	angriest most angry
tall	taller	tallest
good	better	best
bad	worse	worst
many	more	most

Most Latin superlatives end in *-issimus, -a, -um*. But be sure to do Exercise 20-1 as you read.

LECTIŌNĒS:
NOSTER NŌVUS HERCULĒS
and
SCELUS HERCULIS

Aelius and Licinia worry about the future of their unborn child and decide to compare him to the hero Hercules instead of Perseus. Aelius tells his wife stories about Hercules' childhood and great deeds.

Notā Bene:

- Superlatives can also be translated as "very," e.g., *Vir fortissimus* can indicate a "very brave man." A *fēmina fortissima* could be "a most brave woman!"
- **Superlative adverbs** are formed by dropping the 2-1-2 adjective ending and adding *-ē*.

facillimus, -a, -um easiest   ⟶   *facillimē* most/very easily

EXERCEĀMUS!

20-1   Classifying Superlatives

As you read, look for superlative adjectives and adverbs marked in **bold**. Put them into the following four groups according to how they are formed: *-issimus, -a, -um*; *-illimus, -a, -um*; *-rimus, -a, -um*; and all the others (with special or irregular forms). Follow the model.

⟶ *perterritissima*   *-issimus, -a, -um*   *-illimus, -a, -um*   *-rimus, -a, -um*   irregular

🔊 NOSTER NŌVUS HERCULĒS

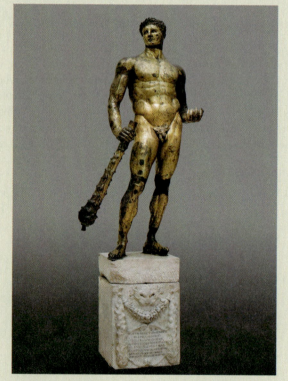

Ūnā nocte Aelius et Licinia sedent et dē verbīs astrologī multa dīcunt. Licinia "Vērumne est?" inquit, "Eritne puer noster hērōs sicut Perseus? Sed quae facta magna hic puer facere poterit? Āh, Aelī, **perterritissima** sum. Et tū? Quid ac-
5 cidet? Eritne necesse filiō nostrō monstra **difficillima** op-pugnāre?"

Aelius lēniter rīdet et mulierem mulcet. "Nōlī," inquit, "timēre, Licinia. Astrologī nōn semper vēra dīcunt. Fīlius nōn Perseus nōvus nōbīs erit, sed nōvus Herculēs, hērōs
10 māior erit! Nulla perīcula eī nocēbunt! Per totum orbem terrārum ībit et **maxima** monstra necābit sicut Herculēs ipse necābat sed nec perīculum nec vulnera habēbit. Deī ipsī fili-olum nostrum et nōs conservābunt! Ecce! Audī fābulam **clārissimam** dē Hercule:
15 "Herculēs, Alcmēnae fīlius, ōlim in Graeciā habitābat. Hic omnium hominum **optimus** hērōs erat. At Iūnō, rēgīna deōrum, Alcmēnam ōderat et Herculem infantem necāre voluit. Mīsit igitur duōs serpentēs **ferōcissimās** et **saevissimās** quae mediā nocte in cubiculum Alcmēnae
20 vēnērunt, ubi Herculēs cum frātre suō dormiēbat. Nec autem in cūnīs nec in lectīs, sed in scūtō **maximō** cubābant. Serpentēs **celerrimī** appropinquantēs scūtum movēbant; itaque puerī ē somnō excitātī sunt.

"Iphiclēs, frāter Herculis, **fortissimē** exclāmāvit; sed
25 Herculēs ipse, **fortissimus** puer, haudquāquam timēbat. **Minimīs** manibus serpentēs ferōcēs statim prehendit, et

Herculēs dē Forō Boāriō

facillimē colla eārum magnā vī compressit. Tālī modō puer serpentēs necāvit. Alcmēna autem, **miserrima** māter puerōrum, **horrendissimum** clāmōrem audīverat, et marītum suum ē somnō excitāverat. Ille **celerrimē** gladium suum rapuit et tum ad puerōs properābat, sed ubi ad locum vēnit, rem **mīrābilissimam** vīdit, Herculēs enim rīdēbat
30 et serpentēs mortuās monstrābat."

VERBA ŪTENDA

accidō, accidere, accidī happen
Alcmēna, -ae f. Alcmena, mother of Hercules
at but, and yet
autem however
clāmor, clāmōris m. shout
clārus, -a, -um famous
collum, -ī n. neck
comprimō, comprimere, compressī press, squeeze together
conservō (1) preserve, keep safe
cubō (1) sleep, lie
cūnae, cūnārum f. pl. cradle
enim for, because
excitō (1) awaken, excite, raise; *excitātī sunt* "were awakened"
exclāmō (1) call out
facilis, facile easy

factum, -ī n. deed
fāma, -ae f. fame, rumor, report
ferox, ferōcis fierce, savage
fīliolus, -ī m. little son (affectionate)
Graecia, -ae f. Greece
haudquāquam by no means
Herculēs, Herculis m. Hercules
hērōs, hērōis m. hero
horrendus, -a, -um horrible, terrible
igitur therefore
itaque therefore
Iūnō, Iūnōnis f. Juno, queen of the gods
lēniter gently
manibus "with his hands"
maximus, -a, -um greatest
medius, -a, -um the middle of
minimus, -a, -um smallest

mīrābilis, mīrābile astonishing, amazing
mittō, mittere, mīsī, missum send
modus, -ī m. way, manner
monstrō (1) show
monstrum, -ī n. monster
mortuus, -a, -um dead
moveō, movēre, mōvī move
mulceō, mulcēre, mulsī soothe, stroke
mulier, mulieris f. woman, wife
necō (1) kill, slay
nōbīs to us; *nōs* us
nox, noctis f. night
ōdī, ōdisse hate
oppugnō (1) attack
optimus, -a, -um best
orbis, orbis m. circle, ring; orbis terrārum circle of

the lands, i.e., "the world"
perīculum, -ī n. danger
perterritus, -a, -um very frightened
prehendō, prehendere, prehendī seize, take hold of
properō (1) hasten
rapiō, rapere, rapuī, raptum snatch, seize
rēgīna, -ae f. queen
rem thing, event
saevus, -a, -um savage, cruel
scūtum, -ī n. shield
serpens, serpentis f. snake, serpent
somnus, -ī m. sleep
statim immediately
tum then
vī "with strength"
vulnus, vulneris n. wound

POSTQUAM LĒGISTĪ

Answer these questions in English.

1. How does the conversation of Aelius and Licinia indicate that they are expectant parents? What does their conversation indicate about their relationship?
2. Why does Aelius prefer to compare his unborn son to Hercules rather than Perseus?
3. What do you think of Juno's behavior in the story about Hercules and the snakes? Does she act the way you would expect a god to act? What does this tell you about Roman gods?
4. What does the story of Hercules and the snakes suggest about Hercules as a hero?

Grammatica A

Superlative Adjectives and Adverbs

Regular Formation

Most Latin adjectives form **superlatives** by adding *-issimus, -a, -um* to the stem. This works for both 2-1-2 and 3rd declension adjectives:

ADJECTIVE	STEM	ENDING	EXAMPLE
laetus, -a, -um	laet-	-issimus, -a, -um	laetissimus, -a, -um
fortis, -e	fort-	-issimus, -a, -um	fortissimus, -a, -um

Exceptions

Any adjective with a masculine nominative singular ending in -er forms a superlative by adding -rimus, -a, -um **not to the stem** but directly to the masculine nominative singular form. This is true for both 2-1-2 and 3rd declension adjectives:

ADJECTIVE	MASCULINE NOMINATIVE SINGULAR	ENDING	EXAMPLE
miser, misera, miserum	miser	-rimus, -a, -um	miserrimus, -a, -um
pulcher, -chra, -chrum	pulcher	-rimus, -a, -um	pulcherrimus, -a, -um
ācer, ācris, ācre	ācer	-rimus, -a, -um	ācerrimus, -a, -um

Six adjectives ending in -lis form their superlatives by adding -limus, -a, -um to the stem:

ADJECTIVE	STEM	ENDING	EXAMPLE
facilis, -e	facil-	-limus, -a, -um	facillimus, -a, -um
difficilis, -e	difficil-	-limus, -a, -um	difficillimus, -a, -um
similis, -e	simil-	-limus, -a, -um	simillimus, -a, -um
dissimilis, -e	dissimil-	-limus, -a, -um	dissimillimus, -a, -um
gracilis, -e	gracil-	-limus, -a, -um	gracillimus, -a, -um
humilis, -e	humil-	-limus, -a, -um	humillimus, -a, -um

Other adjectives ending in -lis form their superlatives regularly, by adding -issimus, -a, -um to the stem:

crūdēlis, -e ⟶ crūdēlissimus, -a, -um.

Irregular Superlatives

Finally, here is a list of irregular superlative adjectives (along with their positive and comparative forms). They are marked in **bold**. All entail stem changes. You will see several of these for the first time in *Lectiō Secunda*. They are all *Verba Discenda*.

bonus, -a, -um	melior, melius	**optimus, -a, -um**	best
malus, -a, -um	pēior, pēius	**pessimus, -a, -um**	worst
magnus, -a, -um	māior, maius	**maximus, -a, -um**	greatest
multus,-a, -um	plūrēs, plūra	**plūrimus, -a, -um**	most
parvus, -a, -um	minor, minus	**minimus, -a, -um**	smallest
no positive	prior, prius	**prīmus, -a, -um**	first
superus, -a, -um	superior, superius	**suprēmus, -a, -um**	highest, final
		summus, -a, -um	highest, greatest

Using the Superlative

Quam is sometimes used with a superlative to mean "as _____ as possible"

quam plūrimī	as many as possible
quam celerrimē	as quickly as possible
quam facillimē	as easily as possible

You will see an example of this in the next *lectiō*.

EXERCEĀMUS!

20-2 **Comparatives and Superlatives**

Match the English word in column A with its Latin equivalent in column B.

A	B
1. greater	A. celerrimus
2. smaller	B. difficillimus
3. fastest	C. facilior
4. prettier	D. intelligentior
5. worst	E. laetissimus
6. better	F. māior
7. happiest	G. maximus
8. greatest	H. melior
9. best	I. minor
10. easier	J. optimus
11. most difficult	K. pessimus
12. more intelligent	L. pulchrior

Lectiō Secunda

Antequam Legis

In *Lectiō Secunda* Aelius continues telling the story of Hercules to his wife. In the story, several years have passed since the events described in *Lectiō Prīma,* and Hercules is now married to his first wife. After finishing his story, Aelius suggests a name for his unborn child.

The Future Perfect Tense

As you read this story about Hercules, you are introduced to your final Latin tense, the future perfect. This is the third tense in the perfect system. The other two are the perfect and pluperfect.

Recognizing the Future Perfect

The name says it all. It is a tense that is in the future, but also has a "perfected" or "done" sense to it. In short, if two things are going to happen in the future, and one clearly happens first, then that one goes into the future perfect tense. Here is an example you will see in *Lectiō Secunda.*

> *Sī nēmō mē **vīderit,** nēmō mē oppugnābit!*
> If no one will have seen me, no one will attack me.

or, more colloquially,

> If no one sees me, no one will attack me.

Both parts of the sentence refer to the future, but one will clearly happen before the other occurs. That "done" one goes into the future perfect tense.

The literal translation of the future perfect is "will have," but this is rare in today's speech. Ask your teacher's preference in translating this tense.

Forming the Future Perfect

perfect stem (3rd PP minus the *-ī*)   +   *-erō*   *-erimus*
                                               -eris   *-eritis*
                                               -erit   *-erint*

For now, when you see a future perfect, think "will have" and translate that thought into appropriate English. All future perfects in the *lectiō* are in ***bold italics***.

EXERCEĀMUS!

20-3 **Recognizing Perfect, Pluperfect, and Future Perfect**

As you read, make a line-by-line list of all the verbs marked in **bold** or ***bold italics***. The verbs in ***bold italics*** are future perfect. Those in **bold** are either perfect or pluperfect. The endings will help you tell the difference. Indicate the tense of each verb. Then translate the verb appropriately into English. Follow the models.

Line	Verb	Tense	Translation
→ 5	incidit	perfect	he fell into
→ 9	vīderit	future perfect	he will have seen

🔊 SCELUS HERCULIS

Aelius "Multōs post annōs," inquit, "mea cāra, Herculēs cum Megarā, uxōre suā, beātam vītam agēbat; sed paucōs post annōs Herculēs subitō in furōrem
5 **incidit** atque Megaram et līberōs suōs **occīdit**. Post breve tempus ad sānitātem **rediit**, et propter hoc scelus mox ex urbe **effūgit** et in silvās sē **recēpit**. "Sī nēmō mē ***vīderit***," inquit, "nēmō mē op-
10 pugnābit!"

"Herculēs tantum scelus expiāre cupiēbat. **Constituit** igitur ad ōrāculum Delphicum īre; hoc enim ōrāculum omnium suprēmum erat. Hīc, in templō
15 Apollinis, in summō monte sedēbat fēmina quaedam, nomine Pȳthia, quae consilium dabat eīs quī ad ōrāculum **vēnerant**.

Templum et Ōrāculum Apollinis Hodiē

"Herculēs 'Sī,' inquit, 'Pȳthia mē ***audīverit***, certē mihi auxilium dabit.'" Ubi Herculēs Pȳthiam certiōrem dē scelere
20 suō **fēcit**, Pȳthia prīmō tacēbat. Tandem tamen 'Sī ad urbem Tīryntha ***īveris***,' inquit, 'et omnia imperia Eurystheī rēgis ***fēceris***, iterum pūrus eris.' Herculēs, ubi haec **audīvit**, quam celerrimē ad urbem illam **contendit**, et Eurystheō rēgī sē in servitūtem **trādidit**.

"Herculēs, 'Pessimus,' inquit, 'hominum sum. Sed sī omnia quae mihi imperās facere ***potuerō***, scelus meum expiābō. Sī Minerva mē ***adiūverit***, omnia tua imperia facere poterō.'

25 "Duodecim annōs crūdēlissimō Eurystheō serviēbat, et duodecim labōrēs, quōs ille **imperāverat, confēcit**; hōc enim modō tantum scelus expiāre **potuit**. Dē hīs labōribus plūrima poetae Graecī atque Rōmānī **scrīpsērunt**."

Aelius **conclūsit**: "Itaque, Licinia, fīlius noster nōn Perseus nōvus erit, sed nōvus Herculēs! Herculēs māior hērōs quam Perseus erat et fīlius noster hērōs maximus erit! Nōmen eī igitur Maximus erit!"

🔊 VERBA ŪTENDA

Apollō, Apollinis m. Apollo, god of prophecy
atque and, and also, and even, yet
auxilium, -iī n. help, aid
beātus, -a, -um blessed, happy
certus, -a, -um certain *certiōrem facere* to inform
conclūdō, conclūdere, conclūsī, conclude, finish
conficiō, conficere, confēcī do, accomplish
consilium, -iī n. advice, plan
constituō, constituere, constituī decide
contendō, contendere, contendī make one's way toward
crūdēlis, crūdēle cruel
Delphicus, -a, -um Delphic, pertaining to Delphi (a shrine of Apollo)
duodecim twelve
effugiō, effugere, effūgī escape, flee
enim for

Eurystheus, Eurystheī m. Eurystheus, king of Tiryns
expiō (1) atone for
furor, -ōris m. fury, rage
Graecus, -a, -um Greek
Herculēs, Herculis m. Hercules
igitur therefore
imperium, -iī n. command, order
imperō (1) order
incidō, incidere, incidī meet, fall (into)
itaque therefore
līberī, -ōrum m. pl. children
Megara, -ae f. Megara, wife of Hercules
Minerva, -ae f. Minerva, goddess of wisdom
modus, -ī m. way, manner
mons, montis m. mountain
occīdō, occīdere, occīdī kill, slay
oppugnō (1) attack
ōrāculum, -ī n. oracle, divine pronouncement
pessimus, -a, -um worst
plūrimus, -a, -um most
prīmō at first
pūrus, -a, -um pure

Pȳthia, -ae f. Pythia, oracular priestess of Apollo at Delphi
quīdam, quaedam, quoddam "a certain"
recipiō, recipere, recēpī take back; *sē recipere* retreat
redeō, redīre, redīvī/rediī go back, return
sānitās, -tātis f. health, sanity
scelus, sceleris n. crime
serviō, servīre, servīvī serve
servitūs, -tūtis f. slavery, servitude
silva, -ae f. woods
summus, -a, -um highest, greatest; *summō monte* on the mountaintop
suprēmus, -a, -um highest, final
tamen nevertheless
tandem at last, at length
tantus, -a, -um so great
templum, -ī n. temple
Tīryntha (acc.) Tiryns, a Greek city in the Argolid
trādō, trādere, trādidī hand over
urbs, urbis f. city

POSTQUAM LĒGISTĪ

Answer these questions in both Latin and English if the question is followed by (L). Otherwise, just respond in English.

1. What does Hercules do while he is insane? (L)
2. After this where does he go first? Why?
3. Why does he eventually go to the Delphic oracle?
4. What does the oracle tell him? (L)
5. What happens after Hercules leaves Delphi?
6. How does Aelius conclude this tale?
7. What name does Aelius suggest for his son? Why?

Grammatica B

The Future Perfect Tense

With the addition of the future perfect, you now know all the tenses in Latin. This also completes the perfect system of the verbs.

PERFECT STEM = 3ᴿᴰ PRINCIPAL PART – "-ī"		
PERFECT	**PLUPERFECT**	**FUTURE PERFECT**
Perfect Stem +	**Perfect Stem +**	**Perfect Stem +**
-ī	-eram	-erō
-istī	-erās	-eris
-it	-erat	-erit
-imus	-erāmus	-erimus
-istis	-erātis	-eritis
-ērunt	-erant	-erint

Here is an overview of the perfect system of *vocō* with the translation of the future perfect forms.

PERFECT	PLUPERFECT	FUTURE PERFECT	FUTURE PERFECT TRANSLATION
vocāvī	vocāv**eram**	vocāv**erō**	I will have called
vocāvistī	vocāv**erās**	vocāv**eris**	you will have called
vocāvit	vocāv**erat**	vocāv**erit**	he/she/it will have called
vocāvimus	vocāv**erāmus**	vocāv**erimus**	we will have called
vocāvistis	vocāv**erātis**	vocāv**eritis**	you will have called
vocāvērunt	vocāv**erant**	vocāv**erint**	they will have called

Notā Bene:

- The rules for forming the perfect system work for all verbs in all conjugations, even "irregular" verbs. Thus *sum, esse, fuī* → *fuī, fueram, fuerō.*

Future Perfect Tips

1. Be careful of your stems. Forms like *erō* (future) and *fuerō* (future perfect) can be confusing. The stems will guide you best. The *fu-* in *fuerō* tells you that this is part of the perfect system since it is based on the 3ʳᵈ principal part. Therefore, the form has to be future perfect. Compare *poterō* versus *potuerō*.

2. Don't confuse the following endings:
   - *vēnērunt* perfect (they came, they have come)
   - *vēnerint* future perfect (they will have come)

3. You have probably figured out that the future perfect endings resemble the future of *sum*. But be careful! The 3ʳᵈ plural is *-erint* not *-erunt.*

4. Also, as you read aloud, do not fall into the temptation to put the stress on the endings. You do not pronounce these forms

   clāmāverŌ, clāmāverIS, clāmāverIT, etc.

   Follow your normal rules for accent:

   clāmĀVerō, clāmĀVeris, clāmĀVerit, etc.

Using the Future Perfect Tense

The most important thing to remember about the future perfect tense is that it is used to show an action that "will have happened" before another action. Look at the two verbs in the following sentence from *Lectiō Secunda*:

> *Sī nēmō mē vīderit, nēmō mē oppugnābit!*

Vīderit is future perfect, whereas *oppugnābit* is future. The future perfect is used to show that the "seeing" will have taken place before the "attacking."

Note that good English does not need to use the "have" in the future perfect. You can translate the sentence above as "If no one sees me, no one will attack me."

EXERCEĀMUS!

20-4 Tense Identification

For each of the following sentences from *Lectiō Secunda*, identify the tenses of the two verbs marked in **bold** and explain the relationship between the two actions. Follow the model.

> → *Sī nēmō mē vīderit, nēmō mē oppugnābit!*
> *vīderit*: future perfect   *oppugnābit*: future
> The future perfect is used to show that "seeing" would have to
> take place before "fighting."

1. Sī Pȳthia mē **audīverit**, certissimē mihi auxilium **dabit**.
2. Sī ad urbem Tīryntha **īveris**, iterum pūrus **eris**.
3. Sī omnia imperia Eurystheī rēgis **fēceris**, iterum pūrus **eris**.
4. Sī omnia quae mihi imperās facere **potuerō**, scelus meum **expiābō**.
5. Sī Minerva mē **adiuverit**, omnia tua imperia facere **poterō**.

More on Adverbs and Conjunctions

Many of the *Verba Discenda* in this chapter are indeclinable adverbs or conjunctions. They are your friends. Their spelling never changes. If you learn their meanings carefully, you can use them as translation aids. Here is a list of all the adverbs and conjunctions you have learned as *Verba Discenda* in either this chapter or earlier ones. They are grouped here thematically.

- **Connecting:** *atque* and, and yet, and even; *et* and; *et … et* both … and; *etiam* and also, even now; *-que* and; *-que … -que* both … and; *sīc* thus, in this way, yes; *sīcut* just as; *tam* so, so much (as)
- **Negative:** *nec* and not; *nec … nec* neither, nor; *nōn* not
- **Contrasting:** *at* but, yet; *autem* however; *sed* but; *sōlum* only; *tamen* nevertheless
- **Causal:** *enim* for; *ergō* therefore; *itaque* therefore; *quia* since; *quod* because; *sī* if
- **Temporal:** *cotīdiē* daily; *crās* tomorrow; *diū* for a long time; *dum* while, as long as; *herī* yesterday; *hodiē* today; *iam* now, already; *iterum* again; *māne* early in the morning; *mox* soon; *numquam* never; *nunc* now; *ōlim* once, formerly; *priusquam* before; *saepe* often; *semper* always; *statim* immediately; *subitō* suddenly; *tandem* at last, at length; *tum* then; *tunc* then; *ubi* when
- **Locational:** *ubi* where

Mōrēs Rōmānī

Herculēs Rōmānus

Hercules is the Latin name of the hero the Greeks knew as Heracles. Actually, the hero and his myth are an amalgamation of Greek and Roman tales. Although the stories you read in this chapter deal with Hercules in Greece, there are many adventures of Hercules that take place in

Herculēs Cācusque ā Baccio Bandinelli (1525–1534) Florentiae

Italy and even in Rome. In particular, ancient Romans told the story of Cacus and the cattle of Geryon. Hercules defeated Geryon, a three-bodied monster, in Spain. Driving the cattle back to Greece, the hero passed through the area where Rome would be founded and encountered another monster called Cacus. Stealing the cattle, Cacus brought them into his cave in the Aventine Hill. He led them in backward so that the tracks seemed to lead out of the cave, not into it. Eventually, Hercules heard his cattle mooing and tracked them to the cave, where he and Cacus wrestled to the death. Hercules, of course, won.

Here is an inscription from an altar dedicated to Hercules in late antiquity in Ostia: On the right is the full, unabbreviated text:

DEO	Deō
INVICTO HERCVLI	Invictō Herculī
HOSTILIVS ANTIPATER	Hostilius Antipater
V P PRAEF ANN	v(ir) p(erfectissimus) praef(ectus) ann(ōnae)
CVRAT REI PVBLIC OST	cūrāt(or) reī pūblic(ae) Ost(iensis)
	(fēcit)

Try reading the inscription as a single sentence.

> Hostīlius Antipater, vir perfectissimus, praefectus annōnae, (et) cūrātor reī publicae Ostiensis, (hoc) deō Invictō Herculī (fēcit).

🔊 VERBA ŪTENDA

annōna, -ae f. grain, the grain supply of Rome
cūrātor, -ōris m. caretaker, manager

invictus, -a, -um unconquered
Ostiensis, -se of Ostia, Ostian
perfectus, -a, -um perfect

praefectus, -ī m. director, supervisor
reī pūblicae of the republic

Latīna Hodierna

Herculēs Hodiē

Nōn sine Diīs Animōsus Infans, Nomisma ā Benjamin Franklin

While serving as ambassador to France during the Revolutionary War, Benjamin Franklin designed a medal to celebrate American independence. The obverse depicts the head of a woman representing the goddess Liberty, with the date 4 July 1776 below and the words *Lībertas Americāna* above. On the reverse baby Hercules is strangling the snakes while the goddess Minerva is fighting with a lion, along with the following Latin inscription:

> *nōn sine diīs animōsus infans*

This quote from Horace's *Odes* III.4.20 can be translated at least two ways: "a courageous infant is not without gods" and "an infant is not courageous without gods."

Hercules, of course, also appears in modern cinema and television, including Disney's 1997 film and the 2005 miniseries starring Paul Telfer as Hercules.

Orbis Terrārum Rōmānus

Herculēs Rōmae

Worship of the hero Hercules was an important part of the public religion of Rome. A round temple in his honor (depicted at right) stands in the *Forum Boārium* (Cattle Forum), an ancient meat and fish market on the Tiber River just west of the Circus Maximus. Nearby there was also the important *Herculis Invictī Āra Maxima* (Very Great Altar of Unconquered Hercules).

There were many temples or altars dedicated to this hero in Rome and throughout the empire. Another important temple of Hercules in Rome was known as the *Aedēs Herculis Mūsārum* (Temple of Hercules and the Muses), located near the Circus Flaminius near the Campus Martius. This temple was built by M. Fulvius Nobilior to celebrate his capture of the Greek city of Ambracia in 189 B.C. It contained statues of the nine Muses (goddesses of inspiration) and of Hercules playing the lyre. The coin at right probably depicts this statue of Hercules. Can you read the inscription on either side of the statue? Unfortunately, there are no visible signs of this temple in Rome today.

Templum Herculis in Forō Boāriō Hodiē

QUID PUTĀS?

1. Why do you think Aelius and Licinia prefer comparing their child to Hercules rather than to Perseus? Which hero do you prefer? Why?
2. Why do you think Hercules has appeared in so many different contexts in ancient Rome and in the modern world?
3. Which translation of the quote from Horace's *Odes* III.4.20 on Benjamin Franklin's Hercules coin do you prefer: "a courageous infant is not without gods" or "an infant is not courageous without gods"? Why?
4. Why do you think Benjamin Franklin chose to depict the infant Hercules on a coin celebrating America's recent independence?

Herculēs Mūsārum

Forum Boārium

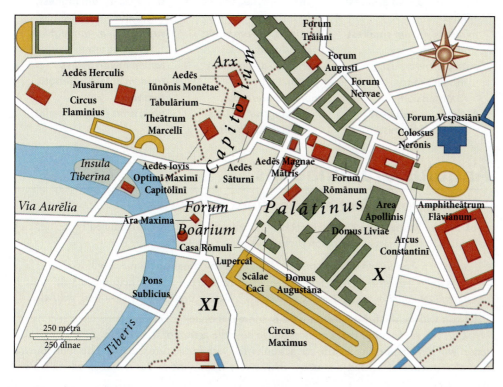

EXERCEĀMUS!

20-5 Scrībāmus

Respond to each of the following questions and supply an appropriate temporal adverb from the list. See how many other temporal adverbs you can use in your response to each question. You will have to change the verb's tense with adverbs like *crās* or *herī*. Follow the model.

Temporal Adverbs

cotīdiē; crās; diū; herī; hodiē; iam; iterum; māne; mox; numquam; nunc; ōlim; saepe; semper; statim; subitō; tum; tunc

→ Spectāsne lūdōs?　　　*Lūdōs numquam spectō.*　　or　　*Lūdōs crās spectābō.*

1. Lūdere vīs?　　　　　　　　　4. Bibisne aquam?
2. Legisne librōs?　　　　　　　　5. Vidēsne canem?
3. Habitāsne in Ītaliā?　　　　　　6. Vidēsne sīmiam?

20-6 Colloquāmur

Now practice asking and answering questions in Exercise 20-5 with other members of your class.

20-7 Verba Discenda

Regroup the *Verba Discenda* according to the following parts of speech: nouns, verbs, adjectives, adverbs, and conjunctions.

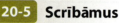
VERBA DISCENDA

at but, yet
atque and, and also, and even, and yet
autem however
clāmor, clāmōris m. shout [clamorous]
enim for
facilis, facile easy [facile]
factum, -ī n. deed [fact]
fāma, -ae f. fame, rumor, report [famous]

igitur therefore
itaque therefore
maximus, -a, -um greatest [maximize]
minimus, -a, -um smallest [minimal]
mittō, mittere, mīsī, missum send [transmission]
optimus, -a, -um best [optimal, optimist]

orbis, orbis m. circle, ring; *orbis terrārum* circle of the lands, i.e., the world [orbit]
pessimus, -a, -um worst [pessimist]
plūrimus, -a, -um most [plurality]
rapiō, rapere, rapuī, raptum snatch, seize [rapacious, raptor]

scelus, sceleris n. crime
statim immediately
summus, -a, -um highest, greatest [summit]
suprēmus, -a, -um highest, final [supreme]
tamen nevertheless
tandem at last, at length
tum then
urbs, urbis f. city [urban]

Angulus Grammaticus

The Future Perfect and Sequence of Tenses

Look for the future perfect tense especially in subordinate clauses introduced by *sī* (if), *cum* (when), and, more rarely, *antequam* (before) or *priusquam* (before).

Sī amīcī mē adiuvāverint, vincam!　　　　If my friends help me, I will win!
Cum amīcī mē adiuvāverint, vincam!　　　When my friends help me, I will win!
Antequam amīcī mē adiuvāverint, vincam!　Before my friends help me, I will win!

Later you will see the future perfect used in more elaborate "if" clauses.

　　Can you see in all of the sentences above how the action of the verb in the future perfect tense "will have happened" before the action of the verb in the future tense? This is an illustration of **sequence of tenses**, a concept that is very important in Latin and to which we will return later.

Appendix

Forms

Nouns

1ST DECLENSION				2ND DECLENSION			
Singular	**Fem.**	**Masc.**	**Masc.**	**Masc.**	**Masc.**	**Masc.**	**Neut.**
Nom.	fēmina	discipulus	vir	fīlius	magister	puer	vīnum
Gen.	fēminae	discipulī	virī	fīliī	magistrī	puerī	vīnī
Dat.	fēminae	discipulō	virō	fīliō	magistrō	puerō	vīnō
Acc.	fēminam	discipulum	virum	fīlium	magistrum	puerum	vīnum
Abl.	fēminā	discipulō	virō	fīliō	magistrō	puerō	vīnō
Voc.	fēmina	discipule	vir	fīlī	magister	puer	vīnum
Plural							
Nom.	fēminae	discipulī	virī	fīliī	magistrī	puerī	vīna
Gen.	fēminārum	discipulōrum	virōrum	fīliōrum	magistrōrum	puerōrum	vīnōrum
Dat.	fēminīs	discipulīs	virīs	fīliīs	magistrīs	puerīs	vīnīs
Acc.	fēminās	discipulōs	virōs	fīliōs	magistrōs	puerōs	vīna
Abl.	fēminīs	discipulīs	vīrīs	fīliīs	magistrīs	puerīs	vīnīs
Voc.	fēminae	discipulī	virī	fīliī	magistrī	puerī	vīna

3RD DECLENSION				I-STEMS	
Singular	**Masc.**	**Fem.**	**Neut.**	**Masc./Fem.**	**Neut.**
Nom.	frāter	soror	nōmen	ignis	mare
Gen.	frātris	sorōris	nōminis	ignis	maris
Dat.	frātrī	sorōrī	nōminī	ignī	marī
Acc.	frātrem	sorōrem	nōmen	ignem	mare
Abl.	frātre	sorōre	nōmine	igne or ignī	marī
Voc.	frāter	soror	nōmen	ignis	mare
Plural					
Nom.	frātrēs	sorōrēs	nōmina	ignēs	maria
Gen.	frātrum	sorōrum	nōminum	ignium	marium
Dat.	frātribus	sorōribus	nōminibus	ignibus	maribus
Acc.	frātrēs	sorōrēs	nōmina	ignēs	maria
Abl.	frātribus	sorōribus	nōminibus	ignibus	maribus
Voc.	frātrēs	sorōrēs	nōmina	ignēs	maria

Adjectives

2-1-2 ADJECTIVES

	2ND DECLENSION	1ST DECLENSION	2ND DECLENSION
Singular	**Masc.**	**Fem.**	**Neut.**
Nom.	bonus	bona	bonum
Gen.	bonī	bonae	bonī
Dat.	bonō	bonae	bonō
Acc.	bonum	bonam	bonum
Abl.	bonō	bonā	bonō
Voc.	bone	bona	bonum
Plural			
Nom.	bonī	bonae	bona
Gen.	bonōrum	bonārum	bonōrum
Dat.	bonīs	bonīs	bonīs
Acc.	bonōs	bonās	bona
Abl.	bonīs	bonīs	bonīs
Voc.	bonī	bonae	bona

	2ND DECLENSION	1ST DECLENSION	2ND DECLENSION
Singular	**Masc.**	**Fem.**	**Neut.**
Nom.	pulcher	pulchra	pulchrum
Gen.	pulchrī	pulchrae	pulchrī
Dat.	pulchrō	pulchrae	pulchrō
Acc.	pulchrum	pulchram	pulchrum
Abl.	pulchrō	pulchrā	pulchrō
Voc.	pulcher	pulchra	pulchrum
Plural			
Nom.	pulchrī	pulchrae	pulchra
Gen.	pulchrōrum	pulchrārum	pulchrōrum
Dat.	pulchrīs	pulchrīs	pulchrīs
Acc.	pulchrōs	pulchrās	pulchra
Abl.	pulchrīs	pulchrīs	pulchrīs
Voc.	pulchrī	pulchrae	pulchra

3RD DECLENSION ADJECTIVES

3 Terminations

Singular	Masc.	Fem.	Neut.
Nom.	celer	celeris	celere
Gen.	celeris	celeris	celeris
Dat.	celerī	celerī	celerī
Acc.	celerem	celerem	celere
Abl.	celerī	celerī	celerī
Voc.	celer	celeris	celere

Plural			
Nom.	celerēs	celerēs	celeria
Gen.	celerium	celerium	celerium
Dat.	celeribus	celeribus	celeribus
Acc.	celerēs	celerēs	celeria
Abl.	celeribus	celeribus	celeribus
Voc.	celerēs	celerēs	celeria

2 Terminations

Singular	Masc./Fem.	Neut.
Nom.	fortis	forte
Gen.	fortis	fortis
Dat.	fortī	fortī
Acc.	fortem	forte
Abl.	fortī	fortī
Voc.	fortis	forte

Plural		
Nom.	fortēs	fortia
Gen.	fortium	fortium
Dat.	fortibus	fortibus
Acc.	fortēs	fortia
Abl.	fortibus	fortibus
Voc.	fortēs	fortia

1 Termination

Singular	Masc./Fem./Neut.
Nom.	fēlix
Gen.	fēlīcis
Dat.	fēlīcī
Acc.	fēlīcem (m./f.) fēlix (n.)
Abl.	fēlīcī
Voc.	fēlix

Plural	
Nom.	fēlīcēs (m./f.) fēlīcia (n.)
Gen.	fēlīcium
Dat.	fēlīcibus
Acc.	fēlīcēs (m./f.) fēlīcia (n.)
Abl.	fēlīcibus
Voc.	fēlīcēs (m./f.) fēlīcia (n.)

Comparative Adjectives

Note: Comparatives are declined like 3rd declension regular (not i-stem) nouns.

Singular	Masc./Fem.	Neut.
Nom.	celerior	celerius
Gen.	celeriōris	celeriōris
Dat.	celeriōrī	celeriōrī
Acc.	celeriōrem	celerius
Abl.	celeriōre	celeriōre
Voc.	celerior	celerius
Plural		
Nom.	celeriōrēs	celeriōra
Gen.	celeriōrum	celeriōrum
Dat.	celeriōribus	celeriōribus
Acc.	celeriōrēs	celeriōra
Abl.	celeriōribus	celeriōribus
Voc.	celeriōrēs	celeriōra

Superlative Adjectives

REGULAR FORMATION

POSITIVE	SUPERLATIVE
laetus, -a, -um	laetissimus, -a, -um
fortis, -e	fortissimus, -a, -um
crūdēlis, -e	crūdēlissimus, -a, -um

IRREGULAR FORMATIONS

A. All adjectives ending in *-er* in the masculine nominative singular:

POSITIVE	SUPERLATIVE
miser, -era, -erum	miserrimus, -a, -um
pulcher, -chra, -chrum	pulcherrimus, -a, -um
celer, -is, -e	celerrimus, -a, -um

B. Some adjectives ending in *-lis* in the masculine nominative singular:

POSITIVE	SUPERLATIVE
facilis, -e	facillimus, -a, -um
difficilis, -e	difficillimus, -a, -um
similis, -e	simillimus, -a, -um
dissimilis, -e	dissimillimus, -a, -um
gracilis, -e	gracillimus, -a, -um
humilis, -e	humillimus, -a, -um

C. Irregular comparative and superlative adjectives:

POSITIVE	COMPARATIVE	SUPERLATIVE
bonus, -a, -um	melior, melius	optimus, -a,- um
malus, -a, -um	pēior, pēius	pessimus, -a, -um
magnus, -a, -um	māior, māius	maximus, -a, -um
multus, -a, -um	plūrēs, plūra	plūrimus, -a, -um
multī, -ae, -a	plūs (neuter form only)	plūrimī, -ae, -a
parvus, -a, -um	minor, minus	minimus, -a, -um
[no positive]	prior, prius	prīmus, -a, -um
superus, -a, -um	superior, superius	suprēmus, -a, -um
		summus, -a, -um

Personal / Reflexive Adjectives

PERSON	LATIN FORMS	TRANSLATION
Singular		
1st	meus, -a, -um	my
2nd	tuus, -a, -um	your
3rd	suus, -a, -um (reflexive)	his/her/its own
Plural		
1st	noster, -tra, -trum	our
2nd	vester, -tra, -trum	your
3rd	suus, -a, -um (reflexive)	their own

UNUS NAUTA Adjectives

Ullus, -a, -um any
Nūllus, -a, -um no, none
Ūnus, -a, -um one
Sōlus, -a, -um alone, only

Neuter, neutra, neutrum—neither
Alius, -a, -ud another, other
Uter, utra, utrum either, which (of two)
Tōtus, -a, -um whole, entire
Alter, altera, alterum the other (of two)

	MASC.	FEM.	NEUT.
Singular			
Nom.	sōlus	sōla	sōlum
Gen.	sōlīus	sōlīus	sōlīus
Dat.	sōlī	sōlī	sōlī
Acc.	sōlum	sōlam	sōlum
Abl.	sōlō	sōlā	sōlō
Plural			
Nom.	sōlī	sōlae	sōla
Gen.	sōlōrum	sōlārum	sōlōrum
Dat.	sōlīs	sōlīs	sōlīs
Acc.	sōlōs	sōlās	sōla
Abl.	sōlīs	sōlīs	sōlīs

Adverbs

REGULAR

	POSITIVE	COMPARATIVE	SUPERLATIVE
Based on 2-1-2 adjective	laetē	laetius	laetissimē
Based on 3rd declension adjective	fortiter	fortius	fortissimē

PARTIALLY IRREGULAR

	POSITIVE	COMPARATIVE	SUPERLATIVE
3rd declension adjectives ending in -*er*	celeriter	celerius	celerrimē
Other 3rd declension adjectives	fortiter	fortius	fortissimē

COMPLETELY IRREGULAR

bene	melius	optimē
male	pēius	pessimē
magnopere	magis	maximē
multum	plūs	plūrimum
parum	minus	minimē

Pronouns

	1ST PERSON	2ND PERSON	3RD PERSON		
Singular					
Nom.	ego	tū	is	ea	id
Gen.	meī	tuī	eius	eius	eius
Dat.	mihi	tibi	eī	eī	eī
Acc.	mē	tē	eum	eam	id
Abl.	mē	tē	eō	eā	eō
Plural					
Nom.	nōs	vōs	eī	eae	ea
Gen.	nostrī/nostrum	vestrī/vestrum	eōrum	eārum	eōrum
Dat.	nōbīs	vōbīs	eīs	eīs	eīs
Acc.	nōs	vōs	eōs	eās	ea
Abl.	nōbīs	vōbīs	eīs	eīs	eīs

RELATIVE PRONOUN AND INTERROGATIVE ADJECTIVE

	MASC.	FEM.	NEUT.
Singular			
Nom.	quī	quae	quod
Gen.	cuius	cuius	cuius
Dat.	cui	cui	cui
Acc.	quem	quam	quod
Abl.	quō	quā	quō
Plural			
Nom.	quī	quae	quae
Gen.	quōrum	quārum	quōrum
Dat.	quibus	quibus	quibus
Acc.	quōs	quās	quae
Abl.	quibus	quibus	quibus

INTERROGATIVE PRONOUN

	MASC./FEM.	NEUT.
Singular		
Nom.	quis	quid
Gen.	cuius	cuius
Dat.	cui	cui
Acc.	quem	quid
Abl.	quō	quō
Plural		
Nom.	quī	quae
Gen.	quōrum	quōrum
Dat.	quibus	quibus
Acc.	quōs	quae
Abl.	quibus	quibus

DEMONSTRATIVE: *hic haec hoc*

	MASC.	FEM.	NEUT.
Singular			
Nom.	hic	haec	hoc
Gen.	huius	huius	huius
Dat.	huic	huic	huic
Acc.	hunc	hanc	hoc
Abl.	hōc	hāc	hōc
Plural			
Nom.	hī	hae	haec
Gen.	hōrum	hārum	hōrum
Dat.	hīs	hīs	hīs
Acc.	hōs	hās	haec
Abl.	hīs	hīs	hīs

NUMBERS

	ROMAN NUMERAL	CARDINAL NUMBER			ORDINAL NUMBER	NOTES
1	I	M.	F.	N.	prīmus, -a, -um	
		ūnus	ūna	ūnum		
		ūnīus	ūnīus	ūnīus		
		ūnī	ūnī	ūnī		
		ūnum	ūnam	ūnum		
		ūnō	ūnā	ūnō		
2	II	duo	duae	duo	secundus, -a, -um	These three cardinal numbers are declinable.
		duōrum	duārum	duōrum		
		duōbus	duābus	duōbus		
		duōs	duās	duo		
		duōbus	duābus	duōbus		
3	III	trēs	trēs	tria	tertius, -a, -um	
		trium	trium	trium		
		tribus	tribus	tribus		
		trēs	trēs	tria		
		tribus	tribus	tribus		

Verbs

INDICATIVE

1st Conjugation   vocō, vocāre, vocāvī, vocātum

PRESENT	IMPERFECT	FUTURE	PERFECT	PLUPERFECT	FUTURE PERFECT
vocō	vocābam	vocābō	vocāvī	vocāveram	vocāverō
vocās	vocābās	vocābis	vocāvistī	vocāverās	vocāveris
vocat	vocābat	vocābit	vocāvit	vocāverat	vocāverit
vocāmus	vocābāmus	vocābimus	vocāvimus	vocāverāmus	vocāverimus
vocātis	vocābātis	vocābitis	vocāvistis	vocāverātis	vocāveritis
vocant	vocābant	vocābunt	vocāvērunt	vocāverant	vocāverint

2nd Conjugation   moneō, monēre, monuī, monītum

PRESENT	IMPERFECT	FUTURE	PERFECT	PLUPERFECT	FUTURE PERFECT
moneō	monēbam	monēbō	monuī	monueram	monuerō
monēs	monēbās	monēbis	monuistī	monuerās	monueris
monet	monēbat	monēbit	monuit	monuerat	monuerit
monēmus	monēbāmus	monēbimus	monuimus	monuerāmus	monuerimus
monētis	monēbātis	monēbitis	monuistis	monuerātis	monueritis
monent	monēbant	monēbunt	monuērunt	monuerant	monuerint

3rd Conjugation Regular: scrībō, scrībere, scripsī, scriptum

PRESENT	IMPERFECT	FUTURE	PERFECT	PLUPERFECT	FUTURE PERFECT
scrībō	scrībēbam	scrībam	scripsī	scripseram	scripserō
scrībis	scrībēbās	scrībēs	scripsistī	scripserās	scripseris
scrībit	scrībēbat	scrībet	scripsit	scripserat	scripserit
scrībimus	scrībēbāmus	scrībēmus	scripsimus	scripserāmus	scripserimus
scrībitis	scrībēbātis	scrībētis	scripsistis	scripserātis	scripseritis
scrībunt	scrībēbant	scrībent	scripsērunt	scripserant	scripserint

3rd Conjugation -iō: capiō, capere, cēpī, captum

PRESENT	IMPERFECT	FUTURE	PERFECT	PLUPERFECT	FUTURE PERFECT
capiō	capiēbam	capiam	cēpī	cēperam	cēperō
capīs	capiēbās	capiēs	cēpistī	cēperās	cēperis
capit	capiēbat	capiet	cēpit	cēperat	cēperit
capīmus	capiēbāmus	capiēmus	cēpimus	cēperāmus	cēperimus
capītis	capiēbātis	capiētis	cēpistis	cēperātis	cēperitis
capiunt	capiēbant	capient	cēpērunt	cēperant	cēperint

4th Conjugation   audiō, audīre, audīvī, audītum

PRESENT	IMPERFECT	FUTURE	PERFECT	PLUPERFECT	FUTURE PERFECT
audiō	audiēbam	audiam	audīvī	audīveram	audīverō
audīs	audiēbās	audiēs	audīvistī	audīverās	audīveris
audit	audiēbat	audiet	audīvit	audīverat	audīverit
audīmus	audiēbāmus	audiēmus	audīvimus	audīverāmus	audīverimus
audītis	audiēbātis	audiētis	audīvistis	audīverātis	audīveritis
audiunt	audiēbant	audient	audīvērunt	audīverant	audīverint

PRESENT INFINITIVE

1ST CONJUGATION	2ND CONJUGATION	3RD CONJUGATION REG.	3RD -IŌ	4TH CONJUGATION
vocāre	monēre	scrībere	capere	audīre

IMPERATIVE

1ST CONJUGATION	2ND CONJUGATION	3RD CONJUGATION	4TH CONJUGATION
Vocā!	Monē!	Scrībe!	Audī!
Vocāte!	Monēte!	Scrībite!	Audīte!

NEGATIVE IMPERATIVE

Nōlī vocāre!	Nōlī monēre!	Nōlī scrībere!	Nōlī audīre!
Nōlīte vocāre!	Nōlīte monēre!	Nōlīte scrībere!	Nōlīte audīre!

IRREGULAR IMPERATIVES

	SING.	PL.
dīcō, dīcere	dīc	dīcite
dūcō, dūcere	dūc	dūcite
faciō, facere	fac	facite
ferō, ferre	fer	ferte

IRREGULAR VERBS

sum, esse, fuī					
PRESENT	IMPERFECT	FUTURE	PERFECT	PLUPERFECT	FUTURE PERFECT
sum	eram	erō	fuī	fueram	fuerō
es	erās	eris	fuistī	fuerās	fueris
est	erat	erit	fuit	fuerat	fuerit
sumus	erāmus	erimus	fuimus	fuerāmus	fuerimus
estis	erātis	eritis	fuistis	fuerātis	fueritis
sunt	erant	erunt	fuērunt	fuerant	fuerint

possum, posse, potuī					
PRESENT	IMPERFECT	FUTURE	PERFECT	PLUPERFECT	FUTURE PERFECT
possum	poteram	poterō	potuī	potueram	potuerō
potes	poterās	poteris	potuistī	potuerās	potueris
potest	poterat	poterit	potuit	potuerat	potuerit
possumus	poterāmus	poterimus	potuimus	potuerāmus	potuerimus
potestis	poterātis	poteritis	potuistis	potuerātis	potueritis
possunt	poterant	poterunt	potuērunt	potuerant	potuerint

volō, velle, voluī

PRESENT	IMPERFECT	FUTURE	PERFECT	PLUPERFECT	FUTURE PERFECT
volō	volēbam	volam	voluī	volueram	voluerō
vīs	volēbās	volēs	voluistī	voluerās	volueris
vult	volēbat	volet	voluit	voluerat	voluerit
volumus	volēbāmus	volēmus	voluimus	voluerāmus	voluerimus
vultis	volēbātis	volētis	voluistis	voluerātis	volueritis
volunt	volēbant	volent	voluērunt	voluerant	voluerint

nōlō, nōlle, nōluī

PRESENT	IMPERFECT	FUTURE	PERFECT	PLUPERFECT	FUTURE PERFECT
nōlō	nolēbam	nōlam	nōluī	nōlueram	nōluerō
nōn vīs	nolēbās	nōlēs	nōluistī	nōluerās	nōlueris
nōn vult	nolēbat	nōlet	nōluit	nōluerat	nōluerit
nōlumus	nolēbāmus	nōlēmus	nōluimus	nōluerāmus	nōluerimus
nōn vultis	nolēbātis	nōlētis	nōluistis	nōluerātis	nōlueritis
nōlunt	nolēbant	nōlent	nōluērunt	nōluerant	nōluerint

mālō, mālle, māluī

PRESENT	IMPERFECT	FUTURE	PERFECT	PLUPERFECT	FUTURE PERFECT
mālō	mālēbam	mālam	māluī	mālueram	māluerō
māvīs	mālēbās	mālēs	māluistī	māluerās	mālueris
māvult	mālēbat	mālet	māluit	māluerat	māluerit
mālumus	mālēbāmus	mālēmus	māluimus	māluerāmus	māluerimus
māvultis	mālēbātis	mālētis	māluistis	māluerātis	mālueritis
mālunt	mālēbant	mālent	māluērunt	māluerant	māluerint

eō, īre, īvī / iī, ītum

PRESENT	IMPERFECT	FUTURE	PERFECT	PLUPERFECT	FUTURE PERFECT
eō	ībam	ībō	īvī	īveram	īverō
is	ībās	ībis	īvistī	īverās	īveris
it	ībat	ībit	īvit	īverat	īverit
īmus	ībāmus	ībimus	īvimus	īverāmus	īverimus
ītis	ībātis	ībitis	īvistis	īverātis	īveritis
eunt	ībant	ībunt	īvērunt	īverant	īverint

edō, ēsse / edere	
edō	edimus
ēs	ēstis
ēst	edunt

Participles

Singular	Masc./Fem.	Neut.
Nom.	vocāns	vocāns
Gen.	vocantis	vocantis
Dat.	vocantī	vocantī
Acc.	vocantem	vocāns
Abl.	vocantī / vocante	vocantī / vocante
Plural		
Nom.	vocantēs	vocantia
Gen.	vocantium	vocantium
Dat.	vocantibus	vocantibus
Acc.	vocantēs	vocantia
Abl.	vocantibus	vocantibus

2nd Conjugation	monēns, monentis
3rd Conjugation Reg.	scrībēns, scrībentis
3rd Conjugation -iō	capiēns, capientis
4th Conjugation	audiēns, audientis

Verba Omnia

Modus Operandī: Words in bold are *Verba Discenda* through Chapter 20. Bracketed numbers indicate the chapter in which this word became a *Verbum Discendum*. Definitions of *verba discenda* aim for comprehensiveness. The definitions of other words are not necessarily comprehensive but rather focus on the meanings in the context of the narrative.

abl. = ablative
acc. = accusative
adj. = adjective
dat. = dative
conj. = conjunction
excl. = exclamation
esp. = especially
f. = feminine
imp. = impersonal
imper. = imperative

indecl. = indeclinable
interj. = interjection
interr. = interrogative
m. = masculine
n. = neuter
pl. = plural
prep. = preposition
subj. = subjunctive
v. = verb

A

ā, ab, abs (+ abl.) **from, away from; by (with persons)** [5]
abdō, abdere, abdidī, abditum **hide, conceal** [19]
abeō, abīre, abīvī / abiī, abitum **go away** [7]
abhinc from here; ago
abitus, -ūs m. departure
abluō, abluere, abluī, ablūtum wash, cleanse
absum, abesse, āfuī **be absent** [19]
abūtor, abūtī, abūsus sum (+ abl.) use up, waste
ac = atque and, and also, and besides
ac and, and besides
acadēmia, -ae f. the academy
accēdō, accēdere, accessī, accessum agree, assent; approach; attack
accendō, accendere, accendī, accensum light, burn
accidō, accidere, accidī, happen; fall at, fall near
accipiō, accipere, accēpī, acceptum accept, receive
accumbō, accumbere, accubuī, accubitum recline at table
accurrō, accurrere, accurrī / accucurrī, accursum run, hasten to
ācer, ācris, ācre sharp, violent, eager, swift
acervus, -ī m. heap
acētum, -ī n. vinegar
acquiescō (1) quiet down, subside
Acrisius, -iī m. Acrisius (Perseus' grandfather)

ācriter sharply
Actiacus, -a, -um of Actium
actor, actōris m. actor
ad (+ acc.) **to, toward, for** [3, 5]
ad dextram to the right
ad lūnam by moonlight
ad sinistram to the left
adamō (1) fall in love, love passionately
addīcō, addīcere, addīxī, addictum consecrate
addō, addere, addidī, additum add, give; say in addition
addūcō, addūcere, adduxī, adductum bring in, lead to
adeō so much, to such a degree
adeō, adīre, adīvī / adiī, aditum **go to** [7]
adeps, adipis m./f. fat
adhūc to this point, still, yet
adiungō, adiungere, adiunxī, adiunctum join to, add to
adiūtor, -ōris m. helper
adiuvō, adiuvāre, adiūvī, adiūtum **help** [16]
adminiculum, -ī n. tool, support, aid
admīror, admīrārī, admīrātus sum admire, wonder at
admoneō, admonēre, admonuī, admonitum warn strongly, admonish
adoleō, adolēre, adoluī, adultum burn
adoptō (1) adopt
adsum, adesse, adfuī **be near, be present; (+ dat.) be "there" for someone, be of assistance, help, aid** [19]
adulescens, -entis m./f. **youth** [15]

advena, -ae m./f. foreigner, stranger

adveniō, advenīre, advēnī, adventum arrive at, come to [11]

adventus, -ūs m. arrival

adversārius, -iī m. opponent, enemy

adversus (+ acc.) opposite to, against

adversus, -a, -um adverse, contrary

aedēs and *aedis, aedis* f. temple, house of a god

aedificium, -iī n. building

aedificō (1) build, make

aedīlitās, -tātis f. aedilship, office of aedile (public works)

aedis, see *aedēs*

aeger, aegra, aegrum sick

aegrescō, aegrescere grow sick

Aegyptus, -ī f. Egypt, a province of Rome

Aelius, -iī m. Aelius, a male name

aēneus, -a, -um bronze

aequē fairly

aequinoctiālis, -e equinoctal, of the equinox

aequor, aequoris n. (level surface of the) sea

aequus, -a, -um even, equal; fair, just; patient, calm

āēr, āeris m. air, atmosphere

aes, aeris n. metal, especially copper or bronze

aestimō (1) value, estimate, consider

aestuōsus, -a, -um hot

aestus, -ūs m. heat

aetās, -tātis f. age, period of time

Aetia, -ōrum n. pl. "The Causes," title of a book by Callimachus

afferō, afferre, attulī, allātum bring to

afficiō, afficere, affēcī, affectum affect, move, influence

affinis, affine related by marriage

afflīgō, afflīgere, afflīxī, afflictum bother

affulgeō, affulgēre, affulsī (+ dat.) shine on, smile on; also spelled *adfulgeō,* etc.

Āfrica, -ae f. Africa, the Roman province of Africa (modern Tunisia)

Āfrus, -a, -um African

Agamemnōn, -nonis m. Agamemnon, king of Mycenae

age, agite come! well! all right!

agedum come! well! all right!

ager, agrī m. field [14]

aggredior, aggredī, aggressus sum go to, approach

agitātor, -ōris m. driver, charioteer

agitātus, -a, -um shaken, disturbed, upset

agitō (1) agitate, disturb

agmen, agminis n. column of troops, battle line; troops, army; herd, flock; crowd

agnoscō, agnoscere, agnōvī, agnōtum recognize, acknowledge

agō, agere, ēgī, actum act, do, lead, drive [4]

Agrippa, Agrippae m. Agrippa, Augustus' general and brother-in-law

Āh ha! ah!

aha ha! (in reproof, amusement, or denial)

āit, āiunt say (in present only)

albus, -a, -um white

Alcinous, -ī m. Alcinous, king of the Phaeacians and host of Odysseus

Alcmēna, -ae f. Alcmena, mother of Hercules

ālea, -ae f. die (singular of dice), dice-playing

Alexander, -ī m. Alexander (the Great), king of Macedonia

Alexandrēa, -ae f. Alexandria; *Alexandrēae* is locative "at Alexandria"

Alexandrēos, -ē, -on Alexandrian (Greek form of *Alexandrīnus*)

Alexandrīnus, -a, -um Alexandrian, pertaining to the city in Egypt

alibī elsewhere, in another place

aliōquī besides

aliquandō sometimes, at length, formerly, someday, hereafter

aliquis, aliquid n. someone, something [18]

aliter otherwise, else, in another way

alius, -a, -ud other, another [9]; *alius . . . alius* one . . . another; in pl. some . . . others

allegō (1) deputize, commission, charge

alloquor, alloquī, allocūtus sum speak to, address

almus, -a, -um nourishing, kind, dear [18]

Alpēs, Alpium f. pl. Alps, the mountains of northern Italy

altē high

alter, altera, alterum the other (of two) [17]

altus, -a, -um high [2]

alumnus, -ī m. foster son

alvus, -ī m. belly, stomach

amābilis, -e lovable

amārus, -a, -um bitter

amātōrius, -a, -um loving, pertaining to love, amatory

ambitiō, -ōnis f. canvassing (for votes), political campaign

ambitiōsus, -a, -um ambitious, ostentatious

ambō, ambae, ambō both (of two); (dat./abl. pl.) *ambōbus/ambābus*

ambulō (1) walk [2]

Amerīcānus, -a, -um American

amīca, -ae f. (female) friend, girlfriend [13]

amīcus, -ī m. friend [7]

āmittō, āmittere, āmīsī, āmissum lose, send away [9]

amō (1) love [13]

amor, amōris m. love [15]

āmoveō, āmovēre, āmōvī, āmōtum remove, move away

amphitheātrum, -ī n. amphitheater [17]

Amphitritē, -ēs f. Amphitrite, wife of Neptune; a lucky name for a ship

Amphitruō, -ōnis m. Amphitryon, husband of Alcmena

amphora, -ae f. amphora

amplector, amplectī, amplexus sum embrace, cherish

amputō (1) cut off

amulētum, -ī n. charm, amulet

an or, whether

ancilla, -ae f. female servant [8]

angiportum, -ī m. alley

angulus, -ī m. corner

angustiae, -ārum f. pl. trouble, difficulty

angustus, -a, -um narrow

anima, -ae f. breath, soul, life

animadvertō, animadvertere, animadvertī,
   animadversum observe, remark, notice, understand

animal, -ālis n. animal [17]

animus, -ī m. mind

annō superiōre last year

annōna, -ae f. year's provision

annuō, annuere, annuī nod (in approval)

annus, -ī m. year [12]

ante in front, before, ahead; (+ acc.) before, in front of

anteā previously

antehāc before this time, earlier

antequam before

antiburschius, -iī m. someone who is anti-studet,
   a student hater

antīquitās, -tātis f. antiquity

antīquus, -a, -um old, ancient [10]

Antōnius, -iī m. Antonius, Antony

ānulus, -ī m. ring

anus, -ūs f. old woman

apage go! scram!

aper, aprī m. boar

aperiō, aperīre, aperuī, apertum open; discover; show

apiārius, -iī m. beekeeper

apodȳtērium, -iī n. dressing room

Apollō, Apollinis m. Apollo, god of prophecy

Appennīnī, -ōrum m. pl. Appennines, the mountains
   along the spine of Italy

appetō, appetere, appetīvī / appetiī, appetītum seek,
   grasp for, grasp after

applaudō, applaudere, applausī applausum applaud

applicō, applicāre, applicāvī / applicuī, applicātum /
   applicitum apply

appōnō, appōnere, apposuī, appositum serve, put to

appropinquō (1) (+ dat.) approach, come near to [11]

aprīcus, -a, -um sunny

aptus, -a, -um attached to, connected to; suitable, fit

apud (+ acc.) at the house of, with, at _____'s [16]

aqua, -ae f. water [2]

aquaeductus, -ūs m. aqueduct

āra, -ae f. altar [19]

arānea, -ae f. spider

arbitror, abitrārī, arbitrātus sum observe, perceive; think

arbor, arboris f. tree

arca, -ae f. chest

Arcadia, -ae f. Arcadia, a region in Greece

arcānus, -a, -um secret

arcessō, arcessere, arcessīvī / arcessī, arcessītum fetch;
   call for; summon; procure

archierus, -ī m. chief priest

arcus, arcūs m. arch

ardeō, ardēre, arsī, arsum burn, glow

ardor, ardōris m. fire, flame

argentārius, -a, -um of silver, pertaining to silver;
   faber argentārius silversmith

argentārius, -iī, m. banker

argenteus, -a, -um of silver, silvery

argentum, -ī n. silver; money

Argī, Argōrum m. pl. Argos, a city in Greece

Argīlētum the Argiletum, (a street leading into
   the Roman Forum)

argūmentum -ī, n. plot, summary (of a play)

arguō, arguere, arguī, argūtum argue

arma, armōrum n. pl. arms, weapons

armō (1) arm

ars, artis f. skill, art [16]

artifex, artificis m. artist, artisan, maker

Artorius, -iī m. Artorius, a male name

artus, -ūs m. limb

as, assis m. as, a small copper coin of minimal value

ascendō, ascendere, ascendī, ascensum climb, ascend

Asia, -ae f. Asia, a Roman province in what is now Turkey

Asinius, -iī m. Asinius

asinus, -ī m. donkey

aspectō (1) gaze, look at

asper, aspera, asperum rough, harsh

aspergō, aspergere, aspersī, aspersum sprinkle

aspiciō, aspicere, aspexī, aspectum look at

assentior, assentīrī, assensus sum approve

assequor, assequī, assecūtus sum pursue, gain

assō (1) roast

assuētus, -a, -um accustomed

astō, astāre, astitī stand (up); stand by, assist

astrologia, -ae f. astrology

astrologus, -ī m. astrologer

astūtus, -a, -um smart

at but, and yet [20]

āter, ātra, ātrum black

Athēnae, Athēnārum f. pl. Athens, a city in Greece

atque and, and also, and even, yet [20]

atquī yet

ātrium, -iī n. atrium, public greeting room
   of a Roman house

atrōciter fiercely

attat Ah! (used to express surprise, fear, or a warning)

attendō, attendere, attendī, attentum listen carefully

attonitus, -a, -um astonished, amazed

auctōritās, -tātis f. authority, power

audācia , -ae f. daring
audeō, audēre, ausus sum dare [9]
audiāmus "Let's listen!", subj.
audiō, audīre, audīvī / audiī, audītum hear, listen to [7]
Augēās, Augēae m. Augeas, king of Elis in Greece
Augēus, -a, -um Augean, pertaining to King Augeas
augustus, -a, -um revered
Augustus, -ī m. "the revered one," a title of Octavius, the
     emperor C. Julius Caesar Octavianus (63 B.C.–14 A.D.),
     known as *Augustus* ("Revered")
aura, -ae f. breeze
aureus, -a, -um golden
auris, auris f. ear
auscultō (1) listen
auspex, auspicis m. diviner, soothsayer
auspicium, -(i)ī n. sign, omen, auspices
aut or; *aut . . . aut* either . . . or [4]
autem however [20]
auxilium, -iī n. help, aid; pl. auxiliary forces
Avē Greetings!
aveō, avēre be eager
avia, -ae f. grandmother
avidē eagerly
avidus, -a, -um eager
avis, avis f. bird
āvolō (1) hasten away, fly away
avus, -ī m. grandfather, ancestor

B

Bacchus, -ī n. Bacchus, the god of wine;
     also known as Liber
Baiae, Baiārum m. pl. Baiae, a resort town near
     Naples, Italy
balneae, ārum f. pl. bath
barba, -ae f. beard
basilica, -ae, basilica, courthouse
beātus, -a, -um blessed, happy
bellum, -ī n. war; *bellum gerere* wage war
bellus, -a, -um handsome, pretty
bene well, nicely [4]
beneficium, -iī n. kindness, benefit, favor
benevolens, benevolentis well-wishing, benevolent
benignē kindly
benignus, -a, -um kind, kind-hearted, bounteous
bestiārius, -iī m. animal fighter
bēta, -ae f. beet
bibliothēca, -ae f. library
bibliothēcē, -ēs f. library (the Greek equivalent
     of *bibliothēca, -ae*)
bibō, bibere, bibī drink [2]
biennium, -iī n. a two-year period
bīga, -ae f. two-horse chariot

bis twice, two times
bonus, -a, -um good [3]
bōs, bovis m./f. cow, bull, ox
brāc(c)hium, -iī n. arm [14]
brevī in a short time
brevis, breve short [18]
Brundisium, -iī n. Brundisium, a city in Calabria
Brūtus, -ī m. Marcus Iunius Brutus (85–42 B.C.),
     one of the leading assassins of Julius Caesar
būbō, būbōnis m. owl
bulla, -ae f. bulla, a locket worn around a child's neck

C

cachinnātiō, -ōnis f. loud laughter
cachinnō (1) laugh loudly
cacūmen, cacūminis n. tree top
cadāver, cadāveris n. corpse, dead body
cadō, cadere, cecidī, cāsum fall (down); be slain; end
Caecilia, -ae f. Caecilia, a female name
caelibāris, -e unmarried
Caelius, -a, -um Caelian, pertaining to one
     of the seven hills of Rome
caelum, -ī n. sky
Caesar, Caesaris m. Caesar
Calabria, -ae f. region in the heel of Italy
caldārium, -iī n. hot bath
calidum, -ī n. a hot drink
calidus, -a, -um warm, hot
Callimachus, -ī m. chief librarian at Alexandria
     and poet (c.280–243 B.C.)
calvus, -a, -um bald
calx, calcis f. goal, chalkline
Campānia, -ae f. Campania, region of southern
     Italy around Naples
campus, -ī m. field
candidātus, -ī m. candidate
candidus, -a, -um dazzling white; bright
canis, canis m./f. dog
canō, canere, cecinī, cantum sing, sing about
cantō (1) sing
cantus, -ūs m. song
capax, capācis spacious, roomy; "full of"
capillus, -ī m. hair
capiō, capere, cēpī, captum take, catch [3]
Capitōlīnus, -a, -um Capitoline, pertaining
     to the Capitoline hill
Capitōlium, -iī n. the Capitoline hill, one of the seven
     hills of Rome
captīvus, -ī m. captive, prisoner
caput, capitis n. head; master
carcer, carceris m. prison; starting gate
careō, carēre, caruī, caritum (+ abl.) lack, be without, lose

cāritās, -ātis f. charity, generosity

carmen, carminis n. song, poem, poetry [17]

carō, carnis f. flesh; meat

carōta, -ae f. carrot

carpō, carpere, carpsī, carptum seize, pluck, enjoy

cārus, -a, -um dear [13]

Cassius, -iī m. C. Cassius Longinus (85–42 B.C.), one of the leading assassins of Julius Caesar

Castor, -oris m. Castor, the divine twin brother of Pollux, one of the Gemini

Castōrum of the Castors, i.e., Castor and Pollux

castra, -ōrum n. pl. camp

cāsus, -ūs m. event; misfortune

catēna, -ae f. chain, fetter

catulus, -ī m. puppy

caudex, caudicis m. piece of wood, as an oath "blockhead!"

causa, -ae f. cause, reason; *causā* (+ gen.) on account of, because of

causidicus, -ī m. lawyer

cautus, -a, -um cautious, careful

cavea, -ae f. cage

caveō, cavēre, cāvī, cautum take care, beware

cēdō, cēdere, cessī, cessum go, walk; (+ dat.) yield to, give way to; succeed; allow, grant

celeber, celebris, celebre frequent, famous

celer, celeris, celere fast, swift [15]

celeriter quickly, swiftly

cella, -ae f. room [18]

cēlō (1) hide

celsus, -a, -um high, lofty, tall

cēna, -ae f. dinner [12]

cēnō (1) dine [12]

censeō, cēnsēre, cēnsuī, cēnsum be of the opinion

centaurus, -ī m. centaur, half-human and half-horse

centum indecl. one hundred

centuria, -ae f. century, i.e., a division of the Roman citizenry based on wealth; the two highest such centuries were the senators and the *equitēs* (knights)

centuriō, -ōnis m. centurion

certāmen, certāminis n. contest, race

certē certainly

certiōrem facere make more certain, inform; *sē certiōrem facere*, make oneself more certain, learn, learn about

certus, -a, -um sure, certain

cēterum besides, for the rest

Chaldaeus, -a, -um Chaldaean, an inhabitant of Mesopotamia

Charōn, Charōnis m. Charon, the ferryman of the Underworld

Chīrōn, -ōnis m. Chiron, a schoolmaster who shares his name with a centaur who taught various heroes.

cibus, -ī m. food [2]

cicātrīcōsus, -a, -um scarred

cicātrix, cicātrīcis f. scar

cingō, cingere, cinxī, cinctum gird, put a belt around

cingulum, -ī n. belt

cinis, cineris m./f. ash

circulus, -ī m. circle

circum (+ acc.) around [6]

circumambulō (1) walk around

circumcingō, circumcingere, circumcinxī, circumcinctum gird around, surround

circumcurrō, circumcurrere run around

circumeō, circumīre, circumīvī / circumiī, circumitum go around

circumsiliō, circumsilīre leap around

circumspectō (1) look around

circumstō, circumstāre, circumstetī stand around, surround

circus, circī m. circle, circus; racetrack

cista, -ae f. chest, box

cisterna, -ae f. cistern, well

cīvis, cīvis m./f. citizen

cīvitās, -ātis f. citizenship, the state

clādēs, -is f. defeat

clāmō (1) shout, cry out [5]

clāmor, clāmōris m. shout, cry, uproar [20]

clāmōsus, -a, -um noisy

clārus, -a, -um clear, bright; loud, distinct; famous

Claudius, -iī m. Claudius, *nōmen* of an old Roman family

claudō, claudere, clausī, clausum shut, close

clēmentia, -ae f. mercy, clemency

Cleopatra, -ae f. Cleopatra, the last Ptolemaic ruler of Egypt

cliens, clientis m. client

cloāca, -ae f. sewer

cōdex, cōdicis m. book

coepī, coepisse, coeptum begin

coetus, -ūs m. assembly, band

cōgitō (1) think, think about [10]

cognātus, -a, -um relative; kinsman

cognoscō, cognoscere, cognōvī, cognitum learn, get to know, observe; in the perfect: "to know"

cōgō, cōgere, coēgī, coactum drive together, force

cōliculus, -ī = cauliculus,-ī m. small cabbage, cabbage sprout

collābor, collābī, collapsus sum fall in a faint, collapse

collāre, collāris n. collar

collēgium, -iī n. club, group, corporation, association

collis, collis m. hill

colloquium, -iī n. talk, conversation

colloquor, colloquī, collocūtus sum talk together, converse

collum, -ī n. neck

colō, colere, coluī, cultum cultivate, take care of; honor, pay court to, worship

colōnia, -ae f. colony

color, -ōris m. color, complexion

columbārium, -iī n. a niche for a cinerary urn

coma, comae f. hair

combūrō, combūrere, combussī, combustum burn, burn up

comes, comitis m./f. companion

comitia, -ōrum n. pl. elections

comitō (1) accompany, attend

comitor, comitārī, comitātus sum accompany, attend

commentāriolum, -ī n. small handbook, short essay

committō, committere, commīsī, commissum entrust

commodus, -a, -um pleasant, comfortable, convenient, suitable

commūnis, commūne common

commutō (1) change

comoedia, -ae f. comedy

compescō, compescere, compescuī confine, restrain

compitālis, -e of the crossroads

complector, complectī, complexus sum embrace

comprehendō, comprehendere, comprehendī, comprehensum seize, grasp, understand

compressus, -a, -um squeezed together, narrow

comprimō, comprimere, compressī, compressum press, squeeze together

computō (1) count up, calculate

concalescō, -ere, -uī to warm up

concēdō, concēdere, concessī, concessum (+ dat.) go way, yield, withdraw, allow, grant

concīdō, concīdere, concīdi, concīsum cut, chop up

concilium, -iī n. council = Roman senate

conclāve, conclāvis n. room

conclūdō, conclūdere, conclūsī, conclūsum conclude, finish

concordia, -ae f. concord, harmony

Concordia, -ae f. the goddess of Concord

condīmentum, -ī n. spice, seasoning

condō, condere, condidī, conditum build, found

condūcō, condūcere, condūxī, conductum rent

conferō, conferre, contulī, collātum discuss, bring together, collect; *sē conferre* go ("betake oneself"); talk together

conficiō, conficere, confēcī, confectum do, accomplish, complete

confirmō (1) reassure, strengthen, confirm, encourage

congiārium, -iī n. largesse, gift

congregō (1) gather

coniciō, conicere, coniēcī, coniectum hurl, cast

coniunctiō, -iōnis f. joining together, union

coniungō, coniungere, coniunxī, coniunctus join, connect, ally

coniunx, coniugis m./f. spouse

cōnor, cōnārī, cōnātus sum try, undertake

consacrō (1) dedicate, consecrate

conscendō, conscendere, conscendī, conscensum ascend; embark

conscrībō, conscrībere, conscripsī, conscriptum enlist

consentiō, consentīre, consensī, consensum consent, agree

consequor, consequī, consecūtus sum obtain, procure

conservō (1) preserve, keep safe

conservus, -ī m. fellow slave

consīderō (1) consider, inspect

consilium, -iī n. plan, advice, counsel, reason, judgment

consistō, consistere, constitī, constitum stop, halt; (+ *ā* or *ex* + abl.) consist of

consōbrīna, -ae f. female first cousin (on the mother's side)

consōlor, consōlārī, consōlātus sum console

conspiciō, conspicere, conspexī, conspectum catch sight of, see, look at, observe [9]

constat imp. "it is known (that)"; it is agreed

consternō (1) confuse, terrify

constituō, constituere, constituī, constitūtum put, appoint, decide, establish

constō, constāre, constitī, constātum stand still; cost [10]; *satis constat* it is agreed that, it is an established fact that

constringō, constringere, constrinxī, constrinctum bind fast; compress

construō, construere, construxī, constructum build

consuētūdō, -inis f. companionship

consul, consulis m. consul

consulāris, -e consular, of consular rank

consulātus, -ūs m. consulship

consūmō, consūmere, consumpsī, consumptum use up, eat, consume

contemnō, contemnere, contempsī, contemptum scorn

contemplor, contemplārī, contemplātus est reflect on, contemplate

contendō, contendere, contendī, contentum make one's way toward

contentus, -a, -um content, satisfied

contineō, continēre, continuī, contentum contain, hold

continuus, -a, -um successive

contrā (+ acc.) against, opposite (to) [19]

contractiō, -ōnis f. contraction

contrahō, contrahere, contraxī, contractum draw together, gather

conventus, -ūs m. gathering, assembly

convīvium, -iī n. feast, banquet

convocō (1) call together

cōpiōsus, -a, -um plentiful

coquō, coquere, coxī, coctum cook, boil, bake, fry

coquus, -ī m. cook

cor, cordis n. heart [17]

Cordus, -ī m. Cordus, a male name

coriandrum, -ī n. coriander

Corinthus, -ī f. Corinth, a city in Greece

cornicen, -cinis m. horn blower

corōna, -ae f. crown, garland

corpus, corporis n. body [15]

corrumpō, corrumpere, corrūpī, corruptum spoil, destroy

cortex, corticis m./f. skin, bark, rind

cōtīdiē (*cottīdiē*) **daily, every day** [19]

crās **tomorrow** [6]

crassus, -a, -um crass, less polite

crēbrō frequently

crēdō, crēdere, crēdidī, crēditum (+ dat.) believe, trust

crepitus, -ūs m. rattling

crepundia, -ōrum n. pl. rattle

Crescens, -entis m. Crescens, a male name

crescō, crescere, crēvī, crētum grow, arise, appear, increase

Crēta, -ae f. Crete, an island in the eastern Mediterranean

crīmen, crīminis n. crime

crīnis, crīnis m. hair

crocodīlus, -ī m. crocodile

crūdēlis, crūdēle harsh, cruel

cruentus. -a, -um bloody, gory

cruor, cruōris m. gore, blood

crūs, crūris n. leg, shin

cubiculum, -ī **n. bedroom** [12]

cubō (1) lie down (in bed) lie asleep, sleep

culīna, -ae f. kitchen

culpa, -ae f. fault, blame

cultellus, -ī m. knife

cultūra, -ae f. agriculture

cum **(+ abl.) with** [6]

cum prīmum as soon as

cum **when** [15]

cumīnum, -ī n. cumin

cūnae, cunārum f. pl. cradle

cunctor, cunctārī, cunctātus est tarry, linger, hesitate, dawdle

cupidus, -a, -um (+ gen.) longing for, eager for, desirous

cupiō, cupere, cupīvī / cupiī, cupītum **wish, want to** [4]

cupressus, -ī f. cypress tree

cūr **why** [11]

cūra, ae f. worry, concern, care, anxiety

cūrātor, -ōris m. caretaker, manager

cūria, -ae f. curia, senate house

cūrō (1) **care for** [13]

currō, currere, cucurrī, cursum **run** [5]

currus, -ūs m. chariot

cursor, cursōris m. runner

cursum amittere to go off course

cursus, -ūs m. course; voyage; journey; race; march; career

custōdiō, custōdīre, custōdīvī / custōdiī, custōdītum watch, guard

custōs, custodis m./f. guard

D

Damascus, ī f. Damascus, city in Roman province of Syria

Danaē, Danaēs f. Danaë, mother of Perseus

daps, dapis f. sacrificial feast, offering

dē **(+ abl.) away from, down from; concerning, about** [7]

dea, -ae **f. goddess** [11]

dealbātor, -ōris m. whitewasher, someone charged with whitewashing walls either to cover up graffiti or to prepare the wall for new graffiti.

dealbō (1) whitewash

dēbellō (1) vanquish

dēbeō, dēbēre, dēbuī, dēbitum **owe, ought, have to** [7]

dēbilis, -e weak

decem **ten** [12]

dēcernō, dēcernere, dēcrēvī, dēcrētum judge, award

decet, decēre, decuit (+ dat. + inf.) imp. it is fitting

dēcipiō, dēcipere, dēcēpī, dēceptum cheat

decōrus, -a, -um fitting, noble

dēdicō (1) dedicate, devote

dēdūcō, dēdūcere, dēdūxī, dēductum lead down, bring away; conduct, escort; *uxōrem dēdūcere* take a wife, marry

dēductiō, -ōnis f. transportation

dēfendō, dēfendere, dēfendī, dēfensum defend

dēfluō, dēfluere, dēfluxī, dēfluxus flow away; disappear

dēfungor, dēfungī, dēfunctus sum die

dehinc after this, next

deinceps in succession

deinde then

dēlectābilis, -e delicious

dēlectō (1) amuse, delight, charm

dēleō, dēlēre, dēlēvī, dēlētum destroy, wipe out

dēlīberō (1) debate, deliberate

dēliciae, -ārum f. pl. delight, darling; pet

dēligō, dēligere, dēlēgī, dēlectum pick out, choose

Delphicus, -a, -um Delphic, pertaining to Delphi (a shrine of Apollo)

delphīnus, delphīnī m. dolphin

dēlūbrum, -ī n. temple, shrine

dēmānō (1) flow out, spread out

dēmittō, dēmittere, dēmīsī, dēmissum send down

demonstrō (1) point at, show, depict

Dēmosthenēs, -is m. Demonsthenes, a famous Greek orator of the 4th century B.C.

dēmum finally, at length, at last

dēnārius, -iī m. denarius, a silver coin

dēnique finally, at last, in fact

dēplōrō (1) lament

dēpōnō, dēpōnere, dēposuī, dēpositum leave, lay down; commit; entrust, deposit

dēprecor, dēprecārī, dēprecātus sum beg pardon from

descendō, descendere, descendī, descensum go down, descend

describō, describere, descripsī, descriptum describe, draw

dēserō, dēserere, dēseruī, dēsertum desert, abandon

dēsīderium, -iī n. desire, wish

dēsīderō (1) wish for

dēsinō, dēsinere, dēsīvī / dēsiī, dēsitum (+ gen.) cease, desist (from)

dēsistō, dēsistere, dēstitī, dēstitum stop, cease, desist

dēspērō (1) despair (of)

destruō, dēstruere, destruxī, destructum destroy
dēsuper from above
dētergeō, dētergēre, dētersī, dētersum wipe away, rub clean
dētrīmentum, -ī n. loss, damage; defeat
***deus, -ī* m. god; *dī* (alternate nom. pl.) [14]**
dēvertō, dēvertere, dēvertī, dēversum turn aside, stop to visit
dēvorō (1) devour, consume
dexter, dext(e)ra, dext(e)rum right *dext(e)ra (manus),*
  -ae f. right hand
dī m. nom. pl. gods = *deī*
diabolus, -ī m. devil
Diāna, -ae f. Diana, goddess of the hunt and of the moon;
  the moon itself
***dīcō, dīcere, dīxī, dictum* say, tell [7]**
dictum, -ī n. word
Dictys, -yos m. Dictys, brother of the king of Seriphos
diēs, diēī m. day
differō, differre, distulī, dilātum delay
***difficilis, difficile* hard, difficult [15]**
difficultās, -tātis f. trouble, difficulty
diffugiō, diffugere, diffūgī flee from
diffundō, diffundere, diffūdī, diffūsum pour forth,
  spread out
digitus, -ī m. finger
dignitās, -tātis f. worthiness, merit; dignity; office; honor
dignus, -a, -um worthy, deserving
dīligens, dīligentis careful, diligent, frugal
dīligenter carefully
dīmidium, -iī n. half
dīmittō, dīmittere, dīmīsī, dīmissum let go, send out;
  dismiss; release; divorce
Dioclēs, Dioclis m. Diocles, a male name
dīrectē directly
dīrectus, -a, -um straight, direct
dīrigō, dīrigere, direxī, dīrectum direct, guide
dīs dat./abl. pl. of *deus*
discēdō, discēdere, discessī, discessum leave, depart
discernō, discernere, discrēvī, discrētum separate, distinguish
disciplīna, -ae f. instruction, knowledge
***discipula, -ae* f. (female) student [2]**
***discipulus, -ī* m. (male) student [2]**
***discō, discere, didicī* learn [6]**
disertus, -a, -um eloquent
dispergō, dispergere, dispersī, dispersum scatter, disperse
dispiciō, dispicere, dispexī, dispectum consider
displiceō, displicēre, displicuī, displicitum (+ dat.) displease;
  displicet imp. "it is displeasing"
disputō (1) argue
disserō, disserere, disseruī, dissertum discuss
dissimilis, -e unlike
***diū* for a long time [16]**
diūtius (comparative of *diū*) for a bit longer
dīversus, -a, -um different, varied

dīvēs, dīvitis rich, talented
dīvidō, dīvidere, dīvīsī, dīvīsum divide
dīvitiae, -ārum f. pl.wealth, riches
dīvus, -a, -um divine
dīvus, -ī m. god = *deus*
***dō, dare, dedī datum* give [2]**
doceō, docēre, docuī, doctum teach; show
doctus, -a, -um learned
documentum, -ī n. instruction, warning
dolor, dolōris m. pain, grief
dolōsus, -a, -um clever, crafty
domī at home
domicilium, -iī n. home
domina, -ae f. mistress (of the house), the woman in charge
***dominus, -ī* m. master [18]**
***domus, -ī* f. home, house; *domum* home, to a house [4]**
domus, -ūs f. house
dōnec as long as, until
dōnum, -ī n. gift
***dormiō, dormīre, dormīvī / dormiī, dormītum* sleep [12]**
dorsum, -ī n. back
dōtālis, -e dowry
Drusus, -ī m. Drusus, *cognōmen* in the Claudian *gens;*
  Tiberius and his descendants were members of this family
dubitō (1) doubt, hesitate
dubium est it is doubtful
dubius, -a, -um doubtful, uncertain
***dūcō, dūcere, duxī, ductum* lead [4]**
dūdum a little while ago
dulcis, -e sweet
dulciter sweetly
***dum* while, as long as; until [10]**
dummodo provided that, as long as
dumtaxat only up to, "only up to 150"
***duo, duae, duo* two [7]**
duōbus two
***duodecim* twelve [12]**
duodēvīgintī eighteen
dūrus, -a, -um hard, harsh, difficult
dux, ducis m. leader

E

***ē, ex* (+ abl.) out of, from [5]**
Eborācum, -ī n. Eboracum, city in Roman province
  of Britannia (modern York, England)
ēbrius, -a, -um drunk
eburneus, -a, -um ivory
***ecce* Behold! Look! [11]**
edax devouring
Edepol! By Pollux!
ēditor, ēditōris m. organizer; *Ēditor ludōrum* public
  official in charge of the games

edō, ēsse / edere, ēdī, ēsum eat [7]

efficiō, efficere, effēcī, effectum execute, accomplish, do

effrēnātus, -a, -um unbridled

effugiō, effugere, effūgī escape, flee

effugium, -iī n. flight, escape

effundō, effundere, effūdī, effūsum pour out

effūsē a lot

effūsus, -a, -um poured forth; widespread

ēgelidus, -a, -um warm

egēnus, -a, -um in need of, in want of, destitute

ego I [7]

ēgredior, ēgredī, ēgressus sum march out, go out

ehem ha! aha! (in pleasant surprise)

ēheu alas! oh no! [16]

eho here you! hey! (often followed by *tū* or a vocative)

ei / hei ah! oh! (in fear or dismay)

ēia / hēia ah! ah ha! good! yes, indeed!; (+ *age*) quick! come on then!

ēiciō, ēicere, ēiēcī, ēiectum throw out

ēlāborō (1) take pains, exert oneself

elephans, elephantis m. elephant

ēlevō (1) raise up, lift up

ēligō, ēligere, ēlēgī, ēlectum pick out, choose

Elis, -idis f. Elis, a region in the Greek Peloponessus

ēlixus, -a, -um boiled

ēloquor ēloquī, ēlocūtus sum speak out, declare

ēlūdō, ēlūdere, ēlūsī, ēlūsum mock, escape

Emerita Augusta, Emeritae Augustae, f. city in Roman Spain (modern Merida)

emō, emere, ēmī, emptum buy [18]

ēn / ēm come on! (in commands); really? (in questions)

enim for [20]

ensis, ensis m. sword

eō, īre, īvī / iī, itum go [7]

Epaphrodītus, -ī m. Epaphroditus, a Greek name for a man

Ephesus, -ī f. Ephesus, city in the Roman province of Asia (modern Turkey)

epistula, -ae f. letter

epulae, -ārum f. pl. food, dishes of food; banquet, feast

epulor, epulārī, epulātus sum feast, dine

eques, equitis m. horseman, knight; pl. cavalry; order of knights

equus, -ī m. horse

ergō therefore [8]

ērigō, ērigere, ērexī, ērectum erect, raise

errō (1) wander

error, errōris m. mistake

ērubescō, ērubescere, ērubuī redden, blush

ērudītus, -a,-um skilled

ērumpō, ērumpere, ērūpī, ērumptum erupt

ēruptiō, -ōnis f. eruption

Erymanthius, -a, -um Erymanthian

Erymanthos, -theī n. Erymanthus, a mountain in Greece

Esquiliae, -ārum f. pl. the Esquiline hill, one of the seven hills of Rome

Esquilīnus, -a, -um Esquiline, one of the seven hills of Rome

est is [1]

ēsuriō, ēsurīre, ēsurītum be hungry

et and [2]; also, even; *et . . . et* both . . . and [4]

etiam still; also, even, too, and also, even now [17]

etsī although, even if

eu fine! great! (sometimes ironic)

euax hurray!

eugae / euge /eugepae terrific! bravo!

Eumolpus, -ī m. Eumolpus, a character in the *Satyricon*

Eurystheus, -eī m. Eurystheus, king of Mycenae in Greece

ēveniō, ēvenīre, ēvēnī, ēventum come about; happen

ēvītō (1) shun, avoid

ēvoluō, ēvoluere, ēvoluī, ēvolūtum unroll, unfold

exāminō (1) examine

excipiō, excipere, excēpī, exceptum receive, welcome

excitō (1) awaken, excite, raise

exclāmō (1) cry out, explain

excubiae, -ārum f. pl. guard, watch

exemplar, exemplāris n. copy, model

exemplum, -ī n. sample

exeō, exīre, exīvī / exiī, exitum go out

exerceō, exercēre, exercuī, exercitum practice

exercitus, -ūs m. army

exhibeō, exhibēre, exhibuī, exhibitum show, exhibit

exīlis, exīle thin, small

eximō, eximere, exēmī, exemptum take out, remove

existō, see *ex(s)istō*

exitiābilis, -e deadly, desctructive

exorn ō (1) adorn

exōticus, -a, -um strange, exotic, foreign

expallescō, expallescere, expalluī turn very pale

expellō, expellere, expulī, expulsum throw out

expergiscor, expergiscī, experrectus sum awake, wake up

expiō (1) atone for

explicō (1) unfold, display; explain

explōrō (1) test, try

expōnō, expōnere, exposuī, expositum set out; exhibit

ex(s)istō, ex(s)istere, ex(s)titī arise, appear

exspectō (1) await, wait for [16]

exspīrō (1) breathe out

ex(s)tinguō, ex(s)tinguere ex(s)tinxī, ex(s)tinctum quench, extinguish

exsultō (1) exult in

extendō, extendere, extendī, extentum / extensum stretch out, extend

extimescō, extimescere, extimuī be alarmed, dread

extinguō see *ex(s)tinguō*

extrā (+ acc.) beyond, outside of

extrahō, extrahere, extraxī, extractum draw out, drag out

extrēmus, -a, -um final, last; *extrēmās poenās habēre* = die

exuō, exuere, exuī, exūtum strip, undress
exūrō, exūrere, exussī, exustum burn up

F

faber argentārius silversmith
faber, fabrī m. craftsman, artisan, smith, carpenter, workman
Fabius, -iī m. Fabius, a Roman *praenōmen*
fabrica, -ae f. workshop; art, craft
fabricō (1) forge, make, shape, build, construct
fābula, -ae f. story, play [9]
faciēs, faciēī f. face, appearance, beauty
facilis, -e easy [20]
faciliter easily
faciō, facere, fēcī, factum make, do [6]
factiō, -ōnis f. team
factum, -ī n. deed [20]
faenum, -ī n. hay
Falernum, -ī n. Falernian wine
Falernus, -a, -um Falernian, referring to a region in Italy producing a particularly good kind of wine
fāma, -ae f. fame, rumor, report [20]
famēs, famis f. hunger
familia, -ae f. family [4]
fāmōsus, -a, -um famous, well known
famulus, -ī m. servant, attendant
farreus, -a, -um of grain, grain
fās est it is right
fatīgō (1) weary, tire
fātum, -ī n. fate, destiny
Faustus, -ī m. Faustus, a male name
faveō, favēre, fāvī, fautum (+ dat.) favor, support, cheer for
favor, -ōris m. favor, goodwill
fax, facis f. torch
febris, febris f. fever
fēlēs, fēlis f. cat
fēlix, fēlīcis lucky, fortunate [18]
fēmina, -ae f. woman [2]
fenestra, -ae f. window
ferē nearly, almost, about; in general
feriō, ferīre strike, hit; kill, slay
ferō, ferre, tulī, lātum bear, carry, lead; *sē ferre* go ("betake oneself")
ferox, ferōcis fierce, savage
ferrum, -ī n. iron, sword
fervidus, -a, -um boiling, hot; fervent
Fescinnīnus, -a, um Fescinnine, pertaining to the Fescinnine verses sung at weddings
fessus, -a, -um tired [8]
festīnō (1) hasten [9]
festus, -a, -um festal, solemn, religious
Festus, -ī m. Festus, a man's name

fētidus, -a, -um filthy, foul smelling
fīcus, -ī f. fig; fig tree
fidēlis, -e faithful, trustworthy
fidēs, fideī f. faith, trust; credibility
fidius see *medius*
fīgō, fīgere, fīxī, fīxum fasten in place
figūra, -ae f. shape, figure [10]
fīlia, -ae f. daughter [8]
fīliola, -ae f. dear daughter
fīliolus, -ī m. little son (affectionate)
fīlius, -ī m. son [4]
fingō, fingere, finxī, fictum shape, form, fashion
fīniō, fīnīre, fīnīvī / fīniī, fīnītum finish, end [8]
fīnis, fīnis m. end; pl. country, territory [14]
fīō, fierī, factus sum be made, be done; happen, become
firmāmentum, -ī n. support
firmus, -a, -um firm, strong
flagrans, flagrantis glowing, blazing, ardent
flamma, -ae f. flame
flammeum, -eī n. bridal veil
Flāvia, -ae f. Flavia, a female name
flectō, flectere, flexī, flexum turn, bend
fleō, flēre, flēvī, flētum weep, cry
flō (1) blow
floccus, -ī m. tuft of wool; *nōn floccī facere* to consider of no importance
flōrus, -a, -um bright, rich
Flōrus, -ī m. Florus, a male name
flōs, flōris m. flower, bloom
fluitō (1) flow, float
flūmen, -inis n. river
focus, -ī m. fireplace, hearth
fodicō (1) nudge, prod; stab
folia, -ae f. leaf
fons, fontis m. spring, fountain
forās outdoors, out
foris, foris (commonly *forēs, -ium* pl.) f. door, gate; *forīs* out of doors, outside; abroad
forma, -ae f. shape, form; beauty; ground plan
formīdō (1) dread
formōsus, -a, -um beautiful, handsome
forsitan perhaps
fortasse perhaps [11]
fortis, forte strong, brave, loud [15]
fortiter strongly, bravely, loudly
fortūna, -ae f. fortune, chance, luck; wealth, prosperity
fortūnātus, -a, -um lucky, fortunate
forum, -ī n. forum, city center [5]
fossa, -ae f. ditch
frangō, frangere, frēgī, fractum break; crush; conquer
frāter, frātris m. brother [13]
frāterculus, -ī m. little brother
fremō, fremere, fremuī, fremitum growl, groan

frequens, -entis frequent, usual
fricō, fricāre, fricuī, frictum rub, rub down
frīgidārium, -iī n. cold water bath
frīgidus, -a, -um cold
frons, frontis f. forehead, brow
fructus, -a, -um enjoyed
Fructus, -ī m. Fructus, a male first name
fruor, fruī, fructus / fruitus sum (+ abl.) enjoy, profit by
frustrā in vain
frustum, -ī n. morsel, scrap
frutex, fruticis m. bush, shrub
fuga, -ae f. flight
fugiō, fugere, fūgī, fugitum flee, run away [12]
fugitīvus, -ī m. runaway, fugitive
fulgeō, fulgēre, fulsī shine, gleam
fulgur, -uris n. lightning
fullō, -ōnis m. fuller, launderer
fullōnica, -ae f. laundry
fūmōsus, -a, -um smokey
fūmus, -ī m. smoke
fundus, -ī m. farm
fūnebris, -e funereal
fungor, fungī, functus sum (+ abl.) perform, discharge
fūnis, fūnis m. cord, rope
fūnus, fūneris, n. burial, funeral
furcifer, furciferī m. scoundel
furnus, -ī m. oven, bakehouse
fūror, -ōris m. fury, rage
furtīvē secretly
furtīvus, -a, -um secret
fūrunculus, -ī m. petty thief
fuscus, -a, -um dark
Fuscus, -ī m. Fuscus, a male name
fustis, fustis m. staff, club, stick
futūrum, -ī n. future [14]

G

Gāia, -ae f. Gaia, ceremonial name of a Roman bride
Gāius, -iī m. Gaius, ceremonial name of a Roman bridegroom
Gallia, -ae f. Gaul, the Roman province now known as France
gallīna, -ae f. hen
garriō, garrīre, garrīvī / garriī, garrītum chatter
garrulus,-a, -um chattering, blabbing
garum, -ī n. fish sauce
gaudeō, gaudēre, gavīsus sum rejoice, be glad
gaudium, -iī n. joy
gelidus, -a, -um icy, cold
geminus, -a, -um twin
gemma, -ae f. gem
gemō, gemere, gemuī, gemitum moan, groan

gener, generī m. son-in-law
geniālis, -e marriage; merry, festive
gens, gentis f. famly, tribe
genū, -ūs n. knee
genus, generis n. race, type
Germānī, -ōrum pl. Germans, the German people
Germānia, -ae f. Germany
Germānicus, -a, -um German
Germānicus, -ī m. Germanicus, the son-in-law of the emperor Tiberius
gerō, gerere, gessī, gestum bear, carry; *bellum gerere* wage war; *sē gerere* act, conduct oneself
gerūsia, -ae f. a council building for elders, senate house
gestiō, gestīre, gestīvī / gestiī, gestītum exult
gladiātor, -ōris m. gladiator [17]
gladius, -iī m. sword [17]
glīs, glīris m. dormouse
glōria, -ae f. glory
gracilis, -e thin, slender, scanty
gradus, -ūs m. step, pace, tier (of a theater)
Graecia, -ae f. Greece
Graecus, -a, -um Greek
grāmen, grāminis n. grass
grandis, -e great, old
grātiā (+ gen.) for the sake of, for the purpose of
grātia, -ae f. grace, favor; (pl.) thanks; *grātiās* agere give thanks [19]
grātiōsus, -a, -um agreeable
grātulātiō, -ōnis f. congratulations
grātus, -a, -um pleasing, thankful
gravidus, -a, -um pregnant
gravis, -e heavy, serious, deep [15]
graviter severely
gremium, iī n. lap
grex, gregis m. flock, herd (of animals); company, group (of people), troop (of actors)
grūs, gruis, m./f. crane (a bird)
gubernō (1) steer (a ship); govern

H

habeō, habēre, habuī, habitum have, hold [5]
habitō (1) live in, inhabit [12]
habitus, -ūs m. dress, clothing
haereō, haerēre, haesī, haesum cling to, stick
hahae hah!
Halicarnassus, -ī f. Halicarnassus, city in Roman province of Asia (modern Turkey)
hama, -ae f. fire bucket
harēna, -ae f. sand; arena
hasta, -ae f. spear
haud not, by no means [16]

haudquāquam by no means
hauriō, haurīre, hausī, haustum drink, swallow, drain
Hephaestus, -ī m. Hephaestus, slave named after
    the blacksmith god
herba, -ae f. herb
Herculāneum, -eī n. Herculaneum, city destroyed
    by eruption of Vesuvius in 79 A.D.
Hercule by Hercules!
Herculēs, Herculis m. Hercules, the Greek hero Heracles
hērēs, hērēdis m./f. heir, heiress
heri yesterday [19]
Hermēs, -ae m. Hermes, a slave named after the Greek
    messenger god
Hermēs, -ēs m. Hermes, the Greek messenger god
hērōs, hērōos m. hero
heu (often + acc.) oh! (in pain or dismay)
heus say there! hey! you there! (to draw attention)
hic, haec, hoc this [19]
hīc here, in this place [10]
Hierosolyma, -ōrum n. pl. Jerusalem, city in Roman
    province of Judaea (modern Israel / Palestine)
hilaris, -e cheerful
hinc from here
hiō (1) yawn
hippopotamus, -ī m. hippopotamus
Hispānia, -ae f. Spain
Hispānus, -a, -um Spanish
historia, -ae f. history
hodiē today [4]
hodiernus, -a, -um today's, modern
holus, holeris n. vegetables
homō, hominis m./f. human being, person, man [13]
honestus, -a, -um worthy, decent, of high rank
honor, -ōris m. honor, office, dignity
honōrō (1) esteem, honor
hōra, -ae f. hour, time [8]
Horātius, -iī m. Horace, a Roman poet
hōrologium, -iī n. clock
horrendus, -a, -um horrible, terrible
horribilis, -e rough, terrible, horrible
hortor, hortārī, hortātus sum urge
hortus, -ī m. garden
hospes, hospitis m. guest, host, stranger
hostis, hostis m./f. stranger, foreigner, enemy;
(pl.) the enemy [14]
hūc here, to this place
huī (exclamation of astonishment or admiration) wow!
humilis, humile low; humble
humus, -ī f. earth, soil
hyaena, -ae f. hyena
Hydra, -ae f. a many-headed serpent-like monster
    with poisonous blood
Hymēn, only found in nom. m. Hymen, the god of

marriage; also, the wedding song or the marriage itself
Hymenaeus, -ī m. Hymenaeus = Hymen
Hymettus, -ī m. Hymettus, a mountain near Athens,
    famous for its honey
hypocauston, -ī n. hypocaust; heating system for a bath

I

iaceō, iacēre, iacuī lie, lie still, lie dead
iaciō, iacere, iēcī, iactum throw, hurl
iactō (1) hurl, throw; boast
iam dūdum for a long time now
iam now, already [8]; *nōn iam* not any longer
iānitor, -ōris m. doorman, porter
iānua, -ae f. door
ibi there
īdem, eadem, idem the same
identidem again and again
idōneus, -a, -um (+ dat.) fit, suitable
iēiūnus, -a, -um hungry [13]
ientāculum, -ī n. breakfast
igitur therefore [20]
ignāvus, -a, -um idle, cowardly
ignis, ignis m. fire [14]
ignōminia, -ae f. dishonor
ignōrō (1) be ignorant of
ignōscō, ignōscere, ignōvī, ignōtum (+ dat.) forgive,
    grant pardon to
ignōtus, -a, -um unknown
Iliacus, -a, -um Trojan
ille, illa, illud he, she, it; they; that, those [17]
illīc there, over there
illīdō, illīdere, illīsī, illīsum strike against
illūc to there
illūminō (1) brighten
Illyricum, -ī n. Illyricum, a Roman province in the Balkans
imāgō, -inis f. image, likeness; statue
imbuō, imbuere, imbuī, imbūtum wet, soak
imitātiō, -ōnis f. imitation, copy
immānis, immāne huge, vast
immittō, immittere, immīsī, immissum send to
immō rather, more precisely
immōbilis, -e immovable, unmoving
immolō (1) offer as a sacrifice
immortālis, -e immortal
impatiens, impatientis impatient (of)
impediō, impedīre, impedīvī / impediī, impedītum hamper,
    hinder, impede
imperātor, -ōris m. commander, general, ruler, emperor
imperium, -iī n. command, order, rule, empire, supreme
    command
imperō (1) (+ dat.) command, order, rule
impetrō (1) obtain by formal request or petition

impetus, -ūs m. attack, assault

impleō, implēre, implēvī, implētum fill

implōrō (1) plead, beg

impōnō, impōnere, imposuī, impositum
 (+ dat.) put on, put upon, assign, impose upon

improbus, -a, -um disloyal, shameless, morally unsound

īmus, -a, -um inmost, deepest, bottommost

in **(+ abl.) in, on, at [2]; (+ acc.) into, onto, against [5]**

inānis, -e poor, useless, vain

inaurēs, inaurium m. pl. earrings

incautus, -a, -um uncautious, not careful

incendium, -iī n. fire, conflagration

incendō, incendere, incendī, incensum set fire to, inflame, burn

incertus, -a, -um uncertain

incidō, incidere, incidī, incāsum fall (into); meet (with);
 occur, arise

incipiō, incipere, incēpī, inceptum **begin [18]**

incitō (1) incite; spur on

inclīnō (1) bend, tilt

includō, inclūdere, inclūsī, inclūsum shut in, enclose

incognitus, -a, -um not known

incola, -ae m./f. inhabitant

incolō, incolere, incoluī inhabit

incommodus, -a, -um disagreeable

incurrō, incurrere, incurrī / incucurrī run into

indecōrē sē gerere misbehave

indecoris, -e shameful

indicō, indīcere, indīxi, indictum declare publically

indīviduus, -a, -um indivisible

induō, induere, induī, indūtum put on

industria, -ae f. industry

industrius, -a, -um industrious, diligent

inertia, -ae f. idleness

infāmia, -ae f. dishonor

infāmis, infāme disreputable

infans, infantis **m./f. infant [14]**

infēlix, -īcis unhappy, unfortunate

inferior, inferius lower

infernus, -a, -um infernal, pertaining to the underworld

inferō, inferre, intulī, illātum bring, serve

inferus, -a, -um "below"; *in inferōs locōs* into "the places
 below," i.e., hell

infortūnātus, -a, -um unlucky, unfortunate

infrā below, underneath, under

ingenium, -iī n. talent

ingens, ingentis huge, great

ingenuus, -a, -um freeborn

ingredior, ingredī, ingressus sum enter, go in

iniciō, inicere, iniēcī, iniectum throw in

inīquus, -a, -um unequal

initium, -iī n. beginning

inquīrō, inquīrere, inquīsīvī / inquīsī, inquīsītum inquire

inquit, inquiunt **say [2]**

insānia, -ae f. madness, insanity

inscriptiō, -ōnis f. inscription, writing on stone

insequor, insequī, insecutus sum pursue

insignis, insigne conspicuous, famous, notable

insiliō, insilīre, insiluī leap into

inspectō **(1)** **look closely at [19]**

inspiciō, inspicere, inspexī, inspectum **look (closely) at;**
 inspect [10]

instar indecl. (+ gen.) equal

instrūmentum, -ī n. tool, instrument

insula, -ae **f. island, apartment block [9]**

insum, inesse, infuī be in

intactus, -a, -um intact

intellegens, intellegentis **smart, intelligent [15]**

intellegō, intellegere, intellēxī, intellectum **understand [13]**

intendō, intendere, intendī, intentum / intēnsum stretch, direct

intentō (1) point (at), threaten

intentus, -a, -um intent, eager

inter **(+ acc.) between, among [5]**

intercēdō, intercēdere, intercessī, intercessum come
 between; interrupt

interdiū by day

intereā meanwhile

interficiō, interficere, interfēcī, interfectum **kill [14]**

interiaceō, interiacēre, interiacuī lie between

interim meanwhile

interpellō (1) interrupt

interrogō (1) ask, question; examine

intrā (+ acc.) within

intrepidus, -a, -um fearless

intrō **(1)** **enter [8]**

introductiō, -ōnis f. introduction

intueor, intuērī, intuitus sum look at, gaze at, consider

inuictus, -a, -um unconquered

inūtilis, -e useless, profitless

inveniō, invenīre, invēnī, inventum **find, discover [14]**

invictus, -a, -um unconquered

invideō, invidēre, invīdī, invīsum (+ dat.) envy, hate,
 grudge; refuse

invidiōsus, -a, -um arousing hatred or envy

invidus, -a, -um envious

invīsus, -a, -um hated

invītō (1) invite

iō a shout of religious emotion

iocor, iocārī, iocātus sum (1) joke

iocōsus, -a, -um funny

iocus, - ī m. joke

Iphiclēs, -eī m. Iphicles, Heracles' brother

Iphigenīa, -ae f. Iphigenia, daughter of Agamemnon

ipse, ipsa, ipsum **he, she, it; they; himself, herself,**
 itself, themselves (emphatic) [17]

īra, -ae, f. anger

īrācundē angrily

īrāscor, īrāscī, īrātus sum be angry at

īrātus, -a, -um **angry [6]**

irreparābilis, -e irrecoverable, irreparable

irrīdeō, irrīdēre, irrīsī, irrīsum laugh at, mock

irrīsor, -ōris m. mocker, "one who mocks"

irrītō (1) upset, annoy, aggravate

irrumpō, irrumpere, irrūpī, irruptum burst, break open

is, ea, id **he, she, it; they [17]**

Īsēon, -ī n. temple of the goddess Isis

Īste, ista, istud **that one of yours (derogatory) [17]**

Īta so, thus; yes

Ītalia, -ae f. Italy

Ītalus, -a, -um Italian

itaque **therefore [20]**

item similarly, likewise

iter, itineris n. road, journey; *iter facere* to make a journey, to journey

iterō (1) repeat, do again

iterum **again [4]**

iubeō, iubēre, iussī, iussum order

iūcundus, -a, -um pleasant, agreeable

Iūdaea, -ae f. Judaea, the Roman province in what is now approximately Israel

Iullus, -ī m. Jullus, Servilia's intended husband

iunctiō, -ōnis f. joining

iungō, iungere, iunxī, iunctum join; *sē iungere* (+ dat.) to join oneself (with), to ally oneself (with)

Iūnō, Iūnōnis f. Juno, queen of the gods

Iuppiter, Iovis m. Jupiter, king of the gods

iūrō (1) swear

iūs, iūris n. law

iussus, -ūs m. order, command (only used in abl.) "by order of"

iustus, -a, -um legal

iuvenis, iuvenis **m./f. youth [15]**

iuventūs, -tūtis f. young men collectively, youth

iuvō, iuvāre, iūvi, iūtum help

iuxtā (+ acc.) near to

K

Kalendae, -ārum f. pl. kalends, the first day of the month

L

L. = *Lūcius*

lābor, lābī, lāpsus sum fall down

labor, labōris **m. work, labor [16]**

labōriōsus, -a, -um working, laborious, tedious

labōrō **(1) work [9]**

labrum, -ī n. basin; lip

Labyrinthus, -ī m. maze, labyrinth, especially the one in Crete in which the Minotaur was imprisoned

Lachesis, -is f. Lachesis, one of the three goddesses of Fate

Lacō, -ōnis m. Laconian, Spartan

lacrima, -ae f. tear

lacrimō **(1) cry, shed tears [17]**

lactō (1) nurse

lacus, -ūs m. lake

laedō, laedere, laesī, laesum hurt, damage

laetitia, -ae f. happiness

laetor, laetarī, laetātus sum be happy, rejoice

laetus, -a, -um **happy [3]**

lalla excl. calming sound

lāneus, -a, -um woolen

lanista, -ae m. trainer, manager of a gladiatorial troop

lanius, -iī m. butcher, butcher shop

lanx, lancis f. dish, place

lapsō (1) slip

laqueus, -ī m. snare, noose

Lar, Laris m. Lar, a household god

lateō, latēre, latuī hide

latericius, -a, -um brick, made of brick

lātifundium, -iī n. large country estate

lātrīna, -ae f. public toilet

latrō, latrōnis m. thief, robber

lātus, -a, -um wide, broad

latus, lateris n. side, ribs; *latus fodicō* poke in the ribs

laurea, -ae f. laurel wreath

laus, laudis f. praise

lavō, lavāre, lāvī, lautum / lavātum / lōtum wash

lectīca, -ae f. litter, a sedan chair

lectīcārius, -iī m. litter bearer

lectiō, -ōnis f. reading

lectus, -ī **m. (dining) couch, bed [18]**

lēgātus, -ī m. lieutenant; legate

legiō, legiōnis f. legion, army

legitmus, -a, -um real, lawful, right

legō, legere, lēgī, lectum **gather, choose; read [15]**

lēniō, lēnīre, lēnīvī / lēniī, lēnītum ease, put at ease; allay, mitigate

lēnis, lēne smooth, soft, mild, gentle

lēniter smoothly, softly, midly, gently

lentē slowly, calmly

lentus, -a, -um slow, calm; tough

leō, leōnis m. lion

lētum, -ī n. death

levis, leve light, gentle

levō (1) lift, lighten

libellum, -ī n. little book

libens, libentis cheerful

libenter freely, willingly

līber, lībera, līberum **free [14]**

liber, librī **m. book [14]**

līberī, -ōrum m. pl. children

līberō (1) (+ abl.) free, free from

lībertās, -ātis f. freedom, liberty

lībertīnus, -ī m. freedman (used as defining social status)

lībertus, -ī m. freedman (in relation to his master)

libet, libēre, libuit, libitum est (+ dat.) imp. it is pleasing (to someone)

libitīnārius, -iī m. undertaker

librārius, -iī m. bookseller, book copier

lībum, -ī n. special holiday cake or pancake

licet, licēre, licuit or, *licitum est* imp. it is permitted

Licinia, -ae f. Licinia, a female name

Licinius, -iī m. Licinius, a male name

ligneus,-a, -um wooden

lignum, -ī m. wood, firewood

līmen, līminis n. threshold

līmus, -ī m. mud, slime

lingua, -ae f. tongue, speech

liquāmen, liquāminis n. liquid, especially fish sauce

liquor, -ōris m. fluid, liquid

līs, lītis f. lawsuit

littera, -ae f. letter of the alphabet

lītus, lītoris n. shore

Livius, -iī m. Livy, the historian

locō (1) put in place, contract for, rent

locus, -ī m. **place [19]**; also *locum, -ī* n.

longē far off, far, a long distance, for a long time [11]

longinquus, -a, -um far away, far off

longus, -a, -um long [19]

loquēla, -ae f. speech, utterance

loquor, loquī, locūtus sum speak, talk, say

lōtium, -ī n. urine

lubet = libet (+ dat.) imp. it is pleasing (to someone)

lūceō, lūcēre, luxī shine

lucerna, -ae f. (oil) lamp

lūcifer,-a, -um light-bearing (an epithet or nickname for the goddess Diana); *Lūcifera Diana* "the light-bearer"

Lūcius, -iī m. Lucius, son of Servilius and Caecilia

lucrum, -ī n. profit

luctātor, luctātōris m. wrestler

lūdia, -ae f. a gladiator's girl

lūdō, lūdere, lūsī, lūsum play, tease

lūdus -ī m. **school, game [4]**

lūgeō, lūgēre, luxī, luctum mourn, lament

lūgubris, -e mourning

lūmen, lūminis n. light, torch

lupa, -ae f. wolf

lūteus, -a, -um yellow, saffron

lutum, -ī n. mud, dirt

lux, lūcis f. light

M

M. = *Marcus*

macellum, -ī n. (grocery) market, store

maculō (1) spot, stain, pollute

madefaciō, madefacere, madefēcī, madefactum make moist, soak

madidus, -a, -um moist, wet

Maecēnās, Maecēnātis m. G. Clinius Maecenas (70–8 B.C.), Augustus' close friend and advisor

maestitia, -ae f. sadness, grief

maestus, -a, -um sad, gloomy [18]

magis more, rather [16]

magister, -trī m. **teacher (male), schoolmaster [2]**

magistra, -ae f. **teacher (female), schoolmistress [2]**

magistrātus, -ūs m. office, magistracy; magistrate

magnificus, -a, -um noble, elegant, magnificent

magnitūdō, -inis f. greatness

magnopere much, greatly, especially

magnus, -a, -um large, great, loud [8]

magus, -ī m. magician

māiestās, -ātis f. majesty, authority

māior, māius older; m. pl. ancestors, elders [15]

male badly

malefactor, -ōris m. evil-doer, criminal

maleficus, -a, -um wicked, criminal, harmful

malleum, -ī n. hammer, mallet

mālō, mālle, māluī prefer [7]

mālus Pūnica, -i f. pomegranate (lit., "Punic apple")

malus, -a, -um bad [6]

mamma, -ae f. breast

māne early in the morning [4]

maneō, manēre, mansī, mansum stay, remain, endure, await

manifestus, -a, -um clear, evident

mansuētus, -a, -um gentle

manubiae, -ārum f. pl. general's share of an army's military plunder

manus, -ūs f. hand

mappa, -ae f. table napkin; starting flag

Marcus, -ī m. Marcus, son of Servilius and Cornelia, brother of Lucius

mare, maris n. **sea [14]**

marītus, -ī m. **husband [16]**

marmor, -oris n. marble

marmoreus, -a, -um marble, made of marble

Mars, Martis m. Mars, god of war

Martius, -a, -um of Mars

mās, maris male

mastīgia, -ae m. rascal, someone worthy of a whipping

māter, mātris f. **mother [13]**

matercula, -ae f. dear mother

māteria, -ae f. material

mātertera, -ae f. aunt, mother's sister

matrimōnium, -iī n. marriage, matrimony

mātrōna, -ae f. married woman

mātūrus, -a, -um timely, early

mātūtīnus, -a, -um of or belonging to the early morning

mausōlēum, -ēī n. mausoleum, tomb
maximē, with *cum* especially
maximus, -a, -um greatest [20]
mē me [3]
Mēdēa, -ae f. Medea, the midwife
medicus, -ī m. doctor, physician
medius fidius / mediusfidius by the gods of truth!
    most certainly!
medius, -a, -um midway, in the middle (of), the middle of
medulla, -ae f. marrow
Megara, -ae f. Megara, wife of Hercules
mehercle by Hercules! (as an oath to express strong feeling)
meī of me [7]
mel, mellis n. honey
melior, melius better [19]
membrum, -ī n. limb (arm or leg), body part; member
meminī, meminisse remember; *mementō, -tōte* (imper.)
    remember!
memor, memoris mindful (of), remembering
memoria, -ae f. memory
mendax, -dācis untruthful; *Mendax*, a beggar living
    in Valeria's *insula*
mendīcus, -a, -um beggar
mens, mentis f. mind; reason; mental disposition
mensa, -ae f. table [16]
mensis, mensis m. month [14]
mentior, mentīrī, mentītus sum lie, deceive
mercātor, -ōris trader, merchant
mercātōrius, -a, -um mercantile, commercial
Mercurius, -iī m. Mercury, the messenger god
mereō, merēre, meruī, meritum deserve
merīdiē at noon
merīdiēs, -ēī (f) midday, noon
merum, -ī n. pure (unmixed) wine
merx, mercis f. a commodity; (pl.) goods, merchandise
Mesopotamia, -ae f. Mesopotamia, the
    land between the Tigris and Euphrates rivers
mēta, -ae f. turning post
metuō, metuere, metuī, metūtum fear, be afraid of
metus, -ūs m. fear
meus, -a, -um my [5]
mī = mihi to me; my (vocative of *meus*)
mihi to me, my, [1]
mīles, -itis m. soldier
mille indecl. thousand; *milia* n. pl. thousands
Minerva, -ae f. Minerva, Roman goddess of wisdom
    and crafts
minimus, -a, -um smallest [20]
minor, minus smaller [19]
Mīnōtaurus, -ī m. Minotaur, half-human, half-bull
    imprisoned in the Labyrinth
mīrābilis, -e amazing, wondrous
mīrāculum, -ī n. miracle

mirmillo, -ōnis m. mirmillo, heavily armed gladiator
mīror, mīrārī, mīrātus sum wonder at, admire
mīrus, -a, -um astonishing, wonderful
misceō, miscēre, miscuī, mixtum unite, blend, mix, stir up
miser, misera, miserum wretched
miserābilis, -e miserable
miserābiliter miserably
misereor, miserērī, miseritus sum pity; *mē miseret* it
    distresses me
miseria, -ae f. misery
misericordia, -ae f. pity
missiō, -ōnis f. discharge (military); permission
    (for gladiators) to cease fighting; *ad missiōnem* to a
    draw; *missiō honesta* an honorable discharge
mītis, mīte soft
mittō, mittere, mīsī, missum send [20]
modicum moderately
modicus, -a, -um a moderate amount of
modo only, just now, but
modus, -ī m. way, manner
molae, -ārum f. pl. mill
molestus, -a, -um troublesome, tiresome
mollis, -e soft
molliter softly
mōmentum, -ī n. importance, (important) moment; effort
moneō, monēre, monuī, monitum warn, advise
monīle, -is n. necklace, collar
mons, montis m. mountain
monstrō (1) show, display, point out
monstrum, -ī n. monster
monumentum, -ī n. memorial, monument; tomb
morbus, -ī m. illness, sickness
mordax, mordācis biting
mordeō, mordēre, momordī, morsum bite
morior, morī, mortuus sum die
mors, -tis f. death
morsum, -ī. morsel
morsus, -ūs m. bite, nibble
mortuus, -a, -um dead
mōs, mōris m. custom; (pl.) character [15]
mōtus, -ūs m. movement, motion
moveō, movēre, mōvī, mōtum, move, affect
mox soon [9]
mūla, -ae f. mule
mulceō, mulcēre, mulsī, mulsum soothe, stroke, pet
mulier, mulieris f. woman, wife
mulsum, -ī n. warm drink of honey and wine
multitūdō, -inis f. great number, multitude
multō much, by far, long
multum a lot, much [16]
multus, -a, -um much; (pl.) many [2]
mūlus, -ī m. mule
mundō (1) clean

mundus, -a, -um clean, refined, elegant

mundus, -ī m. world

mūnicipium, -iī n. town under Roman rule but governed by its own local laws

mūnus, -eris n. function, duty; gift; pl. games, public shows, spectacles [17]

murmillo = mirmillo a heavily armed gladiator

murmur, -uris n. whispering, murmur, growling

murmurō (1) mutter

mūrus, -ī m. wall

mūs, mūris m. mouse

musca, -ae f. fly

musculus, -ī m. muscle

musicus, -ī m. musician

mussitō (1) mutter

mustāceus, -ī m. a grape-cake, a wedding cake baked with must on bay leaves

mūtō (1) alter, change

mūtus, -a, -um speechless, mute

mūtuus, -a, -um shared, mutual

N

Naevia, -ae f. Naevia, Servilia's friend.

Naevius, -iī m. Naevius, Naevius Cordus, object of Servilia's love

nam for

nānus, -ī m. dwarf

nārēs, -rium f. pl. nostrils

narrātiō, -ōnis f. narrative, story

narrō (1) say, tell [14]

nascor, nascī, nātus sum be born

Nāsō,-ōnis m. Naso, Ovid's *cognomen*

nāsus, -ī m. nose

natiō, -ōnis f. nationality

natō (1) swim

nātū by birth

nātūra, -ae f. nature, character, disposition

nātus, -a, -um born; *xx annōs nātus* = xx years old [12]

naufragium, -iī n. shipwreck, crash (of chariots), collision, wreck

nāvicula, -ae f. little boat

nāvigō (1) sail

nāvis, nāvis f. ship

nāvus, -a, -um active, industrious

-ne asks a yes/no question [4]

nē not, that not, in order that not, lest

Neāpolis, f. Naples, a city in southern Italy

nec and not; *nec . . . nec* neither . . . nor [15]

necessārius, -a, -um necessary, indispensable

necesse est (+ dat. + inf.) imp. it is necessary (to) [12]

necō (1) kill, slay

negō (1) deny

negōtium, -iī n. business, task [8]

Nemausus, -ī f. Nemausus, a city in Roman Gaul (modern Nīmes)

nēmō, -inis m. nobody, no one [13]

nepōs, -ōtis m. grandson, grandchild, descendant

neptis, -is f. granddaughter

Neptūnus, -ī m. Neptune, god of the sea

neque and not; *neque . . . neque* neither . . . nor

nesciō, nescīre, nescīvī / nesciī, nescītum not know

neuter, -tra, -trum neither [17]

nī unless

niger, -gra, -grum black

nihil nothing [3]

nihilōminus nevertheless

Nīlōticus, -a, -um of the Nile (river)

nimbus, -ī m. cloud

nimis too much

nimium too, too much, excessively [16]

nisi unless

niteō, nitēre, nituī shine, glitter

nitidus, -a, -um gleaming, shiny

nītor, nītī, nīsus / nixus sum lean on, rest on; endeavor, exert oneself, strain, struggle

nōbilis, -e noble [15]

noceō, nocēre, nocuī, nocitum (+ dat.) harm, hurt, injure, do injury to [12]

nocte for the night (abl.)

noctū at night

nocturnus, -a, -um nocturnal, of the night

nōdus, -ī m. knot

nōlō, nōlle, nōluī not want to, be unwilling [7]

nōmen, -inis n. name [1]

nōmenclātor, -ōris m. nomenclator, one who announces the names of people

nōminō (1) name

nomisma, -atis n. coin

nōn iam not any longer

nōn not [3]

nōn sōlum . . . sed etiam not only . . . but also [18]

nōndum not yet

nōnne asks a question expecting a yes answer [5]

nōnnullī, -ae, -a some, several [9]

nonus, -a, -um ninth

nōs, nostrum / nostrī, nōbīs, nōs, nōbīs we, us

noscō, -ere, nōvī, nōtum know, get to know [11]

noster, -tra, -trum our [9]

nota, -ae f. sign, word

notō (1) mark, note; write down

nōtus, -a, -um known, familiar

novitās, -ātis f. newness, freshness

novus, -a, -um new [8]

nox, noctis f. night [14]

nūbēs, -is f. cloud

nūbō, -bere, -psī, -ptum marry
nūdus, -a, -um naked, nude, unarmed
nūgae, -ārum f. pl. trifles, nonsense
nullus, -a, -um no, not any, none [17]
num asks a question expecting a no answer [5]
nūmen, nūminis n. divine presence; god
numerō (1) count, include
numerus, -ī m. number
nummus, -ī m. coin, money
numquam never [17]
nunc now [3]
nuntiō (1) announce, report
nuntius, -iī m. messenger; news
nūper recently, not long ago
nupta, -ae f. bride
nuptiāe, -ārum f. pl. wedding, marriage
nuptiālis, -e nuptial, marriage for a wedding
nūtriō, nūtrīre, nūtrīvī / nūtriī, nūtritum nurse, nourish, raise
nūtus, nūtūs m. nod
nux, nucis f. nut

O

ō oh! hey!
obeō, obīre, obīvī / obiī, obitum go away, die
obēsus, -a, -um fat
oblāta, -ōrum n. pl. "that which has been served"
oblīviscor, oblīviscī, oblītus sum (+ gen.) forget
obscēnus, -a, -um obscene
obscūrō (1) darken, obscure, conceal
obscūrus, -a, um dark, shady; gloomy; uncertain
obsecrō (1) implore, beg
obserō (1) block, obstruct
observō (1) pay attention (to)
obstetrix, obstetrīcis f. midwife
obtineō, obtinēre, obtinuī, obtentum hold, support, gain [9]
occāsiō, -ōnis f. opportunity, appropriate time
occīdō, occīdere, occīdī, occīsum kill, slay
occlūdō, occlūdere, occlūsī, occlūsum shut, close
occupō (1) occupy, busy
occurrō, occurrere, occurrī / occucurrī, occursum (+ dat.) encounter, run into
ocrea, -ae f. metal greave
Octāviānus, -ī m. Octavian
octāvus, -a, -um eighth
octō eight [12]
octōgintā eighty
oculus, -ī m. eye
ōdēum, -ī n. odeum, a building for musical perforamances
ōdī, ōdisse hate
odor, odōris m. scent, odor
Oedipus, -ī m. Oedipus, king of Thebes

oenogarum, -ī n. a sauce made of garum and wine
offerō, offerre, obtulī, oblātum (+ dat.) bring before, offer
officīna, -ae f. workshop
officium, -iī n. task, duty
oleō, olēre, oluī smell, stink
oleum, -ī n. oil
ōlim once, formerly [19]
olīva, -ae f. olive
olla, -ae f. pot, jar; urn
Ollus archaic form of *ille* That (man)
ōmen, ōminis n. religious sign, omen
omnīnō utterly, altogether, complete
omnis, -e each, every; (pl.) all [15]
onus, oneris n. load, burden
opera, -ae f. work, pain, labor
operam dare (+ dat.) pay attention to
operiō, operīre, operuī, opertum cover
opīmus, -a, -um rich, plentiful
opīniō, -ōnis f. opinion, belief; reputation
opīnor, opīnārī, opīnātus sum think, believe
oportet, oportēre, oportuit (+ inf.) one ought [12]
oppidum, -ī n. town
oppugnō (1) attack
optimus, -a, -um best [20]
optō (1) wish
opulentus, -a, -um rich, wealthy
opus, operis n. work, effort; structure, building; (pl.) goods; *opus est* (+ dat.) there is need for
ōrāculum, -ī n. oracle, divine pronouncement
ōrātiō, -ōnis f. speech [16]
ōrātiōnem habēre give/deliver a speech
ōrātor, -tōris m. speaker
orbis, -is m. circle, ring; orbis terrārum circle of the lands, the world [20]
ordinō (1) put in order
ordō, -inis m. row, line, order; rank; class of citizens
oriens, orientis m. east
orīgō, -inis f. origin, beginning, source
orior, orīrī, ortus sum rise, get up, be born
ornāmentum, -ī n. decoration, mark of distinction
ornātrix, ornātrīcis f. hairdresser
ornātus, -a, -um decorated
ornō (1) adorn, decorate
ōrō (1) pray
ōs, ōris n. mouth, face [13]
os, ossis n. bone
ōsculō (1) kiss
Oscus, -a, -um Oscan
ōsor, -ōris m. hater
ostendō, ostendere, ostendī, ostentum / ostensum show
ostentātiō, -ōnis f. display, flashiness
Ostia, -ae f. Ostia, the harbor of Rome; *Ostiam* "to Ostia"
Ostiensis, -e pertaining to Ostia (Rome's port), "Ostian"

ōtiōsus, -a, -um useless, unoccupied
ōtium, -iī n. leisure
Ovidius, -iī m. Ovid
ovis, -is m./f. sheep
ōvum, -ī n. egg [10]

P

p. = pūblicus, -a -um
paedagōgus, -ī m. a slave assigned to a young boy,
    a tutor [5]
paene almost [18]
paeniteō, paenitēre, paenitui to cause dissatisfaction: *paenitet*
    imp., it gives reason for regret; *mē paenitet* I am sorry
pāgus, -ī m. country district
Palātīnus, -a, -um Palatine, of the Palatine
Palātium, -iī n. the Palatine hill, one of the seven hills
    of Rome
palma, -ae f. palm frond (of victory)
Palmȳra, -ae f. Palmyra, city in Roman province of Syria
palpitō (1) beat, throb
palpō (1) stroke, caresss
pānis, -is m. bread
Pannonius, -a, - um Pannonian, member of a Balkan tribe
pannus, -ī m. cloth, garment, rag
papāver, -eris n. poppy; poppy-seed
papȳrus, -ī f. papyrus
pār, paris equal
pār, paris n. pair, couple
parātus, -a, -um prepared
parcō, parcere, pepercī / parcuī / parsī, parsūrus
    (+ dat.) spare, pardon, show mercy to [12]
Pardalisca, -ae f. Pardalisca, a female name
parens, parentis m./f. parent [16]
pariēs, parietis m. wall
pariō, parere, peperī, partum bring forth, give birth
    (to), bear, create
parma, -ae f. small shield carried by a Thrax gladiator
parō (1) prepare, make ready [12]
pars, partis f. part, piece [19]
parturiō, parturīre, parturīvī / parturiī be pregnant,
    be in labor, give birth
partus, -ūs m. childbirth, birth
parum little, too little, not enough
parvulus, -a, -um very small, tiny, little
parvus, -a, -um small [10]
passer, -eris m. sparrow
passus, -a, -um spread out, dried
pastināca, -ae f. parsnip
pater familiās, patris familiās m. paterfamilias,
    head of the family
pater, patris m. father [13]
patiens, patientis patient

patientia, -ae f. patience
patior, patī, passus sum suffer, allow
patria, -ae f. country, fatherland
patricius, -a, -um noble, patrician
patrōnus, -ī m. patron
paucus, -a, -um few, little [9]
paulisper for a little while
paulō a little, somewhat, by a little
paulō post a little later, somewhat later
paulum a little, somewhat
pauper, pauperis poor
paupertās, -ātis f. poverty
pavīmentum, -ī n. ground, floor, pavement
pax quiet! enough!
pax, pācis f. peace
pectus, -oris n. breast, chest
pecūlium, -iī n. savings, private property
pecūnia, -ae f. money [3]
pēior, pēius worse [19]
pellō, pellere, pepulī, pulsum banish
Penātēs, -ium m. pl. Penates, household gods
penna, -ae f. feather, wing
per (+ acc.) through [5]
peragō, peragere, perēgī, peractum finish, complete
perditus, -a, -um ruined, lost
perdō, perdere, perdidī, perditum lose, destroy
perdūcō, perdūcere, perduxī, perductum conduct, bring
    through, lead through
peregrīnor, peregrīnārī, peregrīnātus sum travel, travel abroad
pereō, perīre, perīvī / periī, peritum perish, vanish
perfectus, -a, -um perfect
perferō, perferre, pertulī, perlātum convey
pergō, pergere, perrexī, perrectum go ahead, advance, proceed
pergrātus, -a, -um very agreeable
perīculōsus, -a, -um dangerous
perīculum, -ī n. danger [20]
peristȳlium, -iī n. peristyle, courtyard, colonnaded garden
perītus, -a, -um experienced (in), skilled (in) + gen.
perlaetus, -a, -um very happy
perlegō, perlegere, perlēgī, perlectum scan, survey
permaximus, -a, -um very great, very loud
permultus, -a, -um very many
perpetuus, -a, -um continuous, uninterrupted;
    in perpetuum forever
persequor, persequī, persecūtus sum pursue, chase
Perseus, -eī m. Perseus, the Greek hero who decapitated
    Medusa
perstō, perstāre, perstitī, perstātum stand firm, stand around
persuādeō, persuādēre, persuāsī, persuāsum (+ dat.) persuade
perterritus, -a, -um very frightened, terrified
pertimescō, pertimescere, pertimuī become very scared
pertineō, pertinēre, pertinuī belong to
perturbātus, -a, -um disturbed, confused, very frightened

perturbō (1) disturb, trouble greatly

pervehō, pervehere, pervexī, pervectum carry, bear

perveniō, pervenīre, pervēnī, perventum arrive at, reach

pervigilō (1) be awake all night, "to be up all night"

pēs, pedis m. foot

pessimus, -a, -um worst [20]

petītiō, -ōnis f. candidacy, petition; lawsuit

petō, petere, petīvī / petiī, petītum seek; look for; attack; run for political office

philosophia, -ae f. philosophy

philosophus, -ī m. philosospher

Pholus, -ī m. Pholus the centaur

pictor, -ōris m. painter, professional artist paid to write (political) graffiti on public wall

pictūra, -ae f. picture

Pieridēs, -um f. pl. the inhabitants of Pieria, i.e., the Muses

pietās, -ātis f. reverence, respect

piger, pigra, pigrum low, sluggish, lazy

piget imp. it displeases

pigmentum, -ī n. color, pigment

pila, -ae f. ball

pilleus, -eī m. felt cap worn by a freed slave

pingō, pingere, pinxī, pictum paint

pīpiō (1) chirp

pīrāta, -ae m. pirate

piscātor, -ōris m. fisherman

piscīna, -ae f. fishpond

piscis, -is m. fish

pistor, -ōris m. miller

pistrīnum, -ī n. mill

pius, -a, -um pious, devout

placenta, -ae f. a flat cake (Roman cakes looked more like pancakes)

placeō, placēre, placuī, placitum (+ dat.) be pleasing to; esp. placet (+ inf.) imp. it is pleasing [12]

placidus, -a, -um calm, peaceful

plānē clearly

planta, -ae f. sole of the foot

plānus, -a, -um plane, flat; even; obvious;

Plātō, -ōnis m. Plato, a Greek philosopher

plaudō, plaudere, plausī, plausum clap, applaud

plaustrum, -ī n. cart, wagon

plausus, -ūs m. applause, recipient of applause

plēbēius, -a, -um plebian, pertaining to the common people

plēnus, -a, -um (+ abl.) full, full of

plōrō (1) weep, cry

Plōtia, -ae f. Plotia, Valeria's mother

pluō, pluere, pluvī to rain; *pluit* imp. it is raining

plūrēs, plūra more (in number) [19]

plūrimus, -a, -um most [20]

plūs more (in amount) [19]

pōculum, -ī n. cup

poena, -ae f. punishment, penalty

poēta, -ae m. poet [14]

poliō, polīre, polīvī, polītum polish

polliceor, pollicērī, pollicitus sum promise

Polliō, -ōnis m. Pollio, a wealthy patron of Vergil and advisor of Augustus

Pollux, -ūcis m. Pollux, divine twin brother of Castor, one of the Gemini

Polydectēs, -ae m. Polydectes, king of the island of Seriphus

pōmerium, -iī n. open space surrounding the walls of a Roman town

pompa, -ae f. ceremonial procession

Pompēiānus, -a, -um Pompeian

Pompēiī, -ōrum m. pl. Pompeii, city in Campania destroyed by eruption of Mt. Vesuvius in 79 A.D.

pōmum, -ī n. fruit, apple

pōne behind; (+ acc.) behind

pōnō, pōnere, posuī, positum put, place [4]

pontifex, -icis m. priest

populus, -ī m. people [4]

porrō and besides, further

porrus, -ī m. leek

porta, -ae f. door, gate

portitor, -ōris m. ferryman

portō (1) carry [8]

portus, -ūs m. gate

poscō, poscere, poposcī ask for, demand, request [5]

possum, posse, potuī be able, can [7]

post (+ acc.) after, behind [5]

posteā afterward, then

posterus, -a, -um following, next

postis, -is f. doorpost

postquam after, since

postrēmō at last, finally

postrīdiē the next day

postulō (1) ask for, beg, demand, require, request

potens, potentis powerful [15]

potestās, -ātis f. power, authority

potior, potīrī, potītus sum (+ abl. or gen.) take possession of, get, acquire

pōtō (1) drink

pōtus, -ūs m. (a) drink

praecipiō, praecipere, praecēpī, praeceptum order

praecipuus, -a, -um special, particular

praeclārus, -a, -um very clear, famous, noble, excellent, beautiful [16]

praecox, praecocis naïve, premature

praefectus, -ī m. director, supervisor

praefica, -ae f. hired female mourner

praegredior, praegredī, praegressus sum go before, precede

praemium, -iī n. plunder; prize; reward; (pl.) discharge benefits

Praeneste, -is n. Praeneste, a town in Latium

Praenestīnus, -a, -um of Praeneste, a town in in Latium

praeparō (1) prepare

praesentiō, praesentīre, praesensī, praesensum to perceive
beforeheand

praesertim especially, particularly

praeses, -idis m. guardian, warden

praesideō, praesidēre, praesēdī preside (over)

**praestō, praestāre, praestitī, praestātum (+ dat.)
be superior to; stand out from; surpass [10]**

praeter (+ acc.) along, beyond; except

praetereā besides, moreover

praetereō, praeterīre, praeterīvī / praterīī, praeteritum
go past; escape notice of; neglect

praetextus, -a, -um bordered; *toga praetexta* a toga
with a purple border

praetor, -ōris m. judge, praetor

praetōriānus, -ī m. a man who has been praetor but
has not yet become consul

praetrepidō (1) be nervous in ancitipation

praetūra, -ae f. praetorship, judgeship

prandium, -ī n. noon meal, luncheon

prasinus, -a, -um green

precor, precārī, precātus sum pray

prehendō, prehendere, prehendī, prehensum take hold of, seize

prēlum, -ī n. wine- or oil-press

pretiōsus, -a, -um valuable, expensive

pretium, -iī m. price

prex, prēcis f. prayer

prīdiē on the day before

prīmigenius, -a, -um original

prīmō at first

prīmum first, at first

prīmus, -a, -um first [18], *prīmum digitum* fingertip

princeps, -cipis m. head, leader, chief; title of Augustus
and his imperial successors

prior, prius former [19]

priscus, -a, -um old, ancient

prius formerly, before, in the past

priusquam before [19]

prīvātus, -a, -um private (citizen)

prīvō (1), to deprive of

prīvignus, -ī m. stepson

prō (+ abl.) before, in front of, for, instead of [6]

proavus, -ī m. great-grandfather, remote ancestor

probus, -a, -um good, honest

procax, procācis pushy, undisciplined

**prōcēdō, prōcēdere, prōcessī, prōcessum proceed,
advance [10]**

prōcreō (1) procreate, create

procul far, far away, from far away

prōcūrātor, -ōris m. administrator, procurator

prodigus, -a, -um wasteful, extravagant

proelium, -iī n. battle

profectō without question, undoubtedly

professor, -ōris m. professor

proficiscor, proficiscī, profectus sum set out, depart

prōgeniēs, -ēī f. family, children, progeny

prōgredior, prōgredī, prōgressus sum go to, advance,
march forward, proceed

prohibeō, prohibēre, prohibuī, prohibitum keep off;
prevent; restrain; forbid

prōiciō, prōicere, prōiēcī, prōiectum throw down

prōmittō, prōmittere, prōmīsī, prōmissum send forth; promise

promptus, -a, -um ready

pronepōs, -ōtis m. great-grandson

proneptis, -is f. great-granddaughter

prōnuba, -ae f. bridesmaid

prōnuntiō (1) proclaim, announce, say, recite, report

propāgō (1) increase, enlarge

prope (+ acc.) near [5]

prōpellō, prōpellere, prōpulī, prōpulsum drive, push forward

properō (1) hasten

Propertius, -iī m. Propertius, a Roman elegiac poet
of the 1st century A.D.

propinquus, -a, -um neighboring, nearby

propitius, -a, -um favorable, propitious

proprius, -a, -um one's own, personal, unique

propter (+ acc.) on account of [9]

prōra, -ae f. prow

prorsus straight ahead; forward

proscaenium, -iī n. stage

prōsequor, prōsequī, prōsecūtus sum accompany, follow

prospectus, -ūs m. view

prōsum, prōdesse, prōfuī (+ dat.) benefit, profit, be useful to

prōtegō, prōtegere, prōtexī, prōtectum cover, protect

prōvincia, -ae f. province

prōvocō (1) challenge

proximus, -a, -um nearest, next

prūdens, prūdentis foreseeing, prudent

prūnum, -ī n. plum

pūblicus, -a, -um public, common

pudeō, pudēre, puduī, puditum be ashamed; *mē pudet*
I am ashamed

pudor, -ōris m. shame, modesty, decency

puella, -ae f. girl [6]

puellāris, -e pertaining to a girl

puer, puerī m. boy [6]

pugna, -ae f. fight

pugnō (1) fight [12]

pugnus, -ī m. fist

pulcher, pulchra, pulchrum pretty, handsome [13]

pullus, -a, -um dingy, somber; *toga pulla* a dark gray
toga worn in mourning

pulsō (1) strike, beat; push, drive; "strike the ground
with feet," i.e., dance

pulvīnar, -āris m. cushioned couch (used for a religious statue)

pūmilio, -ōnis m./f. dwarf

pūpa, -ae f. doll, girl
puppis, puppis f. stern (of a ship)
purgō (1) clean, cleanse
pūrus, -a, -um pure, plain, without an iron tip
puteus, puteī m. well, pit
Puticulī, -ōrum m.pl. a nickname for a burial area outside the Esquiline hill
putō (1) think
Pȳthia, -ae f. Pythia, oracular priestess of Apollo at Delphi

Q

quā dē causā? for what reason? why?
quā where, in so far as
quadrāgēsimus, -a, -um fortieth
quadrātus, -a, -um square
quadrīga, -ae f. pl. chariot with four horses
quaerō, quaerere, quaesivī / quaesiī, quaesītum ask [18]
quaestiō, -ōnis f. question
quaestūra, -ae f. quaestorship
quālis, quāle? what kind of? what sort of?; see also *tālis*
quam how! [13]
quam than [10]
quamdiū for how long
quamquam although, yet
quamvīs although
quandō when
Quantī constat? How much does it cost?
quantus, -a, -um how much, how many [10]
quārē for, because; interr. in what way? how?; whereby; wherefore, why
quartus, -a, -um fourth
quasi as if, practically
quater four times
quatiō, -ere, quassī, quassum shake, wave about
quattuor four [10]
-que and; *-que . . . -que* both . . . *and* [4]
queror, querī, questus sum complain
quī, quae, quod who, which [18]
quia since, because [18]
quid what? [1]
Quid agis? How are you? How are you doing?
Quid fit? What is going on? What's happening?
Quid plūra? Why say more?
quīdam, quaedam, quoddam certain (indefinite, as in "a certain person")
quidem certainly
quiēs, -ētis f. quiet, calm, rest, peace
quiescō, quiescere, quiēvī, quiētum rest [14]
quiētus, -a, -um calm, quiet
quīlibet, quaelibet, quidlibet/quodlibet whoever, whatever
quīn that not (with subj. "from X'ing"); indeed; why not?
Quinctilius, -iī m. Quinctilius, a male name

quindecim fifteen
quinquāgintā fifty
quinque five [10]
quintum for the fifth time
quintus, -a, -um fifth
Quirīnālis, -e Quirinal, pertaining to one of the seven hills of Rome
Quirīs, -ītis m. archaic form of *civis* citizen
quis = aliquis after *sī*
quis, quid who? what? [6]
quisque, quaeque, quodque/quicque/quidque each, every
quisquis, quicquid/quidquid whoever, whatever
quīvīs, quaevīs, quidvīs anyone, anything
quō? where?
quod because [3]
quōmodo how [17]
quoque also [8]
quot? indecl. how many?
quōusque how long

R

rādō, radere, rāsī, rasum scrape, scratch, shave, erase
rāmus, -ī m. branch
rapiō, rapere, rapuī, raptum snatch, seize [20]
rārō rarely, seldom
rārus, -a, -um rare; thin; scattered
ratiō, -ōnis f. account, transaction; *ratiōnem habēre* "to have a sense of"
recēdō, recēdere, recessī, recessum retire, withdraw
recenter recently
recipiō, recipere, recēpī, receptum accept, receive, take back; *se recipere* retreat
recordor, recordārī, recordātus sum remember
recreō (1) relax, restore
rectē straightly, correctly
rectus, -a, -um straight, correct [6]
recumbō, recumbere, recubuī lie down, recline
redeō, redīre, redīvī / rediī, reditum come back, go back, return
redigō, redigere, redēgī, redactum drive back, restore
reditus, -ūs m. return
referō, referre, rettulī, relātum carry, carry back, bring back
refrīgerō (1) make cool
refugiō, refugere, refūgī run away
rēgia, -ae f. palace
rēgīna, -ae f. queen
regiō, -ōnis f. region, district
regnō (1) reign, hold power over
regnum, -ī n. kingdom
regō, regere, rexī, rectum rule, govern
regredior, regredī, regressus sum return
rēiciō, rēicere, rēiēcī, rēiectum throw

religiōsissimē most piously

religiōsus, -a, -um pious, devout

relinquō, relinquere, relīquī, relictum leave, leave behind

reliquus, -a, -um remaining

remaneō, remanēre, remansī remain, stay behind

remittō, remittere, remīsī, remissum send back

removeō, remōvēre, remōvī, remōtum move back; remove

repellō, repellere, reppulī, repulsum push back, repel, repulse

repetō, repetere, repetīvī/repetiī, repetītum repeat

repleō, replēre, replēvī, replētum fill up, fill again

reportō (1) bring home

repōtia, -ōrum n. pl. celebration on the day following a festivity like a marriage

repugnō (1) fight back; resist

requiescō, requiesere, requiēvī, requiētum rest

requīrō, requīrere, requīsīvī / requīsiī, requīsītum seek, look for, search for

rēs gestae f. pl. deeds

rēs pūblica, reī pūblicae f. republic

rēs, reī f. thing, matter; business, affair; reason

resideō, residēre, resēdī sit, remain in a place

respiciō, respicere, respexī, respectum take notice of, read (omens)

respīrō (1) breathe

respondeō, respondēre, respondī, responsum (+ dat.) reply, answer [3]

restituō, restituere, restituī, restitūtum replace, restore; give back

restitūtus, -a, -um restored

rēte, rētis n. net

rētiārius, -iī m. gladiatorial fighter with a net

retineō, retinēre, retinuī, retentum hold fast, retain; cling to

reveniō, revenīre, revēnī, reventum come back, return

revertō, revertere, revertī come back, turn back, return; also *revertor, revertī, reversus sum* turn back, return

revocō (1) call back

rex, rēgis m. king [14]

rhētor, rhētoris teacher of rhetoric (public speaking) [16]

rhētorica, -ae f. rhetoric

rhētoricus, -a, -um rhetorical [16]

rīdeō, rīdere, rīsī, rīsum laugh [7]

rīdiculōsus, -a, -um laughable, riduculous

rigor, rigōris m. straight line; *Rigor Valī Aelī* Hadrian's Wall in Britain

rixa, -ae f. (loud) quarrel, violent quarrel, brawl

rōbustus, -a, -um strong

rogō (1) ask (for) [10]

Rōma, -ae f. Rome [11]

Rōmānus, -a, -um Roman [11]

Romulus, -a, -um of Romulus (the founder of Rome); Roman

rostra, -ōrum n. pl. speaker's platform

rostrum, -ī n. beak

rota, -ae f. wheel

ruber, rubra, rubrum red

Rūfus, -ī m. Rufus ("Red")

rumpō, rumpere, rūpī, ruptum burst, break down

ruō, ruere, ruī rush, rush at; fall to ruin

rursus again [16]

rūs, rūris n. country, country estate; *rurī* "in the country" (note the lack of a prep.)

russātus, -a, -um red

rusticus, -a, -um rural, rustic

S

S.D. = *salūtem dīcit*

Sabīnus, -a, -um Sabine, pertaining to the Sabines, neighbors of Rome

saccus, -ī m. wallet, bag sack, pocket book [11]

sacer, sacra, sacrum sacred, holy

sacrāmentum, -ī n. oath, sacred obligation (especially one sworn by soldiers)

sacrificō (1) sacrifice

saeculum, -ī n. age, era

saepe often [6]

saevus, -a, -um raging, violent, savage, cruel, furious

sagax, sagācis wise, sharp

sagitta, -ae f. arrow

sāl, salis m./n. salt

Saliāris, -e of the Salii (priests of Mars, god of war)

saliō, salīre, saliī/saluī, saltum leap, jump [11]

saltātor, -ōris m. dancer

saltem at least

salūs, -ūtis f. health, safety

salūtātiō, -ōnis f. greeting, formal morning visit by a client to a patron

salūtō (1) greet, say "Salvē!" [4]

Salvē/Salvēte! Hello. Hi. Be well! [3]

salvus, -a, -um alright, safe, well [16]

sanguis, sanguinis m. blood

sānitās, -ātis f. health, sanity

sānō (1) restore to health

sānus, -a, -um healthy

sapiō, sapere, sapīvī/sapiī show good sense

satis enough, sufficient

satura, -ae f. satire

scālae, -ārum f. pl. stairs, staircase

scalpō, scalpere, scalpsī, scalptum scratch

scelerātus, -a, -um wicked

scelus, -eris n. crime [20]

sciō, scīre, scīvī / sciī, scītum know, know about

Scorpus, -ī m. Scorpus, a male name

scrība, -ae m. scribe, secretary

scrībō, scrībere, scripsī, scriptum write [6]

scriptor, -ōris m. writer

scrūta, -ōrum n. pl. trash

scutum, -ī n. shield

Scybalē, -ēs f. Scybale, a female name

schola, -ae f. school, leisure

sē (see *suī*)

secō, secāre, secuī, sectum cut, cut off, cut up

secundus, -a, -um second; favorable

Secundus, -ī m. Secundus, a male name

sed but [3]

sēdecim sixteen [8]

sedeō, sedēre, sēdī, sessum sit [5]

sēdēs, -is f. seat, home, residence [14]

sēligō, sēligere, sēlēgī, sēlectum select, choose

sella, -ae f. chair

semel once

semper always [3]

senātor, -ōris m. senator, member of the senate

senātus, -ūs m. senate

senectūs, -ūtis f. old age

senex, senis m. old man

senex, senis m. old, aged

sensus, -ūs m. feeling

sententia, -ae f. proverb, saying

sentiō, sentīre, sensī, sensum feel, hear, see, sense, perceive

sepeliō, sepelīre, sepelīvī / sepeliī, sepultum bury

septimum for the seventh time

septuāgintā indecl. seventy

sepulcrum, -ī n. tomb

sepultūra, -ae f. burial, grave

sequor, sequī, secūtus sum follow

serēnitās, -ātis f. cheerful tranquility

sērius later, too late, rather late [17]

sermō, -ōnis m. speech, talk

sermōcinor, sermōcinārī, sermōcinātus sum converse, talk, chat

sērō late, too late

serpens, serpentis f. snake, serpent

servātor, -ōris n. savior

Servīlia, -ae f. Servilia, daughter of Servilius

Servīliānus, -a, -um Servilian, of the Servilii

Servīlius, -iī m. Servilius, head of the *Servīliī*

serviō, servīre, servīvī / serviī, servītum serve, be a slave to

servitūs, -ūtis f. slavery, servitude

servō (1) save, protect, observe; observe, pay attention to

servus, -ī m. slave, servant [7]

Sevērus, -ī m. Severus, a male name

sex six [10]

sextus, -a, -um sixth

Sextus, -ī m. Sextus, a male *praenōmen*

sī if [7]

sī placet Please! lit., "if it pleases" [7]

sī vōbīs placeat Please!

sīc so, thus, in this way; yes [11]

siccus, -a, -um dry

Sicō, Sicōnis m. Sico, a male name

sīcut just as, like [7]

significō (1) mean

signō (1) mark, seal, stamp

signum, -ī n. mark, token, sign, seal

silenter silently

silentium, -iī n. stillness, silence, tranquility;
    silentium tenēre to keep silent

silescō, silescere, silescuī grow quiet

silva, -ae f. woods, forest

sīmia, -ae m./f. monkey [5]

similis, -e similar, like to

simplex, simplicis simple, naïve

simul atque also *simul ac* as soon as

simul together, altogether, at the same time, all at once

Sinae, -ārum f. pl. China

sināpis, -is f. mustard

sine (+ abl.) without [6]

singulāris, -e single

singulātim one by one

singulī, -ae, -a individual, one to each (in a group);
    one by one; *singulō* one by one

sinister, -tra, -trum left; *sinistra (manus), -ae* f. the left hand

sinō, sinere, sīvī / siī, situm allow, permit

sinus, -ūs m. lap

sīp(h)ō, -ōnis m. siphon, water hose

sistō, sistere, stetī / stitī, statum stand still [8]

sitiens, sitientis thirsty

sitiō, sitīre be thirsty

sitis, -is f. thirst

situs, -a, -um located, buried

sīve or

soccus, -ī m. loose-fitting slipper

socius, -iī m. partner, companion

Sōcratēs, -is m. 5th century B.C. Athenian philosopher

socrus, -ūs f. mother-in-law

sodālis, -is m. companion

sōl, sōlis m. sun; day

sōlāciolum, -ī n. relief, comfort

sōlārium, -iī n. sundial

soleō, solēre, solitus sum be accustomed (to)

solidum, -ī n. something firm, solid; "a substantial sum"

sōlum only [3]

solum, -ī n. earth, soil

sōlus, -a, -um only, alone [6]

solvō, solvere, solvī, solūtum loosen, unbind; fulfil, perform;
    pay, deliver; *nāvem solvō* set sail

sollicitō (1) upset, shake up

sollicitus, -a, -um uneasy, apprehensive, nervous,
    anxious that/lest

somniculōsus, -a, -um sleepy

somnus, -ī m. sleep, rest; laziness

sonitus, -ūs m. sound

sonus, -ī m. sound [6]

sordidus, -a, -um filthy

soror, sorōris f. sister [13]

spargō, spargere, sparsī, sparsum spread, scatter, sprinkle

spatiōsus, -a, -um wide

spatium, -iī n. space

speciālis, speciāle individual, particular, special

speciēs, -ēī f. appearance, look, type

spectāculum, -ī n. sight, spectacle, game

spectātor, -ōris m. spectator, observer

spectō (1) look at, watch [10]

speculum, -ī n. mirror

spēlunca, -ae f. cave

spernō, spernere, sprēvī, sprētum reject, scorn, disregard

spērō (1) hope, hope for, look forward to [9]

spēs, speī f. hope, expectation

spīna, -ae f. thorn; spine; center barrier of the circus

spiritus, -ūs m. soul

spīrō (1) breathe

splendidus, -a, -um bright, shining, illustrious, splendid, shiny

spolium, -iī n. spoils (of war); *spolia opīma* spoils taken by one general from another in single combat

sponsa, -ae f. a woman engaged to be married

sponsiō, -ōnis f. bet, wager; *sponsiōnem facere* to make a bet

sportula, -ae f. little basket; gift of money or food from patron to client

squālidus, -a, -um dirty, filthy

squālor, squālōris m. filth

st shh! shush!

stabulum, -ī n. stable

stāmen, stāminis m. thread

statim immediately [20]

statūra, -ae f. stature

status, -ūs m. condition, position

stercus, -oris n. dung, excrement

sternō, sternere, strāvī, strātum spread out

stertō, stertere, stertuī snore

stilus, -ī m. stilus, pen

stīpendium, -iī n. tax, contribution, pay

stō, stāre, stetī, statum stand [5]

strangulō (1) choke, strangle

strēnuē actively, vigorously

strēnuus, -a, -um active, vigorous, hard, strenuous

strepitus, -ūs m. noise

struō, struere, struxī, structum build, construct

studeō, studēre, studuī (+ dat.) devote one's self to, be eager for, study [12]

studiōsus, -a, -um (+ gen.) eager (to), devoted (to)

studium, -iī n. study, eagerness, zeal [6]

stultus, -a, -um stupid

stuprum, -ī n. dishonor, shame

Stygius, -a, -um Stygian, pertaining to the River Styx in the Underworld

Stymphālus, -ī m. Stymphalus, a Greek lake and town of the same name

Styx, Stygis f. river Styx, river bordering the Underworld

suāsōria, -ae f. persuasive speech

suāvis, suāve pleasant, agreeable, delightful

sub (+ abl.) under, from under; (+ acc.) under [6]

sūbiciō, sūbicere, sūbiēcī, sūbiectum throw from beneath, put under foot.

subitō suddenly [11]

sublevō (1) lift, raise, support, lighten, alleviate

submissus, -a, -um low (voice)

submittō, submittere, submīsī, submissum raise, rear; let grow; make subject to; *sē submittere* (+ dat.) to lower oneself to

subsīdō, subsīdere, subsēdī crouch

Subūra, -ae f. Subura, a neighborhood in Rome

succēdō, succēdere, successī, successum go below, go under; come to; succeed (to)

sūdo (1) sweat, perspire

suffrāgātiō, -ōnis f. public espression of support

suī, sibi, sē, sē himself, herself, itself, themselves

sum, esse, fuī be [6]

summittō, summittere, summīsī, summissum (with *sē* + dat.) lower oneself to

summus, -a, -um highest, greatest [20]

sumptuōsus, -a, -um expensive, costly

sunt (they) are [2]

super above; (+ acc. or abl.) over, on top of [10]

super left over

superbus, -a, -um proud, haughty

superēmineō, superēminēre, stand out over

superficiēs, -ēī f. surface

superior, superius higher [19]

superō (1) surpass, conquer

supersum, superesse, superfuī be left over; survive; have strength (for)

superus, -a, -um "above"; *in superōs (locōs)* = in heaven

suppetō, suppetere, suppetīvī / suppetiī, suppetītum be available for

suprā (+ acc.) over, above

suprēmus, -a, -um highest, final [20]

surdus, -a, -um deaf

surgō, surgere, surrexī, surrectum get up, rise up

sūs, suis m./f. pig, sow

suscipiō, suscipere, suscēpī, susceptum accept

suspendō, suspendere, suspendī, suspensum hang

suspīrium, -iī n. sigh, heartthrob

suspīrō (1) sigh

sustineō, sustinere, sustinuī, sustentum hold up, support, withstand

susurrō (1) whisper

suōpte = stronger form of *suō*

sūtor, -ōris m. cobbler, shoemaker

suus, -a, -um his/her/its/their own [9]

Syria, -ae f. Roman province located approximately
 where modern Syria is today

T

T. = *Titus*

***taberna, -ae* f. (snack) shop [2]**

tabula, -ae f. counter, slate, tablet

tabulārium, -iī n. office

***taceō, tacēre, tacuī, tacitum* be quiet, be silent [13]**

tacitus, -a, -um silent, secret

taeda, -ae f. pine-torch

taediōsus, -a, -um boring

taedit, taedēre, taesum est (+ gen.) or (+ inf.) imp.
 be tired (of), be sick (of)

taedium, -iī n. boredom, weariness; object of weariness,
 boring thing; *taedium habēre* to be bored

Talassio, -ōnis m. Talasio! an ancient wedding cry

tālis, tāle such, of such a kind, of such a sort; *tālis,*
 -e . . . quālis, -e of such a sort . . . as

***tam* so, so much (as) [11]**

***tamen* nevertheless [20]**

tamquam just as, just like

***tandem* at last, at length, finally [20]**

tangō, tangere, tetigī, tactum touch; reach; affect, move,
 mention

tantum so much, to such a degree

tantus, -a, -um so great, so much

tardus, -a, um late

taurus, -ī m. bull

tectum, -ī n. roof, house

tegō, tegere, texī, tectum to protect, hide, conceal, cover

tēla, -ae f. loom, web

tellūs, tellūris f. earth, ground, land

tempestās, -ātis f. time, weather, season, storm

tempestīvē on time

tempestīvus, -a, -um opportune, seasonable, timely

templum, -ī n. temple

temptō (1) feel; try; test

***tempus, -oris* n. time, season [13]**

***teneō, tenēre, tenuī, tentum* hold [6]**

tener, -era, -erum soft, delicate

tenuis, -e thin

tepidārium, -iī n. warm bath

tepor, -ōris m. warmth, heat

ter three times

tergum, -ī n. back; *ā tergō* behind

terminō (1) conclude, end

***terra, -ae* f. land [8]**

terreō, terrēre, terruī, territum frighten, terrify

terribilis, -e frightening, terrible

terrificus, -a, -um terrifying

territus, -a, -um afraid, scared [14]

tertius, -a, -um third

tessellātus, -a, -um mosaic

testor, testārī, testātus sum bear witness to, testify to

theātrum, -ī n. theater

Thēbae, Thēbārum f. pl. Thebes, a city in Greece

thermae, -ārum f. pl. public baths

Thracia, -ae f. Thrace, a Roman province located in what
 is now part of Greece, Bulgaria, and Turkey

Thrax, Thrācis m. Thracian; a gladiator with lighter armor,
 including a helmet and greaves on both legs

Tiberis, -is m. Tiber, the river running through Rome

Tiberius, -iī m. Tiberius, Augustus' stepson, adopted son,
 and successor

***tibi* your, to you [1]**

tībīcen, -inis m. piper

***timeō, timēre, timuī* fear, be afraid [10]**

timidē timidly

timidus, -a, -um afraid, timid

timor, timōris m. fear; object of fear

tintinnō (1) ring

Tīrō a male name, especially the slave and trusted scribe
 of Cicero

tīrō, -ōnis m. recruit

Tīryns, -nthos f. acc. *Tīryntha* f. a Greek city in the Argolid

Titus, -ī m. Titus, a male name

toga, -ae f. toga

togātus, -a, -um dressed in a toga

tolerō (1) bear, endure

***tollō, tollere, sustulī, sublātum* lift, raise [11]**

tonō (1) thunder, make to resound

tonsor, -ōris m. barber

torpeō, torpēre, torpuī grow numb

torreō, torrēre, torruī, tostum bake

tortus, -a, -um twisted, crooked

torus, -ī m. bed

tot indecl. so many

***tōtus, -a, -um* whole, all, entire [17]**

tractō (1) treat, handle

trādō, trādere, trādidī, trāditum hand down, entrust, deliver

tragicomoedia, -ae f. tragicomedy

tragoedia, -ae f. tragedy

trahō, trahere, traxī, tractum drag, haul, draw, remove

tranquillitās, -ātis f. calmness, stillness; fair weather

tranquillus, -a, -um calm, still, peaceful

***trans* (+ acc.) across [5]**

transeō, transīre, transīvī / transiī, transitum go over,
 go across

transfigō, transfigere, transfixī, transfixum pierce through

transportō (1) carry (across), transport, convey, transport

trecentī, -ae, -a three hundred

tremō, tremere, tremuī tremble

trepidus, -a, -um nervous, anxious

trēs, tria three [6]

tribūnicius, -a, -um m. belonging to a tribune

tribūnus, -ī m. tribune; *tribūnus militum* military tribune

tribūtim by tribes

triclīnium, -iī n. triclinium, dining room

tridens, tridentis m. trident

triennium, -iī n. a three-year period

trieteris, -idis f. triennial, unit of three years

trigintā thirty

tristis, -e sad [15]

tristitia, -ae f. sadness

triumphālis, -e triumphal

triumphātor, -ōris m. one who celebrates a triumph

triumphō (1) triumph, celebrate a triumph

triumphus, -ī m. triumph, triumphal procession, military triumph

trivium, triv(i)ī n. an intersection, a place where three roads meet

Trōia, -ae f. Troy, city in the Roman province of Asia (modern Turkey)

tropaeum, tropaeī m. trophy, victory monument

tū, tuī, tibi, tē, tē you (sing.) yourself [3]

tuba, -ae f. horn, trumpet

tubicen, tubicenis m. trumpeter

tueor, tuērī, tuitus sum look at, watch over, look after, protect

Tulliānum, -ī n. Tullianum, the state prison in Rome

tum then [20]

tumeō, tumēre swell

tumultus, -ī m. uproar, disturbance

tunc then [3]

tunica, -ae f. tunic

turba, -ae f. crowd, disorder, confusion

turbō (1) disturb, disorder

turbō, turbinis m. whirlwind

turpis, -e ugly, foul, loathsome

Tuscus, -a, -um Etruscan

tūtus, -a, -um safe [14]

tuus, -a, -um your (sing.) [6]

Tyrus, -ī f. Tyre, city in Roman province of Syria (modern Lebanon)

U

ubi where; when [5]

ubīque everywhere

ūdus, -a, -um wet

Ulixēs, -is or *-ēī* m. Ulysses, the hero of Homer's *Odyssey*, known in Greek as Odysseus

ūllus, -a, -um any [17]

ulna, -ae f. yard (unit of measurement)

ulula, -ae f. screech owl

ululō (1) wail, weep

umbilīcus, -ī m. navel, belly button, center, umbilical cord

umbra, -ae f. shade, soul

umerus, -ī m. shoulder

umquam at any time, ever

unda, -ae f. wave

unde from where

unguentārius, -iī m. perfume seller

ūnicus, -a, -um one and only, sole

ūnus, -a, -um one [7]

urbānus, -a, -um polished, refined; witty; of the city

urbs, -is f. city, esp. the city of Rome [20]

ūrīna, -ae f. urine

urna, -ae f. large water jar

ūrō, ūrere, ussī, ustum burn

usque as far as

ut as, how, in order that, so that; how; when

uterus, -ī m. womb, belly

utilis, -e useful

utinam if only! would that!

ūtor, ūtī, ūsus sum (+ abl.) use, employ, enjoy, experience

utrum whether

ūva, -ae f. grape; *ūva passa* dried grape, raisin

uxor, -ōris f. wife [18]

V

vādō, vādere go, advance, proceed

vae (often + dat.) woe! (in pain or dread)

vāgītus, -ūs m. cry, wail

vagor, vagārī, vagātus sum wander

vah / vaha ah! oh! (in astonishment, joy, anger)

val(l)um, val(l)ī n. a line of palisades

valdē very (much), a lot [11]

valeō, valēre, valuī be strong, be well; *Valē/Valēte!* Farewell. Good-bye. Be well! [2, 3]

Valeria, -ae f. Valeria, owner of the snack shop

vāpulō (1) be beaten

varius, -a, -um various, changeable, mixed

vastō (1) plunder, lay waste

vastus, -a, -um huge

Vatia, -ae f. Vatia, a Roman *nōmen*

Vaticānus, -ī m. Vatican, a hill on the right bank of the Tiber in Rome

vehemens, -entis violent, strong, intense, vehement

Vēiī, Vēiōrum m. pl. Veii, a very old Etruscan city north of Rome

vēlōciter quickly

velut just as, just like

vēnātiō, -ōnis f. hunt

vēnātor, -ōris m. hunter

venditiō, -ōnis f. sale

venditor, -ōris m. merchant

vendō, vendere, vendidī, venditum sell

venēnātus, -a, -um poisonous
venēnum, -ī n. poison
venetus, -a, -um blue
veniō, venīre, vēnī, ventum come [2]
venter, -tris m. belly, abdomen, womb
ventus, -ī m. wind
Venus, -eris f. Venus, goddess of love
venustus, -a, -um charming, attractive
vēr, vēris n. springtime
verber, verberis n lash, blow
verberō (1) assail, flog, batter, lash, scourge, beat
verbum, -ī n. word [11]
vērē truly [15]
vereor, verērī, veritus sum be afraid of, fear, show reverence to
Vergilius, -iī m. Vergil, the poet
vēritās, -ātis f. truth
vērō indeed, in truth, truly
Vērōna, -ae f. Verona, a town in northern Italy
Vērōnensis, -ense Veronan, from Verona
verrō, verrere, versum sweep clean
versō (1) keep turning around, spin, whirl
versor, versārī, come and go, frequent
versus, -ūs m. verse, line of poetry
vertō, vertere, vertī, versum turn, overturn
vērus, -a, -um true [15]
vescor, vescī (+ abl.) take food, feed devour
vesper, -eris m. evening
vesperascō, vesperascere, vesperāvī grow towards evening
Vesta, -ae f. Vesta, goddess of the hearth
vester, vestra, vestrum your (pl.) [6]
vestīmentum, -ī n. garment, clothing
vestiō, vestīre, vestīvī / vestiī, vestītum dress, clothe
vestis, -is f. garments, clothing
Vesuvius, -iī m. Vesuvius, volcanic mountain in Campania
vetō, vetāre, vetuī, vetitum forbid, prohibit
vetus, -eris aged, old
vexātus, -a, -um upset
vexillum, -ī n. standard, banner
vexō (1) agitate, harry, upset, disturb
via, -ae f. road, street, way [5]
Vibius, -iī m. Vibius, a male name
vīcennālis, -e made for a period of twenty years, 20th anniversary
vīcīnitās, -ātis f. neighborhood
vīcīnus, -ī m. neighbor
victor, -ōris m. victor, conqueror
victōria, -ae f. victory
victrix, -īcis f. female conquerer
videō, vidēre, vīdī, vīsum see, perceive [3]
videor, vidērī, vīsus sum seem, appear; be seen; *vidētur* (+ inf.) imp. it seems good, seems like a good idea
vigeō, vigēre, viguī be strong, thrive
vigescō, vigescere become strong

vigil, -is m./f. sentry, guard; firefighter; (pl.) fire brigade
vigilō (1) watch, keep watch; stay awake, stay awake all night; wake up
vīgintī twenty [12]
villa, -ae f. villa, country estate
Vīminālis, -e Viminal (hill in Rome), pertaining to the Viminal
Vīminālis, -is m. Viminal (hill), one of the seven hills of Rome
vinciō, vincīre, vinxī, vinctum tie up, fetter, bind
vincō, vincere, vīcī, victum conquer [12]
vīnum, -ī n. wine [3]
violentia, -ae f. force, violence
Vipsānius, -iī m. Vipsanius
vir, virī m. man [2]; husband
virga, -ae f. rod
virgō, -inis f. young girl
virītim, man by man, per person
vīs, vis f. strength, power, force; (pl.) *vīrēs, vīrium* strength, troops, forces
vīscera, -um n. pl. internal organs, entrails
vīsitō (1) visit
vīta, -ae f. life [13]
vitta, -ae f. ribbon
vīvo, vīvere, vixī, victum live
vīvus, -a, -um alive, living
vix scarcely, hardly
vōcālis, vōcāle speaking, vocal
vōciferor, vōciferārī, vōciferātus sum yell, cry out
vocō (1) call [8]
Volcānus, -ī m. Vulcan, the god of fire and smiths
volō (1) fly; hasten
volō, velle, voluī want to, be willing to [7]
vōs, vestrum / vestrī, vōbīs, vōs, vōbīs you (pl.); yourselves
vōtum, -ī n. vow; votive offering
voveō, vovēre, vōvī, vōtum vow
vox, vōcis f. voice [15]
vulnerō (1) wound
vulnus, -eris n. wound
vulturīnus, -a, -um of a vulture
vultus, vultūs m. face; also spelled *voltus*
vulva, -ae f. womb

X

Xerxēs, Xerxis m. Xerxes, king of Persia

Z

Zephyrus, -ī m. the West Wind, which brings mild weather
Zēthus, -ī, m. Zethus ("Westy"), a male name

Verba Discenda

English-Latin Lexicon: This English-Latin Lexicon is based on the *Verba Discenda* in Chapters 1–20. Numbers in brackets indicate the chapter in which the Latin word becomes a *verbum discendum*. Before you use a word in a Latin sentence, it is a good idea to check its entire meaning in the *Verba Omnia*.

abl. = ablative
acc. = accusative
adj. = adjective
dat. = dative
conj. = conjunction
esp. = especially
f. = feminine

inf. = infinitive
interj. = interjection
m. = masculine
n. = neuter
pl. = plural
prep. = preposition
v. = verb

A

a lot *multum* [16]; *valdē* [11]
about *dē* (+ abl.) [7]
across *trāns* (+ acc.) [5]
act *agō, agere, ēgī, actum* [4]
advance *prōcēdō, prōcēdere, prōcessī, prōcessum* [10]
afraid *territus, -a, -um* [14]
after *post* (+ acc.) [5]
again *iterum* [4]; *rursus* [16]
against *in* (+ acc.) [5]; *contrā* (+ acc.) [19]
aid *adsum, adesse, adfuī* (+ dat.) [19]
alas! *ēheu* [16]
all *omnēs, -ia* [15]; *tōtus, -a, -um* [17]
almost *paene* [18]
alone *sōlus, -a, -um* [6]
already *iam* [8]
alright *salvus, -a, -um* [16] cf. "correct"
also *etiam* [17]; *quoque* [8]
altar *āra, -ae* f. [19]
always *semper* [3]
among *inter* (+ acc.) [5]
amphitheater *amphitheātrum, -ī* n. [17]
ancestors *māiōrēs, māiōrum* m. pl. [15]
ancient *antīquus, -a, -um* [10]
and *et* [2]; *atque* [20]; *-que* [4]
and also *atque* [20]; *et* [2]; *etiam* [17]
and even *atque* [20]
and not *nec* [15]
angry *īrātus, -a, -um* [6]

animal *animal, -ālis* n. [17]
another *alius, -a, -ud* [9]
another (of two) *alter, altera, alterum* [17]
answer *respondeō, respondēre, respondī, responsum* (+ dat.) [3]
any *ūllus, -a, -um* [17]
apartment block *insula, -ae* f. [9]
approach *appropinquō* (1) (+ dat.) [11]
are (they) *sunt* [2]
arm *brāc(c)hium, -iī* n. [14]
around *circum* (+ acc.) [6]
arrive at *adveniō, advenīre, advēnī, adventum* [11]
art *ars, artis* f. [16]
as long as *dum* [10]
ask *quaerō, quaerere, quaesivī / quaesiī, quaesītum* [18]
ask (for) *poscō, poscere, poposcī* [5]; *rogō* (1) [10]
asking a question expecting a no answer *num* [5]
asking a question expecting a yes answer *nōnne* [5]
asking a simple question *-ne* [4]
at _____'s *apud* (+ acc.) [16]
at *in* (+ abl.) [2, 5]
at last, at length *tandem* [20]
at the house of *apud* (+ acc.) [16]
await *exspectō* (1) [16]
away from *ā, ab, abs* (+ abl.) [5]; *dē* (+ abl.) [7]

B

bad *malus, -a, -um* [6]
bag *saccus, -ī* m. [11]

be *sum, esse, fuī* [6]
be able *possum, posse, potuī* [7]
be absent *absum, abesse, āfuī* [19]
be afraid *timeō, timēre, timuī* [10]
be eager for *studeō, studēre, studuī* (+ dat.) [12]
be near *adsum, adesse, adfuī* (+ dat.) [19]
be of assistance to *adsum, adesse, adfuī* (+ dat.) [19]
be pleasing to *placeō, placēre, placuī, placitum* (+ dat.);
   esp., it is pleasing *placet* (+ inf.) [12]
be quiet, silent *taceō, tacēre, tacuī, tacitum* [13]
be strong *valeō, valēre, valuī, valitum* [3]
be "there" for someone *adsum, adesse, adfuī* (+ dat.) [19]
be superior to *praestō, praestāre, praestitī,*
   praestitum/praestātum (+ dat.) [10]
be unwilling *nōlō, nōlle, nōluī* [7]
be well *valeō, valēre, valuī, valitum* [3]
Be well! *Salvē/Salvēte!* [3]; *Valē/Valēte!* [2]
be willing to *volō, velle, voluī* [7]
beautiful *pulcher, -chra, -chrum* [13]
because *quia* [18]; *quod* [3]
bed *lectus, -ī* m. [18]
bedroom *cubiculum, -ī* n. [12]
before (conj.) *priusquam* [19]
before (prep.) *prō* (+ abl.) [6]
begin *incipiō, incipere, incēpī, inceptum* [18]
behind *post* (+ acc.) [5]
Behold! *Ecce!* [11]
best *optimus, -a, -um* [20]
better *melior, melius* [19]
body *corpus, corporis* n. [15]
book *liber, librī* m. [14]
born *nātus, -a, -um* [12]
both . . . and *et . . . et* [4]; *-que . . . -que* [4]
boy *puer, puerī* m. [6]
brave *fortis, forte* [15]
brother *frāter, frātris* m. [13]
business *negōtium, -ī* n. [8]
but *at* [20]; *sed* [3]
but also *sed etiam* (with *nōn sōlum* . . . not only . . .) [18]
buy *emō, emere, ēmī, emptum* [18]
by (with persons) *ā, ab, abs* (+ abl.) [5]
by no means *haud* [16]

C

call *vocō* (1) [8]
can *possum, posse, potuī* [7]
care for *cūrō* (1) [13]
carry *portō* (1) [8]
character *mōrēs, mōrum* m. pl. [15]
choose *legō, legere, lēgī, lectum* [15]
circle *orbis, orbis* m.

city, esp. the city of Rome *urbs, urbis* f. [20]
city center *forum, -ī* [5]
come *veniō, venīre, vēnī, ventum* [2]
come near to *appropinquō* (1) (+ dat.) [11]
come to *adveniō, advenīre, advēnī, adventum* [11]
conceal *abdō, abdere, abdidī, abditum* [19]
concerning *dē* (+ abl.) [7]
conquer *vincō, vincere, vīcī, victum* [12]
correct *rectus, -a, -um* [6]
cost *constō, constāre, constitī, constātūrum* [10]
couch (dining) *lectus, -ī* m. [18]
country *fīnēs, fīnium* m. pl. [14]
crime *scelus, sceleris* n. [20]
cry out *clāmō* (1) [5]
custom *mōs, mōris* m. [15]

D

daily *cōtidiē (cottidiē)* [19]
danger *perīculum, -ī* n. [20]
dare *audeō, audēre, ausus sum* [9]
daughter *fīlia, -ae* f. [8]
dear *almus, -a, -um* [18]; *cārus, -a, -um* [13]
deed *factum, -ī* n. [20]
demand *poscō, poscere, poposcī* [5]
devote one's self to *studeō, studēre, studuī*
   (+ dat.) [12]
difficult *difficilis, difficile* [15]
dine *cēnō* (1) [12]
dining couch *lectus, -ī* m. [18]
dinner *cēna, -ae* f. [12]
discover *inveniō, invenīre, invēnī, inventum* [14]
do *agō, agere, ēgī, actum* [4]; *faciō, facere,*
   fēcī, factum [6]
do injury to *noceō, nocēre, nocuī, nocitum*
   (+ dat.) [12]
down from *dē* (+ abl.) [7]
drink *bibō, bibere, bibī* [2]
drive *agō, agere, ēgī, actum* [4]
duty *mūnus, mūneris* n. [17]

E

each *omnis, -e* [15]
eagerness *studium, -iī* n. [6]
early in the morning *māne* [4]
easy *facilis, -e* [20]
eat *edō, ēsse / edere, ēdī, ēsum* [7]
egg *ōvum, -ī* n. [10]
either . . . or *aut . . . aut* [4]
end (v.) *fīniō, fīnīre, fīnīvī / fīniī, fīnītum* [8]
end (noun) *fīnis, fīnis* m. [14]

enemy; pl. the enemy *hostis, hostis*
    m./f. [14]

enter *intrō* (1) [8]

entire *tōtus, -a, -um* [17]

even, even now *et* [2]; *etiam* [17]

every *omnis, -e* [15]

every day *cōtidiē (cottidiē)* [19]

excellent *praeclārus, -a, -um* [16]

excessively *nimium* [16]

F

face *ōs, ōris* n. [13]

fame *fāma, -ae* f. [20]

family *familia, -ae* f. [4]

famous *praeclārus, -a, -um* [16]

far, far off *longē* [11]

Farewell! *Valē/Valēte!* [2]

fast *celer, celeris, celere* [15]

father *pater, patris* m. [13]

favor *grātia, -ae* f. [19]

fear *timeō, timēre, timuī* [10]

female servant *ancilla, -ae* f. [8]

few *paucī, -ae, -a* [9]

field *ager, agrī* m. [14]

fight *pugnō* (1) [12]

figure *figūra, -ae* f. [10]

final *suprēmus, -a, -um* [20]

finally *tandem* [20]

find *inveniō, invenīre, invēnī, inventum* [14]

finish *fīniō, fīnīre, fīnīvī / fīniī, fīnītum* [8]

fire *ignis, ignis* m. [14]

first *prīmus, -a, -um* [18]

five *quinque* [10]

flee *fugiō, fugere, fūgī, fugitum* [12]

food *cibus, -ī* m. [2]

for a long time *diū* [16]; *longē* [11]

for a second time *iterum* [4]

for (conj.) *enim* [20]

for (prep.) *ad* (+ acc.) [2, 5]; *prō* (+ abl.) [6]

foreigner *hostis, hostis* m./f. [14]

former *prior, prius* [19]

formerly *ōlim* [19]

fortunate *fēlix, fēlīcis* [18]

forum *forum, -ī* [5]

four *quattuor* [10]

friend (male) *amīcus, -ī* m. [7]

friend (female) *amīca, -ae* f. [13]

from *ā, ab, abs* (+ abl.) [5]; *ē, ex* (+ abl.) [5]

from under; *sub* (+ abl.) [6]

function *mūnus, mūneris* n. [17]

future *futūrum, -ī* n. [14]

G

gain *obtineō, obtinēre, obtinuī, obtentum* [9]

game *lūdus -ī*, m. [4]; public games *mūnera,*
    mūnerum n. pl. [17]

gather *legō, legere, lēgī, lectum* [15]

get to know *noscō, noscere, nōvī, nōtum* [11]

gift (public) *mūnus, mūneris* n. [17]

girl *puella, -ae* f. [6]

girlfriend *amīca, -ae* f. [13]

give *dō, dare, dedī, datum* [2]

give thanks *grātiās agere* [19]

gladiator *gladiātor, -ōris* m. [17]

gloomy *maestus, -a, -um* [18]

go *eō, īre, īvī / iī, itum* [7]
    go away *abeō, abīre, abīvī/abiī, abitum* [7]
    go to *adeō, adīre, adīvī/adiī, adītum* [7]

god *deus, -ī* m.; *dī* (alternate nom. pl.) [14]

goddess *dea, -ae* f. [11]

good *bonus, -a, -um* [3]

Good-bye! *Valē/Valēte!* [2]

grace *grātia, -ae* f. [19]

great *magnus, -a, -um* [8]

greater *māїor, māїōris* [15]

greatest *maximus, -a, -um* [20];
    summus, -a, -um [20]

greet *salūtō* (1)

H

handsome *pulcher, pulchra, pulchrum* [13]

happy *laetus, -a, -um* [3]

hard *difficilis, difficile* [15]

harm *noceō, nocēre, nocuī, nocitum* (+ dat.) [12]

hasten *festīnō* (1) [9]

have *habeō, habēre, habuī, habitum* [5]

have to *dēbeō, dēbēre, dēbuī, dēbitum* [7]

he *ille, illīus* [17]; *is, eius* [17]

hear *audiō, audīre, audīvī / audiī, audītum* [7]

heart *cor, cordis* n. [17]

heavy *gravis, grave* [15]

Hello! *Salvē/Salvēte!* [3]

help *adiuvō, adiuvāre, adiūvī, adiūtum* [16]

her own *suus, -a, -um* [9]

here *hīc* [10]

herself (emphatic) *ipsa* [17]

Hi! *Salvē/Salvēte!* [3]

hide *abdō, abdere, abdidī, abditum* [19]

high *altus, -a, -um* [2]

higher *superior, superius* [19]

highest *summus, -a, -um* [20];
    suprēmus, -a, -um [20]

himself (emphatic) *ipse* [17]
his own *suus, -a, -um* [9]
hold *habeō, habēre, habuī, habitum* [5];
    obtineō, obtinēre, obtinuī, obtentum [9];
    teneō, tenēre, tenuī, tentum [6]
home *domus, -ī* f.; *sēdēs, sēdis* f. [14]
home, to a house *domum* [4]
hope, hope for *spērō* (1) [9]
hour *hōra, -ae* f. [8]
house *domus, -ī* f. [4]
how much, how many *quantus, -a, -um* [10]
how (conj.) *quōmodo* [17]
how! (interj.) *quam* [13]
however *autem* [20]
human being *homō, hominis* m./f. [13]
hungry *iēiūnus, -a, -um* [13]
hurt *noceō, nocēre, nocuī, nocitum* (+ dat.) [12]
husband *marītus, -ī* m. [16]

I

I *ego* [7]
if *sī* [7]
immediately *statim* [20]
in *in* (+ abl.) [2, 5]
in front of *prō* (+ abl.) [6]
in this place *hīc* [10]
in this way *sīc* [11]
infant *infans, infantis* m./f. [14]
injure *noceō, nocēre, nocuī, nocitum*
    (+ dat.) [12]
inspect *inspiciō, inspicere, inspexī,*
    inspectum [10]
intelligent *intellegens, intellegentis* [15]
into *in* (+ acc.) [5]
is *est* [1]
island *insula, -ae* f. [9]
it *id, eius* [17]; *illud, illīus* [17]
it is necessary (to) *necesse est* (+ inf.) [12]
its own *suus, -a, -um* [9]
itself (emphatic) *ipsum* [17]

J

jump *saliō, salīre, saliī / saluī, saltum* [11]
just as *sīcut* [7]

K

kill *interficiō, interficere, interfēcī, interfectum* [14]
kind *almus, -a, -um* [18]

king *rex, rēgis* m. [14]
know *noscō, noscere, nōvī, nōtum* [11]

L

labor *labor, labōris* m. [16]
land *terra, -ae* f. [8]
large *magnus, -a, -um* [8]
later *sērius* [17]
laugh *rīdeō, rīdēre, rīsī, rīsum* [7]
lead *agō, agere, ēgī, actum* [4]; *dūcō, dūcere, dūxī, ductum* [4]
leap *saliō, salīre, saliī / saluī, saltum* [11]
learn *discō, discere, didicī* [6]
life *vīta, -ae* f. [13]
lift *tollō, tollere, sustulī, sublātum* [11]
like *sīcut* [7]
little *paucus, -a, -um* [9]
live *habitō* (1) [12]
long *longus, -a, -um* [19]
long distance *longē* [11]
look at *conspiciō, conspicere, conspexī, conspectum*
    [9]; *spectō* (1) [10]
look closely at *inspectō* (1) [19]; *inspiciō, inspicere,*
    inspexī, inspectum [10]
look forward to *spērō* (1) [9]
Look! *Ecce!* [11]
lord *dominus, -ī* m. [18]
lose *āmittō, āmittere, āmīsī, āmissum* [9]
loud *magnus, -a, -um* [8]
love (noun) *amor, amōris* m. [15]
love (v.) *amō* (1) [13]
lucky *fēlix, fēlīcis* [18]

M

make *faciō, facere, fēcī, factum* [6]
make ready *parō* (1) [12]
man *vir, virī* m. [2]
many *multī, -ae, -a* [2]
master *dominus, -ī* m. [18]
me *mē* (acc., abl.) [3]; *mihi* (dat.) [1]
money *pecūnia, -ae* f. [3]
monkey *sīmia, -ae* m./f. [5]
month *mensis, mensis* m. [14]
more *magis* [16]; (in amount) *plūs* [19];
    (in number) *plūres, plūra* [19]
most *plūrimus, -a, -um* [20]
mother *māter, mātris* f. [13]
mouth *ōs, ōris* n. [13]
much (adj.) *multus, -a, -um* [2]
much (adv.) *multum* [16]
my *meus, -a, -um* [5]

N

name *nōmen, nōminis* n. [1]
near *prope* (+ acc.) [5]
neither *neuter, neutra, neutrum* [17]
neither . . . nor *nec . . . nec* [15]
never *numquam* [17]
nevertheless *tamen* [20]
new *novus, -a, -um* [8]
night *nox, noctis* f. [14]
no *nūllus, -a, -um* [17]
no one *nēmō, nēminis* m. [13]
noble *nōbilis, -e* [15]; *praeclārus, -a, -um* [16]
nobody *nēmō, nēminis* m. [13]
none, not any *nūllus, -a, -um* [17]
not *nōn* [3]; *haud* [16]
not only . . . but also *nōn sōlum . . . sed etiam*
not want to *nōlō, nōlle, nōluī* [7]
nothing *nihil* [3]
nourishing *almus, -a, -um* [18]
now *iam* [8]; *nunc* [3]

O

observe *conspiciō, conspicere, conspexī, conspectum* [9]
often *saepe* [6]
oh no! *ēheu!* [16]
old *antīquus, -a, -um* [10]
older *māiōr, māiōris* (often with *nātū*) [15]
on account of *propter* (+ acc.) [9]
on *in* (+ abl.) [2, 5]
on top of *super* (+ acc.) [10]
once *ōlim* [19]
one ought, must *oportet, oportēre, oportuit* (+ acc. + inf.)
    [12] e.g., Mē cēnāre oportet.
one *ūnus, -a, -um* [7]
only (adj.) *sōlus, -a, -um* [6]
only (adv.) *sōlum* [3]
or *aut* [4]
other *alius, -a, -ud* [9]
ought *dēbeō, dēbēre, dēbuī, dēbitum* [7]
our *noster, nostra, nostrum* [15]
out of *ē, ex* (+ abl.) [5]
over *super* (+ acc.) [10]
owe *dēbeō, dēbēre, dēbuī, dēbitum* [7]

P

pardon *parcō, parcere, pepercī/parsī/parcuī,*
    parsūrus (+ dat.) [12]
parent *parens, parentis* m./f. [16]
part *pars, partis* f. [19]

people *populus, -ī* m. [4]
perceive *videō, vidēre, vīdī, vīsum* [3]
perhaps *fortasse* [11]
person *homō, hominis* m./f. [13]
piece *pars, partis* f. [19]
place (noun) *locus, -ī* m. [19]
place (v.) *pōnō, pōnere, posuī, positum* [4]
play *fābula, -ae* f. [9]
Please! *sī placet* [7]
pocketbook *saccus, -ī* m. [11]
poem *carmen, carminis* n. [17]
poet *poēta, -ae* m. [14]
powerful *potens, potentis* [15]
prefer *mālō, mālle, māluī* [7]
prepare *parō* (1) [12]
pretty *pulcher, pulchra, pulchrum* [13]
proceed *prōcēdō, prōcēdere, prōcessī, prōcessum* [10]
public show *mūnus, mūneris* n. [17]
put *pōnō, pōnere, posuī, positum* [4]

R

raise *tollō, tollere, sustulī, sublātum* [11]
rather *magis* [16]
rather late *sērius* [17]
read *legō, legere, lēgī, lēctum* [15]
reply *respondeō, respondēre, respondī, responsum* (+ dat.) [3]
report *fāma, -ae* f. [20]
request *poscō, poscere, poposcī* [5]
residence *sēdēs, sēdis* f. [14]
rest *quiescō, quiescere, quiēvī, quiētum* [14]
rhetorical *rhētoricus, -a, -um* [16]
ring *orbis, orbis* m.
road *via, -ae* f. [5]
Roman *Rōmānus, -a, -um* [11]
Rome *Rōma, -ae* f. [11]
room *cella, -ae* f. [18]
rumor *fāma, -ae* f. [20]
run *currō, currere, cucurrī, cursum* [5]

S

sack *saccus, -ī* m. [11]
sad *maestus, -a, -um* [18]; *tristis, -e* [15]
safe *salvus, -a, -um* [16]; *tūtus, -a, -um* [14]
say *dīcō, dīcere, dīxī, dictum* [7]; *inquit, inquiunt* [2];
    nārrō (1) [14]
say hello *salūtō* (1) [4]
scared *territus, -a, -um* [14]
school *lūdus, -ī* m. [4]
schoolmaster *magister, -trī* m. [2]
schoolmistress *magistra, -ae* f. [2]

sea *mare, maris* n. [14]

season *tempus, temporis* n. [13]

seat *sēdēs, sēdis* f. [14]

see *conspiciō, conspicere, conspexī, conspectum* [9]; *videō, vidēre, vīdī, vīsum* [3]

seize *rapiō, rapere, rapuī, raptum* [20]

send *mittō, mittere, mīsī, missum* [20]

send away *āmittō, āmittere, āmīsī, āmissum* [9]

serious *gravis, grave* [15]

servant (male) *servus, -ī* m. [7]

servant (female) *ancilla, -ae* f. [8]

several *nōnnūllī, -ae, -a* [9]

shape *figūra, -ae* f. [10]

she *ea, eius* [17]; *illa, illīus* [17]

shed tears *lacrimō* (1) [17]

shop *taberna, -ae* f. [2]

short *brevis, breve* [18]

shout (noun) *clāmor, clāmōris* m. [20]

shout (v.) *clāmō* (1) [5]

show mercy to *parcō, parcere, pepercī / parsī / parcuī, parsūrus* (+ dat.) [12]

since *quia* [18]

sister *soror, sorōris* f. [13]

sit *sedeō, sedēre, sēdī, sessum* [5]

six *sex* [10]

sixteen *sēdecim* [8]

skill *ars, artis* f. [16]

slave *servus, -ī* m. [7]

sleep *dormiō, dormīre, dormīvī / dormiī, dormītum* [12]

small *parvus, -a, -um* [10]

smaller *minor, minus* [19]

smallest *minimus, -a, -um* [20]

snack shop *taberna, -ae* f. [2]

snatch *rapiō, rapere, rapuī, raptum* [20]

so, so much (as) *tam* [11]

some *nōnnūllī, -ae, -a* [9]

someone, something *aliquis, aliquid* n. [18]

son *fīlius, -iī* m. [4]

song *carmen, carminis* n. [17]

soon *mox* [9]

spare *parcō, parcere, pepercī / parsī / parcuī, parsūrus* (+ dat.) [12]

speech *ōrātiō, ōrātiōnis* f. [16]

stand *stō, stāre, stetī, statum* [5]

    stand out from *praestō, praestāre, praestitī, praestitum/praestātum* (+ dat.) [10]

    stand still *constō, constāre, constitī, constātum* [10]; *sistō, sistere, stetī/stitī, statum* [8]

still *etiam* [17]

story *fābula, -ae* f. [9]

straight *rectus, -a, -um* [6]

stranger *hostis, hostis* m./f. [14]

street *via, -ae* f. [5]

strong *fortis, forte* [15]

student (female) *discipula, -ae* f. [2]

student (male) *discipulus, -ī* m. [2]

study (noun) *studium, -iī* n. [6]

study (v.) *studeō, studēre, studuī* (+ dat.) [12]

suddenly *subitō* [11]

support *obtineō, obtinēre, obtinuī, obtentum* [9]

surpass *praestō, praestāre, praestitī, praestātum* (+ dat.) [10]

swift *celer, celeris, celere* [15]

sword *gladius, -iī* m. [17]

T

table *mensa, -ae* f. [16]

take *capiō, capere, cēpī, captum* [3]

task *negōtium, -iī* n. [8]

teacher (female) *magistra, -ae* f. [2]

teacher (male) *magister, -trī* m. [2]

teacher of rhetoric (public speaking) *rhētor, rhētoris* [16]

tell *nārrō* (1) [14]

ten *decem* [12]

territory *fīnēs, fīnium* m. pl. [14]

than *quam* [10]

thanks *grātiae, -ārum* f. pl. [19]

that man *ille, illīus* [17]

that one of yours *iste, ista, istud* (derogatory) [17]

that thing *illud, illīus* [17]

that woman *illa, illīus* [17]

their own *suus, -a, -um* [9]

themselves (emphatic) *ipsī, ipsae, ipsa* [17]

then *tum* [20]; *tunc* [3]

therefore *ergō* [8]; *igitur* [20]; *itaque* [20]

they *eī, eae, ea* [17]; *illī, illae, illa* [17]

think *cōgitō* (1) [10]

this *hic, haec, hoc* [19]

those *illī, illae, illa* [17]

three *trēs, tria* [6]

through *per* (+ acc.) [5]

thus *sīc* [11]

time *hōra, -ae* f. [8]; *tempus, temporis* n. [13]

tired *fessus, -a, -um* [8]

to *ad* (+ acc.) [2, 5]

to me *mihi* [1]

to you *tibi* [1]

today *hodiē* [4]

tomorrow *crās* [6]

too (also) *etiam* [17]

too late *sērius* [17]

too, too much *nimium* [16]

toward *ad* (+ acc.) [2, 5]

true *vērus, -a, -um* [15]

truly *vērē* [15]
tutor *paedagōgus, -ī* m. [5]
twelve *duodecim* [12]
twenty *vīgintī* [12]
two *duo, duae, duo* [7]

U

under *sub* (+ abl.) [6]; *sub* (+ acc.) [6]
understand *intellegō, intellegere, intellēxī, intellēctum* [13]

V

very (much) *valdē* [11]
voice *vox, vōcis* f. [15]

W

wait for *exspectō* (1) [16]
walk *ambulō* (1) [2]
wallet *saccus, -ī* m. [11]
want to *cupiō, cupere, cupīvī/cupiī, cupītum* [4];
    volō, velle, voluī [7]
wants (he, she, it) *vult* [5]
watch *spectō* (1) [10]
water *aqua, -ae* f. [2]
way *via, -ae* f. [5]
well (adj.) *salvus, -a, -um* [16]
well (adv.) *bene* [4]
what? *quid* [1, 18]
when *cum* [15]; *ubi* [5]
where *ubi* [5]
which *quī, quae, quod* [18]
while *dum* [10]

who *quī, quae, quod* [18]
who? *quis* [1, 18]
whole *tōtus, -a, -um* [17]
why *cūr* [11]
wife *uxor, uxōris* f. [18]
wine *vīnum, -ī* n. [3]
wish *cupiō, cupere, cupīvī / cupiī, cupītum* [4]
with *apud* (+ acc.) [16]; with *cum* (+ abl.) [6]
without *sine* (+ abl.) [6]
woman *fēmina, -ae* f. [2]
word *verbum, -ī* n. [11]
work (noun) *labor, labōris* m. [16]
work (v.) *labōrō* (1) [9]
world *orbis terrārum* [20]
worse *pēior, pēius* [19]
worst *pessimus, -a, -um* [20]
write *scrībō, scrībere, scripsī, scriptum* [6]

Y

year *annus, -ī* m. [12]
years old *annōs nātus, -a, -um* [12]
yesterday *heri* [19]
yet *at* [20]; *atque* [20]
you (all) *vōbīs* (dat./abl.) [17]
you (sing.) *tū* [3]
your (pl.) *vester, vestra, vestrum* [6];
    (sing.) *tuus, -a, -um* [6]
your *tibi* [1]
youth *adulescens, -entis* m./f. [15];
    iuvenis, iuvenis m./f. [15]

Z

zeal *studium, -iī* n. [6]

Photo Credits

Index

A

ŌCEANUS
GERMĀNICUS

Rigor Valī Aelī

Britannia

Londīnium

ŌCEANUS

ATLANTICUS

Germānia
Inferior

Rhēnus

Lugdūnensis

Belgica

Augusta Trēvirōrum

Dānuvius

Germānia
Superior

Raetia

Nōricum

Aquītānia

Lugdūnum

Rhodanus

Narbōnensis

Ītalia

Mare Hadri

Tarracōnensis

Massilia

Lūsitānia

Corsica

Rōma

Tiberis

Ēmerita Augusta

Baleārēs

Baetica

Sardinia

Gādēs

Carthāgō Nova

Mare

Sicilia

Maurītānia

Carthāgō

Āfrica
Prōconsulāris

In

Leptis Magna

400 km

400 mīlia Anglica

Roman Empire

Dācia

Dānuvius

Moesia
Superior

Moesia
Inferior

Thrācia

Constantīnopolis

Pontus Euxīnus

Bithȳnia
et Pontus

Galatia

Cappadocia

Armenia

Macedonia

Ēpīrus

Pergamum

Asia

Athēnae

Achaea

Lycia et
Pamphȳlia

Cilicia

Syria

Tigris

Mesopotamia

Euphrātēs

Crēta

Cyprus

Damascus

Iūdaea

Jerusalem

r   n   u   m

aica

Alexandrīa

Arabia

Cȳrēnē

Aegyptus

Sinu

incum

Imperial Rome

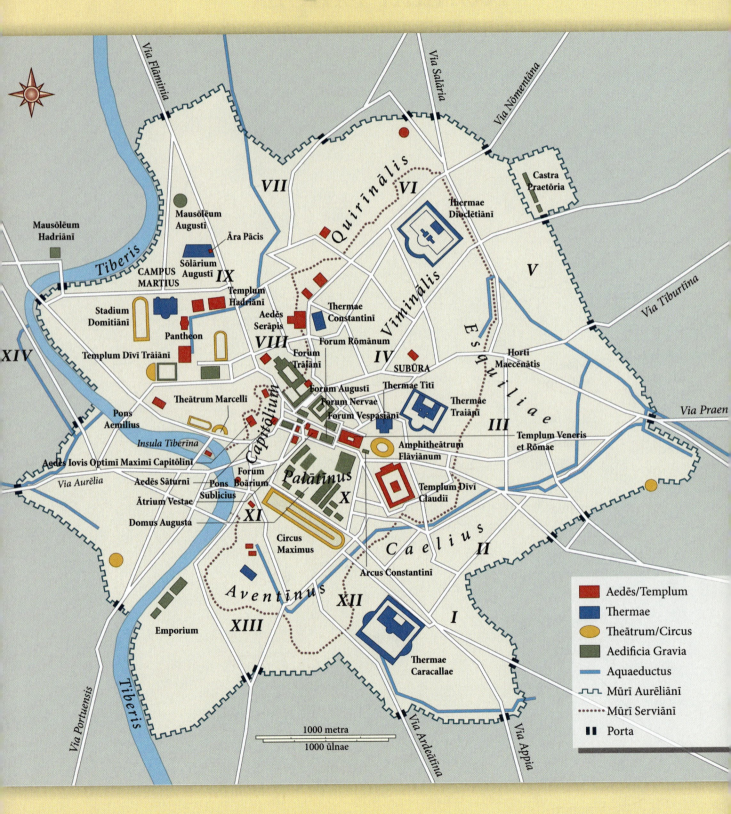

Tiberis

Via Flāminia
Via Salāria
Via Nōmentāna
Via Tīburtīna
Via Praen
Via Ardeātīna
Via Appia
Via Portuensis
Via Aurēlia

VII
VI
V
IX
VIII
IV
III
II
I
X
XI
XII
XIII
XIV

Quirinālis
Vīminālis
Esquīliae
Capitōlium
Palātīnus
Caelius
Aventīnus

CAMPUS MARTIUS
SUBŪRA

Mausōlēum Hadriānī
Mausōlēum Augustī
Āra Pācis
Sōlārium Augustī
Templum Hadriānī
Aedēs Serāpis
Thermae Constantīnī
Thermae Dioclētiānī
Castra Praetōria
Stadium Domitiānī
Pantheon
Templum Dīvī Trāiānī
Forum Rōmānum
Horti Maecēnātis
Theātrum Marcellī
Forum Trāiānī
Forum Augustī
Forum Nervae
Forum Vespasiānī
Thermae Titī
Thermae Traiānī
Pons Aemilius
Insula Tiberina
Aedēs Iovis Optimī Maximī Capitōlīnī
Aedēs Sāturnī
Ātrium Vestae
Domus Augusta
Forum Boārium
Pons Sublicius
Amphitheātrum Flāviānum
Templum Veneris et Rōmae
Templum Dīvī Claudiī
Circus Maximus
Arcus Constantīnī
Emporium
Thermae Caracallae

Legend

🟥	Aedēs/Templum
🟦	Thermae
🟡	Theātrum/Circus
🟩	Aedificia Gravia
—	Aquaeductus
⊐⊏	Mūrī Aurēliānī
⋯	Mūrī Serviānī
‖	Porta

1000 metra
1000 ūlnae